2009 CASE SUPPLEMENT AND STATUTORY APPENDIX

CASES AND MATERIALS

TRADEMARK AND UNFAIR COMPETITION LAW

FOURTH EDITION

by

JANE C. GINSBURG
Morton L. Janklow Professor of
Literary and Artistic Property Law
Columbia University Law School

JESSICA LITMAN
John F. Nickoll Professor of Law
University of Michigan Law School

MARY L. KEVLIN
Cowan, Liebowitz and Latman, P.C.
Adjunct Professor New York University School of Law

FOUNDATION PRESS
2009

THOMSON REUTERS™

© 2001, 2003, 2004 FOUNDATION PRESS

© 2005, 2006, 2007, 2008 By THOMSON REUTERS/FOUNDATION PRESS

© 2009 By THOMSON REUTERS/FOUNDATION PRESS

    195 Broadway, 9th Floor
    New York, NY 10007
    Phone Toll Free 1–877–888–1330
    Fax (212) 367–6799
    foundation–press.com

Printed in the United States of America

ISBN 978–1–59941–678–6

TABLE OF CONTENTS

*

TABLE OF CASES

Principal cases are in bold type. Non-principal cases are in roman type. References are to Pages.

*

2009 CASE SUPPLEMENT
AND STATUTORY APPENDIX

CASES AND MATERIALS

TRADEMARK AND
UNFAIR COMPETITION
LAW

*

PRELUDE

Top Tobacco, L.P v. North Atlantic Operating Company, Inc.

509 F.3d 380 (7th Cir. 2007).

■ EASTERBROOK, *Chief Judge.* This case illustrates the power of pictures. One glance is enough to decide the appeal.

Top Tobacco, L.P., sells tobacco to people who want to roll cigarettes by hand or make them using a cranked machine. This is known as the roll-your-own, make-your-own or RYO/MYO business. Top Tobacco and its predecessors have been in this segment of the cigarette market for more than 100 years, and the mark TOP®, printed above a drawing of a spinning top, is well known among merchants and customers of cigarette tobacco. North Atlantic Operating Company and its predecessors also have been in the roll-your-own, make-your-own business for more than 100 years, though initially only as manufacturers of cigarette paper. Not until 1999 did North Atlantic bring its own tobacco to market. The redesigned can that it introduced in 2001 bears the phrase Fresh–Top™ Canister. Top Tobacco maintains in this suit under the Lanham Act that none of its rivals may use the word "top" as a trademark.

Trademarks are designed to inform potential buyers who makes the goods on sale. See *KP Permanent Make–Up, Inc. v. Lasting Impression I, Inc.,* 543 U.S. 111 (2004); *Dastar Corp. v. Twentieth Century Fox Film Corp.,* 539 U.S. 23 (2003). Knowledge of origin may convey information about a product's attributes and quality, and consistent attribution of origin is vital when vendors' reputations matter. Without a way to know who makes what, reputations cannot be created and evaluated, and the process of competition will be less effective. See generally William M. Landes & Richard A. Posner, *The Economic Structure of Intellectual Property Law* 166–209 (2003).

Top Tobacco insists that it has exclusive rights to the word "top" for use on tobacco in this market. But many words have multiple meanings: "Top" may mean the best, or a spinning toy, or a can's lid. Top Tobacco uses the word "top" in the second sense and may hope that consumers will hear the first as well; North Atlantic uses the word in its third sense, to refer to a pull-tab design that keeps tobacco fresh. If English used different words to encode these different meanings, there could not be a trademark problem. Because our language gives the word "top" so many different

1

meanings, however, there is a potential for confusion. But no one who saw these cans side by side could be confused about who makes which:

The phrase "Fresh–Top Canister" on North American's can does not stand out; no consumer could miss the difference between Top Tobacco's TOP brand, with a spinning top, and North Atlantic's ZIG–ZAG (R) brand, with a picture of a Zouave soldier. The trade dress (including colors and typography) of each producer's can is distinctive. Here is a larger version of the ZIG–ZAG brand can.

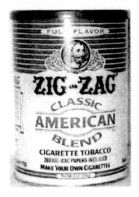

The left panel shows the can as it was between 2001 and 2004, when Fresh–Top Canister was on the front (right under "Classic American Blend"), and the two right panels show the can as it was from 2004 through 2006, when the phrase Fresh–Top Canister was on the side. The phrase was removed in 2006 when North Atlantic replaced the aluminum pull-tab design with a plastic lid. (This change does not make the case moot, because the possibility of damages remains.)

The district court granted summary judgment for the defendants, 2007 U.S. Dist. LEXIS 2838 (N.D. Ill. Jan. 4, 2007), and the pictures show why. It is next to impossible to believe that any consumer, however careless, would confuse these products. "Next to impossible" doesn't mean "absolutely impossible"; judges are not perceptual psychologists or marketing experts and may misunderstand how trade dress affects purchasing decisions. But the pictures are all we have. Top Tobacco did not conduct a survey of consumers' reactions to the cans and did not produce an affidavit from even a single consumer or merchant demonstrating confusion.

What Top Tobacco wants us to do is to ignore the pictures and the lack of any reason to believe that anyone ever has been befuddled. Like other courts, this circuit has articulated a multi-factor approach to assessing the probability of confusion. See, e.g., *Barbecue Marx, Inc. v. 551 Ogden, Inc.*, 235 F.3d 1041 (7th Cir. 2000). These factors include whether the trademarks use the same word, whether they sound alike, and so on. Top Tobacco insists that "Fresh Top" is spelled and sounds the same as fresh "TOP", and thus it traipses through the list. It conveniently omits the fact that the phrase on the ZIG–ZAG can is "Fresh–Top Canister", with "Fresh–Top" serving as a phrasal adjective modifying the word "canister" rather than as the product's brand. But it's unnecessary to belabor the point. A list of factors designed as *proxies* for the likelihood of confusion can't supersede the statutory inquiry. If we know for sure that consumers are not confused about a product's origin, there is no need to consult even a single proxy.

Top Tobacco says that merchants may have been confused, because a few of the price lists that North Atlantic sent to its wholesalers and retailers omitted the ZIG–ZAG brand and gave prices for a "6 oz. Fresh–Top TM Can" and a ".75 oz. Pocket Pouch TM". Yet all of these lists prominently include the seller's name (North Atlantic or National Tobacco), and if any commercial buyer thought that North Atlantic was selling the TOP brand the record does not contain a shred of evidence to that effect.

Finally, only a few words are required to address Top Tobacco's claim that it has a "famous" brand that was diluted by the "Fresh–Top Canister" phrase. See 15 U.S.C. § 1125(c)(2)(A) (special protection for famous marks "widely recognized by the general public of the United States as a designator of source of the goods or services of the mark's owner"). There can be no doubt that TOP is an old and recognized brand in the loose-cigarette-tobacco market. There is also no doubt that "top" is commonly used in the tobacco business, so that the appearance of that word on a package does not affect the reputation of Top Tobacco. One brand of chewing tobacco bears a large "Top Leaf" stamp. "Top Hat" is a well-known brand of cigar tobacco. Marlboro sells cigarettes in a "Flip–Top (R) Box". Another brand of cigarettes is sold under the mark "Top Score". The "Tip–Top" brand of cigarette paper is available from the same sources as Top Tobacco's tobacco. When Top Tobacco obtained a federal registration for its brand of loose cigarette tobacco, it assured the Patent and Trademark Office that it was claiming only limited rights in the word "top." It could hardly be otherwise: the word "top" is too common, and too widely used to refer to the lids of packages—as well as parts of clothing ensembles, masts of ships, summits of mountains, bundles of wool used in spinning, half-innings of baseball, positions in appellate litigation (the top-side brief), and flavors of quark—to be appropriated by a single firm.

The portion of § 1125 from which we have quoted was amended in October 2006 to use "the general public" as the benchmark. This change eliminated any possibility of "niche fame," which some courts had recognized before the amendment. See *Syndicate Sales, Inc. v. Hampshire Paper Corp.*, 192 F.3d 633 (7th Cir. 1999). Top Tobacco insists that even if the amendment (and North Atlantic's new packaging) preclude equitable relief, it is still entitled to damages under the old version of § 1125. But what we have said is enough to show that the word "top" is not famously distinctive "as a designator of source" in any sensibly specified niche of tobacco products.

AFFIRMED.

QUESTIONS

1. What might Top have hoped to accomplish by bringing this lawsuit?

2. Should Top be able to prevent other tobacco producers from using its mark on their packaging without regard to whether consumers are confused? Why or why not?

3. How should a court evaluate whether the use of a word is likely to confuse consumers? Judge Easterbook notes that the 7th Circuit, like other circuits, "has articulated a multi-factor approach to assessing the probability of confusion." What factors might be relevant to the assessment? See *infra* Chapter 6.A. (Likelihood of Confusion).

4. Top also claimed that it was a famous brand, which entitled it to protect its trademark from dilution. Should trademark law treat famous marks differently from marks that are less well known? If so, how should a court decide whether a trademark is famous? See *infra* Chapter 9 (Dilution).

5. How important to the decision was the observation that the word "top" was commonly used in the tobacco business? Should trademarks consisting of common words be treated differently from trademarks that are unusual or unique? See *infra* Chapter 2.B (Distinctiveness).

6. As the court notes, many words have multiple meanings. Should competitors always be free to use a trademarked word so long as they use it to express a meaning that's different from the meaning invoked in the trademark? Can you think of examples?

7. In what circumstances should competitors be entitled to use a trademarked word to express the same meaning as the meaning associated with the mark? In what circumstances should they be permitted to use a trademark to refer to the product sold under the mark? See *infra* Chapter 6.C.2.b (Fair Use), Chapter 6.C.2.c. (Nominative Fair Use).

CHAPTER 1

CONCEPTS OF TRADEMARKS AND UNFAIR COMPETITION

A. COMPETITION

Page 13. Insert following *NBA v. Motorola*:

Associated Press v. All Headline News Corp., 608 F.Supp.2d 454 (S.D.N.Y. 2009). The Associated Press sued All Headline News for "free riding on the AP's news articles," claiming that defendant's employees searched for breaking news stories on the Internet and then rewrote AP stories for dissemination to AHN's customers' websites. AHN argued that AP's common law misappropriation claim was preempted. The court disagreed:

> The cause of action for misappropriation of "hot news" has its origins in *International News Service v. Associated Press*, 248 U.S. 215, 39 S. Ct. 68, 63 L. Ed. 211 (1918), a decision arising under federal common law and one that pre-dates *Erie R. Co. v. Tompkins*, 304 U.S. 64, 58 S. Ct. 817, 82 L. Ed. 1188 (1938). The defendants move to dismiss this claim. . . . [T]hey contend that a claim for misappropriation of hot news is preempted by the federal Copyright Act.
>
> *International News Service* held that breaking news (sometimes described as "hot news") was the "*quasi* property" of a news-gathering organization, 248 U. S. at 236, and thus subject to protection against a competitor's interference. The Supreme Court held that allowing one news agency to appropriate and profit from the work of another would "render publication profitless, or so little profitable as in effect to cut off the service by rendering the cost prohibitive in comparison with the return." *Id.* at 241. Newsgathering carries with it "the expenditure of labor, skill, and money," and the Supreme Court held that its appropriation by another "is endeavoring to reap what it has not sown." *Id.* at 239–40. Although *Erie* would render the federal common law origins of *International News Service* non-binding in the federal courts, the cause of action is still recognized under the laws of various states, including the state of New York. *See generally Nat'l Basketball Ass'n v. Motorola, Inc.*, 105 F.3d 841, 845 (2d Cir. 1997) (claim for misappropriation of hot news is valid under New York law and not preempted by the federal Copyright Act); *see also Electrolux*

Corp. v. Val–Worth, Inc., 6 N.Y.2d 556, 567–68, 161 N.E.2d 197, 190 N.Y.S.2d 977 (1959); *Bond Buyer v. Dealers Digest Publishing Co.*, 25 A.D.2d 158, 159–60, 267 N.Y.S.2d 944 (1st Dep't 1966); *Capitol Records, Inc. v. Naxos of America, Inc.*, 262 F. Supp. 2d 204, 209–10 (S.D.N.Y. 2003).

. . .

... A cause of action for misappropriation of hot news remains viable under New York law, and the Second Circuit has unambiguously held that it is not preempted by federal law. . . . .

NBA's five elements are set forth in the Amended Complaint. The defendants have set forth no persuasive reason why the Second Circuit's preemption analysis in *NBA* should be rejected or overruled by this Court, and fails to explain how a district court would be empowered to do so in any event.

The defendants' motion to dismiss Claim One is denied.

QUESTIONS

1. As readers and advertising dollars migrate to online publications, newspapers across the country are finding their previously profitable business models unsustainable and ceasing publication. Is the availability of a common law "hot news" misappropriation suit likely to help conventional news organizations stay in business?

2. How narrow is the "hot news" *INS*-like claim that the Court of Appeals for the Second Circuit held survives federal preemption? What other fact patterns can you imagine that would fit the five factors articulated in *NBA v. Motorola*?

B. TRADEMARKS

Page 29. Insert after the Questions following Champion Spark Plug v. Sanders:

Custom Manufacturing v. Midway Services, Inc., 508 F.3d 641 (11th Cir. 2007). Midway hired Custom to design water meters for its apartment buildings. Midway was dissatisfied with the system Custom designed. It canceled the contract and hired a different firm to redesign and install the meters. The new contractor modified Custom circuit boards and installed them in the redesigned system. The modified circuit boards bore Custom's mark. Custom sued Midway and its new contractor, arguing that repair technicians and fire marshals would see Custom's trademark and be misled into believing that Custom had produced the modified circuit boards. The court was not persuaded. Noting that Custom's mark was not visible without first disassembling the water meters, and that neither repair technicians nor fire marshals should be viewed as likely customers, the court held that Custom had failed to show a likelihood of confusion.

QUESTION

If prospective customers for the trademark owner's product are unlikely to see the allegedly infringing mark, has the trademark owner any legitimate basis for complaint? See *Rescuecom Corp. v. Google, Inc.*, 562 F.3d 123 (2d Cir. 2009), and notes and questions following, *infra* this Supplement pp. 72–82.

CHAPTER 2

WHAT IS A TRADEMARK?

B. DISTINCTIVENESS

Pages 84–85. Replace *In re Oppedahl & Larson*, with the following:

In re Chippendales USA, 90 U.S.P.Q. 2d 1535, 2009 WL 804141 (T.T.A.B. 2009). The "exotic" male dancing group, the "Chippendales," sought to register a mark consisting of "a three-dimensional [nude] human [male] torso with cuffs around the wrists and neck collar comprising a bow tie" as an inherently distinctive trademark for entertainment services. Although the Board stated that trade dress may be inherently distinctive when used in connection with services as well as goods, a majority upheld the Examiner's determination that the mark at issue lacked inherent distinctiveness. The Board applied the test elaborated in *Seabrook Foods, Inc. v. Bar–Well Foods, Ltd.*, 568 F.2d 1342 (CCPA 1977), inquiring whether, when the mark was first adopted in 1979, it was "a common basic shape or design;" whether it was "unique or unusual in the particular field;" and whether it was "a mere refinement of a commonly-adopted and well-known form of ornamentation for a particular class of goods or services viewed by the public as a dress or ornamentation for the goods or services."

[W]e conclude that the cuffs and collar costume/uniform, when viewed apart from applicant's use and promotion of the Cuffs & Collar Mark, is the same basic type of revealing and provocative attire worn by adult entertainers. Thus, we conclude that, when viewed in context, the Cuffs & Collar Mark is a common basic shape or design.

Next we must consider whether the Cuffs & Collar Mark is or was unique or unusual in the particular field. The Examining Attorney argues again that the Cuffs & Collar Mark is not unique for these services inasmuch as it is of the same general type as others and not unusual in the field. By contrast, applicant argues that, because all strippers begin their routine with some kind of fantasy outfit, these examples demonstrate non-trademark symbols for the easily-recognizable occupations of real life characters used as part of a story. Applicant argues that this contrasts with the cuffs and collar expressly designed to be part and parcel of applicant's identity. . . .

The discussion above regarding "common designs" also points to the answer to the question as to whether applicant's mark was unique or unusual from the outset—the answer is no. That is, as we noted, the Cuffs & Collar Mark is a simple variation on revealing and provocative costumes or uniforms generally in use in the adult-entertainment, exotic-dancing field.

... [E]ven if applicant was the first, and the one and only, party to use the cuffs and collar uniform in the field, whether it be in the male or female adult entertainment field, that fact alone would not be sufficient to render it inherently distinctive. [citation omitted] The more important fact in our overall analysis is that the cuffs and collar are not unusual in the field of adult entertainment generally, nor in the field of adult entertainment for women. . . .

Next we must consider whether the Cuffs & Collar Mark was a refinement of an existing form of ornamentation for the particular class of services. We find that it was such a refinement for the same reasons, and based on the same evidence, discussed in our treatment of the first two factors.

Judge Bucher dissented. Inquiring "whether the design, shape or combination of elements is so unique, unusual or unexpected in this market that one can assume without proof that it will automatically be perceived by customers as an indicia of origin—a trademark," he credited applicant's expert's assessment of the inherent brand designation of the cuffs-and-collar mark. The expert's field was dramaturgy and theatre arts; she had "conducted extensive research on the history of striptease in the United States:"

Dr. Shteir points out that upon its first use by applicant in 1979, the cuffs and collar design likely symbolized promiscuous, liberated, sexual woman drawn to class, prestige and wealth:

> Chippendales has taken two everyday articles that virtually always appear connected to a garment and, by featuring them alone, has given them new meaning. The separation of a cuffs and collar from a shirt invokes the image of a tuxedo but now the space where the shirt used to be has new meaning: sexuality, fantasy, and fulfillment. One reason that the connection between the Cuffs and Collar trade dress and Chippendales is so strong is that it is more than merely acquired recognition but is instead reflective of the many ways that the symbol perfectly matches the brand.

Dr. Shteir's declaration, P64

Applicant explains that this "skeleton of a tuxedo," allowed audience members

> ... to simultaneously hearken back to the fantasy of the wealthy man combined with the fantasy of the man whose true wealth is his ability to please. This, too, is consistent with the iconic role that the Chippendales dancer plays over the course of the evening. He is larger than life and can represent whatever each individual in the audience desires him to represent.

> How anyone could call a symbol laden with such rich emotional imagery merely a refinement of an existing ornamentation for a

particular class of services is difficult to fathom. Rarely has any symbol so perfectly captured the very essence of a brand. And when a symbol captures so much so quickly, it is not functioning as mere ornamentation but as a designation of source.

In re Vertex Group, LLC, 89 U.S.P.Q.2d (BNA) 1694 (T.T.A.B. 2009). Applicant sought to register the sound of a personal security alarm for children. The Board upheld the refusal to register on the ground that, while sounds could serve as trademarks, the alarm sound at issue failed to function as a trademark.

> Would the sound sought to be registered be perceived as a source indicator or merely as a sound emitted by the personal alarm to call public attention to the conduct prompting the alarm? Applicant argues that the sound would be perceived as an indication of the source of its product.... [A]larms ... are somewhat ubiquitous. Applicant has shown this by placing in the record evidence of numerous other producers of personal alarms, all of which are described as loud, and most of which, according to applicant, "utilize differing frequencies and differing arrangements of frequencies," just as applicant's alarm does. Sound pulses are not at all an uncommon way for a phone to ring, an alarm clock to sound, an appliance timer to go off, a smoke alarm to signal the possibility of fire, or for any number of other products to provide an audible signal designed to attract attention. As *General Electric* instructs, "a distinction must be made between unique, different, or distinctive sounds and those that resemble or imitate 'commonplace' sounds or those to which listeners have been exposed under different circumstances." 199 USPQ at 563. Clearly, alarm sounds consisting of a series of sound pulses, including those at frequency or decibel levels approximating those employed by applicant's alarms, are commonplace and the types of sounds to which prospective consumers of applicant's products would have been exposed in various circumstances. To state the obvious, every audible alarm emits some sort of sound, many similar to that of applicant's product; and we do not find that consumers are predisposed to equate such sounds with the sources of the products that emit them.

Accord, *Nextel Comm., Inc. v. Motorola, Inc.*, 2009 WL 174923 (T.T.A.B., 2009) (cellular telephones are "goods that make sound in their normal course of operation"; Applicant's "chirp" sound therefore "falls into the category of sounds that cannot be inherently distinctive").

See also Chapter 4.C.6, *infra* this Supplement (refusal to register based on functionality of alarm sound).

Page 87. Add a new question m.:

m. FARMACY for retail store selling organics and herbs. See *In re Tea & Sympathy*, 88 U.S.P.Q.2d (BNA) 1062 (T.T.A.B. 2008) (suggestive).

Page 89.–Seventh line should read:

... when they would mislead the plaintiff's customers to another shop.

CHAPTER 3

OWNERSHIP AND USE

A. OWNERSHIP

Page 112. Add new Question 2:

2. Clever Company, an advertising agency, devised a slogan, "my life, my card," which it proposed to several credit card companies, including American Express. Amex did not reply to Clever's solicitation. Several months later, however, after working with a different advertising agency, Amex began to air advertisements incorporating the "My life. My card." slogan. Clever has initiated a trademark infringement action against Amex. Amex moves to dismiss on the ground that Clever has no trademark rights in the slogan because Clever has not used the slogan as a trademark. How should the court rule? What would it mean for Clever to use the slogan as a trademark? *See American Express Co. v. Stephen G. Goetz*, 515 F.3d 156 (2d Cir. 2008).

Page 112. Following Questions, add the following excerpted decision:

Estate of Francisco Coll–Monge v. Inner Peace Movement, 524 F.3d 1341 (D.C. Cir. 2008):

Ordinarily, a party establishes ownership of a mark by being the first to use the mark in commerce. [Citations omitted.] Alternatively, the Lanham Act permits an applicant to establish ownership under the "related companies" doctrine by showing that it controlled the first user of the mark. *See Secular Orgs. for Sobriety, Inc. v. Ullrich*, 213 F.3d 1125, 1130 (9th Cir. 2000) ("[T]o prevail on its trademark claim, [plaintiff] must demonstrate that it was the first user of the disputed marks or, in the alternative, that if [defendant organization] was using the marks first, it was doing so as a related entity and the benefits of any such use should therefore inure to [plaintiff]."). "Under the doctrine of 'related companies,' the first use of a mark by a person 'controlled by the registrant or applicant for registration of the mark' shall inure to the benefit of the controlling entity." *Id.* at 1131 (quoting 15 U.S.C. § 1055). In this case, it is undisputed that the Non–Profits were the "first users" of the marks at issue but the Estate contends that Coll controlled the Non–Profits' use of the marks, which use therefore inured to his benefit. The district court rejected this argument, reasoning that "[b]ecause the defendants are non-profit organizations with no owners and their actions are controlled solely by their Board of Directors, no one person has control over any actions of the defendants, much less control over the uses of the trademark." Summ. J. Order 3. We conclude the court erred in holding that a nonprofit corporation cannot be a related company whose use of the trademark is controlled by a mark's registrant.

The related companies doctrine is embodied in section 5 of the Lanham Act, which provides:

> Where a registered mark or a mark sought to be registered is or may be used legitimately by related companies, such use shall inure to the benefit of the registrant or applicant for registration, and such use shall not affect the validity of such mark or of its registration, provided such mark is not used in such manner as to deceive the public. If first use of a mark by a person is controlled by the registrant or applicant for registration of the mark with respect to the nature and quality of the goods or services, such first use shall inure to the benefit of the registrant or applicant, as the case may be.

15 U.S.C. § 1055. The Lanham Act defines a "related company" as "any person whose use of a mark is controlled by the owner of the mark with respect to the nature and quality of the goods or services on or in connection with which the mark is used." *Id.* § 1127. The statute does not expressly require formal corporate control, as the district court suggested. Instead, the statute requires control over only the "use of a mark ... with respect to the nature and quality of the goods or services," *id.*, which may include not only corporate control but also licensing agreements and other types of oversight. [Citations omitted.] The Estate has offered sufficient evidence of such control to survive summary judgment.

QUESTION

A company licensed to use another's trademark in connection with goods and services is a "related company" whose use is attributed to the licensor, at least so long as the licensor maintains control over the licensee. Who owns the mark if the licensor fails to control the licensee? See *infra*, Chapter 5.B. Abandonment.

B. Use

Page 122. After Questions, insert the following decision:

Many years after *Procter & Gamble v. Johnson & Johnson*, some entrepreneurs continue to hoard trademarks, but with no greater success when their ownership is contested. Consider the following:

Central Mfg. Inc. v. Brett

492 F.3d 876 (7th Cir. 2007).

■ Evans, Circuit Judge.

The Pine Tar Incident

It's undisputed: George Brett was a great baseball player. The statistics from his 21 years in The Show, all with the Kansas City Royals, seal the deal: 3,154 hits, 317 home runs, and a career batting average of .305. Only three other players—Stan Musial, Hank Aaron, and Willie Mays—ended their careers with more than 3,000 hits and 300 home runs, while still maintaining a lifetime batting average over .300. Brett's selection to the Hall of Fame, on the first ballot in 1999, was richly deserved. Yet for all his accomplishments, many who love baseball will always think of the "Pine Tar Incident" as the capstone of his career. It is a joy to recall.

It was July 24, 1983, and the Royals, trailing 4–3 to the New York Yankees, had a man on first but were down to their final out in the top half of the ninth inning. Brett was at the plate. The Yankees' ace closer, "Goose" Gossage, was on the mound. And Brett crushed an 0–1 fastball over the 353–foot mark into the right field seats, giving Kansas City the lead, 5–4. Pandemonium broke out in the Royals' dugout. The Yankee Stadium crowd fell silent. But things were about to change.

While the Royals were celebrating, the Yankees' fiery manager, Billy Martin, walked calmly (unusual for him) to home plate where he engaged the umpire, Tim McClelland, in quiet conversation. Martin pointed to an obscure rule (and we sometimes think the Federal Rules of Appellate Procedure are obscure!), which provides that any substance (including pine tar) that a player might rub on his bat handle for a better grip cannot extend more than 18 inches. See Major League Baseball Official Rules § 1.10(b). Martin, pointing to a lot of pine tar on the bat Brett left behind as he circled the bases, asked McClelland to check it out. McClelland, using home plate as a ruler, determined that pine tar covered 24 inches of the bat handle. So the bat, McClelland ruled, was illegal.

With his ruling ready for delivery, McClelland took a few steps toward the jubilant Royals' dugout and gave the signal: for using an illegal bat, the home run was nullified, and Brett was out. Game over. Yankees win 4–3. And all hell broke loose. An infuriated George Brett charged out of the dugout and rushed McClelland as Martin, who looked like the cat who ate the canary, stood off to the side. It was one of the great all-time rhubarbs in baseball history. And that's how it ended, at least for July 24, 1983.

But baseball, like our legal system, has appellate review. The Royals protested the game and, as luck would have it, American League President Lee MacPhail (to use a phrase with which we are accustomed) "reversed and remanded for further proceedings." The game resumed three weeks later with Kansas City ahead, 5–4. It ended after 12 minutes when Royals' closer Dan Quisenberry shut the door on the Yankees in their half of the ninth to seal the win. The whole colorful episode is preserved, in all its glory, on YouTube, at http://www.youtube.com/watch?v=4Cu1WXylkto (last visited June 6, 2007). See also Retrosheet Boxscore, Kansas City Royals 5, New York Yankees 4, at http://www.retrosheet.org/boxesetc/1983/B07240NYA1983.htm (last visited June 6, 2007).

Our Case Today

And so, at last, we come to this case which presents another (albeit a less compelling) appeal of a dispute involving George Brett and a baseball bat. We begin with the facts.

In 2001, Brett joined Tridiamond Sports, Inc., a manufacturer of baseballs, baseball bats, gloves, and other related accessories, to form Brett Brothers Sports International, Inc. (Brett Brothers). Tridiamond was incorporated in 1997 by Joe Sample, a former airline executive who had served as vice-president and president of International Ambassador, a company specializing in the organization of travel programs. International Ambassador was purchased in 1996 by former Major League Baseball Commissioner Peter Ueberroth, and informal conversations with Ueberroth soon gave Sample an idea. Ueberroth mentioned the difficulty some players had in adjusting from the use of metal baseball bats at the high school and collegiate levels to the wood bats of professional baseball. Initially introduced in the early 1970s as a cost-saving alternative for leagues operating under a smaller budget due to the breakability of wood bats, metal bats were eventually believed to generally outperform wood ones [citations omitted]. Because the use of metal bats may inflate hitting statistics, a player's professional prospects may be misevaluated, and the shift to wood bats may reveal a great player to be merely a very good one—the difference, potentially, between a highly compensated major league career and a decade spent on buses shuttling from Appleton to the Quad Cities.

Sample realized that the uncertainty of the switch potentially created a market niche for a bat that combined the best of both worlds: the production and feel of the wood bat with the break-resistance of the metal bat. He thus formed Tridiamond and initiated research on the construction of a more durable wood bat. Eventually the company developed a specialized process of grading, lamination, and fiberglass reinforcement that enabled the product they were looking for. Tridiamond initially sold three bat models with names inspired by Sample's background in aviation: the Mirador, the Stealth, and the Bomber.

Brett Brothers now sells eight different models of wood bats used throughout all levels of amateur and professional baseball. Relevant for our purposes is the Stealth model . . . The first recorded sale of the Stealth bat occurred on July 13, 1999, when twelve bats were sold to Tim Nolan of Pro–Cut in Rockford, Illinois. Brett Brothers has since sold more than 25,000 Stealth bats to all manner of customers worldwide, including through retail outlets in 48 states and via its Web site.

The plaintiffs in this action, Central Manufacturing, Inc. and Stealth Industries (collectively "Central"), are both controlled by Leo Stoller, who serves as president and sole shareholder. Stoller similarly operates a number of other companies, including Rentamark.com, S Industries, Inc., and Sentra Manufacturing. Stoller alleges that his companies have been using the "Stealth" trade name and mark for a wide range of products since at least 1982. Indeed, Stoller has registered the Stealth mark for things like boats, motorcycles, bicycles, microwave-absorbing automobile paint, billiard and dart equipment, auto locks, window locks, comic books, lawn sprinklers, metal alloys, pest elimination devices, and other products. [Citation omitted] In 1984, Stoller, through Sentra Manufacturing, filed a trademark registration with the United States Patent and Trademark Office (PTO) claiming ownership of the Stealth mark for "[s]porting goods, specifically, tennis rackets, golf clubs, tennis balls, basketballs, baseballs, soccer balls, golf balls, cross bows, tennis racket strings and shuttle cocks." Sentra was awarded the mark in 1985; it was eventually transferred to Central in 1997.

In 2001, Central filed a mark application with the PTO for using the Stealth word mark on "baseball bats, softball bats and t-ball bats." Later that year, Central entered into a licensing agreement with Blackwrap, Inc. for the use of the Stealth word mark on its bats; a similar agreement was reached (for $800) with Easton Sports, Inc. in 2003. In 2004 (five years after the first Brett Brothers sale of Stealth-model bats), the U.S. PTO granted the mark for baseball bats. Central soon became aware of Brett Brothers' use of the Stealth word mark and filed suit in the Northern District of Illinois, alleging violations of the Lanham Act, 15 U.S.C. § 1051 et seq., and the Illinois Deceptive Trade Practices Act, 815 ILCS 510/1 et seq. Central believes that because they registered the "Stealth" mark for baseballs and other sporting goods in 1985, they have priority of use of the mark for baseball bats, and Brett Brothers is guilty of infringement and unfair competition. . . .

Leo Stoller is no stranger to trademark litigation. Indeed, one might say it is the essential part of his business strategy. In fact, were there a Hall of Fame for hyperactive trademark litigators, Stoller would be in it. And, like George Brett, he would have gotten in on the first ballot. Acting as a sort of intellectual property entrepreneur, Stoller has federally registered scores of trademarks with the U.S. PTO (Central lists upwards of 50 that are actual or pending for just the "Stealth" mark), many containing everyday words that regularly pop up in commercial enterprise. When other companies or individuals inevitably make use of these words, Stoller issues cease-and-desist letters in the hopes that the user will blanche at the prospect of litigation and either agree to pay him a "licensing fee" or yield to his claims of ownership and stop using the alleged mark altogether. . . .

. . . Upon learning of Brett Brothers' Stealth bat, Stoller sent the company a cease-and-desist letter claiming ownership of the "Stealth" mark for use on baseball bats, alleging infringement, and demanding a $100,000 licensing fee. Brett Brothers refused, and Stoller (through Central) instituted this litigation.

An action for trademark infringement can only succeed if, among other things, the plaintiff owns the mark. Registration provides prima facie evidence of ownership, but this can be rebutted by competent evidence. *See* 15 U.S.C. § 1115(a). Ultimately, it is not the fact of registration that matters so much as the use of the mark in commerce; "[b]y insisting that firms use marks to obtain rights in them, the law prevents entrepreneurs from reserving brand names in order to make their rivals' marketing more costly." *Zazu Designs v. L'Oreal, S.A.*, 979 F.2d 499, 503 (7th Cir. 1992). Established use by a non-registrant is a valid defense to a registrant's infringement claim. 15 U.S.C. § 1115(b)(5).

With this in mind, the district court judge (the Honorable David H. Coar) had no trouble concluding that Brett Brothers' established use of the "Stealth" mark on baseball bats since 1999 precluded any infringement on the basis of Central's 2004 registration (thus also destroying the probative value, if any, of Central's 2003 and 2004 licensing agreements with Black-wrap and Easton). Central relies instead on the theory that its 1985 registration of the "Stealth" mark for baseballs and other sporting goods gave it rights to the mark on baseball bats as "closely related" products. [Citation omitted.] Rather than address the relationship between bats and balls, Brett Brothers challenged the validity of the 1985 trademark in the first place and sought to introduce evidence establishing that Central and its predecessors never used the mark in commerce.

As part of this effort, Brett Brothers requested that Stoller produce any documents related to the development, commercial use, and sales volume of any goods bearing the "Stealth" mark. Receiving no answer, they moved to compel compliance. Judge Coar granted the motion and gave Stoller three weeks to respond. Stoller missed the deadline, and his eventual response made only vague promises of documents to come. Finally, at his deposition, Stoller produced a single softball bearing the "Stealth" mark and an advertising flyer with a picture of a similar ball. He testified that he had at various points sold baseball bats to Walmart, Kmart, Montgomery Ward, Venture, Sears, Sportmart, Brown's Sporting Goods, and Zaire's, among others. He insisted that he had some invoices and purchase orders related to these sales, but he could not specify where these were or to which customers they corresponded. (Stoller never followed through on promises to produce these documents.) Asked for a sales total of Stealth bats, Stoller offered the number $10,000 from "memory" but could not confirm possession of records to support that figure. He also could not name the bat manufacturer.

Stoller eventually produced several documents. First was a sheet titled "Stealth Brand Baseball Sales" (not "Baseball Bat Sales") that simply provided a dollar amount for each year from 1996 to 2003. It offered nothing about any specific transactions—nothing about quantity, particular products, names of buyers, or dates of sale. Next were four similar looking "Sales Quote Sheets"—effectively price lists for four different alleged customers, all of whom are now out of business. One was addressed to Best Products in 1988, another to Venture Stores in 1991, a third to F.W. Woolworth in 1994, and one more to Montgomery Ward in 1997. Despite the apparent three-year interval between each document, the prices varied little. The aluminum bats were listed at $102 per bat in 1988, $103 in 1991, $104 in 1994, and $105 in 1997. Other products were also priced with small changes of identical increment. None of the quote sheets evidenced any actual orders or sales of the listed products. Finally, Stoller produced a spreadsheet listing itemized annual sales of a wide array of "Stealth" sports-related products. Though it lists baseballs, no baseball bats are referenced anywhere.

> . . .

Even if the sufficiency of Central's use were not a question of fact warranting deferential treatment on appellate review, see *Zazu Designs*, 979 F.2d at 505, it would not be a close question: there is absolutely nothing in the record upon which any reasonable person could conclude that Central and its predecessors actually sold "Stealth" baseballs prior to Brett Brothers first use of the mark in 1999. Stoller has repeatedly sought ways to get around trademark law's prohibition on the stockpiling of unused marks, and this case is no different. It is unfathomable that a company claiming to have engaged in thousands of dollars of sales of a product for more than a decade would be unable to produce even a single purchase order or invoice as proof. Self-serving deposition testimony is not enough to defeat a motion for summary judgment. By exposing Central's failure to make bona fide use of the "Stealth" mark for baseballs, Brett Brothers met its burden to overcome the presumption afforded by the 1985 registration, and summary judgment in its favor was the appropriate course.

Judge Coar went further. Invoking the authority granted by 15 U.S.C. § 1119, he ordered the cancellation of Central's 2005 registration of the "Stealth" mark for baseball bats. We find no error in this decision, which we review for abuse of discretion. Brett Brothers could have asserted its rights earlier by petitioning the PTO for cancellation, *see id.* § 1064, but nothing in § 1119 requires such a step. Instead, the provision arms courts with the power to effectively put the public on notice of its trademark-related judgments. Because a court's decision may raise doubts about the validity of a trademark registration, § 1119 arms the court with the power to update the federal trademark register to account for a mark's actual legal status (or lack thereof) after it has been adjudicated, thereby reducing the potential for future uncertainty over the rights in a particular mark. Where, as here, a registrant's asserted rights to a mark are shown to be invalid, cancellation is not merely appropriate, it is the best course. . . .

Page 126. Insert after Questions:

Aycock Engineering, Inc. v. AirFlite, Inc., 90 U.S.P.Q. 2d 1301 (Fed. Cir. 2009) Aycock Engineering registered AIRFLITE in 1974 for the service of arranging individual bookings with air taxi operators. In 2007, the TTAB ruled the registration void for failure to "use in commerce" the AIRFLITE mark. Reviewing the case law on use of service marks, the Federal Circuit stated:

> The language of the statute, by requiring that the mark be "used or displayed in the sale or advertising of services, and the services are rendered in commerce," makes plain that advertisement and actual use of the mark in commerce are required; mere preparations to use that mark sometime in the future will not do. Thus, we hold that an

applicant's preparations to use a mark in commerce are insufficient to constitute use in commerce. Rather, the mark must be actually used in conjunction with the services described in the application for the mark. . . .

The court held that Aycock merely engaged in preparations to use the mark:

Mr. Aycock had to develop his company to the point where he made an open and notorious public offering of his AIRFLITE service to intended customers. [citation omitted] However, at no point in time did Mr. Aycock give a potential customer the chance to use his AIRFLITE service. He never arranged for a single flight between a customer and an air taxi operator. This is because Mr. Aycock, as stated in his deposition, believed he needed at least 300 air taxi operators under contract before his service could become operational. Reasonably, because he never had more than twelve air taxi operators under contract at any one time, Mr. Aycock chose not to open his doors to the public.

Furthermore, while the two toll-free telephone numbers he obtained could have been used at some point in time as a means of offering the service to the public, they were never actually used for this purpose. Nothing in the record suggests that Mr. Aycock ever gave potential customers an opportunity to use the phone lines to make flight reservations, or that a single customer seeking to book a flight actually called the toll-free number. The record also fails to indicate that Mr. Aycock, or anyone else associated with Aycock Engineering ever spoke with a member of the general public about making a flight reservation through the AIRFLITE service.

That Mr. Aycock advertised to, contracted with, and was paid by air taxi operators does not transform the service from its preparatory stages to being rendered in commerce. Instead, these actions were Mr. Aycock's attempts to build the service's infrastructure, which, when completed, could then be offered to the public (and thus "rendered in commerce").

Judge Newman dissented, contending that the Board and the majority misdescribed the services that Aycock was in fact, and for over 30 years had been, rendering. The relevant service, she urged, was not booking passengers with air taxi services, but signing up air taxi services to carry passengers.

The services for which the mark was registered were described during the examination, shown in the specimens submitted with the application, and reasonably reflected in the description that the examiner required. If indeed a flaw in the registration is now discovered, after thirty-five years, it should be clarified and corrected, not voided ab initio. The cancellation of this long-standing registration is seriously flawed, and is seriously unjust. . . .

After improperly ruling that the service of providing a network of air taxi operators cannot support a registrable service mark, the Board held that the description of services in the AIRFLITE registration requires the booking of flights in airplanes. The TTAB held that since no individuals had booked flights in Aycock's network, Aycock was not performing the service described in the registration, and cancelled the registration. My colleagues on this panel appear to agree with the Board that the registration requires the transportation of passengers, and thereby define the registration into invalidity. However, the Lanham Act was designed to support the marks of commerce. [Citations omitted] The definition should be construed to support the registration, when it is reasonable to do so. . . .

The specimens filed with the application show display of the mark AIRFLITE in Aycock's advertising of its services to air taxi operators nationwide, and the record states that Aycock obtained contracts with about a dozen air taxi operators. Mr. Aycock testified that this is far fewer than the number that he needs, and that the business has not progressed as he had hoped. However, there was no finding of discontinuance or abandonment of the activity. Slow commercial progress, or absence of income or profit, is not a ground of cancellation of registration. [Citations omitted] The Lanham Act authorizes cancellation of abandoned marks, but a mark is not abandoned because the proprietor is encountering difficulties in the business.

QUESTION

If "the services" that are advertised and rendered in commerce turn out to be related to but different from those described in the registration, has the mark been "used" sufficiently to maintain the registration? How strictly should the relevant services be defined? What policies underlie the positions of the *Aycock* majority and dissent?

Nextel Comm., Inc. v. Motorola, Inc., 2009 WL 174923 (T.T.A.B., 2009). Having ruled that applicant's "chirp" sound for cellular telephones was not inherently distinctive (see *supra* this Supplement, Chapter 2.B.), the Board determined that the sound had not acquired distinctiveness either, because applicant failed to "use [the sound] in commerce." The Lanham Act definition of use in commerce includes a requirement that the mark be "affixed" to the goods or their labels, or on "documents associated with the goods or their sale." The Board appears to have understood the "affixation" requirement to mean that the applicant must in some way have called attention to the subject matter claimed as a mark. Without the source-denoting role of affixation, "the chirp emitted by applicant's cellular telephones in the normal course of their operation will be perceived merely as a signal to the user that one of the handset's features has been activated." Thus, the chirp may have been "used" in the sense of the functioning of the cellphone, but not "used in commerce [*as a trademark*]."

C. ANALOGOUS USE

Page 130. Add new Question 3:

3. Thoroughbred Legends claims to own a service mark in Ruffian, the name of a celebrated race horse. Legends sought to make a movie about the famous filly. It approached ESPN and other television networks and producers, offering a license to the Ruffian name for use in a film. It directed a well-known horse racing broadcaster to film interviews of Ruffian's jockey and trainer, and obtained commitments from most relevant individuals involved in Ruffian's racing career to participate in the film. It acquired historic memorabilia like the saddle Ruffian wore during her final match. Legends also entered into an agreement with Paradies Shops to license the Ruffian name for clothing and printed matter and paper goods for marketing, distribution and sale in the stores. It does not appear that those sales in fact took place. Disney has now, without Legends' participation, produced a movie about the career of Ruffian. In response to Legends' trademark action, Disney asserts that Legends has not used Ruffian as a trademark. How should the court rule? *See Thoroughbred Legends, LLC v. Disney*, 2008 WL 616253 (N.D.Ga.2008).

Page 130. Insert after Questions:

Aktieselskabet AF 21. November 2001 v. Fame Jeans

525 F.3d 8 (D.C. Cir. 2008).

■ BROWN, CIRCUIT JUDGE.

For some reason, a pair of jeans labeled Jack & Jones will sell for the equivalent of $96. Clearly there is magic in the name, and Fame Jeans tried to capture that magic by registering Jack & Jones as a trademark in the United States. Aktieselskabet (Bestseller), which generated the magic by selling Jack & Jones jeans elsewhere in the world, opposed Fame's trademark application. . . .

Bestseller, a Danish corporation, has been selling Jack & Jones jeans since 1990. By 2005, its business with the brand had expanded to include jeans, T-shirts and jackets, distributed in Europe, the Middle East, South America, and Asia. In the European Union alone, Bestseller sold nineteen million articles of branded clothing in 2005. It has registered Jack & Jones and related marks in forty-six countries, and it owns twenty-one domain names incorporating variations of the name.

In 2003, Bestseller decided to expand into North America; its competitor Fame Jeans appears, so far, to have stalled that expansion into the United States by assiduous effort at the U.S Patent and Trademark Office (PTO). Bestseller planned to begin operations in Canada, from which it would develop the brand into the United States. Accordingly, it applied to register the Jack & Jones mark in Canada in August 2004 and in the United States on December 6, 2004. Unfortunately for Bestseller, Fame had already applied to register Jack & Jones in the United States on January 9, 2004. As of their respective filing dates, neither party had tested the susceptibility of American consumers to the allure of Jack & Jones by actually trying to sell any jeans under the brand. Fame, therefore, filed its application under Lanham Act § 1(b), 15 U.S.C. § 1051(b), avowing its intent to use the trademark in commerce. Bestseller, on its part, filed under Lanham Act § 44(e), 15 U.S.C. § 1126(e), swearing it intended to use the mark and citing its 1990 Danish registrations.

Nine days after filing its U.S. application to register Jack & Jones, Bestseller filed an opposition to Fame's application to register the mark, alleging that Fame's registration was likely to cause confusion with Bestseller's Jack & Jones mark and interfere with Bestseller's application to register the mark. On January 30, 2006, the TTAB granted summary judgment on Bestseller's opposition. First, the TTAB pointed out Bestseller had admitted it never used the mark in commerce in the United States, and it explained foreign use alone gave Bestseller no right of priority here. Second, the TTAB held Bestseller's December 6, 2004, application junior to Fame's January 9, 2004, application.

Bestseller sought district court review of the TTAB decision, under Lanham Act § 21(b), 15 U.S.C. § 1071(b).... The district court dismissed all the claims....

B

Since Fame Jeans filed its application on January 9, 2004, Bestseller must establish use, either actual or constructive, before that date. Constructive use can arise under § 7(c), which grants priority, based on filing date, to a U.S. application or to a foreign application that was followed by a timely U.S. application under § 44(d). Bestseller filed a U.S. application on December 6, 2004, based on its 1991 Danish registration. It neither complied with the six-month timeliness requirement of § 44(d) nor even filed its application under § 44(d). Therefore, Bestseller cannot demonstrate any constructive use prior to Fame's filing date. However, Bestseller has adequately alleged actual use. Although the complaint does not set forth trademark use to earn Bestseller rights in the Jack & Jones mark, an opposer who has made enough "analogous" use can still defeat a registration. *See Malcolm Nicol & Co. v. Witco Corp.*, 881 F.2d 1063, 1065 (Fed. Cir. 1989) (quoting 3 MCCARTHY, *supra*, § 20:4 (1984)).

First, Bestseller fails to allege actual use in the most straightforward way, by showing its own protectible right to the Jack & Jones trademark in the United States. At common law, "prior ownership of a mark is only established as of the first actual use of a mark in a genuine commercial transaction." *Allard Enters., Inc. v. Adv. Programming Res., Inc.*, 146 F.3d 350, 358 (6th Cir. 1998). The 1988 amendments to the Lanham Act codified a standard of "use in commerce," necessary for a valid trademark registration, which means "the bona fide use of a mark in the ordinary course of trade," including, for a trademark, attaching the trademark to goods. 15 U.S.C. § 1127. In any case, "sporadic or minimal" sales are not sufficient. *Allard Enters.*, 146 F.3d at 359; *see also Zazu Designs v. L'Oreal, S.A.*, 979 F.2d 499, 503 (7th Cir. 1992) ("A few bottles sold over the counter ... and a few more mailed to friends" are not sufficient use.). While a single sale may indicate the first use of a mark, it must be the beginning of "continuous commercial utilization." *Allard*, 146 F.3d at 358. Obviously, as § 1052(d) requires, such use must also be "in the United States." *See Person's Co. v. Christman*, 900 F.2d 1565, 1568–69 (Fed. Cir. 1990) (T-shirt sales in Japan are not "use in United States commerce").

However, Bestseller need not "meet the technical statutory requirements to register ... [a mark] to have a basis for objection to another's registration." *Nat'l Cable Television Ass'n v. Am. Cinema Editors, Inc.*, 937 F.2d 1572, 1578 (Fed. Cir. 1991). Section 2(d) requires only "use[] in the United States," and adoption of the mark by use analogous to strict trademark use will therefore suffice. *T.A.B. Sys., Inc. v. Pactel Teletrac*, 77 F.3d 1372, 1375 (Fed. Cir. 1996). An opposer may rely on myriad forms of activity besides sales themselves, including, among others, regular business contacts, after-sales services, advertising of various forms, and marketing. *First Niagara Ins. Brokers, Inc. v. First Niagara Fin. Group*, 476 F.3d 867, 868–69 (Fed. Cir. 2007); *Johnny Blastoff, Inc. v. L.A. Rams Football Co.*, 188 F.3d 427, 434 (7th Cir. 1999); *Malcolm Nicol*, 881 F.2d at 1064. Even marketing of a trademarked product before the product is ready for sale has the potential to defeat a rival's registration. *See Old Swiss House, Inc. v. Anheuser–Busch, Inc.*, 569 F.2d 1130, 1133 (C.C.P.A. 1978). Still, desultory marketing such as sending out occasional press releases is not enough. *Id.* Analogous use must be "of such a nature and extent as to create public identification of the target term with the opposer's product." *T.A.B. Sys.*, 77 F.3d at 1375.

Bestseller's allegations fall short of showing a sale, whether in the United States or to an American abroad, as the beginning of a continuous commercial exploitation of the Jack & Jones mark in the United States; but they do give fair notice of a claim to analogous use. While Bestseller clearly sells millions of dollars worth of Jack & Jones branded clothing elsewhere in the world, it fails to allege any sales in the United States or to Americans. The closest Bestseller comes is saying this clothing "has been available to U.S. consumers through Bestseller's foreign customers and stores as well as through re-sales on eBay.com." Am. Compl. P 14. This allegation does not imply any American sales at all, much less continuous commercial sales.

By contrast, Bestseller actually does say it conducted "research and marketing for use of the mark within the United States." Am. Compl. P 29. The complaint does not say this marketing was sufficiently extensive to create an awareness of the Jack & Jones brand among American consumers, but it is reasonable to infer such an awareness from Bestseller's other allegations. Presumably, Bestseller will need to produce more substantial evidence if Fame contests this conclusion.... Simply put, the allegation of marketing in the United States, together with the inference of public association, is enough to give Fame fair notice of what it must contest. No more is required of a complaint. . . .

QUESTION

How persuasive is the claim of analogous use? If Fame Jeans was trying to usurp the fame of the Jack & Jones brand, but the foreign trademark owner had not yet sold jeans under the mark in the US, what other recourse would Bestseller have? Consider *International Bancorp v. Société des Bains de Mer de Monte Carlo*, casebook pp. 133–40, and *ITC v. Punchgini, infra* this Supplement, Chapter 3.E.

D. EXTRATERRITORIAL USE

Page 140.   Add new Question 5.

5. Recall *Aktieselskabet AF 21. November 2001 v. Fame Jeans, supra* this Supplement, Chapter 3.C. Could the Fourth Circuit have found that the Monte Carlo Casino had made analogous use of the Casino de Monte Carlo mark in the U.S.? Would such a finding have aided the Casino's U.S. trademark infringement claim against the off-shore gambling defendant?

E. PRIORITY

Pages 148–57.   Replace Second Circuit opinion in *ITC v. Punchgini* with following decisions in the same controversy:

ITC Limited v. Punchgini, Inc.

880 N.E.2d 852 (N.Y. 2007).

■ READ, J.

The United States Court of Appeals for the Second Circuit has asked us to resolve two questions regarding New York common law claims for unfair competition. We conclude that New York recognizes common law unfair competition claims, but not the "famous" or "well-known" marks doctrine.

I.

ITC Limited, a corporation organized under the laws of India, owns and operates the Maurya Sheraton & Towers, a five-star luxury hotel in New Delhi, India, through its subsidiary, ITC Hotels Limited. One of the Maurya Sheraton's seven restaurants is Bukhara, a five-star restaurant named after a city in Uzbekistan located on the famous Silk Road between China and the West. The New Delhi Bukhara, which has attained some measure of renown among those with an avid interest in fine cuisine, was named one of the 50 best restaurants in the world by London-based "Restaurant" magazine in 2002 and 2003. In the three decades since the New Delhi Bukhara opened in 1977, ITC has sought to capitalize on the restaurant's prestige, with mixed results: although ITC has opened or franchised Bukhara restaurants in Hong Kong, Bangkok, Bahrain, Montreal, Bangladesh, Singapore, Kathmandu, Ajman and the United States, as of May 2004 only the original restaurant in New Delhi and the restaurants in Singapore, Kathmandu and Ajman remained in business.

ITC established a Bukhara restaurant in Manhattan in 1986; in 1987 a Bukhara restaurant was opened in Chicago by a franchisee. On October 13, 1987 ITC obtained United States trademark registration for a Bukhara mark in connection with restaurant services; however, ITC closed its Bukhara restaurant in Manhattan on December 17, 1991, and cancelled the Chicago restaurant's franchise on August 28, 1997. ITC has not owned, operated or licensed any restaurant in the United States using the Bukhara mark since terminating the Chicago franchisee's licensing agreement in 1997.

In 1999, defendants Raja Jhanjee, Vicky Vij and Dhandu Ram, together with defendants Paragnesh Desai and Vijay Roa, incorporated Punchgini, Inc. for the purpose of opening an Indian restaurant in mid-town Manhattan, which they called Bukhara Grill. Jhanjee, Vij and Ram had all worked at the New Delhi Bukhara, and Vij had also worked at ITC's Bukhara restaurant in Manhattan. As Vij explained the origin of the new restaurant's name, in 1999 there was "no restaurant Bukhara in New York, and we just thought we [would] take the name" (*ITC Limited v. Punchgini, Inc.,* 482 F.3d 135, 144 [2d Cir. 2007]). In 2001, several Punchgini shareholders and defendants Mahendra Singh and Bachan Rawat, also alumni of ITC's Bukhara, opened a second Indian restaurant in mid-town Manhattan, called Bukhara Grill II (*id.; ITC Ltd. v. Punchgini, Inc.,* 373 F.Supp.2d 275, 277 [SD NY 2005]). Defendants have identified five other restaurants in the United States using Bukhara in their names, including one in Brooklyn. These restaurants are not affiliated with ITC. In addition, defendants have learned of more than 20 Bukhara restaurants unrelated to ITC outside the United States, including restaurants located in Uzbekistan, Australia, Egypt, Pakistan, the United Kingdom and "a high-end ... chain" in South Africa, which "also sells prepackaged foods under the 'Bukhara' name" and "owns the website www.bukhara.com."

The Bukhara Grill features many of the New Delhi Bukhara's signature dishes—which showcase the cuisine of the Northwest frontier region of India—and replicates many of its particular design elements. Indeed, one press report quoted Jhanjee as describing the Bukhara Grill as "quite like Delhi's Bukhara," commenting that "[t]he food is similar ... and the waiters too are dressed in similar Pathani suits."

On March 22, 2000, ITC's attorney sent Jhanji a letter accusing him of "passing off [his] new business [i.e., Bukhara Grill] as that of" ITC, "piggy[]back[ing] on the tremendous reputation" of ITC's Bukhara restaurants, and "partak[ing] of the fame, goodwill and custom earned by [ITC] by the mere adoption of the identical name." He demanded that Jhanji acknowledge ITC's exclusive rights to the Bukhara mark and refrain from further use of it; disclose how long he had used the Bukhara mark and render an accounting of sales and/or profits for this time period; and remit to ITC any such profits, plus estimated damages and attorneys' fees.

. . .

On February 26, 2003, . . . ITC filed a lawsuit against defendants in the United States District Court for the Southern District of New York. The amended complaint alleged trademark infringement under section 32(1)(a) of the Lanham Act; unfair competition and false advertising under sections 43(a) and 44(h) of the Lanham Act; and parallel actions under New York common law. As an affirmative defense, defendants charged ITC with abandonment of any rights in the United States to the Bukhara mark, and filed a counterclaim seeking cancellation of the mark's registration on that ground.

Following discovery, defendants moved for summary judgment. As an initial matter, the District Court Judge ruled that ITC could not pursue a trademark infringement claim because the record conclusively demonstrated its abandonment of the Bukhara mark and dress for restaurants in the United States. He then considered ITC's "assert[ions] that its unfair competition claims under section 43(a) of the Lanham Act and the New York common law provide a basis for liability independent of trademark law"; that is, ITC claimed that "[e]ven if it abandoned the 'Bukhara' mark and dress within the United States . . . it [was] nonetheless protected from unfair competition by virtue of the 'well known' or 'famous' marks doctrine" (373 F Supp 2d at 285–286).[1]

"The very existence of th[e well-known marks] doctrine is controversial," the District Court Judge opined, "as is its scope. Neither party cites, nor has the Court found, any Supreme Court or Second Circuit authority upholding liability on this theory, and it has been applied infrequently by the federal district courts" (*id.* at 286). He noted that the Ninth Circuit had recently countenanced the doctrine, but that it did so under "circumstances . . . arguably different from those in this case" (*id.,* citing *Grupo Gigante S.A. de C.V. v. Dallo & Co.,* 391 F.3d 1088 [9th Cir. 2004] [apparently as matter of policy, court permitted Mexican grocery chain to establish whether its "Gigante" mark was sufficiently widely known among Mexican–Americans in Southern California to be protected from use by California grocery chain]).

1. There is some ambiguity regarding the proper name for what has been variously called the "famous marks doctrine," the "well-known marks doctrine" and the "famous mark doctrine" (*see e.g.* McCarthy on Trademarks and Unfair Competition § 29:4 [using the above names interchangeably]). Apparently, the use of "well-known" in place of "famous" took hold after the passage of the Federal Trademark Anti–Dilution Act, which uses "famous" as a term of art (*see* 15 USC § 1125 [c] et seq.). At any rate, "famous" and "well-known," "mark" and "marks," have been used interchangeably to describe the putative doctrine, and no distinction is intended by our choice of words here.

The Judge, however, remarked that "[t]wo early cases in New York state courts, with fact patterns strikingly similar to the events alleged here by ITC, exemplify the doctrine" (375 F. Supp. 2d at 286, citing *Maison Prunier v. Prunier's Restaurant & Cafe, Inc.,* 159 Misc. 551, 288 N.Y.S. 529 [Sup Ct, New York County 1936]; *Vaudable v. Montmartre, Inc.,* 20 Misc. 2d 757, 193 N.Y.S.2d 332 [Sup Ct, New York County 1959]). But "[a]ssuming without deciding that these cases support the existence of an unfair competition claim, even in the absence of a viable US trademark, on the basis of a foreign mark that is 'well known' or 'famous,' it remains unclear how to determine what foreign marks are sufficiently famous to qualify" (375 F. Supp. 2d at 287). After reviewing various possible standards for a mark to qualify for the putative doctrine, the District Court Judge recognized that "an apparent consensus" existed as to what "at the very least . . . must be established in the relevant American market for a mark to qualify under the 'well known' or 'famous' mark doctrine"; and that "ITC [had] failed even to establish a triable issue" under that minimum standard (*id.* at 288). He also concluded that ITC lacked standing to press its claim under the Lanham Act for false advertising. The District Court therefore granted defendants summary judgment dismissing ITC's complaint in its entirety, and cancelled ITC's registration of the Bukhara mark, as defendants had requested in their counterclaim.

On March 28, 2007, the Second Circuit affirmed the District Court's award of summary judgment on ITC's infringement, unfair competition and false advertising claims under federal law. The court acknowledged, however, that "New York common law allows a plaintiff to sue for unfair competition where a property right or commercial advantage has been misappropriated," and stated that "in light of ITC's abandonment of the Bukhara mark and dress for restaurants in the United States, its common law assertion of a property right or a commercial advantage in these designations based on their foreign use depends on whether New York recognizes the famous marks doctrine in the circumstances here at issue" (482 F3d at 165 [quotation marks and citation omitted]).

Citing *Vaudable* and *Prunier,* two "decades-old trial court decisions" that are "routinely identif[ied] . . . as foundational in the development of the famous marks doctrine" (*id.* at 166), the court observed that

> "[n]either the New York Court of Appeals nor any intermediate New York appellate court . . . has ever specifically adopted the views expressed in [these cases] to accord common law protection to the owners of famous marks. Moreover, no New York court has clearly delineated a standard for determining when a mark becomes sufficiently famous to warrant protection" (*id.* at 165–66).

Further, "recognition of the famous marks doctrine as part of New York common law is plainly an important policy issue for a state that plays a pivotal role in international commerce" (*id.* at 166). Finally, because "certification [would] conclusively resolve the question of whether ITC's state unfair competition claim was, in fact, properly dismissed" (*id.* at 166–

167), the Second Circuit certified two questions to us regarding the New York common law claims.

II.

Certified Question No. 1

"Does New York common law permit the owner of a famous mark or trade dress to assert property rights therein by virtue of the owner's prior use of the mark or dress in a foreign country?" (482 F.3d at 166.)

The Second Circuit's first certified question calls upon us to define property rights in the context of a common law unfair competition claim grounded on a theory of misappropriation (*see* 482 F.3d at 165). Thus, we must consider whether a famous foreign mark constitutes property or a commercial advantage protected from unfair competition under New York law.

We have long recognized two theories of common law unfair competition: palming off and misappropriation (*see Electrolux Corp. v. Val–Worth, Inc.,* 6 N.Y.2d 556, 567–568, 161 N.E.2d 197, 190 N.Y.S.2d 977 [1959] [discussing the acceptance of these theories of unfair competition in New York courts and collecting cases]). "Palming off"—that is, the sale of the goods of one manufacturer as those of another—was the first theory of unfair competition endorsed by New York courts, and "has been extended ... to situations where the parties are not even in competition" [citations omitted].

After the United States Supreme Court sanctioned the misappropriation theory of unfair competition in *International News Serv. v. Associated Press* (248 U.S. 215, 39 S. Ct. 68, 63 L. Ed. 211 [1918]), "[t]he principle that one may not misappropriate the results of the skill, expenditures and labors of a competitor has ... often been implemented in [New York] courts" (*Electrolux,* 6 N.Y.2d at 567, citing *Germanow v. Standard Unbreakable Watch Crystals,* 283 N.Y. 1, 18, 27 N.E.2d 212 [1940]; *Fisher v. Star Co.,* 231 N.Y. 414, 428, 132 N.E. 133 [1921]; *see also Meyers v. Waverly Fabrics,* 65 N.Y.2d 75, 79–80, 479 N.E.2d 236, 489 N.Y.S.2d 891 [1985] [acknowledging defendant's possible liability for "violation of the law of unfair competition by misrepresenting the [uncopyrighted] design, which it knew to be plaintiff's, as its own"] [numerous citations omitted]; *National Basketball Assn. v. Motorola, Inc.,* 105 F.3d 841, 847–853 [2d Cir. 1997] [accepting misappropriation as a theory under New York common law]). Indeed, the New York cases cited by the District Court and the Second Circuit as embodying the famous or well-known marks doctrine in New York common law—*Prunier* and *Vaudable*—were, in fact, decided wholly on misappropriation theories.

In *Prunier,* the plaintiff operated celebrated haute cuisine restaurants in Paris and London, but none in the United States. The defendants opened a restaurant in New York and "appropriated to themselves the plaintiff's name.... Indeed, it was admitted ... that the name was intentionally selected because of plaintiff's well-known reputation and good will which has been built up as the result of decades of honest business effort. The defendants den[ied], however, that they ever held themselves out as being Prunier's of Paris" (159 Misc. at 553). The court upheld the legal viability of an unfair competition claim by the plaintiff—even though the two restaurants were not in direct competition—so long as "plaintiff['s] conten[tion] that its reputation extends far beyond the territorial limits of Paris and London and that it has a substantial following *in New York City* and in other parts of the world" was proved (*id.* at 559 [emphasis added]).

In *Vaudable,* the plaintiff's restaurant in Paris—Maxim's—was internationally famous "in the high-class restaurant field" (20 Misc 2d at 758–759). The defendants "appropriate[d] the good will plaintiffs [had] created in the name Maxim's as a restaurant," and were therefore held liable for unfair competition based on misappropriation even though the parties were "not in present actual competition" (*id.* at 759). "The trend of the law, both statutory and decisional," the court opined, "has been to extend the scope of the doctrine of unfair competition, whose basic principle is that commercial unfairness should be restrained whenever it appears that there has been a misappropriation, for the advantage of one person, of a property right belonging to another" (*id.* at 759 [citations omitted]; *see also Roy Export Co. v. Columbia Broadcasting System* (672 F.2d 1095, 1105 [2d Cir. 1982] [with decline of general federal common law after inception of misappropriation branch of unfair competition tort in *International News Serv.,* "the doctrine was developed by the states, New York in particular; there it has flourished in a variety of factual settings"]).

While expositors of the famous marks doctrine point to *Prunier* and *Vaudable* (*see* 5 McCarthy on Trademarks and Unfair Competition § 29:4 n 2 [4th ed. Sept. 2007] [citing *Prunier* and *Vaudable* as "perhaps the most famous examples" of the "well known" marks doctrine]), *Prunier* and *Vaudable* themselves in no way explain or proclaim—let alone rely on—any famous or well-known marks doctrine for their holdings. Instead, *Prunier* and *Vaudable* fit logically and squarely within our time-honored misappropriation theory, which prohibits a defendant from using a plaintiff's property right or commercial advantage—in *Prunier* and *Vaudable,* the goodwill attached to a famous name—to compete unfairly against the plaintiff in New York.

Under New York law, "[a]n unfair competition claim involving misappropriation usually concerns the taking and use of the plaintiff's property to compete against plaintiff's own use of the same property" (*Roy Export,* 672 F.2d at 1105). The term "commercial advantage" has been used interchangeably with "property" within the meaning of the misappropriation theory (*see Flexitized, Inc. v. National Flexitized Corp.,* 335 F.2d 774, 781–82 [2d Cir. 1964]). What *Prunier* and *Vaudable* stand for, then, is the proposition that for certain kinds of businesses (particularly cachet goods/services with highly mobile clienteles), goodwill can, and does, cross state and national boundary lines.

Accordingly, while we answer "Yes" to the first certified question, we are not thereby recognizing the famous or well-known marks doctrine, or any other new theory of liability under the New York law of unfair competition. Instead, we simply reaffirm that when a business, through renown in New York, possesses goodwill constituting property or a commercial advantage in this State, that goodwill is protected from misappropriation under New York unfair competition law. This is so whether the business is domestic or foreign.

III.

Certified Question No. 2

"How famous must a foreign mark or trade dress be to permit its owner to sue for unfair competition?" (482 F.3d at 167.)

Protection from misappropriation of a famous foreign mark presupposes the existence of actual goodwill in New York (*see e.g. Roy Export,* 672 F.2d at 1105 [misappropriation under New York law usually requires use in state of plaintiff's property or commercial advantage to compete against plaintiff]). If a foreign plaintiff has no goodwill in this state to appropriate, there can be no viable claim for unfair competition under a theory of misappropriation. At the very least, a plaintiff's mark, when used in New York, must call to mind its goodwill. Otherwise, a plaintiff's property right or commercial advantage based on the goodwill associated with its mark is not appropriated in this state when its unregistered mark is used here. Thus, at a minimum, consumers of the good or service provided under a certain mark by a defendant in New York must primarily associate the mark with the foreign plaintiff (*cf. Allied Maintenance Corp. v. Allied Mechanical Trades, Inc.,* 42 N.Y.2d 538, 545, 369 N.E.2d 1162, 399 N.Y.S.2d 628 [1977]).

Whether consumers of a defendant's goods or services primarily associate such goods or services with those provided by a foreign plaintiff is an inquiry that will, of necessity, vary with the facts of each case. Accordingly, we cannot—and do not—provide an exhaustive list of the factors relevant to such an inquiry. That said, some factors that would be relevant include evidence that the defendant intentionally associated its goods with those of the foreign plaintiff in the minds of the public, such as public statements or advertising stating or implying a connection with the foreign plaintiff; direct evidence, such as consumer surveys, indicating that consumers of defendant's goods or services believe them to be associated with the plaintiff; and evidence of actual overlap between customers of the New York defendant and the foreign plaintiff.

If the customers of a New York defendant do not identify a mark with the foreign plaintiff, then no use is being made of the plaintiff's goodwill, and no cause of action lies under New York common law for unfair competition. As a result, to prevail against defendants on an unfair competition theory under New York law, ITC would have to show first, as an independent prerequisite, that defendants appropriated (i.e., deliberately copied), ITC's Bukhara mark or dress for their New York restaurants. If they successfully make this showing, defendants would then have to establish that the relevant consumer market for New York's Bukhara restaurant primarily associates the Bukhara mark or dress with those Bukhara restaurants owned and operated by ITC.

Accordingly, the certified questions should be answered in accordance with this opinion....

ITC Ltd. v. Punchgini

518 F.3d 159 (2d Cir. 2008).

■ Reena Raggi, Circuit Judge:

... Having received the Court of Appeals' response, 9 N.Y.3d 467, 880 N.E.2d 851, 850 N.Y.S.2d 366, 2007 N.Y. Slip Op. 09813, 2007 WL 4334177 (N.Y. 2007), we now affirm the district court's award of summary judgment in its entirety.

I. The New York Court of Appeals' Answers to the Certified Questions

[The Court summarized the decision of the New York Court of Appeals.]

In short, to pursue an unfair competition claim, ITC must adduce proof of both deliberate copying and "secondary meaning." See ITC Ltd. v. Punchgini, Inc., 482 F.3d at 167 (observing that " '[s]econdary meaning' is a term of art referencing a trademark's ability to 'identify the source of the product rather than the product itself' ") (quoting Two Pesos, Inc. v. Taco Cabana, Inc., 505 U.S. 763, 766 n.4 (1992)).

II. ITC's Failure to Raise a Genuine Issue of Material Fact as to Secondary Meaning

Reviewing the challenged summary judgment award on ITC's state law claim of unfair competition in light of this response, we easily conclude, as the district court did, that ITC adduced sufficient evidence of deliberate copying to satisfy that element of this claim. Thus, we focus in this opinion on the sufficiency of defendants' showing of secondary meaning.

The district court concluded that ITC "failed even to establish a triable issue as to the existence of 'secondary meaning' in the New York market in which defendants operate." Id. at 288. In challenging this conclusion, ITC has abandoned its original appellate argument that no proof of secondary meaning is required when a New York unfair competition claim is based on intentional copying. Recognizing that the New York Court of Appeals' opinion ruled otherwise, ITC now contends that the district court erred in concluding that it could not establish secondary meaning. Specifically, ITC faults the district court for applying a different and stricter standard to its secondary meaning analysis than the New York Court of Appeals has now identified. ITC submits that, if it had had the benefit of the Court of Appeals decision, it would have submitted additional and certainly sufficient evidence to withstand summary judgment. The argument, which is conclusory rather than specific, is unconvincing both on the facts and the law.

First, assuming arguendo that the district court did apply a stricter standard of secondary meaning than required by New York law, that hardly explains ITC's decision to withhold evidence supportive of secondary meaning, particularly because any evidence of secondary meaning would also have been material to plaintiffs' theory of famous marks protection under federal and state law. Second, and perhaps more important, the record demonstrates that the district court did not, in fact, hold ITC to an unduly strict standard of secondary meaning. To the contrary, it considered whether there was sufficient evidence to demonstrate secondary meaning how ever that term was construed. Toward this end, the district court reviewed the record evidence in light of the six factors classically recognized as relevant to secondary meaning: "(1) advertising expenditures, (2) consumer studies linking the mark to a source, (3) unsolicited media coverage of the product, (4) sales success, (5) attempts to plagiarize the mark, and (6) length and exclusivity of the mark's use." *Id.* (*quoting Genesee Brewing Co. v. Stroh Brewing Co.*, 124 F.3d 137, 143 (2d Cir. 1997)). We discern no material difference between the standard established by these factors and those enumerated by the New York Court of Appeals and quoted earlier in this opinion.

ITC argues that the district court nevertheless erred in requiring secondary meaning in "the New York market," *id.*, whereas the New York Court of Appeals focused more narrowly on defendants' customers in New York. In fact, it is evident from a review of both decisions that the two courts were referring to the same market, i.e., potential customers for defendants' New York restaurant. We do not understand the Court of Appeals to have limited the relevant market to persons who had already eaten in defendants' restaurants, nor do we understand the district court to have expanded the relevant market to every New Yorker, whether or not inclined to eat in restaurants generally or Indian restaurants in particular. See, e.g., *ITC Ltd. v. Punchgini, Inc.*, 373 F. Supp. 2d at 286 (describing relevant market examined in *Vaudable v. Montmartre, Inc.*, 20 Misc. 2d 757, 193 N.Y.S.2d 332, 334–35 (N.Y. Sup. Ct. 1959), as "the class of people residing in the cosmopolitan city of New York who dine out"); id. at 287–88 (describing test in *Grupo Gigante S.A. de C.V. v. Dallo & Co.*, 391 F.3d 1088, 1097–98 (9th Cir. 2004), as "whether customers of the American firm are likely to think they are patronizing the same firm that uses the mark in another country").

In any event, even if we were to conclude that the district court somehow erred in its market definition, ITC has failed to adduce evidence sufficient to create a genuine issue of material fact on the question of whether the Bukhara mark, when used in New York, calls to mind for defendants' potential customers ITC's goodwill, or that defendants' customers primarily associate the Bukhara mark with ITC. See *ITC Ltd. v. Punchgini, Inc.*, 2007 N.Y. Slip Op. 09813 at *14. Like the district court, we observe that ITC's proffered evidence of goodwill derived entirely from foreign media reports and sources and was unaccompanied by any evidence that would permit an inference that such reports or sources reach the relevant consumer market in New York. See *ITC Ltd. v. Punchgini, Inc.*,

373 F. Supp. 2d at 290. ITC proffered no evidence that it had "directly targeted advertising of its Indian or other foreign 'Bukhara' restaurants to the United States." *Id.* at 288–89. It made no attempt to prove its goodwill in the relevant market through consumer study evidence linking the Bukhara mark to itself, and it presented no research reports demonstrating strong brand name recognition for the Bukhara mark anywhere in the United States. See *id.* at 289 & n.15. Moreover, the record is devoid of any evidence of actual overlap between customers of defendants' restaurant and ITC's Bukhara, aside from ITC's own inadmissible speculation. Absent admissible evidence, however, a reasonable factfinder could not conclude that potential customers of defendants' restaurant would primarily associate the Bukhara mark with ITC, particularly in light of evidence that numerous Indian restaurants in Massachusetts, Washington, Virginia, and around the world have used the name "Bukhara," all without any affiliation or association with ITC.

ITC's belated efforts to identify admissible evidence of secondary meaning are unavailing. First, ITC points to record evidence that a significant number of defendants' customers are Indian or "well-traveled [people who] know what authentic Indian food tastes like." Appellants' Supp. Br. Jan. 7, 2008, at 7. Even if these facts support a reasonable inference that this consumer market is "more knowledgeable about India than the general New York population," *id.*, ITC provides no evidence-apart from its own conjecture-to support the conclusion that, as a consequence, these persons "primarily associate" the name "Bukhara" with ITC. Conjecture, of course, is insufficient to withstand summary judgment. Second, ITC argues that the district court failed to consider evidence of "public statements or advertising stating or implying a connection with the foreign plaintiff." Appellants' Supp. Br. Jan. 7, 2008, at *7. We are not persuaded. The district court plainly considered this evidence and concluded that it supported ITC's claim of intentional copying. Moreover, the district court recognized that "there may be some circumstances in which intentional copying is sufficient to show 'secondary meaning.' " *ITC Ltd. v. Punchgini, Inc.*, 373 F. Supp. 2d at 291. But it cogently explained why this was not such a case: "it would be tautological to conclude that copying alone demonstrates 'secondary meaning' sufficient to permit an unfair competition claim as to a foreign mark here, where that copying is only prohibited by the 'well known' or 'famous' mark exception if the mark has 'secondary meaning.' " *Id.* We adopt this reasoning as consistent with the New York Court of Appeals' conclusion that more than copying is necessary for a famous foreign mark holder to pursue a state law claim for unfair competition. That foreign holder must further offer evidence that the defendant's potential customers "primarily associate[]" the mark with the foreign holder. *ITC Ltd. v. Punchgini, Inc.*, 2007 N.Y. Slip Op. 09813 at *14. ITC cannot satisfy this burden simply by pointing to evidence of obvious similarities between defendants' Bukhara Grill and ITC's own Bukhara restaurant, because such evidence is no proof that defendants' potential customers were even aware of the existence of ITC's Bukhara.

Finally, ITC faults the district court for ignoring evidence of the goodwill created by ITC's New York and Chicago restaurants during the years they operated. Even if we were to assume the possibility of a company maintaining goodwill for years after abandoning a trademark, ITC cannot point to any record support—even from a single one of defendants' customers—that the goodwill of ITC's New York and Chicago restaurants lingered so that defendants' potential customers "primarily associated" New York's Bukhara Grill with ITC establishments. *Id.*

III.   Conclusion

For the reasons stated, we conclude that the record evidence is insufficient as a matter of law to raise a triable question of fact on the issue of secondary meaning necessary to establish a New York State claim for unfair competition in a foreign mark. Accordingly, we hold that the district court correctly granted summary judgment in favor of defendants on this claim, and we now conclude our consideration of this appeal by affirming the judgment of the district court in all respects.

AFFIRMED.

QUESTIONS

1. Paris Conv. art. 6*bis* requires member States, *inter alia*, to "prohibit the use of a trademark which constitutes a reproduction, an imitation, or a translation, liable to create confusion, of a mark considered by the competent authority of the country of . . . use to be well known in that country as being already the mark of a person entitled to the benefits of this Convention and used for identical or similar goods." TRIPs art. 16.2, which extends Paris Conv. art. 6*bis* to services, further specifies, "In determining whether a trademark is well-known, Members shall take account of the knowledge of the trademark in the relevant sector of the public, including knowledge in the Member concerned, which has been obtained as a result of promotion of the trademark." Is the New York Court of Appeals' decision (which cites neither international agreement) consistent with these standards?

2. If a foreign mark must have generated goodwill in New York, what is the relevant segment of the New York public? Suppose plaintiff's establishment is a very famous sushi restaurant in Tokyo, which is not known to most New Yorkers. The Tokyo restaurant is, however, certainly known to Japanese business people who visit or temporarily reside in New York City. If the NYC version is an imposter (and the trademark owner is not itself doing business in NYC), would the Tokyo original have a claim in New York on the ground that the local establishment is targeting itinerant Japanese (as well as any New York residents who have traveled to Tokyo and learned of the restaurant there)? Does it matter if the New York restaurant's clientele includes not only Japanese business people, but New Yorkers who are unaware of the Tokyo restaurant?

3. Under the NY Court of Appeals' and Second Circuit's approach, is there any basis on which to hold liable a merchant who identifies a trademark and/or trade dress well-known in its country of origin, but not in the US, and then assiduously copies the mark and/or trade dress in purveying identical goods or rendering identical services?

Empresa Cubana del Tabaco v. Culbro, 587 F. Supp.2d 622 (S.D.N.Y. 2008). Applying the criteria announced by the New York Court of Appeals in *Punchgini*, the Southern District of New York held that Culbro misappropriated the COHIBA cigar mark used in Cuba and elsewhere (but, because of the embargo, not in the U.S.).

> [In an earlier proceeding] this Court made several findings of fact [establishing] that General Cigar "intentionally copied" the COHIBA mark. While rejecting Plaintiff's contention that Defendant acted in bad faith, this Court found that General Cigar launched a super-premium cigar product using the name COHIBA "in part to capitalize on the success of the Cuban COHIBA brand and especially the good ratings and the notoriety that it had received in *Cigar Aficionado*." *Empresa Cubana*, 70 U.S.P.Q.2d at 1659. In addition, the record showed that General Cigar's conduct constituted "copying the COHIBA mark and attempting to exploit the reputation of the Cuban COHIBA." *Id.* at 1688. The Court found that General Cigar attempted "to plagiarize the mark," and engaged in "intentional copying," on account of the Cuban COHIBA's fame in the United States. *Id.* at 1681–82. General Cigar's statements, the Court found, established that "development of the COHIBA brand was an attempt to somehow capitalize on the success of the Cuban brand." *Id.* at 1686 (quotation omitted). Notwithstanding this evidence, the Court found that the record did not demonstrate that General Cigar "believed they did not own the COHIBA mark." *Id.* at 1688. After *ITC*, whatever additional evidence this Court determined was necessary to establish "bad faith" in the context of the famous marks doctrine is no longer necessary. The evidence in the record, therefore, is more than sufficient to demonstrate that General Cigar deliberately copied the COHIBA mark, as required by *ITC*.
>
> To prove misappropriation, Cubatabaco must also establish that the "relevant consumer market … primarily associates" the COHIBA trademark with the Cuban COHIBA. *ITC*, 880 N.E.2d at 860. After trial, this Court found that the Cuban COHIBA had acquired recognition consistent with "secondary meaning" in the U.S., that is, it was "uniquely associated" with the Cuban COHIBA, or that this was its "primary significance." *Empresa Cubana*, 70 U.S.P.Q.2d at 1677, 1682. Relying on *Vaudable* [*v. Montmartre, Inc.*, 20 Misc.2d 757 (N.Y. Sup. Ct. 1959)], which the Court of Appeals cited to in *ITC*, this Court concluded that the Cuban COHIBA had achieved "a level of fame consistent with secondary meaning as described in *Vaudable*." [Citations omitted] Accordingly, Cubatabaco has established the second and final prong of an unfair competition by misappropriation claim under New York law and is entitled to relief.

CHAPTER 4

REGISTRATION OF TRADEMARKS

B.   PRIORITY, INTENT TO USE AND FOREIGN MARKS

Page 190.   Insert Question 3 before *Zirco*:

3.   The excerpt from the preceding Senate Report states that the intent-to-use provisions require a bona fide intent on the part of the applicant measured by "an objective good-faith test." Where the individual ITU applicant in *Boston Red Sox Baseball Club Limited Partnership v. Sherman, infra* 4.C. this Supplement, included over 100 items of apparel in the application, but produced no documents evidencing a bona fide intent contemporaneously with filing his application, such as business plans, evidence of capability of manufacturing such items or any other documents, the Board held the applicant lacked a bona fide intent. Non-domestic applicants that file based on a foreign application or registration under Section 44 or that extend an international registration to the U.S. under section 66 are also required to possess and to declare a bona fide intent to use the mark in U.S. commerce on the covered goods. Should evidence showing information about activities outside the U.S. be considered in determining such applicants' bona fide intent to use the mark in U.S. commerce? *See Honda Motor Co. v. Winkelmann,* 90 U.S.P.Q.2d 1660 (T.T.A.B. 2009)

Page 190.   Delete *Zirco v. AT&T* and Question and substitute the following case and Question:

Compagnie Gervais Danone v. Precision Formulations, LLC

89 U.S.P.Q.2d 1251 (T.T.A.B. 2009).

BY THE BOARD:

MOTION FOR SUMMARY JUDGMENT IN OPPOSITION NO. 91179589

Precision seeks to register the mark FRUITOLOGY for various cosmetic products in International Class 3, various nutritional goods and medicated skin creams in International Class 5, and various beverage goods in International Class 32.

Danone has moved for summary judgment . . . on its claim of priority and likelihood of confusion regarding Precision's nutritional goods of International Class 5 and the goods of International Class 32. Danone has not opposed Precision's application to register the mark in International Class 3.

There are no questions as to standing or similarity of the marks and goods in these cases, as the parties' submissions show they have filed trademark applications for nearly identical marks, for overlapping or legally identical goods, and each party has claimed there is a likelihood of confusion. Moreover, in its answer to the notice of opposition Precision admitted that the parties' marks are "identical in sight, sound, connotation and commercial impression" and that "there is direct overlap between some" of the parties' goods. The parties have therefore effectively conceded that confusion is likely between the opposed goods in each opposed class. The sole issue that remains is one of priority.

. . .

We begin by looking at Precision's priority date. A party that has filed an intent-to-use application may rely on the filing date of its application to establish priority. *See Larami Corp. v. Talk To Me Programs Inc.,* 36 USPQ2d 1840, 1845 n. 7 (TTAB 1995) (constructive use provisions may be used both defensively and offensively to establish priority); *see also, Zirco Corp. v. American Telephone & Telegraph Co.,* 21 USPQ2d 1542, 1544 (TTAB 1991) (right to rely on constructive use date comes into existence with filing of intent-to-use application). Precision may, therefore, claim priority back to the February 21, 2007 date on which it filed the intent-to-use application. Precision has not relied on any earlier date for priority purposes.

We next consider Danone's priority date. We note that Danone filed its application on May 22, 2007 pursuant to Section 66, 15 U.S.C. § 1141f, of the Trademark Act.[1] Section 66(b), 15 U.S.C. § 1141f(b), provides that a Section 66(a) application:

... shall constitute constructive use of the mark, conferring the same rights as those specified in section 7(c), as of the earliest of the following:

(1) The international registration date, if the request for extension of protection was filed in the international application.

(2) The date of recordal of the request for extension of protection, if the request for extension of protection was made after the international registration date.

(3) The date of priority claimed pursuant to section 67.

Section 67 of the Trademark Act, 15 U.S.C. § 1141g, states that an applicant is entitled to claim a date of priority when it holds an international registration, makes a request for extension of protection (application) to the U.S., includes a claim of priority based on a right of priority under Article 4 of the Paris Convention for the Protection of Industrial Property,

---

1. The filing date of Danone's § 66(a) application is the international registration date of May 22, 2007. *See* TMEP § 1904.01(b).

and the date of the international registration is within six months of the filing date of the application underlying the international registration. Danone's International Registration No. 0930814 issued May 22, 2007. The International Registration is based on an underlying French application (No. 06 3 467 672) filed December 6, 2006, which issued on May 11, 2007, as French Registration No. 06 3 467 672. Danone claimed priority based on the December 6, 2006 filing date of the French application. Thus, pursuant to Sections 66(b) and 67, Danone is entitled to a priority date of December 6, 2006. *See General Motors Corp. v. Aristide & Co., Antiquaire de Marques,* 87 USPQ2d 1179, 1181 (TTAB 2008).

Because Danone's application has an effective filing date of December 6, 2006, and that date is earlier than Precision's filing date of February 21, 2007, Danone may rely on its effective filing date to establish priority. Thus, we find that there are no genuine issues of material fact as to the issue of priority.

Accordingly, Danone's motion for summary judgment is granted, contingent upon application Serial No. 79041120 maturing into a registration.[2] If application Serial No. 79041120 matures into a registration, the Board will enter judgment against Precision, sustain the opposition, and refuse registration to Precision for International Classes 5 and 32.

QUESTION

If Precision rather than Danone had priority and received a contingent judgment, Danone could potentially be forced to wait up to 3 years if Precision submitted all available extensions of time to file a statement of use. After that time, it might nevertheless allow the application to go abandoned. Would it be fair to make Danone wait so long before it knew whether it could register its mark? Consider the *WarnerVision* case that follows. Would Precision be able to sue Danone for infringement, relying only on its ITU filing date priority if Danone started using the mark?

C. BARS TO REGISTRATION

Page 205. Insert after *In re Bad Frog Brewery, Inc.*:

Boston Red Sox Baseball Club Limited Partnership v. Sherman

2008 WL 4149008 (TTAB 2008).

■ HOLTZMAN, ADMINISTRATIVE TRADEMARK JUDGE:

Applicant, Brad Francis Sherman, has filed an application to register the mark shown below.

---

2. Section 66(b), 15 U.S.C. § 1141f(b), confers the same rights as those specified in Section 7(c) of the Trademark Act, 15 U.S.C. § 1057(c). Section 7(c) provides that filing an application for registration on the Principal Register establishes constructive use and na-tionwide priority, contingent upon issuance of a registration. Thus, we do not enter judgment at this time, but rather grant Danone's summary judgment motion contingent on the issuance of a registration in application Serial No. 79041120.

Applicant seeks registration of the mark for the following goods:

Clothing, namely, shirts, T-shirts, under shirts, night shirts, rugby shirts, polo shirts, cardigans, jerseys, uniforms, athletic uniforms, pants, trousers, slacks, jeans, denim jeans, overalls, coveralls, jumpers, jump suits, shorts, boxer shorts, tops, crop tops, tank tops, halter tops, sweat shirts, sweat shorts, sweat pants, wraps, warm-up suits, jogging suits, track suits, blouses, skirts, dresses, gowns, sweaters, vests, fleece vests, pullovers, snow suits, parkas, capes, anoraks, ponchos, jackets, reversible jackets, coats, blazers, suits, turtlenecks, cloth ski bibs, swimwear, beachwear, tennis wear, surf wear, ski wear, infantwear, baby bibs not of paper, caps, swim caps, berets, beanies, hats, visors, headbands, wrist bands, sweat bands, headwear, ear muffs, aprons, scarves, bandanas, belts, suspenders, neckwear, neckties, ties, neckerchiefs, ascots, underwear, briefs, swim and bathing trunks, bras, sports bras, brassieres, bustiers, corsets, panties, garters and garter belts, teddies, girdles, foundation garments, singlets, socks, loungewear, robes, bathrobes, underclothes, pajamas, sleepwear, night gowns, lingerie, camisoles, negligees, chemises, chemisettes, slips, sarongs, leg warmers, hosiery, pantyhose, body stockings, knee highs, leggings, tights, leotards, body suits, unitards, body shapers, gloves, mittens, footwear, shoes, sneakers, boots, galoshes, sandals, zori, slippers, rainwear, baseball caps, wool hats, knit hats, in Class 25.

The application was filed on July 19, 2005 based on an allegation of a bona fide intention to use the mark in commerce.

Opposer, Boston Red Sox Baseball Club Limited Partnership, filed a notice of opposition on August 2, 2006. Opposer alleges that since long prior to applicant's constructive first use date, opposer has used various marks that consist of or incorporate the words RED SOX ("RED SOX Marks"), including a mark in the particular stylized font shown below, in connection with baseball game and exhibition services and a wide variety of goods including clothing, paper goods and printed matter, toys and sporting goods.

RED SOX

. . .

As its original grounds for opposition, opposer alleged priority and likelihood of confusion under Section 2(d) of the Trademark Act; and three grounds under Section 2(a) of the Act: (1) that the mark consists of immoral and scandalous matter; (2) that the mark disparages opposer and/or brings it into contempt or disrepute; and (3) that the mark falsely suggests a connection with opposer. Opposer subsequently amended the opposition to additionally allege that applicant did not have a bona fide intention to use the mark at the time of filing the application.*

. . .

SECTION 2(a)—IMMORAL OR SCANDALOUS MATTER

Opposer argues that SEX ROD comprises matter that would be considered vulgar to a substantial composite of the public when used on t-shirts and other items of apparel identified in the application; and that the mark would be particularly offensive when used on goods intended for children and infants such as the "infantwear" and "baby bibs" included in the description of goods. To support its position, opposer submitted a listing from the Random House Unabridged Dictionary (2d ed. 1993) defining the word "rod" as "*Slang* ... b. *Vulgar*, the penis."

Applicant admits that the term SEX ROD "is intended to possess a sexual connotation," but maintains that the term is only "sexually suggestive." Describing his mark "SEX ROD" as a parody of the RED SOX stylized mark, applicant argues that his mark is "an elegant and symmetrical transposition" of RED SOX; that it is a subtle play on words which "enhances the humor"; and that "the elegance of the execution mitigates any perceived vulgarity of the resulting turn of the phrase." In applicant's view, the mark "represents the at once clever yet sophomoric sense of humor that prevails in those venues in which apparel bearing the SEX ROD Stylized mark would likely be worn, e.g., ballparks, sports bars, and university campuses."

Registration of a mark which consists of or comprises immoral or scandalous matter is prohibited under Section 2(a) of the Trademark Act. Whether a mark is immoral or scandalous must be determined from the standpoint of, not necessarily a majority, but a substantial composite of the general public; and in the context of the goods, the relevant marketplace

---

* Editors' Note: The Board also sustained the opposition on the ground that applicant lacked a bona fide intent to use his mark on the over 100 goods from "anoraks to zoris."

and contemporary attitudes. *In re Boulevard Entertainment, Inc.*, 334 F.3d 1336, 67 USPQ2d 1475, 1477 (Fed. Cir. 2003); and *In re Mavety Media Group, Ltd.*, 33 F.3d 1367, 31 USPQ2d 1923, 1925–26 (Fed. Cir. 1994).

"A showing that a mark is vulgar is sufficient to establish that it 'consists of or comprises immoral ... or scandalous matter' within the meaning of section 1052(a)." *Boulevard Entertainment, supra*, observing that the Court in *Mavety Media, supra*, analyzed the mark in terms of "vulgarity" ...

Dictionary evidence alone can be sufficient to establish that a term has a vulgar meaning. *Boulevard Entertainment, supra at* 1478. In this case opposer has submitted an entry from a mainstream dictionary, the Random House Unabridged Dictionary (2d ed. 1993), demonstrating that the word "rod" has a vulgar meaning. We take judicial notice of an additional mainstream resource, The New Oxford American Dictionary (2d ed. 2005), wherein the term "rod" is similarly characterized as *"vulgar slang* a penis."

There are obviously other non-vulgar definitions of "rod." However, none of the other definitions is relevant here. The significance of "rod" when preceded by the word "sex" denotes only one meaning. In the context of applicant's goods, with the mark perhaps emblazoned across a t-shirt or some other item of apparel, and in the context of the marketplace, which would include all public places where the clothing would be worn or purchased, the mark would convey, not a sexually suggestive connotation as applicant contends, but rather a sexually explicit message to the viewer. We agree with opposer that the use of the term on children's and infant clothing makes the term particularly lurid and offensive.

The evidence is sufficient to show prima facie that "SEX ROD" is vulgar, and applicant has submitted no evidence of a non-vulgar meaning of the term or any other evidence to rebut opposer's showing.

Applicant's testimony as to his opinion of the perception of the mark is simply not sufficient. Whether applicant intended the mark to be humorous, or even whether some people would actually find it to be humorous, is immaterial. The fact remains that the term would be perceived and understood as vulgar by a substantial portion of the purchasing public. Even assuming for the sake of argument that SEX ROD is a parody of opposer's "RED SOX" marks, as applicant asserts, there is nothing in the parody itself which changes or detracts from the vulgar meaning inherent in the term. In other words, the parody, to the extent there is one, is itself vulgar.

SECTION 2(a)—DISPARAGEMENT

Section 2(a) of the Trademark Act also prohibits registration of a mark that "consists of or comprises ... matter which may disparage ... persons, living or dead, institutions, beliefs, or national symbols, or bring them into contempt, or disrepute." As noted in *University of Notre Dame du Lac v. J.C. Food Imports*, 703 F.2d 1372, 217 USPQ 505 (Fed. Cir. 1983), Section 2(a) embodies concepts of the right to privacy and publicity, that is, the right to protect and to control the use of one's identity. In effect, this provision of Section 2(a) protects against appropriation of one's identity by another and subjecting it to contempt or ridicule. *See Greyhound Corp. v. Both Worlds Inc.,* 6 USPQ2d 1635, 1639 (TTAB 1988) ("Disparagement is essentially a violation of one's right of privacy—the right to be 'let alone' from contempt or ridicule.").

The Board in *Greyhound* set forth the two elements of a claim of disparagement: 1) that the communication reasonably would be understood as referring to the plaintiff; and 2) that the communication is disparaging, that is, would be considered offensive or objectionable by a reasonable person of ordinary sensibilities.[7]

Thus, as an initial matter, we must determine whether the designation which opposer claims applicant is attempting to appropriate would be understood as opposer's identity.

As previously noted, opposer, Boston Red Sox Baseball Club Limited Partnership, is the owner of the "Boston Red Sox Major League Baseball" club. The club has operated under the nickname "Red Sox" for 100 years. Since 1908 the name "Red Sox" has been used by the media, press, fans and the public to refer to both the club itself and to the source of its baseball game services. There is no question that the name "Red Sox" is the identity of the baseball club, apart from being a trademark for the entertainment services the club provides.

The stylized version of the "Red Sox" name has been used by the organization for more than 70 years to identify the team. The name appears in large letters across the front of the players' uniforms; it has been heavily promoted to the public through use on a wide range of merchandise and materials; and it has received extensive public exposure over the years in all forms of visual media. As such, opposer's name in this format has come to be recognized by the public not only as a mark identifying the source of opposer's baseball games, but as an alternative form of its "Red Sox" nickname and another symbol of the Red Sox organization. Indeed, applicant admits that the designation "is identified and associated with opposer".

Applicant has copied the form, style and structure of the Club's corporate symbol, and because his mark is so visually similar to the original, many consumers, and in particular Red Sox fans, upon seeing the mark displayed on a t-shirt or a jersey, will recognize it as referring to the Red Sox symbol.

---

7. As the Board noted in *Harjo v. Pro-Football, Inc.,* 50 USPQ2d 1705, 1740 (TTAB 1999), there are different tests for disparagement depending upon whether the party alleging disparagement is an individual or commercial corporate entity, as in *Greyhound,* or a non-commercial group, such as a religious or racial group, as in *Harjo.* [30 USPQ2d 1828 (TTAB 1994)], *rev'd on other grounds,* 284 F.Supp.2d 96, 68 USPQ2d 1225 (D.D.C. 2003), *remanded,* 415 F.3d 44, 367 U.S. App. D.C. 276, 75 USPQ2d 1525 (D.C. Cir. 2005), *dismissed on remand,* 567 F. Supp. 2d 46 (D.D.C. 2008). Because opposer is a commercial corporate entity, the test enunciated in *Greyhound* is applicable here.

Furthermore, applicant admits that the design of his mark is intended to refer to opposer and to evoke the Club. Applicant's intent is strong evidence that he will accomplish his purpose, and that the mark will be perceived by the public as referring to opposer. *See Dunkin' Donuts of America, Inc. v. Metallurgical Exoproducts Corp.,* 840 F.2d 917, 6 USPQ2d 1026 (Fed. Cir. 1988) (evidence of intent is pertinent to Section 2(a) claim of disparagement). *See also Notre Dame, supra at* 509, regarding intent in the context of a Section 2(a) claim of false connection ("Evidence of such intent would be highly persuasive that the public will make the intended false association. The defense that the result intended was not achieved would be hollow indeed.").

We turn then to the question of whether applicant's mark disparages opposer's identity. As the Board stated in *Greyhound,* disparagement is "the publication of a statement which the publisher intends to be understood, or which the recipient reasonably should understand, as tending 'to cast doubt upon the quality of another's land, chattels, or intangible things.'" *Greyhound* citing *Restatement (Second) of Torts § 629* (1977). In the context of Section 2(a), a disparaging mark will cast doubt upon the quality of a plaintiff's corporate goodwill. *See Harjo, supra at* 1740.

We have already determined that SEX ROD would be perceived as a vulgar term by a substantial number of consumers. Inasmuch as applicant's mark in the identical style and format would be understood as a reference to opposer, the mark would be viewed as a sexually vulgar version of the club's symbol and as making an offensive comment on or about the club.

Applicant argues that although the mark "is indeed intended to evoke the Club" the mark "neither contains any profanity nor tarnishes the reputation of the Club." Applicant points to the fact that the team's "members were popularly know[n] as the 'Idiots' just three years ago due to the edgy image that they portrayed both on and off the field, often with the tacit consent of the Club." Opposer acknowledges that the Red Sox players and fans referred to the team "affectionately" as the "idiots," and further notes that the Club itself, has used suggestive phrases such as "You Have RED SOX Envy" on its t-shirts.

While the line between what is or is not offensive may not always be clear, in this case it is. The difference between opposer's expressions of subtle or good-natured ribbing and applicant's crude, overtly sexual mark SEX ROD is obvious. Because applicant's mark is offensive, and because the public will associate the offensive message with opposer, the mark, in the language of the Statute, "may disparage" opposer.

[The Board then concluded that there was no likelihood of confusion or false association with Opposer]

QUESTIONS

1. In concluding that SEX ROD would be perceived as scandalous and immoral by a substantial portion of the purchasing public, is it adequate to rely exclusively on dictionary definitions? Should a party be required to prove this element by survey evidence?

2. Do you agree with the line drawn by the Board between "subtle or good-natured ribbing and applicant's crude, overtly sexual mark"?

3. Should/would the SEX ROD decision be different if applicant did not include children's clothing among the goods on which it intended to use the mark, but instead limited the goods to the kinds of items typically sold to adults (or to males in the 18–40 age group)?

Page 207.

The Board's decision in *McDermott v. San Francisco Women's Motorcycle Contingent* was affirmed in a non-precedential opinion by the Federal Circuit, 240 Fed.Appx. 865 (2007).

Page 217.   Delete Question 6 and add the following two Questions:

6. The measure of scandalous and immoral marks is the perception of a substantial composite of the general public; whereas, marks disparaging to a particular group are viewed through the lens of a substantial composite of that group. What if the disparaged group consists of a religion with 1,000 adherents, will the negative perceptions of 400 of them be sufficient to block a registration? Compare the standard for marks disparaging to a commercial entity or individual, which looks to the reaction of a "reasonable person of ordinary sensibilities." *See Boston Red Sox Baseball Club Limited Partnership v. Sherman, supra* this Supplement.

7. Where there is conflicting evidence as to the perception of the term HEEB as disparaging or not among different groups within the Jewish community, what should be the measure of a substantial composite of the referenced group? Should it matter that the applicant is targeting its goods/services to the group that does not regard the term as offensive or disparaging? *See In re Heeb Media*, 2008 WL 5065114 (T.T.A.B. 2008).

Page 224.   Delete *In re White* and Question following that case and substitute the following case and Questions:

Hornby v. TJX Companies, Inc.

87 U.S.P.Q.2d 1411 (T.T.A.B. 2008).

■ SEEHERMAN, ADMINISTRATIVE TRADEMARK JUDGE:

Lesley Hornby a/k/a Lesley Lawson a/k/a Twiggy, an individual, (hereafter "petitioner") has petitioned to cancel a registration owned by TJX Companies, Inc. (hereafter "respondent") for the mark TWIGGY for "clothing, namely, children's pants, tops, slacks, skirts, vests, sweaters, shirts and blouses." The grounds asserted in the petition to cancel . . . are likelihood of confusion (one element of which, of course, is priority of use), false suggestion of a connection, fraud, and dilution.

. . .

[The Board found against petitioner on the grounds of fraud, likelihood of confusion and likelihood of dilution and found against respondent as to its laches defense].

False Suggestion of a Connection

The final ground which we must decide is whether respondent's use of the mark TWIGGY for children's clothing may falsely suggest a connection with petitioner. The Federal Circuit explained in *University of Notre Dame du Lac v. J.C. Gourmet Food Imports Co., Inc.,* 703 F.2d 1372, 217 USPQ 505, 508 (Fed. Cir. 1983), that the purpose of the false suggestion of a connection language of Section 2(a) was to protect "the name of an individual or institution which was not a 'technical' trademark or 'trade name' upon which an objection could be made under Section 2(d)," and that this statutory section embraces the concepts of the right of privacy and the related right of publicity. *See In re White,* 80 USPQ2d 1654 (TTAB 2006). The Federal Circuit further stated that to succeed on such a ground the plaintiff must demonstrate that the name or equivalent thereof claimed to be appropriated by another must be unmistakably associated with a particular personality or "persona" and must point uniquely to the plaintiff. The Board, in *Buffett v. Chi–Chi's, Inc.,* 226 USPQ 428 (TTAB 1985), in accordance with the principles set forth in *Notre Dame,* required that a plaintiff asserting a claim of a false suggestion of a connection demonstrate 1) that the defendant's mark is the same or a close approximation of plaintiff's previously used name or identity; 2) that the mark would be recognized as such; 3) that the plaintiff is not connected with the activities performed by the defendant under the mark; and 4) that the plaintiff's name or identity is of sufficient fame or reputation that when the defendant's mark is used on its goods or services, a connection with the plaintiff would be presumed. ... However, in some of the decisions involving the false suggestion of a connection ground, the language of the second factor has been modified somewhat, to state "that the marks would be recognized as [the same as, or a close approximation of, the name or identity previously used by the other person], in that they point uniquely and unmistakably to that person." *See L. & J.G. Stickley Inc. v. Cosser,* [81 USPQ2d 1956,] at 1972; *In re White,* [80 USPQ2d 1654]; *In re Urbano,* 51 USPQ2d 1776 (TTAB 1999); *In re Wielinski,* 49 USPQ2d 1754 (TTAB 1998). This modified language recognizes the requirement set forth by the Federal Circuit that the name claimed to be appropriated by the defendant must point uniquely to the plaintiff.

There is no real dispute in this case as to factors one and three. The evidence clearly shows that petitioner is known, both personally and professionally, as "Twiggy," and that respondent's mark TWIGGY is identical to petitioner's name. It is also clear that she is not connected with respondent, and did not give respondent permission to use her name as a trademark for its goods.

With respect to the fourth factor, respondent asserts that its mark TWIGGY would not be recognized as petitioner's name because petitioner's name or identity is not of sufficient fame or reputation that consumers seeing it on children's clothing would presume a connection with petitioner. Petitioner, obviously, takes the opposite position.

. . . [T]he fame or reputation of petitioner must be determined as of the time respondent's registration for TWIGGY issued. Thus, although petitioner may have been a major celebrity in the late 1960s, the burden on petitioner is to show that she had sufficient fame and/or reputation as of July 4, 2000.

There is no question that petitioner was a huge sensation in the late 1960s, a model who was also a celebrity. Certainly if her fame and reputation were considered during the period of 1967–1970, that fame would easily satisfy the prong of the *Buffett* test requiring that the plaintiff's name or identity be of sufficient fame or reputation that when the defendant's mark is used on its goods or services, a connection with the plaintiff would be presumed. What we must consider, then, is whether since that time she has retained a sufficient degree of fame or reputation that, as of July 4, 2000, a connection with her would still be presumed by consumers seeing the mark TWIGGY on children's clothing. We find that she has.

Petitioner is not simply a model who made a name for herself more than 30 years ago and then disappeared from public view. On the contrary, through the years she has continued to play a public role, and has appeared before the public in vehicles which gave her significant national exposure. As noted previously, during the 1970s she starred in a U.S. film called "The Boyfriend," for which she won two Golden Globe awards, and appeared on various television shows that were broadcast nationally in the United States, including "The Sonny and Cher Show" and the "Mike Douglas Show," on which she was a co-host for a week. In the 1980s she starred in a major Broadway hit and Tony-award winning show for 18 months, and was herself nominated for a Tony award. She performed on one of the Academy Award telecasts, and was also a presenter. She also made many appearances on nationally seen television interview shows, including "Johnny Carson" and "Merv Griffin." She starred in movies opposite such "name" actors as Robin Williams and Shirley Maclaine. In the 1990s she had a presence on U.S. television, starring for one year (1991) in a U.S. television series, and in a TV movie in 1996. She also performed in theatrical productions in the United States, starring in a 1997 summer theater production that was reviewed in "The New York Times" (a newspaper with national circulation), and starring for five months in 1999 in an off-Broadway production that was positively reviewed.

She did interviews through the years, for example, when she had a show coming out, and she also did a publicity tour of U.S. cities to publicize her film "Madame Sousatzka. "In connection with the sitcom "Princesses," she had interviews in "People," "Vogue" and "US" magazine.

These various entertainment activities, and the promotional efforts surrounding them, have successfully kept her name before the U.S. public, and have built on the extraordinary initial reputation and celebrity that was created in the period from 1967–1970. We do not say that her post–1970 activities would, on their own, be sufficient to demonstrate the requisite recognition, but they are sufficient when taken together with the phenomenal amount of publicity and recognition she received in that initial period. As further evidence of her reputation and recognition in 2000, the year that respondent's registration issued, we take judicial notice that the fourth edition of The American Heritage Dictionary of the English Language, published in 2000, listed "Twiggy" as an entry, as follows:

> Originally Lesley Hornby. British model who epitomized the ultrathin look popular from 1966 to 1976.

In addition, we think it is significant that in 1999 the Franklin Mint asked petitioner to license her name and likeness for a collectible doll. The other dolls in this collection were Jackie Kennedy, Princess Diana, Marilyn Monroe and Elvis Presley. Although the doll did not go on the market until after respondent's mark was registered, the fact that the Franklin Mint asked petitioner to be part of its doll collection, and the stature of the other dolls in the collection, indicates that her fame was considerable and still ongoing during 1999, the year prior to the issuance of respondent's registration, and that consumers would, at that time, recognize her name. The subsequent sale of a million TWIGGY dolls confirms this. Although the sales of the dolls occurred shortly after the issuance of respondent's registration, they are still indicative of her reputation in 2000.

In sum, we find that petitioner and her name, Twiggy, had sufficient fame and reputation in 1999 and 2000, both prior to and at the time respondent's mark was registered, that purchasers of children's clothing would, upon seeing the mark TWIGGY on such goods, presume an association with her...

Respondent has argued that purchasers of children's clothing would not be aware of petitioner's activities in 1967–1970, when she was a phenomenon. Essentially respondent is asserting that people who knew of petitioner in that time period are now too old to buy children's clothing, and that there is no evidence that "a new generation of adult consumers" would be aware of the 1960s model Twiggy. We accept that purchasers who were too young to have been exposed to the "Twiggy phenomenon," or were born after 1970, would not necessarily be aware of petitioner or her name through her various entertainment activities subsequent to 1970. We also accept that in 2000, the year respondent's mark was registered, and therefore the date as of which we must determine whether the mark falsely suggested a connection with petitioner, some of these people would be purchasers of children's clothing. For example, a girl born in 1970 would have been 30 in 2000, and could have a child age 6–10 for whom she would buy children's clothing. However, girls who were 8–17 years old in 1970 would have been aware of petitioner at that time, and, at least at the younger age range, would have been the purchasers of the board game

Twiggy the Queen of Models, the dress-up paper dolls and the other licensed products. These same girls would have been 38–47 years old in 2000, and are likely to have had children at that time who would wear "children's clothing," since such clothing can be worn by 12–13 year olds. In other words, these women could have given birth when they were in the age range of 25 to 34 and, therefore, have been purchasers of children's clothing in 2000. And not to belabor the point, but it is not unusual for women to continue to have children when in their late 30s or early 40s, and therefore even women who were in their late teens or early 20s in 1967–1970 could have been consumers of respondent's goods in 2000. Further, even if their own children were too old in 2000 to wear children's clothing, the people who knew of petitioner in 1967–1970 are still potential purchasers of children's clothing, for their friends' children or even for their own grandchildren. Moreover, while we have addressed our comments to women as the purchasers of children's clothing, we must also recognize that fathers may purchase clothing for their children, and they do not have the biological issues that women do. Because of petitioner's great celebrity during 1967–1970, men as well as women, and boys as well as girls, would have been very aware of her, and may, in 2000, have been purchasing clothing for their children.

Accordingly, petitioner has satisfied the fourth factor set forth in *Buffett*, that petitioner's name is of sufficient fame or reputation that when the respondent's mark is used on children's clothing, a connection with petitioner would be presumed.

Finally, we consider the second factor, whether respondent's mark would be recognized as pointing uniquely and unmistakably to the petitioner. As we have discussed at length, "Twiggy" had been the personal and professional name of petitioner for more than 30 years at the time respondent's registration issued, and her name was of sufficient fame or reputation that consumers would make a connection between children's clothing sold under the mark TWIGGY and petitioner. The evidence supporting our finding that her name has fame and/or reputation also demonstrates that the name "Twiggy" is unmistakably associated with petitioner. Further, on this record, we find that TWIGGY points uniquely to petitioner. Respondent has pointed out that "twiggy" has a dictionary meaning and, although it has not submitted a copy of it, we take judicial notice that "twiggy" means "1. Resembling a twig or twigs, as in slenderness or fragility. 2. Abounding in twigs: *a twiggy branch*." Respondent has also submitted three third-party registrations, two for the mark TWIGGY for bicycles and for entertainment services presenting a live squirrel water skiing behind a boat, and one for the mark TWIGGY STARDOM for entertainment services consisting of live musical performances and a web site featuring musical performances, etc.

The requirement that a respondent's mark point "uniquely" to petitioner does not mean that TWIGGY must be a unique term. Rather, in the context of the respondent's goods, we must determine whether consumers would view the mark as pointing only to petitioner, or whether they would perceive it to have a different meaning. Thus, if the respondent's goods were a plant food or a plant, the mark TWIGGY used on them could very well be understood as having the dictionary meaning quoted above. However, there is nothing in the record from which we can conclude that TWIGGY for children's clothing would have such a meaning. Although it is not respondent's burden to explain why it adopted its mark, respondent's choice not to do so means we do not have any explanation which might show that the term has another significance when used for children's clothing. In fact, the obvious connection between models and clothing is further support for our conclusion that respondent's mark for children's clothing points uniquely to petitioner.[19]

As for the third-party registrations submitted by respondent, we repeat the Board's statements in *In re White, supra* at 1659–60 (citations omitted):

> Further, the actual copies of third-party registrations and applications are not evidence that the marks which are the subjects thereof are in use and that the public is familiar with the use of those marks. In this regard, we note that applicant has pointed to no case law holding that third-party registrations and/or applications should be accorded significant weight in our analysis of a Section 2(a) false suggestion refusal.
>
> . . .

. . . [T]he three registrations submitted by respondent are not for goods or services even remotely related to clothing, so they are of no value in showing that TWIGGY for children's clothing would have a meaning that does not point to petitioner. In short, the three third-party registrations have no probative value in showing that the name "Twiggy" does not point uniquely to petitioner.

After considering all of the evidence of record in connection with the Section 2(a) false suggestion of a connection factors, we find that respondent's mark TWIGGY for children's clothing may falsely suggest a connection with petitioner.

Conclusion

We find that petitioner has proven her Section 2(a) ground of false suggestion of a connection, but has failed to prove her pleaded grounds of likelihood of confusion, dilution, and fraud. We also find that respondent has failed to prove its affirmative defense of laches.

QUESTIONS

1. In *Hornby*, the Board differentiates a false suggestion of a connection claim under section 2(a) and a likelihood of confusion claim under section

---

19. In saying this, we want to be clear that it is not necessary, in order to succeed on a Section 2(a) false suggestion of a connection ground, that the plaintiff show that consumers would believe the defendant's goods emanate from the plaintiff. That is a requirement for a Section 2(d) likelihood of confusion claim, but not a Section 2(a) claim. We point to petitioner's fame as a model not to show that consumers would expect her to be associated with the sale of clothing, but because consumers are likely to associate clothing and models, and therefore to view the mark TWIGGY as pointing to petitioner.

2(d). If relevant purchasers falsely believe there may be a connection, would they also not likely to be confused as to the sponsorship of such goods/services? Is the real difference in the claims found in the Board's statement that false suggestion of a connection protects names or institutions that are not a "technical" trademark or trade name?

2. The false suggestion of a connection prong of section 2(a) applies *inter alia* to "persons, living or dead." How long after a person dies should this provision be applicable? Does it matter if the deceased person has no heirs or estate managing rights to the name? *See In re MC MC S.r.l.*, Application No. 79022561 for MARIA CALLAS (T.T.A.B. Sept. 26, 2008) and pending opposition *Strathopoulos v. MC MC S.r.l.*, Opp. No. 91187914.

3. Consider the claim of the Boston Red Sox that the SEX ROD mark falsely suggests a connection with the team. Should the fact that the Board found the mark to be scandalous and disparaging affect the outcome of this claim? *See Boston Red Sox Baseball Club Limited Partnership v. Sherman*, *supra* this Supplement, Chapter 4.C.1.a.

Page 229.   Number Question as 1 and add Question 2 as follows:

2. What level of "fame or reputation" must a person or institution possess to establish a false association claim? Is it the same level of fame required for a federal dilution claim, i.e. a wide recognition "by the general consuming public of the United States"? *See Association pour la Defense de Marc Chagall v. Bondarchuk*, 82 U.S.P.Q.2d 1838 (T.T.A.B. 2007) (applying a lesser standard of fame than the dilution standard). Does MARC CHAGALL for vodka suggest a false association with the post-impressionist, Russian artist Marc Chagall, who died in 1985, where the mark owner has no connection with the artist or his heirs? What if Chagall had died over 100 years ago when most state publicity rights would no longer pertain?

Page 235.   Add Questions 4 and 5 as follows:

4. In assessing the similarity of marks, the Board compares the similarity of their sight, sound and meaning. Where the sight and sound of two marks are different, but the meaning of the challenged mark is the foreign language equivalent of the other, how heavily should this similarity of meaning weigh? *See, e.g., In re La Peregrina Ltd.*, 86 U.S.P.Q.2d 1645 (T.T.A.B. 2008) (LA PEREGRINA for jewelry found confusingly similar to PILGRIM for jewelry where "la peregrina" means "the pilgrim" in Spanish).

5. Is it legitimate to compare different portions of a mark to two separate marks of another if those marks are often used on the same product and in its advertising? *See Schering–Plough Healthcare Products, Inc. v. Huang*, 2007 WL 1751193 (T.T.A.B. 2007)(DR. AIR for shoe insoles as compared with DR. SCHOLL'S and AIR PILLO for the same products).

Page 252.   Add the following at the end of the Question:

What if the residence of an individual ITU applicant is Montecito, a wealthy area in Southern California with fewer than 10,000 residents but several celebrities? Is it appropriate to presume a goods/place association with publications and nutritional services for the mark THE MONTECITO DIET? *See In re Mankovitz*, 90 U.S.P.Q.2d 1246 (T.T.A.B. 2009). What if goods come from close to a place named in a mark? *See In re Spirits of New Merced LLC*, 2007 WL 4365811 (T.T.A.B. 2007) (YOSEMITE BEER for beer brewed in a town 80 miles away from Yosemite National Park where town depends on the Park for much of its commercial activity).

Page 259. Add Questions 4, 5 and 6 as follows:

4. *California Innovations* indicates that non-geographic meanings of a mark should be considered in determining whether its primary significance is geographic. How should we regard GUANTANAMERA, which means having to do with the city or province of Guantanamo, Cuba, if it also is the title of a previously popular Spanish song? Does it matter that the goods are cigars? *See Corporacion Habanos, S.A. v. Guantanamera Cigars Co.*, 86 U.S.P.Q.2d 1473, (T.T.A.B. 2008).

5. *California Innovations* states that a false belief is likely to be material if the place named is "noted for" the goods or the goods are a "principal product" of the area. Do you believe NAPA VALLEY MUSTARD CO. for mustard that does not come from Napa Valley, California should be barred from registration? What evidence of materiality would be necessary? *See In re Beaverton Foods, Inc.*, 84 U.S.P.Q.2d 1253, (T.T.A.B. 2008).

6. Should the mark LA GIANNA HAVANA be considered geographically deceptively misdescriptive for cigars not from Cuba where the only possible connection with Cuba is that the cigars may have been grown from seeds descended from Cuban seeds more than 45 years earlier? *See Corporacion Habanos, S.A. v. Garofalo*, Opp. No. 91186535 (Jan. 2, 2009 T.T.A.B.).

In re Spirits International, N.V.

563 F.3d 1347 (Fed. Cir. 2009).

■ DYK, CIRCUIT JUDGE:

Spirits International B.V. ("Spirits"), appeals a decision of the Trademark Trial and Appeal Board ("Board") ... refusing to register Spirits' mark—MOSKOVSKAYA—for vodka. *In re Spirits Int'l N.V.*, 86 USPQ2d 1078 (TTAB 2008). The Board concluded that the mark was primarily geographically deceptively misdescriptive under 15 U.S.C. § 1052(e)(3). Because the Board applied an incorrect test for materiality in determining that the mark was geographically deceptive, we vacate and remand.

BACKGROUND

Spirits filed an application for use of the mark MOSKOVSKAYA for vodka on April 22, 1993, based on an allegation of bona fide intention to use the mark in commerce. Spirits admitted that the vodka "will not be manufactured, produced or sold in Moscow and will not have any other connection with Moscow." *Id.* at 1081....

... Like the examining attorney, the Board, under the doctrine of foreign equivalents, translated the mark into English and found that the primary significance of the mark was a generally known geographic location, establishing the first element of the prima facie case. The Board also found that Moscow is well known for vodka, and that this established the second element. *Id.* at 1086.

The Board also found that Moscow is reputed for high quality vodka, and thus that the public would likely be materially influenced by the mark in the purchasing decision. *Id.* In analyzing the materiality element, the Board stated that "an appreciable number of consumers for the goods or services at issue" must be deceived. *Id.* at 1085. But the Board concluded that "it is never necessary to show that all, or even most, of the relevant consumers would be deceived. All that is required is a showing that *some portion* of relevant consumers will be deceived." *Id.* at 1084 (emphasis added). The Board found that the mark met the materiality requirement because of its deception to Russian speakers.

. . .

I

. . .

California Innovations did not address the question of whether the materiality test of subsection (e)(3) embodies a requirement that a significant portion of the relevant consumers be deceived. We hold that subsection (e)(3) does incorporate such a requirement, and that the appropriate inquiry for materiality purposes is whether a substantial portion of the relevant consumers is likely to be deceived, not whether any absolute number or particular segment of the relevant consumers (such as foreign language speakers) is likely to be deceived.

In interpreting the materiality requirement of 15 U.S.C. § 1052 (e)(3), it is appropriate to look to the history of subsection (a), which includes the same materiality requirement as modern subsection (e)(3). *Cal. Innovations,* 329 F.3d at 1340. Subsection (a), together with the original version of subsection (e) covering primarily deceptively misdescriptive marks, was created by § 2 of the Lanham Act. Pub. L. No. 79–489 § 2, 60 Stat. 427, 428–29 (1946)....

As the legislative history of the Lanham Act makes clear, subsection (a) was designed to codify common law standards for trademark infringement in the context of the registrability of trademarks under federal law...

We thus must examine the common law to determine the scope of subsection (a). Before the Lanham Act, deceptive common law trademarks were unenforceable. This fell under the rubric of the doctrine of "unclean hands," an equitable defense under the common law. *Worden & Co. v. Cal. Fig Syrup Co.,* 187 U.S. 516, 528, 23 S. Ct. 161, 47 L. Ed. 282, 1903 Dec. Comm'r Pat. 637 (1903). This meant that "if the plaintiff makes any material false statement in connection with ... any symbol or label claimed as a trade-mark ... no property can be claimed on it, or, in other words, the right to the exclusive use of it cannot be maintained." *Id*. But the common law doctrine did not apply in situations where a relatively small number of consumers was misled, as was made clear by Justice Holmes' opinion in *Coca-Cola Co. v. Koke Co. of America*, 254 U.S. 143, 144–47, 41 S. Ct. 113, 65 L. Ed. 189 (1920). There the Supreme Court held that the trademark "Coca–Cola" was not deceptive, and thus did not give rise to a defense of unclean hands to trademark infringement. *Id*. The Court first described the historical formulation of the beverage involving substantial quantities of the extract of the coca leaf (cocaine) and the extract of the cola nut. *Id*. The Court noted that the formulation of the beverage had changed over the years, and no longer contained significant quantities of coca or cola. *Id*. On this basis the defendant asserted that the mark was now deceptive. The Court stated that "[o]f course a man is not to be protected in the use of a device the very purpose and effect of which is to swindle the public" but that this defense was not "a very broad" one and "should be scrutinized with a critical eye." *Id*. Although the Court noted that there may be some people "here and there" who would drink the beverage because they thought it contained cocaine, this was insufficient to invoke the unclean hands doctrine because the mark "conveyed little or nothing [about the contents of the drink] *to most who saw it." Id*. (emphasis added).

. . .

Under the circumstances it is clear that section (e)(3) . . . requires that a significant portion of the relevant consuming public be deceived. That population is often the entire U.S. population interested in purchasing the product or service. We note that, in some cases, the use of a non-English language mark can be evidence that the product in question is targeted at the community of those who understand that language. In such cases, the relevant consuming public will be composed of those who are members of that targeted community, and, as a result, people who speak the non-English language could comprise a substantial portion of the relevant consumers. (Citation omitted). There is no such contention here.

II

. . . Here the Board properly recognized that in order to be deceptive, foreign language marks must meet the requirement that "an appreciable number of consumers for the goods or services at issue will be deceived." *In re Spirits*, 86 USPQ2d at 1085. The problem with the Board's decision is that it elsewhere rejected a requirement of proportionality, and discussed instead the fact that Russian is a "common, modern language[] of the world [that] will be spoken or understood by an appreciable number of U.S. consumers for the product or service at issue," such number being in this case 706,000 people, according to the 2000 Census. *Id*. The Board, however, failed to consider whether Russian speakers were a "substantial portion of the intended audience." Because the Board applied an incorrect test, a remand is required.

We express no opinion on the ultimate question of whether a substantial portion of the intended audience would be materially deceived. We note that only 0.25% of the U.S. population speaks Russian. If only one quarter of one percent of the relevant consumers was deceived, this would not be, by any measure, a substantial portion. However, it may be that Russian speakers are a greater percentage of the vodka-consuming public; that some number of non-Russian speakers would understand the mark to suggest that the vodka came from Moscow; and that these groups would together be a substantial portion of the intended audience.

We remand to the Board for a determination of whether there is a prima facie case of material deception under the correct legal test in the first instance. Because of our disposition on the question of the prima facie case, we do not reach the questions raised by the appellant as to the Board's rejection of the survey as rebutting the prima facie case, though we note that the Board's holding as to this issue was heavily influenced by its incorrect view of materiality.

VACATED and REMANDED

QUESTIONS

1. What evidence can an Examiner put forward to show the proportion of the relevant purchasing group for a particular product? How would the Examiner show that vodka purchasers in the U.S. are aware of Russia's connections to vodka or that even non-Russian speakers would understand Moskovskaya to mean somewhere in Russia?

2. Recall the Board's conclusion that BAIKALSKAYA was primarily geographically descriptive for vodka. *In re Joint–Stock Company "Baik,"* Casebook page 248. Does the Federal Circuit's requirement of analysis of the relevant purchasing group of MOSKOVSKAYA vodka impact how the *Baik* case would now be decided?

Page 263.   Insert after Questions 1 and 2:

In re Joint–Stock Company "Baik", 2007 WL 2460997 (T.T.A.B. 2007). In a decision holding that BAIK, a relatively rare surname, is not primarily merely a surname, Judge Seeherman's concurring opinion discusses how the "look and feel" of a surname factor should be interpreted in assessing whether a mark is primarily merely a surname:

> ... if a term does not have the "look and feel" of a surname, it should not be refused registration even if there is evidence to show that it is, in fact, a surname.
>
> However, I do not think that, in the converse situation, registration should be refused simply because the mark at issue is similar in sound or appearance to other surnames. The purpose behind prohibiting the registration of marks that are primarily merely surnames is not to protect the public from exposure to surnames, as though there were something offensive in viewing a surname. Rather, the purpose behind Section 2(e)(4) is to keep surnames available for people who wish to

use their own surnames in their businesses, in the same manner that merely descriptive terms are prohibited from registration because competitors should be able to use a descriptive term to describe their own goods or services.

Because the purpose of Section 2(e)(4) is not to protect the public from being exposed to surname marks, the fact that the public may view a mark as a surname because it has the "look and feel" of a surname should not be the basis for refusing registration of rare surnames. If a surname is extremely rare, it is also extremely unlikely that someone other than the applicant will want to use the surname for the same or related goods or services as that of the applicant. Therefore, if the Office is not able to muster sufficient evidence to show that the mark is the surname of a reasonable number of people, and must instead resort to finding other surnames which rhyme with the mark or differ from the mark by one or two letters, I believe that it is not proper to refuse registration. Interpreting the "look and feel" factor to refuse registration of marks simply because they are similar to recognized surnames does not serve the intention of the statute.

Do you agree with Judge Seeherman's analysis? Why or why not?

Page 273. Insert the following case and Question after the Question:

In re Vertex Group LLC

89 U.S.P.Q.2d 1694 (T.T.A.B. 2009).

■ Rogers, Administrative Trademark Judge:

Applicant Vertex Group LLC seeks to register as a trademark on the Principal Register a sound described as follows:

> . . . a descending frequency sound pulse (from 2.3kHz to approximately 1.5kHz) that follows an exponential, RC charging curve, wherein said descending frequency sound pulse occurs four to five times per second, and that over a one second period of time, there is alternating sound pulses and silence with each occurring approximately 50% of the time during a one second period of time. [2]

Registration of the sound is sought for goods identified as a "Personal security alarm in the nature of a child's bracelet to deter and prevent child abductions," in Class 9 (application Serial No. 76601697; the "child's bracelet application") and as "Personal security alarms," in Class 9 (application Serial No. 78940163; the "personal alarms application"). . . .

. . .

2. A recording of the sound can be heard by accessing an audio file accessible through the USPTO website, at the following address: http:/www.uspto.gov/go/kids/sound ex/78940163_0001.mp3.

Functionality

The Trademark Act provides that a proposed mark may be refused registration if it "comprises any matter that, as a whole, is functional." Section 2(e)(5), 15 U.S.C. § 1052(e)(5). The Supreme Court has stated " '[i]n general terms, a product feature is functional,' and cannot serve as a trademark, 'if it is essential to the use or purpose of the article or if it affects the cost or quality of the article,' that is, if exclusive use of the feature would put competitors at a significant non-reputation-related disadvantage." *Qualitex v. Jacobson,* 34 USPQ2d at 1163–64, quoting *Inwood Laboratories, Inc. v. Ives Laboratories, Inc.,* 456 U.S. 844, 102 S. Ct. 2182, 72 L. Ed. 2d 606, 214 USPQ 1, 4 n.10 (1982). See also, *TrafFix Devices Inc. v. Marketing Displays Inc.,* 532 U.S. 23, 121 S. Ct. 1255, 149 L. Ed. 2d 164, 58 USPQ2d 1001, 1006 (2001). We note that this standard contemplates at least two possible bases upon which a finding of functionality may be made. First, if the product feature is essential to the use or purpose of the article it may be found functional. See *TrafFix Devices,* 58 U.S.P.Q.2d at 1006 ("Where the design is functional under the *Inwood* formulation there is no need to proceed further to consider if there is a competitive necessity for the feature."). Second, if the product feature affects the cost or quality of the article, so that exclusive right to use it would put a competitor at a disadvantage, this, too, may support a conclusion that the product feature is functional.

The Federal Circuit, our primary reviewing court, looks at four factors, originally set out by a predecessor court, when it considers the issue of functionality, and the factors are particularly helpful for analyzing functionality under the second approach: (1) the existence of a utility patent disclosing the utilitarian advantages of the design; (2) advertising materials in which the originator of the design touts the design's utilitarian advantages; (3) the availability to competitors of functionally equivalent designs; and (4) facts indicating that the design results in a comparatively simple or cheap method of manufacturing the product. *In re Morton–Norwich Products, Inc.,* 671 F.2d 1332, 213 USPQ 9, 15–16 (CCPA 1982). *See also Valu Engineering Inc. v. Rexnord Corp.,* 278 F.3d 1268, 61 USPQ2d 1422, 1426 (Fed. Cir. 2002).

In the cases at hand, we conclude that the sound proposed for registration is functional and not entitled to registration under either view of functionality. Quite simply, the use of an audible alarm is essential to the use or purpose of applicant's products. It is clear, for example, that applicant touts the loud volume of the sound emitted by its alarm watch (and emphasizes the loudness much more than the flashing LEDs). Similarly, the evidence regarding competitive personal security devices that applicant put into the record also shows the predominant use of loud sound as an alarm. In addition, the sound involves alternating sound pulses and silence, which the ... evidence shows is a more effective way to use sound as an alarm than is a steady sound.

Applicant has argued that it is not seeking to register a sound of any particular loudness. Equally significant, however, is that the description of the sound is not limited to a particular volume. Thus, we must consider it to encompass all reasonable degrees of loudness for an alarm sound. *Cf. Phillips Petroleum Co. v. C. J. Webb, Inc.,* 442 F.2d 1376, 58 C.C.P.A. 1255, 170 USPQ 35, 36 (CCPA 1971) ("Webb's application is not limited to the mark depicted in any special form. In trying to visualize what other forms the mark might appear in, we are aided by the specimens submitted with Webb's application."). Moreover, it is clear from the record that applicant's alarm emits a loud sound and that the loudness of the sound is an essential feature of the product. For example, the specimen of use shows that applicant's sound is typically used in a loud manner. In addition, applicant has admitted "[t]he volume of the alarm is critical." See September 14, 2005 response to office action, child's bracelet application. Indeed, a soft alarm sound would not draw much attention.

In short, the ability of applicant's products to emit a loud, pulsing sound is essential to their use or purpose. For that reason alone, the functionality refusal must be affirmed in regard to each application. However, we shall also consider the question whether the proposed mark is functional under the *Morton–Norwich* analysis.

The first *Morton–Norwich* factor focuses on whether a utility patent exists disclosing the advantages of the proposed mark. Applicant argues that it has a utility patent application for its product, not for its sound. This argument, however, is undercut by the application's focus on a digital wristwatch with a "loud alarm" as an exemplary embodiment for the product, and the application's description of an alarm of 80–125 decibels. The application does not note the degree of brightness for lights that could potentially be utilized in a visual alarm, or the types of odors that could be used for an olfactory alarm; but it does specify a decibel range for the audible alarm that would be characterized as loud. Moreover, even if applicant is correct in its argument that the existence of its patent application for its product is not relevant to a *Morton–Norwich* analysis regarding the registrability of its sound, the absence of a patent for the sound would only mean this factor would be neutral in the analysis of functionality. *See TrafFix Devices,* 58 USPQ2d at 1006, and *In re N.V. Organon,* 79 USPQ2d at 1646.

The second *Morton–Norwich* factor focuses on whether advertising materials tout utilitarian advantages. Applicant's advertising clearly extols the loudness of the alarm sound, much more than the engineering of the product that produces the sound. Applicant has admitted as much. See January 22, 2008 response, child's bracelet application ("the advertising touts the degree of *loudness*")(emphasis in original). The advertising material does not tout the particular frequencies of the sound pulses or the pattern of the pulses, but applicant has admitted "[t]he volume of the alarm is critical." See September 14, 2005 response to office action, child's bracelet application. Thus, applicant's advertising touts a critical feature of its sound, as emitted by the identified goods. This factor favors a finding of functionality.

The third *Morton–Norwich* factor focuses on whether competitors would have functionally equivalent sounds available to them if applicant were accorded the exclusive rights attendant to registration. Of course, as already noted, when a proposed mark has been found functional on other grounds, it is not necessary for the record to also show use of applicant's particular sound would be a competitive necessity. *See Valu Engineering,* 61 USPQ2d at 1427. Nonetheless, it is clear from the record that alarm sounds work best when they alternate pulses of sound and silence, when the sound pulses fall within a particular range of frequencies, and when the sound is loud. Applicant argues that there are thousands of specific frequencies within the range that is most suitable for use in alarms. That range may be taken as between 1000 and 3000 Hz, based on the information of record. Thus, under applicant's analysis the thousands of frequencies within this range can be combined into countless variations and therefore applicant's particular combination of frequencies need not be employed by other makers of personal alarms. What applicant's argument fails to appreciate, however, is that the description of its mark only specifies that its sound pulses will be between 1500 Hz and 2300 Hz. Based on this description, applicant would be free to combine sound pulses for any of the frequencies within this range, a large swath of the optimal range of 1000 Hz to 3000 Hz. While there may indeed be countless combinations of frequencies available for personal alarms utilizing the frequencies within the optimal range, registration of applicant's sound as described would deprive competitors of many of those options. It matters not that applicant's actual sound may currently use only a handful of particular frequencies, for it would be free to change the combinations at any time and still have its sound fall within the ambit of the description. This factor favors a finding of functionality.

The final *Morton–Norwich* factor considers whether the sound yields applicant a comparatively simple or cheap method of manufacturing personal alarms. Applicant has explained, and the record shows, that the sound of its product has no bearing on the cost or ease of manufacture of its alarms. This factor is neutral.

Weighing all the *Morton–Norwich* factors in the balance, we conclude that the mark applicant has described in its application and proposes to register is functional and unregistrable. The functionality refusal is affirmed in each application, based on both the *Inwood* formulation of the sound being essential to the use or purpose of applicant's goods and under the *Morton–Norwich* analysis.

QUESTION

Would the applicant have fared any better under the Board's functionality analysis if it had specified the volume and pulsing more narrowly? Under the *Inwood* test? Under the *Morton-Norwich* factors?

CHAPTER 5

LOSS OF TRADEMARK RIGHTS

A. GENERICISM

Page 278. Insert before "Protecting Trademarks Against Genericism":

Boston Duck Tours v. Super Duck Tour, 531 F.3d 1 (1st Cir. 2008). Both Boston Duck and Super Duck offer land and water sightseeing tours in Boston, using amphibious vehicles commonly called "ducks." Other companies give similar amphibious tours, often under the name "duck tours," in other cities, including San Francisco, Philadelphia and Chicago. In response to Boston Duck's infringement action, Super Duck asserted that the two marks were unlikely to be confused because "duck tours" was generic. The court referred to several local newspaper articles using the term "duck tours" generically; to the term's widespread generic use in other cities; and to plaintiff Boston Duck's own generic use: "all of this evidence, especially the widespread use of 'duck' and 'duck tours' by companies in the industry, indicates that no other 'commonly used' and effective 'alternative[s]' denote the sightseeing services both parties offer.... To grant Boston Duck exclusive rights to use the phrase in the Boston area would be to erect a barrier of entry into the marketplace, thereby preventing other entities, such as Super Duck, from calling their product by its name. Super Duck, as well as other potential competitors, would be placed at a significant market disadvantage." In a concurring opinion, District Judge di Clerico observed that Boston Duck was not claiming a trademark in "duck tours" but rather in the mark "Boston Duck Tours" ("duck" and "tours" separately disclaimed), and that the majority accordingly should have assessed likelihood of confusion with respect to the entire mark.

QUESTION

The Bay Quackers offers amphibious tours of San Francisco; visitors riding its "ducks" salute passers-by with Bay Quacker-issued kazoos. Ride the Ducks, another duck tour operator, also gives its customers kazoos, labeled "Wacky Quackers," and has since the mid–1990s held a federal trademark registration for the duck-call sound emitted by the kazoos (or other noisemakers). Ride the Duck has now opened operations in San Francisco, and has filed a federal trademark action seeking to enjoin Bay Quackers from using kazoos or otherwise enabling its customers to make duck-like noises as part of its tours. What arguments and defenses would you anticipate regarding Ride the Ducks' soundmark? Who is likely to prevail?

Page 290.   Add to end of Question:

For recent example of a decision addressing both a *Teflon-Eflon*-type survey, and a *Thermos*-type survey, see *Premier Nutrition, Inc. v. Organic Food Bar, Inc.,* 86 U.S.P.Q.2d 1344 (C.D. Cal. 2008). Premier Nutrition sought a declaratory judgment of the genericism of "organic food bar." In that instance, Premier proffered a "brand name/common name" survey showing a high level of "common name" responses to the alleged mark. Defendant countered with a survey showing subjects a variety of nutrition bars, and inquiring "what they would ask for if they were looking for this product in a grocery store."

Page 290.   Insert before "3. Genericism and Confusion":

Welding Services Inc. v. Forman, 509 F.3d 1351 (11th Cir. 2007). Having held the plaintiff's claimed mark "Welding Services, Inc." to be generic for welding services, the court next considered whether a different analysis should apply to a claimed mark consisting of the initials of the company name, WSI:

> Although we conclude that the words "welding services" are not protectable, this does not decide the precise question before us because Welding Services, Inc. does not seek protection for the words them-selves, but for the abbreviation "WSI" and the stylized logo using that abbreviation. The protectability of the initials and of the stylized logo present different issues, so we will consider them in turn.
>
> Abbreviations of generic words may become protectable if the party claiming protection for such an abbreviation shows that the abbreviation has a meaning distinct from the underlying words in the mind of the public. *G. Heileman Brewing Co. v. Anheuser–Busch, Inc.,* 873 F.2d 985, 993–94 (7th Cir. 1989) ("heavy burden" on trademark claimant seeking to show an independent meaning for initials of descriptive words apart from the fact that they are abbreviations for the descriptive words); 2 *McCarthy, supra,* § 12:37 (distinguishing between abbreviations "which still convey[] to the buyer the original generic connotation of the abbreviated name" and those which are "not recognizable as the original generic term"). *But cf. Anheuser–Busch, Inc. v. Stroh Brewery Co.,* 750 F.2d 631, 635–36 (8th Cir. 1984) (abbreviation of generic words protectable if "some operation of the imagination is required to connect the initials with the product"); *Modern Optics, Inc. v. Univis Lens Co.,* 234 F.2d 504, 506, 43 C.C.P.A. 970, 1956 Dec. Comm'r Pat. 350 (C.C.P.A. 1956) ("[I]nitials cannot be considered descriptive unless they have become so generally under-stood as representing descriptive words as to be accepted as substan-tially synonymous therewith.").

Welding Services introduced the affidavit of its marketing director, Michael Welch, stating that the company had used the abbreviation since 1990 and the stylized logo for nine years before Welding Technologies began using its marks. Welch said Welding Services had spent $5 million advertising its marks over the course of fourteen years (from 1990 to 2004) and had generated more than $1 billion in revenues. Welch said that the WSI marks are recognized as a "highly significant indicator of WSI's welding services." On the basis of this evidence, the district court declined to hold that Welding Services' marks were not protectable.

But Welch's affidavit does not address the question of whether the company's investment in advertising its marks served to give the abbreviation "WSI" a meaning distinct from the words "Welding Services Inc." While investment in advertising is relevant to the question of secondary meaning generally, *Investacorp, Inc. v. Arabian Inv. Banking Corp.*, 931 F.2d 1519, 1525 (11th Cir. 1991), the question of whether the abbreviation has a discrete meaning in the minds of the public from the generic words for which it stands requires a different kind of evidence. The only evidence in the record relevant to this question shows Welding Services has not created a separate meaning for the abbreviation. Crucially, exhibit B to Welding Services' statement of material facts shows the logo with the initials on advertising material displayed immediately next to the words "Welding Services Inc." Thus, Welding Services' own motion papers indicate that the abbreviation is used in association with the generic words, rather than being used in a way that would give rise to a meaning distinct from those words. Accordingly, we hold that Welding Services had not shown "WSI" to be protectable.

Page 302.   Insert following *Harley–Davidson v. Grottanelli*:

H–D Michigan v. Top Quality Serv., 496 F.3d 755 (7th Cir. 2007). Harley–Davidson motorcycle owners Dean and Debbie Anderson formed Top Quality Services, and organized a cruise for fellow Harley owners, which they advertised as HOGS ON THE HIGH SEAS.

> [The advertisement] said, "1st Annual Harley Owners' Cruise Rally" in large print immediately above a circular logo that contained the words "HOGS ON THE HIGH SEAS" and a cartoon pig riding a large motorcycle on an ocean wave. Top Quality's website said, "Bring your Harley friends, HOG group members, riding buddies, there won't be a stranger on the ship." Top Quality advised potential vendors that the trip was an "all Harley Owners Cruise Ship Rally." Ninety-seven percent of the passengers on the first cruise owned Harley motorcycles.

When the Andersons sought to register HOGS ON THE HIGH SEAS, Harley–Davidson both filed an opposition proceeding and a trademark infringement action. The District Court ruled for the Andersons, holding the issue of the protectability of HOG precluded by the judgment in *Grottanelli*. The Seventh Circuit reversed.

In this case, the parties only dispute whether the issue litigated in *Grottanelli* is the same as the one here. Harley contends that the issues are different because in *Grottanelli*, the Second Circuit evaluated whether the word "hog" was generic as applied to large motorcycles, whereas in this case, the issue is whether "hog" was generic as applied to a motorcyclist club. Top Quality contends that *Grottanelli* held that "hog" is generic as applied to all motorcycle products and services, thus precluding Harley's infringement claim. . . .

The first sentence in *Grottanelli* strongly suggests that the issue in that case was different than the one here. The court said, "This appeal primarily involves trademark issues as to whether the mark 'HOG' *as applied to large motorcycles* is generic. . . . " *Id.* at 808 (emphasis added). The court then summarized its holding by stating, "[W]e conclude that the word 'hog' had become generic *as applied to large motorcycles* before Harley–Davidson began to make trademark use of 'HOG.' " *Id.* (emphasis added). A few paragraphs later, the court discussed the history of "The Word 'Hog' Applied to Motorcycles" and, in the remainder of the opinion, referred to the generic nature of the word 'hog' "as applied to motorcycles" or "as applied to large motorcycles" at least ten different times. The court never stated that "hog" was generic as applied to a motorcyclist club or to motorcycle products or services.

The Second Circuit also noted that Harley conceded that its claim failed if the word "hog" was generic as applied to large motorcycles, further suggesting that the court had no occasion to decide the issue in this case. *Id.* at 810. Finally, the parties' Second Circuit briefs did not discuss whether "hog" was generic as applied to a motorcyclist club, focusing instead on whether "hog" means large motorcycle. [citation omitted]

Grottanelli did mention that the "HOG" trademark was used to refer to Harley's motorcyclist club, but the court did not state, or even suggest, that Harley's use of the word "hog" was generic as applied to the Harley Owners Group. In short, the *Grottanelli* opinion and the parties' briefs convince us that the Second Circuit did not resolve the issue here: whether "hog" is a generic word for a motorcyclist club. Accordingly, Harley is not collaterally estopped from bringing the claims in this case.

Top Quality argues that *Grottanelli* must have held that "hog" was generic for all motorcycle products and services because it allowed Grottanelli to continue using the word "hog" when promoting his "Hog Holiday" motorcycle rally, "Hog Wash" engine degreaser, and "Hog Trivia" board game. Top Quality seems to suggest that by allowing Grottanelli's continued use of his trade names, the Second Circuit found that both Harley's and Grottanelli's use of the word "hog" was generic. However, that is simply not the case. The Second

Circuit had no occasion to decide whether Grottanelli's use of the word "hog" was generic, because it already had held that Harley's mark as applied to large motorcycles was not protectable, and Harley conceded that this doomed its claim. A plaintiff's generic use of a word has no bearing on whether the defendant's use of the word is also generic.

B. Protectability

Having resolved that collateral estoppel does not preclude Harley's suit, we must address the merits. From our previous discussion, it should be evident that Harley's use of the word "hog" is not generic as applied to its motorcyclist club. As noted above, a generic term is commonly used as a name for the seller's goods, while a descriptive term names a characteristic of a particular product or service. [Citations omitted.] The word "hog" is not commonly used as a name for a motorcyclist club. It is a name for a motorcycle. As such, Harley's use of the word "hog" to refer to the Harley Owners Group is not generic; rather, it is descriptive because it describes the club's members: people who enjoy motorcycles. [Citations omitted.]

Top Quality argues that it uses the word 'hogs' generically, and thus cannot be infringing on Harley's mark. However, this argument lacks merit as well. Though a consumer might conclude that Top Quality's trade name means "Motorcycles on the High Seas," that is not what Top Quality is selling. Top Quality's service does not invite motorcycles to travel on the ocean; it invites *motorcyclists* to travel on the ocean. As a result, its mark is not generic. [Citations omitted.]

QUESTION

How persuasive is the court's distinction between HOG as a generic term for a large motorcycle, and HOG as a descriptive term when used to mean owners of large motorcycles (or of Harley–Davidson motorcycles)? Would Bayer have a claim against the (fictitious) Association of Aspirin Advocates, an organization that urges ingestion of acetylsalicylic acid to diminish the risk of blood clots?

Page 305. Insert at end of Note before Questions:

Compare *In re Reed Elsevier*, 482 F.3d 1376 (Fed. Cir. 2007), upholding refusal on grounds of genericism to register www.lawyers.com as a service mark "for providing an online interactive database featuring information exchange in the fields of law, legal news, and legal services."

B. ABANDONMENT

Page 313. Add after Questions:
STANDARD OF PROOF OF ABANDONMENT

A party alleging abandonment must show that the trademark owner has not used the mark and does not intend to resume its use. But the Lanham

Act does not specify whether this showing must be supported by a preponderance of the evidence (the usual standard of proof in a civil action) or by "clear and convincing evidence." In concurring opinions in **Grocery Outlet Inc. v. Albertson's Inc.**, 497 F.3d 949 (9th Cir. 2007), Judge Wallace urged the latter, while Judge McKeown contended that the Lanham Act did not support a higher burden of proof.

WALLACE, Senior Circuit Judge

I . . . write separately on the burden-of-proof issue. We have held that under the Lanham Act, 60 Stat. 427, 15 U.S.C. §§ 1051–1127 (1946), the burden of proving abandonment is "strict." *Prudential Ins. Co. of Am. v. Gibraltar Fin. Corp. of Cal.*, 694 F.2d 1150, 1156 (9th Cir. 1982). We have also indicated that this strict burden is equivalent to a "high" one. See *Edwin K. Williams & Co., Inc. v. Edwin K. Williams & Co.-East*, 542 F.2d 1053, 1059 (9th Cir. 1976), *citing American Foods, Inc. v. Golden Flake, Inc.*, 312 F.2d 619, 625 (5th Cir. 1963) (holding that defendant failed to meet the "burden of strict proof" required to show abandonment).

Despite these statements, Judge McKeown repeats the incorrect argument she recently made in *Electro Source, LLC v. Brandess–Kalt–Aetna Group, Inc.*, 458 F.3d 931, 935 n.2 (9th Cir. 2006), that the burden of proof in abandonment cases is a question unanswered in our circuit. True, we are more accustomed to applying the "clear and convincing evidence" and "preponderance of the evidence" standards. But merely because Prudential and Williams invoke an unfamiliar or forgotten standard does not mean that the burden-of-proof is-sue is unresolved or that we may disregard those cases.

In my view, meeting a strict burden requires proof by clear and convincing evidence. Before the enactment of the Lanham Act, courts often required strict proof to establish a forfeiture. [Citations omitted.] This was also the standard applied to abandonment of trademarks. [Citations omitted.]

In equally disparate cases, however, pre-Lanham Act courts required clear and convincing evidence to establish a forfeiture. [Citations omitted.] And at least one court expressly required clear and convincing evidence of abandonment of a trademark. See *Mathy v. Republic Metalware Co.*, 1910 Dec. Comm'r Pat. 387, 35 App. D.C. 151, 1910 WL 20792, at *3 (D.C. Cir. 1910); see also *Hoosier Drill*, 78 Ind. 408, 1881 WL 6748, at *3 (requiring "clear and unmistakable evidence").

Strict proof was no different than clear and convincing evidence, and they were the same burden. Unsurprisingly, when the Court of Appeals of New York required "strict proof" of trademark abandonment, see *Neva–Wet Corp. of Am. v. Never Wet Processing Corp.*, 277 N.Y. 163, 13 N.E.2d 755, 761 (N.Y. 1938), it relied on *Mathy* and *Hoosier Drill*.

It is not difficult to imagine why there were simultaneously two equivalent standards of proof under the common law. Statutes or contracts underlying a forfeiture were "strictly" construed. [Citations omitted.] The same language used to describe the rule of construction may also have come to describe the "higher degree of proof than a mere preponderance" that was the "natural corollary" of that rule. [Citation omitted.]

I will not presume, as Judge McKeown does, that *Prudential* and *Williams* idly required "strict proof" or that a "high burden" be met. I have no doubt that our court meant that abandonment under the Lanham Act must be shown by clear and convincing evidence. This is the only plausible translation of strict proof and high burden, and Judge McKeown offers no other.

I agree with Judge McKeown that 15 U.S.C. § 1127 says nothing about the burden of proof, but she mistakenly concludes that the preponderance of the evidence standard was the "traditional" one. The traditional standard was clear and convincing evidence (or strict proof), and there is nothing in the Lanham Act indicating that Congress relaxed this burden. See *Chappell v. Robbins*, 73 F.3d 918, 924 (9th Cir. 1996) ("We may fairly presume that Congress is aware of the common-law background against which it legislates. . . . ").

Judge McKeown also correctly observes that the abandonment defense under the Lanham Act is different than the one under the common law. The Lanham Act requires proof of "intent not to resume . . . use" and permits a presumption of abandonment in certain cases, see 15 U.S.C. § 1127, while the common law required proof of "intent to abandon," *Mathy*, 1910 Dec. Comm'r Pat. 387, 35 App. D.C. 151, 1910 WL 20792, at *3. But that does not mean that the Lanham Act adjusted the burden required to prove the defense. In any event, *Prudential* and *Williams* require a different conclusion. I would follow our cases.

McKEOWN, Circuit Judge, concurring:

Given the standard of review on appeal and Grocery's concession as to the standard of proof for abandonment, I concur in the court's per curiam opinion. I write separately to express my view on a question unanswered in our circuit. Although we have previously held that "[a]bandonment of a trademark, being in the nature of forfeiture, must be strictly proved," *Prudential Insurance Company of America v. Gibraltar Financial Corporation of California*, 694 F.2d 1150, 1156 (9th Cir. 1982), and that "[b]ecause a finding of insufficient control [of a tradename] essentially works a forfeiture, a person who asserts insufficient control must meet a high burden of proof," *Edwin K. Williams & Co., Inc. v. Edwin K. Williams & Co.-East*, 542 F.2d 1053, 1054 (9th Cir. 1976), we have not elaborated on the meaning of "strict proof" or "high burden." See *Electro Source, LLC v. Brandess–Kalt–Aetna Group, Inc.*, 458 F.3d 931, 935 n.2 (9th Cir. 2006) (reserving the issue of the standard of proof to show trademark abandonment).

In my view, the language of 15 U.S.C. § 1127 does not support an elevated standard of "clear and convincing." The statute does not impose a burden beyond the traditional preponderance of the evidence standard applicable in civil matters. Nor is there any evidence that Congress intended to raise the bar to clear and convincing evidence,[3] as argued by Albertson's. The federal courts of appeals that have considered the issue are in accord and have consistently applied the preponderance of the evidence standard in the trademark abandonment context. [Citations omitted.] These cases are predicated on the statutory language of the Lanham Act, not on the common law or some judicially-created hybrid standard.

In addressing the Lanham Act's changes from the common law with respect to the law of abandonment, the Federal Circuit noted that

[a]t common law there was no similar presumption of abandonment of a mark simply from proof of nonuse. A challenger had to prove not only nonuse of the mark but also that the former user intended to abandon the mark. However, with respect to rights under the Lanham Act, proof of abandonment was facilitated by the creation of the . . . statutory presumption.

Imperial Tobacco, Ltd., Assignee of Imperial Group PLC v. Philip Morris, Inc., 899 F.2d 1575, 1579 (Fed. Cir. 1990) (appeal from trademark cancellation proceeding before TTAB) (citations omitted). Thus, the Federal Circuit cautioned that "statements from opinions under the common law of abandonment concerning the nature of the element of intent and who had the burden of proof cannot be applied indiscriminately to an abandonment case under the Lanham Act." *Id*. Although the vacuum in our circuit with respect to a square holding on the burden of proof in abandonment cases may cause some litigants and judges to fall back on pre-Lanham Act cases, we are bound by the statute, not the common law.[4]

---

3. Rather, the statute recognizes that proving the subjective intent of a trademark holder may be burdensome for a defendant and provides two aids for demonstrating intent not to resume use: (1) intent may be inferred from the circumstances, and (2) a rebuttable presumption of abandonment arises after three consecutive years of nonuse. 15 U.S.C. § 1127; see *Cumulus Media, Inc. v. Clear Channel Communications, Inc.*, 304 F.3d 1167, 1174 (11th Cir. 2002). With that acknowledgment expressed in the statute, I do not presume that Congress intended to raise the burden of proof without specifying its intention to do so.

4. In his separate concurrence, Judge Wallace argues that the applicable burden is clear and convincing evidence, relying on a case decided more than 30 years before the Lanham Act. See *Mathy v. Republic Metalware Co.*, No. 623, 35 App. D.C. 151, 1910 WL 20792, at *3 (D.C. Cir. 1910). That case is inapposite, however, as it was decided under the common law regime requiring proof of "intent to abandon," see id., rather than the Lanham Act, which requires proof of "intent not to resume use" and permits a presumption of abandonment after three consecutive years of nonuse. See 15 U.S.C. § 1127; see also *Exxon Corp. v. Humble Exploration Co., Inc.*, 695 F.2d 96, 102–03 (5th Cir. 1983) ("There is a difference between intent not to abandon or relinquish and intent to resume use in that an owner may not wish to abandon its mark but may have no intent to resume its use.... An 'intent to resume' requires the trademark owner to have plans to resume commercial use of the mark. Stopping at an 'intent not to abandon' tolerates an owner's protecting a mark with neither commercial use nor plans to resume commercial use. Such a license is not permitted by the Lanham Act.'') (emphasis added). Nor do the other non-trademark cases, also decided before adoption of the Lanham Act, shed light on the applicable burden of proof under the statute.

CHAPTER 6

INFRINGEMENT

A. LIKELIHOOD OF CONFUSION

Page 355. Add before Questions:

Leelanau Wine Cellars, Ltd v. Black & Red, Inc., 502 F.3d 504 (6th Cir. 2007). "In 1981, Michigan's Leelanau Peninsula was designated an Approved American Viticultural Area (AVA). 27 C.F.R. § 9.40. Federal regulation defines a 'viticultural area' as a 'delimited grape-growing region distinguishable by geographical features, the boundaries of which have been delineated.... ' 27 C.F.R. § 9.11. An area's designation as an AVA permits the name of the area to be used as an 'appellation of origin' on wine labels and in advertising." Both plaintiff LWC and defendant B & R own and operate wineries located in the Leelanau Peninsula. Plaintiff has been making wine since 1977 and in 1997 obtained a federal trademark registration for LEELANAU CELLARS. Defendant began making wine in 1999 and in 2000 adopted the name "Chateau de Leelanau Vineyard and Winery." In 2001 LWC filed an action under federal and state trademark law seeking to enjoin B & R from using the term "Leelanau" in any trade or brand name for the sale of wine. The district court found confusion unlikely; the Sixth Circuit affirmed. The court was particularly critical of plaintiff's survey.

> On the issue of actual confusion, LWC, on remand from this court, produced a consumer survey conducted by Dr. Parikh at four malls throughout Michigan: two in Detroit, one in Grand Rapids, and one in Traverse City. In the study, interviewees were taken into a room and shown an advertisement for Leelanau Cellars wine. Interviewees were then asked to put the advertisement away and look at five bottles of Chardonnay, all of which originated in Michigan. The study included a "test cell" and a "control cell." The test and control cells both contained Turner Road, St. Julian, Wilhurst, and Zafarana wines. In the test cell, the fifth wine was Chateau de Leelanau. In the control cell, the fifth wine was Bel Lago. Participants in the study were, after viewing the advertisement and the wines, asked, "Do you believe there is *OR* is not a bottle of wine in this display that is the same as, or comes from the same source, that is, the same winery that puts out the wine in the advertisement that you just looked at?" Of those subjected to the test cell, 64 percent responded in the affirmative to the proposed question, and 54 percent identified Chateau de Leelanau as the wine they believed matched the ad. Of those who selected Chateau de

Leelanau, 38 percent justified their belief on the basis of the use of the name "Leelanau" in both the Leelanau Cellars ad and on the Chateau de Leelanau bottle. Among the individuals who did not identify a match between the wine in the ad and a wine in the display, 10 percent nevertheless believed that there was a "relationship, sponsorship, or association" between the winery in the ad and the winery producing one of the bottles in the display. Eight percent of those individuals identified Chateau de Leelanau only as the associated wine. By contrast, only 31 percent of those individuals exposed to the control cell identified Bel Lago as coming from the same or a related source as Leelanau Cellars and reached that conclusion based on similarities in the labels. After adjusting her results for survey noise or guessing, Dr. Parikh concluded that, the "net confusion level" ranged between 27 percent and 31 percent.

The district court permitted the admission of the Parikh study, but refused to give Parikh's survey significant weight, citing three reasons: (1) the universe of respondents was overbroad and failed to include individuals who were potential purchasers of B & R's wines; (2) the survey did not replicate conditions that consumers would encounter in the marketplace; and (3) the survey questions were suggestive and misleading. These were legitimate bases for declining to rely heavily on the findings of the Parikh study. The district court correctly recognized that the study failed to limit the respondent population to those persons likely to purchase defendant's products. ... Although the study included adults who had or were likely to purchase a bottle of wine in the $5 to $14 price range, there was no attempt to survey only those people who would purchase moderately priced wines produced in the state of Michigan, undoubtedly a distinct group. Nor was the survey limited to wine purchasers who acquire wine through wine tasting rooms, the primary distribution source of B & R. The district court was also correct in concluding that the study failed to replicate actual market conditions. B & R sells its wines almost exclusively through its tasting rooms. Thus, it is unlikely that a purchaser of Chateau de Leelanau would find herself faced with the need to distinguish among various wines or, having walked into a B & R tasting room, erroneously believe that she was in fact at Leelanau Cellars.

These deficiencies undermine the persuasiveness of the Parikh survey. Where a survey presented on the issue of actual confusion reflects methodological errors, a court may choose to limit the importance it accords the study in its likelihood of confusion analysis. *See Borinquen Biscuit Corp. v. M.V. Trading Corp.*, 443 F.3d 112, 121 n.6 (1st Cir. 2006) (noting as to a consumer survey submitted in trademark litigation that the "small sample size and large margin of error combined to cast considerable doubt on its statistical integrity"); *Ashland Oil, Inc.*, 1995 U.S. App. LEXIS 24652, 1995 WL 499466 at *4 ("It is the trial court's responsibility to determine the probative value of a consumer survey, and it is appropriate for the trial court to accord little or no weight to a defective survey."). The district court did not err in refusing to assign the consumer study presented by LWC considerable weight in its likelihood of confusion analysis. Because of its shortcomings, the Parikh study cannot serve as dispositive proof of the likelihood of confusion.

The court also observed that consumers were unlikely to encounter the respective wines in the same commercial setting.

Courts consider the respective marketing channels of the parties to a trademark infringement action to determine "how and to whom the respective goods or services of the parties are sold." *Gen. Motors Corp. v. Keystone Auto. Indus., Inc.*, 453 F.3d 351, 357 (6th Cir. 2006) (internal quotation marks omitted). There is less likelihood of confusion where the goods are sold through different avenues. *See id.*

There is very limited overlap between the distribution channels B & R and LWC utilize. B & R sells approximately 85 percent of its wine through its tasting rooms. Indeed, Kurtz testified that B & R wine almost "never leaves our tasting room." B & R does not sell to major retail operations. LWC, by contrast, sells 25 to 30 percent of its wines through its tasting rooms and the remaining 70 to 75 percent through retail stores like Sam's Club or Meijer's. Thus, despite their operation within a common geographical area, Chateau de Leelanau and LWC are sold, for the most part, in entirely distinct environments. This factor suggests a lesser likelihood of purchaser confusion.

Page 377. Insert after *Playboy v. Netscape*:

In **Designer Skin, LLC v. S & L Vitamins,** 560 F.Supp.2d 811, (D.Ariz. 2008) a controversy involving the inclusion of plaintiff's trademark in the meta tag of the defendant, who is an unauthorized distributor of genuine Designer Skin products, the court observed that initial interest confusion cases finding liability do so when the defendant has engaged in "bait and switch" tactics:

Deception, it bears emphasizing, is essential to a finding of initial interest confusion. . . . In contrast to the deceptive conduct that forms the basis of a finding of initial interest confusion, S & L vitamins uses Designer Skin's marks to truthfully inform internet searchers where they can find Designer Skin's products. . . . Indeed, in practical effect S & L Vitamins invites Designer Skin's customers to purchase Designer Skin's products. The fact that these customers will have the opportunity to purchase competing products when they arrive at S & L Vitamins' sites is irrelevant. The customers searching for Designer Skin's products find exactly what they are looking for when they arrive at these sites. S & L Vitamins is not deceiving consumers in any way. Thus, its use of the marks does not cause initial interest confusion.

The Court recognizes that this holding is at odds with the Tenth Circuit's decision in *Australian Gold, Inc. v. Hatfield*, 436 F.3d 1228 (10th Cir. 2006). There, under facts virtually identical to those in this case, the Tenth Circuit held that the defendant's use of the trademarks caused initial interest confusion because it "used the goodwill associated with Plaintiffs' trademarks in such a way that consumers might be lured to the lotions from Plaintiffs' competitors." *Id.* at 1239. With all due respect to the Tenth Circuit, this Court does not find *Hatfield* persuasive. In this Court's view, there is a meaningful distinction between (1) using a mark to attract potential customers to a website that only offers products of the mark holder's competitors and (2) using a mark to attract potential customers to a website that offers the mark holder's genuine products as well as the products of competitors. As discussed above, in the latter situation no "bait and switch" occurs.

For examples of "bait and switch" tactics, see *Venture Tape Corp. v. McGills Glass Warehouse*, 540 F.3d 56 (1st Cir. 2008) (meta tags); *Finance Express LLC v. Nowcom Corp.*, 564 F.Supp.2d 1160 (C.D. Cal. 2008). In the latter case, the defendant registered domain names incorporating its competitor's trademarks, embedded its competitor's trademarks in its meta tags ("keyword stuffing") and purchased keywords containing its competitor's trademarks in order to generate banner advertisements when a user enters the trademark as a search term ("keying"). The court preliminarily found that all of these practices were likely to cause at least initial interest confusion. Having observed that "the only purpose Nowcom could have had in registering Finance Express' domain name [and in 'keying' and 'keyword stuffing'] was to direct potential consumers of Finance Express' products to Nowcom's website," the court rejected the defendant's attempt to distinguish *Playboy v. Netscape*:

> Nowcom attempts to distinguish *Playboy* from the instant case on the grounds that the banner advertisements in *Playboy* were unlabeled, and the court made note of this fact by stating that it was not "addressing a situation in which a banner advertisement clearly identifies it source with its sponsor's name ... Doing so might eliminate the likelihood of initial interest confusion that exists in this case." 354 F.3d at 1030 & n. 44. While it is true that a clearly-labeled banner advertisement might not create initial interest confusion, Nowcom's banner advertisement cannot be fairly characterized as one which "clearly identifies its source with its sponsor's name." Nowcom's banner advertisement states in large, underlined font: "Manage Your Dealership." Underneath that heading, on the second and third lines of the advertisement, it states in smaller font "Use Just One Software Program. Get A Free Trial of Dealer Desktop." On the fourth line down, in even smaller font, appears a link to Nowcom's website: "www.Nowcom.com" This advertisement is not clearly labeled. The only indication as to the identity of the advertisement's sponsor lies in the website address, which is located in small print on the last line of the advertisement. While Nowcom's argument might be tenable if its name appeared in large font in the first line of the advertisement, or perhaps even if it appeared anywhere in the text of the advertisement, this is not the case. A website address located in small font at the bottom of the advertisement is not sufficient to overcome the initial interest confusion that results from Nowcom's practice of keying.

Page 377. Add a new Question 5:

5. Internet merchants may employ a variety of diversionary tactics, including meta tagging, typosquatting, pop up advertisements and sponsored search results, to take a consumer to the merchant's webpage. Should the assessment of confusion turn on whether:

—The website is offering genuine goods (from an unauthorized distributor)

—The website is offering clearly labeled competing goods

—The website is offering clearly labeled "replicas" of the trademark owner's goods

Pages 381–91. Delete *1–800 Cigar* **and** *JG Wentworth.* **Substitute the following:**

Rescuecom Corp. v. Google, Inc.

562 F.3d 123 (2d Cir. 2009).

■ LEVAL, CIRCUIT JUDGE.

Appeal by Plaintiff Rescuecom Corp. from a judgment of the United States District Court for the Northern District of New York (Mordue, *Chief Judge*) dismissing its action against Google, Inc., under Rule 12(b)(6) for failure to state a claim upon which relief may be granted. Rescuecom's Complaint alleges that Google is liable under §§ 32 and 43 of the Lanham Act, 15 U.S.C. §§ 1114 & 1125, for infringement, false designation of origin, and dilution of Rescuecom's eponymous trademark. The district court believed the dismissal of the action was compelled by our holding in *1–800 Contacts, Inc. v. WhenU.com, Inc.,* ("*1–800*"), because, according to the district court's understanding of that opinion, Rescuecom failed to allege that Google's use of its mark was a "use in commerce" within the meaning of § 45 of the Lanham Act, 15 U.S.C. § 1127. We believe this misunderstood the holding of *1–800.* While we express no view as to whether Rescuecom can prove a Lanham Act violation, an actionable claim is adequately alleged in its pleadings. Accordingly, we vacate the judgment dismissing the action and remand for further proceedings. . . .

Rescuecom conducts a substantial amount of business over the Internet and receives between 17,000 to 30,000 visitors to its website each month. It also advertises over the Internet, using many web-based services, including those offered by Google. Since 1998, "Rescuecom" has been a registered federal trademark, and there is no dispute as to its validity.

Google operates a popular Internet search engine, which users access by visiting www.google.com. Using Google's website, a person searching for the website of a particular entity in trade (or simply for information about it) can enter that entity's name or trademark into Google's search engine and launch a search. Google's proprietary system responds to such a search request in two ways. First, Google provides a list of links to websites, ordered in what Google deems to be of descending relevance to the user's search terms based on its proprietary algorithms. Google's search engine assists the public not only in obtaining information about a provider, but also in purchasing products and services. If a prospective purchaser, looking for goods or services of a particular provider, enters the provider's trademark as a search term on Google's website and clicks to activate a search, within seconds, the Google search engine will provide on the searcher's computer screen a link to the webpage maintained by that provider (as well as a host of other links to sites that Google's program determines to be relevant to the search term entered). By clicking on the link of the provider, the searcher will be directed to the provider's website, where the searcher can obtain information supplied by the provider about its products and services and can perhaps also make purchases from the provider by placing orders.

The second way Google responds to a search request is by showing context-based advertising. When a searcher uses Google's search engine by submitting a search term, Google may place advertisements on the user's screen. Google will do so if an advertiser, having determined that its ad is likely to be of interest to a searcher who enters the particular term, has purchased from Google the placement of its ad on the screen of the searcher who entered that search term. What Google places on the searcher's screen is more than simply an advertisement. It is also a link to the advertiser's website, so that in response to such an ad, if the searcher clicks on the link, he will open the advertiser's website, which offers not only additional information about the advertiser, but also perhaps the option to purchase the goods and services of the advertiser over the Internet. Google uses at least two programs to offer such context-based links: AdWords and Keyword Suggestion Tool.

AdWords is Google's program through which advertisers purchase terms (or keywords). When entered as a search term, the keyword triggers the appearance of the advertiser's ad and link. An advertiser's purchase of a particular term causes the advertiser's ad and link to be displayed on the user's screen whenever a searcher launches a Google search based on the purchased search term. Advertisers pay Google based on the number of times Internet users "click" on the advertisement, so as to link to the advertiser's website. . . .

In addition to Adwords, Google also employs Keyword Suggestion Tool, a program that recommends keywords to advertisers to be purchased. The program is designed to improve the effectiveness of advertising by helping advertisers identify keywords related to their area of commerce, resulting in the placement of their ads before users who are likely to be responsive to it. . . .

Once an advertiser buys a particular keyword, Google links the keyword to that advertiser's advertisement. The advertisements consist of a combination of content and a link to the advertiser's webpage. Google displays these advertisements on the search result page either in the right margin or in a horizontal band immediately above the column of relevance-based search results. These advertisements are generally associated with a label, which says "sponsored link." Rescuecom alleges, however, that a user might easily be misled to believe that the advertisements which appear on the screen are in fact part of the relevance-based search result and that the appearance of a competitor's ad and link in response to a searcher's search for Rescuecom is likely to cause trademark confusion as to affiliation, origin, sponsorship, or approval of service. This can occur, according to the Complaint, because Google fails to label the ads in a manner which would clearly identify them as purchased ads rather than search results. The Complaint alleges that when the sponsored links appear in a horizontal bar at the top of the search results, they may appear to the searcher to be the first, and therefore the most relevant, entries responding to the search, as opposed to paid advertisements.

Google's objective in its AdWords and Keyword Suggestion Tool programs is to sell keywords to advertisers. Rescuecom alleges that Google makes 97% of its revenue from selling advertisements through its AdWords program. Google therefore has an economic incentive to increase the number of advertisements and links that appear for every term entered into its search engine.

Many of Rescuecom's competitors advertise on the Internet. Through its Keyword Suggestion Tool, Google has recommended the Rescuecom trademark to Rescuecom's competitors as a search term to be purchased. Rescuecom's competitors, some responding to Google's recommendation, have purchased Rescuecom's trademark as a keyword in Google's AdWords program, so that whenever a user launches a search for the term "Rescuecom," seeking to be connected to Rescuecom's website, the competitors' advertisement and link will appear on the searcher's screen. This practice allegedly allows Rescuecom's competitors to deceive and divert users searching for Rescuecom's website. According to Rescuecom's allegations, when a Google user launches a search for the term "Rescuecom" because the searcher wishes to purchase Rescuecom's services, links to websites of its competitors will appear on the searcher's screen in a manner likely to cause the searcher to believe mistakenly that a competitor's advertisement (and website link) is sponsored by, endorsed by, approved by, or affiliated with Rescuecom. . . .

I. Google's Use of Rescuecom's Mark Was a "Use in Commerce"

Our court ruled in *1–800* that a complaint fails to state a claim under the Lanham Act unless it alleges that the defendant has made "use in commerce" of the plaintiff's trademark as the term "use in commerce" is defined in 15 U.S.C. § 1127. The district court believed that this case was on all fours with *1–800*, and that its dismissal was required for the same reasons as given in *1–800*. We believe the cases are materially different. The allegations of Rescuecom's complaint adequately plead a use in commerce.

In *1–800*, the plaintiff alleged that the defendant infringed the plaintiff's trademark through its proprietary software, which the defendant freely distributed to computer users who would download and install the program on their computer. The program provided contextually relevant advertising to the user by generating pop-up advertisements to the user depending on the website or search term the user entered in his browser. *Id.* at 404–05. For example, if a user typed "eye care" into his browser, the defendant's program would randomly display a pop-up advertisement of a company engaged in the field of eye care. Similarly, if the searcher launched a search for a particular company engaged in eye care, the defendant's program would display the pop-up ad of a company associated with eye care. *See id.* at 412. The pop-up ad appeared in a separate browser window from the website the user accessed, and the defendant's brand was displayed in the window frame surrounding the ad, so that there was no confusion as to the nature of the pop-up as an advertisement, nor as to the fact that the defendant, not the trademark owner, was responsible for displaying the ad, in response to the particular term searched. *Id.* at 405.

Sections 32 and 43 of the Act, which we also refer to by their codified designations, 15 U.S.C. §§ 1114 & 1125, *inter alia*, impose liability for unpermitted "use in commerce" of another's mark which is "likely to cause confusion, or to cause mistake, or to deceive," § 1114, "as to the affiliation . . . or as to the origin, sponsorship or approval of his or her goods [or] services . . . by another person." § 1125(a)(1)(A). The *1–800* opinion looked to the definition of the term "use in commerce" provided in § 45 of the Act, 15 U.S.C. § 1127. That definition provides in part that "a mark shall be deemed to be in use in commerce . . . (2) on services when it is used or displayed in the sale or advertising of services and the services are rendered in commerce." 15 U.S.C. § 1127. Our court found that the plaintiff failed to show that the defendant made a "use in commerce" of the plaintiff's mark, within that definition.

At the outset, we note two significant aspects of our holding in *1–800*, which distinguish it from the present case. A key element of our court's decision in *1–800* was that under the plaintiff's allegations, the defendant did not use, reproduce, or display the plaintiff's mark *at all*. The search term that was alleged to trigger the pop-up ad was the plaintiff's *website address*. *1–800* noted, notwithstanding the similarities between the website address and the mark, that the website address was not used or claimed by the plaintiff as a trademark. Thus, the transactions alleged to be infringing were not transactions involving use of the plaintiff's trademark. *Id.* at 408– 09. *1–800* suggested in dictum that is highly relevant to our case that had the defendant used the plaintiff's *trademark* as the trigger to pop-up an advertisement, such conduct might, depending on other elements, have been actionable. 414 F.3d at 409 & n.11.

Second, as an alternate basis for its decision, *1–800* explained why the defendant's program, which might randomly trigger pop-up advertisements upon a searcher's input of the plaintiff's website address, did not constitute a "use in commerce," as defined in § 1127. *Id.* at 408–09. In explaining why the plaintiff's mark was not "used or displayed in the sale or advertising of services," *1–800* pointed out that, under the defendant's program, advertisers could not request or purchase keywords to trigger their ads. *Id.* at 409, 412. Even if an advertiser wanted to display its advertisement to a searcher using the plaintiff's trademark as a search term, the defendant's program did not offer this possibility. In fact, the defendant "did not disclose the proprietary contents of [its] directory to its advertising clients. . . ." *Id.* at 409. In addition to not selling trademarks of others to its customers to trigger these ads, the defendant did not "otherwise manipulate which category-related advertisement will pop up in response to any particular terms on the internal directory." *Id.* at 411. The display of a particular advertisement was controlled by the category associated with the website or keyword, rather than the website or keyword itself. The defendant's program relied upon categorical associations such as "eye care" to select a pop-up ad randomly from a predefined list of ads appropriate to that category. To the extent that an advertisement for a competitor of the plaintiff was displayed when a user opened the plaintiff's website, the trigger to display the ad was not based on the defendant's sale or recommendation of a particular trademark.

The present case contrasts starkly with those important aspects of the *1–800* decision. First, in contrast to *1–800*, where we emphasized that the defendant made no use whatsoever of the plaintiff's trademark, here what Google is recommending and selling to its advertisers is Rescuecom's trademark. Second, in contrast with the facts of *1–800* where the defendant did not "use or display," much less sell, trademarks as search terms to its advertisers, here Google displays, offers, and sells Rescuecom's mark to Google's advertising customers when selling its advertising services. In addition, Google encourages the purchase of Rescuecom's mark through its Keyword Suggestion Tool. Google's utilization of Rescuecom's mark fits literally within the terms specified by 15 U.S.C. § 1127. According to the Complaint, Google uses and sells Rescuecom's mark "in the sale . . . of [Google's advertising] services . . . rendered in commerce." § 1127.

Google, supported by amici, argues that *1–800* suggests that the inclusion of a trademark in an internal computer directory cannot constitute trademark use. Several district court decisions in this Circuit appear to have reached this conclusion. *See e.g., S & L Vitamins, Inc. v. Australian Gold, Inc.*, 521 F. Supp. 2d 188, 199–202 (E.D.N.Y. 2007) (holding that use of a trademark in metadata did not constitute trademark use within the meaning of the Lanham Act because the use "is strictly internal and not communicated to the public"); *Merck & Co., Inc. v. Mediplan Health Consulting, Inc.*, 425 F. Supp. 2d 402, 415 (S.D.N.Y. 2006) (holding that the internal use of a keyword to trigger advertisements did not qualify as trademark use). This over-reads the *1–800* decision. First, regardless of whether Google's use of Rescuecom's mark in its internal search algorithm could constitute an actionable trademark use, Google's recommendation and sale of Rescuecom's mark to its advertising customers are not internal uses. Furthermore, *1–800* did not imply that use of a trademark in a software program's internal directory precludes a finding of trademark use. Rather, influenced by the fact that the defendant was not using the plaintiff's trademark at all, much less using it as the basis of a commercial transaction, the court asserted that the particular use before it did not constitute a use in commerce. *See 1–800*, 414 F.3d at 409–12. We did not imply in *1–800* that an alleged infringer's use of a trademark in an internal software program insulates the alleged infringer from a charge of infringement, no matter how likely the use is to cause confusion in the marketplace. If we were to adopt Google and its amici's argument, the operators of search engines would be free to use trademarks in ways designed to deceive and cause consumer confusion.[4] This is surely neither within the intention nor the letter of the Lanham Act.

Google and its amici contend further that its use of the Rescuecom trademark is no different from that of a retail vendor who uses "product placement" to allow one vender to benefit from a competitors' name recognition. An example of product placement occurs when a store-brand generic product is placed next to a trademarked product to induce a customer who specifically sought out the trademarked product to consider the typically less expensive, generic brand as an alternative. *See 1–800*, 414 F.3d at 411. Google's argument misses the point. From the fact that proper, non-deceptive product placement does not result in liability under the Lanham Act, it does not follow that the label "product placement" is a magic shield against liability, so that even a deceptive plan of product placement designed to confuse consumers would similarly escape liability. It is not by reason of absence of a use of a mark in commerce that benign product placement escapes liability; it escapes liability because it is a benign practice which does not cause a likelihood of consumer confusion. In contrast, if a retail seller were to be paid by an off-brand purveyor to arrange product display and delivery in such a way that customers seeking to purchase a famous brand would receive the off-brand, believing they had gotten the brand they were seeking, we see no reason to believe the practice would escape liability merely because it could claim the mantle of "product placement." The practices attributed to Google by the Complaint, which at this stage we must accept as true, are significantly different from benign product placement that does not violate the Act.

Unlike the practices discussed in *1–800*, the practices here attributed to Google by Rescuecom's complaint are that Google has made use in commerce of Rescuecom's mark. Needless to say, a defendant must do more than use another's mark in commerce to violate the Lanham Act. ... We have no idea whether Rescuecom can prove that Google's use of Rescuecom's trademark in its AdWords program causes likelihood of confusion or mistake. ... What Rescuecom alleges is that by the manner of Google's display of sponsored links of competing brands in response to a search for Rescuecom's brand name (which fails adequately to identify the sponsored link as an advertisement, rather than a relevant search result), Google

4. For example, instead of having a separate "sponsored links" or paid advertisement section, search engines could allow advertisers to pay to appear at the top of the "relevance" list based on a user entering a competitor's trademark—a functionality that would be highly likely to cause consumer confusion. Alternatively, sellers of products or services could pay to have the operators of search engines automatically divert users to their website when the users enter a competitor's trademark as a search term. Such conduct is surely not beyond judicial review merely because it is engineered through the internal workings of a computer program.

creates a likelihood of consumer confusion as to trademarks. . . . Whether Google's actual practice is in fact benign or confusing is not for us to judge at this time. We consider at the 12(b)(6) stage only what is alleged in the Complaint.

We conclude that the district court was mistaken in believing that our precedent in *1–800* requires dismissal.

The *Rescuecom* court took the unusual step of including an Appendix "On the Meaning of 'Use in Commerce' in Sections 32 and 43 of the Lanham Act." The Appendix analyzes the statutory text and its evolution from the original 1946 Lanham Act text through the current version enacted in the 1988 amendments. The Appendix argues that the term "use in commerce" was likely intended as a "qualification for registration" rather than as a limitation on the scope of infringing conduct:

> . . . the history of the development of the Lanham Act confirms what is also indicated by a common-sense understanding of the provisions. The definition of the term "use in commerce" provided by § 1127, was intended to continue to apply, as it did when the definition was conceived in the 1941 bill, to the sections governing qualification for registration and for the benefits of the Act. In that version, the term "use in commerce" did not appear in § 32, which established the elements of liability for infringing upon a federally registered mark. The eventual appearance of that phrase in that section did not represent an intention that the phrase carry the restrictive definition which defined an owner's entitlement to registration. The appearance rather resulted from happenstance pairing of the verb "use" with the term "in commerce," whose purpose is to claim the jurisdictional authority of the Commerce Clause. Section 1127, as noted, does not prescribe that its definitions necessarily apply throughout the Act. They apply "unless the contrary is plainly apparent from the context." . . .

> . . . Congress did not intend that this definition apply to the sections of the Lanham Act which define infringing conduct. The definition was rather intended to apply to the sections which used the phrase in prescribing eligibility for registration and for the Act's protections. However, Congress does not enact intentions. It enacts statutes. And the process of enacting legislation is of such complexity that understandably the words of statutes do not always conform perfectly to the motivating intentions. This can create for courts difficult problems of interpretation. . . .

> . . . Between 1962 and 1988, notwithstanding the likelihood shown by the legislative history that Congress *intended* the definition to apply only to registration and qualification for benefits and not to infringement, a court addressing the issue nonetheless would probably have concluded that the section applied to alleged infringement, as well. . . .

[The 1988 amendment] left the preexisting language about placement of the mark unchanged, but added a prior sentence requiring that a "use in commerce" be "a bona fide use in the ordinary course of trade, and not made merely to reserve a right in a mark." While it is "plainly apparent from the context" that the new first sentence cannot reasonably apply to statutory sections defining infringing conduct, the question remains whether the addition of this new sentence changed the meaning of the second sentence of the definition without changing its words.

We see at least two possible answers to the question, neither of which is entirely satisfactory. One interpretation would be that, by adding the new first sentence, Congress changed the meaning of the second sentence of the definition to conform to the new first sentence, without altering the words. The language of the definition, which, prior to the addition of the new first sentence, would have been construed to apply both to sections defining infringement, and to sections specifying eligibility for registration, would change its meaning, despite the absence of any change in its words, so that the entire definition now no longer applied to the sections defining infringement. Change of meaning without change of words is obviously problematic.

The alternative solution would be to interpret the two sentences of the statutory definition as of different scope. The second sentence of the definition, which survived the 1988 amendment unchanged, would retain its prior meaning and continue to apply as before the amendment to sections defining infringement, as well as to sections relating to a mark owner's eligibility for registration and for enjoyment of the protections of the Act. The new first sentence, which plainly was not intended to apply to infringements, would apply only to sections in the latter category—those relating to an owner's eligibility to register its mark and enjoy the Act's protection. Under this interpretation, liability for infringement under §§ 1114 and 1125(a) would continue, as before 1988, to require a showing of the infringer's placement of another's mark in the manner specified in the second sentence of the § 1127 definition. It would not require a showing that the alleged infringer made "bona fide use of the mark in the ordinary course of trade, and not merely to reserve a right in the mark." On the other hand, eligibility of mark owners for registration and for the protections of the Act would depend on their showing compliance with the requirements of both sentences of the definition.

We recognize that neither of the two available solutions is altogether satisfactory. Each has advantages and disadvantages. At least for this Circuit, especially given our prior *1–800* precedent, which applied the second sentence of the definition to infringement, the latter solution, according a different scope of application to the two sentences of the definition, seems to be preferable.[12]

---

12. We express no view which of the alternative available solutions would seem preferable if our Circuit had not previously applied the second sentence to sections of the Act defining infringement.

The judges of the *1–800* panel have read this Appendix and have authorized us to state that they agree with it. At the same time we note that the discussion in this Appendix does not affect the result of this case. We assumed in the body of the opinion, in accordance with the holding of *1–800*, that the requirements of the second sentence of the definition of "use in commerce" in § 1127 apply to infringing conduct and found that such use in commerce was adequately pleaded. The discussion in this Appendix is therefore dictum and not a binding opinion of the court. It would be helpful for Congress to study and clear up this ambiguity

Note: The trend of decisions rendered in other Circuits after the Second Circuit's *1–800* decision and before *Rescuecom*, generally declined to follow the *1–800* approach to "use in commerce." In these cases, the defendants were not the search engines, but competitors who had incorporated third party trademarks in the metadata of their websites (meta tagging), or purchased key words linked to advertisements; courts held these acts to be "use[s] in commerce" of the plaintiff's trademark. For example, in *North American Medical Corp. v. Axiom Worldwide, Inc.*, 522 F.3d 1211 (11th Cir. 2008), Axiom included two of North American's registered trademarks, "Accu–Spina" and "IDD Therapy" on its website within meta tags. The court observed that Axiom

> included the terms within its meta tags to influence Internet search engines. For instance, evidence in this case indicated that, before Axiom removed these meta tags from its website, if a computer user entered the trademarked terms into Google's Internet search engine, Google listed Axiom's website as the second most relevant search result. In addition, Google provided the searcher with a brief description of Axiom's website, and the description included these terms and highlighted them. . . .

> In deciding whether Axiom has made an infringing "use," we focus on the plain language of § 1114(1)(a), which, as noted above, requires a "use in commerce . . . of a registered mark in connection with the sale . . . or advertising of any goods." 15 U.S.C. § 1114(1)(a). The facts of the instant case are absolutely clear that Axiom used NAM's two trademarks as meta tags as part of its effort to promote and advertise its products on the Internet. Under the plain meaning of the language of the statute, such use constitutes a use in commerce in connection with the advertising of any goods.

The Eleventh Circuit declined to follow *1–800* both because in that case, unlike Axiom's, plaintiff's trademark was neither incorporated into the code for defendant's website nor was displayed in a search report or on the website. The court also expressed doubt that the "use" component of a Lanham Act claim requires display of the plaintiff's mark. Accord, *Finance*

Express LLC v. Nowcom Corp., 564 F.Supp.2d 1160 (CD Cal. 2008) (meta-tagging and keying). Similarly, in *Hysitron, Inc. v. MTS Sys. Corp.*, 2008 WL 3161969 (D. Minn. 2008), the court found defendant's purchase of Google Adwords consisting of plaintiff's trademark to be a "use in commerce."

> The majority of courts that have addressed the issue have disagreed with the Second Circuit's reasoning and found that using a competitor's trademark to create a sponsored link or other advertising does constitute a "use in commerce." [Citations omitted.] These cases reason that a company's use of a trademark to generate advertising is a "use in commerce," even when the customer never sees the mark.
>
> This Court adopts the majority view that using a trademark to generate advertising constitutes a "use in commerce" under the Lanham Act. This approach adheres to the plain meaning of the Lanham Act's definition of "use in commerce." The language used in the definition suggests that a "use in commerce" is not limited to affixing another's mark to one's own goods but also encompasses any use of another's mark to advertise or sell one's own goods and services. MTS used the HYSITRON mark to generate a sponsored link as part of its effort to advertise and sell its own goods over the internet. Under the plain language of the Lanham Act, MTS used the HYSITRON mark in commerce.

QUESTIONS

1. Would/should the analysis in *Rescuecom* be different if Google sold keyword trigger rights in words corresponding to third party trademarks, but no longer proposed the Keyword Selection Tool?

2. Does/should it make a difference if the defendant is the advertiser or the search engine? How does/should the analysis change depending on whether the defendant is alleged to infringe by *purchasing* keyword triggers or *embedding* third party trademarks in its mega tags, or instead is alleged to infringe by *selling* trigger rights in third party trademarks?

3. What should other courts, within or without the Second Circuit, make of the *Rescuecom* Appendix? Does it matter whether admitted dictum is expressed as part of an opinion or as a law review-esque addendum?

4. *Rescuecom* may culminate a shift in courts' analysis of sale of keyword trigger rights as "use in commerce." When courts dismissed trademark owners' claims at the outset so long as the search engine did not display the trademark owner's mark, Google's policy was to structure the advertisements to avoid showing the third party mark. If, as a result of *Rescuecom* and similar decisions, "use" is now established, and Google's defense accordingly turns on likelihood of confusion, courts are less likely to enter summary judgment for Google. Under those circumstances, might one anticipate that Google will no longer limit Adwords to keyword triggers that do not show third party trademarks in the resulting advertisements? If Google will not be ordered to cease selling trademarks as Adwords unless the particular advertisement is likely to cause confusion, but such a determination will not be made until after the claim is tried (and Google may also calculate that not every third party trademark owner will sue in any event), does it make sense as a matter of commercial strategy for Google to allow the third party trademark to appear in the Adwords client's advertisements, in order to collect the additional advertising revenue pending adjudication of the infringement claim? Is there any legal restraint on such a strategy?

Page 402.   Question 1, insert after reference to _American Rice v. Arkansas Rice Growers_:

The Fifth Circuit has adhered to its approach: in a more recent case involving the same plaintiff, _American Rice, Inc. v. Producers Rice Mill, Inc._, 518 F.3d 321 (5th Cir. 2008) the court again held that the Lanham Act would apply to American Rice's claim that its American rival in Saudi Arabia had adopted a confusingly similar mark.

B.   SECONDARY LIABILITY FOR TRADEMARK INFRINGEMENT

Page 433.   Insert after Questions:

Vulcan Golf, LLC v. Google Inc.

552 F.Supp.2d 752 (N.D. Ill. 2008).

■ BLANCHE M. MANNING, US DIST. JUDGE.

. . .

I.   Background

According to the lengthy First Amended Complaint ("FAC") ... the defendants have engaged in a massive scheme to use deceptive domain names on the internet to generate billions of advertising dollars at the expense of the plaintiffs. The specifics of the scheme are somewhat complicated, but in its most simple form, the FAC alleges that certain of the defendants register, license and/or "park", among other things, domain names that are the same as or substantially and confusingly similar to the plaintiffs' distinctive trade names or marks. The defendants do this because they know that when an internet user types a domain name into the address bar on the Google web browser, there is a possibility that the user will either guess the domain name for the plaintiff (and guess wrong) or misspell the name he or she is looking for.

For example, the FAC alleges that Dotster has registered and/or otherwise controls the domain name "www.VulcanGolf.com." This domain name is obviously very similar to the domain name "www.VulcanGolf. com," which is registered to and has been used by plaintiff Vulcan since May 1997. According to the plaintiffs' theory, Dotster has intentionally registered this domain name without the period after the "www" expecting that a certain number of internet users will mistype the name and will land on the webpage Dotster has created that is associated with the "incorrect" and allegedly deceptive domain name. When that happens, the defendants, having registered similar and purportedly deceptive domain names, profit if the internet user clicks on the advertising that is placed on the "deceptive" domain site. The advertising is allegedly created, sponsored, and maintained by Google which, according to the FAC, has developed "the largest single online marketing/advertising business in the world." The FAC alleges that Google "partners" with domain registrants as well as parking companies and others and consequently has "millions of domain names under its direct or indirect license, use, control, and management" including the purportedly deceptive domains.

Google allegedly uses sophisticated software that "processes" these domain names and assists in deciding what advertisements would be profitable on each domain. Google and the parking company defendants "collaborate in the placement of advertisements on domains and in the design/optimization of the landing pages associated with those domains." "To encourage Internet users to click [on the advertisements], Defendant Google, and in some instances other Parking Company Defendants, use targeting solutions that intelligently select the most relevant ads and categories for the domain names." When a user clicks on the advertising, Google and the parking companies and/or the domain owners receive revenue from that advertiser. . . .

In essence, then, the plaintiffs allege that Google and the other defendants have engaged in a wide-ranging scheme whereby they receive "billions of dollars in ill-gotten advertising and marketing revenue" by knowingly and intentionally registering, licensing and monetizing purportedly deceptive domain names at the expense of the plaintiff-mark owners.

* * *

4. Contributory Infringement

[The Complaint identifies Sedo and Oversee as "parking companies," defined as "a company that aggregates numerous domain names from individual domain registrants and contracts with an advertising service to license and monetize those domain names."] Sedo claims that Vulcan and Jackson have failed to properly allege a claim for contributory trademark infringement. Oversee makes the same argument as to all of the plaintiffs. In order to prove contributory infringement, "a plaintiff must demonstrate that a defendant: (1) intentionally induced a third party to infringe the plaintiff's mark; or (2) supplied a product to a third party with actual or constructive knowledge that the product was being used to directly infringe the mark." *Monotype Imaging, Inc. v. Bitstream, Inc.*, 03 C 4349, 2005 WL 936882, at *3 (N.D. Ill. Apr. 21, 2005)(citations omitted). "Contributory infringement therefore requires proof of direct infringement by a third party, as well as defendants' intent and knowledge of the wrongful activities of its distributors." *Id.* (citation omitted). . . .

Here, the plaintiffs allege that:

The Parking Company Defendants intentionally taste, register, and otherwise assist Domain registrants in procuring Deceptive Domains for the express purpose of monetization with Defendant Google advertisements; (FAC P 155)

The Parking Company Defendants enter into license agreements with the Domain registrants for the license and rights to control, monitor, maintain, use and place advertising on their domains, including Deceptive Domains; (FAC P 148)

Defendant Google, Parking Company Defendants and/or the Domain registrants enter into agreements where Defendant Google and the Parking Company Defendants share advertising/marketing revenue generated on parked domains; (FAC P 147);

The Parking Company Defendants cause popups or popunder advertisements on the Deceptive Domains and receive money for each popup or popunder displayed, in furtherance of the Deceptive Domain Scheme alleged herein. FAC P 160

In addition, the plaintiffs allege that the "[d]efendants induce, cause, and/or materially contribute to the Deceptive Domain Scheme and other unlawful conduct alleged herein" and list statements or actions that the defendants use to "direct" or "promote" the Deceptive Domain Scheme. As such, the court rejects Sedo and Oversee's argument that the plaintiffs have not sufficiently alleged that the defendants intentionally induced another to infringe on a trademark. Specifically, the court finds that the plaintiffs have sufficiently pled a claim for contributory infringement to the extent that the FAC alleges that the defendants "intentionally induced a third party to infringe the plaintiff's mark."

Oversee also asserts that the plaintiffs fail to sufficiently allege the second element of a contributory infringement claim, that is that it "continues to supply a product knowing that the recipient is using the product to engage in trademark infringement." However, contrary to Oversee's implication that both elements must be satisfied, the contributory infringement test is an "either/or" test. Because the court has found that the plaintiffs have alleged that the defendants intentionally induced another to infringe a trademark, that is all that is necessary to allow the claim to move forward.

5. Vicarious Infringement

a. Sedo

Sedo contends that Vulcan and Jackson have failed to allege a claim of vicarious trademark infringement. Liability for vicarious trademark infringement "requires a finding that the defendant and the infringer have an apparent or actual partnership, have authority to bind one another in transactions with third parties or exercise joint ownership or control over the infringing product." *Hard Rock Cafe Licensing Corp.*, 955 F.2d at 1150 (citation omitted). According to Sedo, the plaintiffs have not alleged any facts that Sedo and the domain owners who use its service can bind one another in a transaction or exercise joint ownership over anything.

However, as already noted above, [in addition to the facts previously alleged] the FAC alleges that:

... Defendant Parking Companies enter into agreements with Defendant Google and license to Defendant Google the rights to control, monitor, maintain, use and place advertising on all of the domains under the Parking Company's control, including Deceptive Domains. (FAC P 149).

These allegations are sufficient to support a claim that the alleged infringers at least have an "apparent or actual partnership" or have the "authority to bind one another." As such, the motion to dismiss on this basis is denied.

b. Google

Google also avails itself of the *Hard Rock* case asserting that the "theory of vicarious trademark infringement liability pleaded in the First Amended Complaint was expressly rejected by the Seventh Circuit." Specifically, Google refers to the "right and ability to supervise standard," taken from the copyright violation context, which was advocated by the plaintiff in *Hard Rock* but rejected by the Seventh Circuit.

As described above, the *Hard Rock* court initially stated that liability for vicarious trademark infringement "requires a finding that the defendant and the infringer have an apparent or actual partnership, have authority to bind one another in transactions with third parties or exercise joint ownership or control over the infringing product." *Hard Rock*, 955 F.2d at 1150. In the immediate next sentence, however, the *Hard Rock* court noted that "[t]he case before us does not fit into the joint tortfeasor model, and *Hard Rock* does not argue that it does." *Id.* The *Hard Rock* court then went on to discuss (and reject) the alternative "right to supervise" standard relied by the plaintiff in that case.

Here, the plaintiffs do not appear to be seeking relief based on the "right to supervise" doctrine. Instead, as already stated above, the allegations in the FAC are sufficient to state a claim that the alleged infringers at least have an "apparent or actual partnership" or have the "authority to bind one another" as required by the rule articulated by the Seventh Circuit. Thus, Google's reliance on the Seventh Circuit's rejection of the "right to supervise" standard is misplaced and the court rejects this basis for dismissal of the vicarious trademark infringement claim against Google.

* * *

Tiffany, Inc. v. eBay, Inc., 576 F.Supp.2d 463 (S.D.N.Y. 2008). Tiffany, Inc. claimed that sellers using eBay's online auction sites were offering counterfeit Tiffany silver jewelry. Although eBay responded to Tiffany's notices by closing access to offending sites, Tiffany contended that principles of secondary liability imposed on eBay an obligation "preemptively [to] refus[e] to post any listing offering five or more Tiffany items."

> [T]he Court finds that eBay is not liable for contributory trademark infringement. In determining whether eBay is liable, the standard is not whether eBay could reasonably anticipate possible infringement, but rather whether eBay continued to supply its services to sellers when it knew or had reason to know of infringement by those sellers. *See Inwood Labs., Inc. v. Ives Labs., Inc.,* 456 U.S. 844, 854 (1982). Indeed, the Supreme Court has specifically disavowed the

reasonable anticipation standard as a "watered down" and incorrect standard. *Id.* at 854 n.13. Here, when Tiffany put eBay on notice of specific items that Tiffany believed to be infringing, eBay immediately removed those listings. eBay refused, however, to monitor its website and preemptively remove listings of Tiffany jewelry before the listings became public. The law does not impose liability for contributory trademark infringement on eBay for its refusal to take such preemptive steps in light of eBay's "reasonable anticipation" or generalized knowledge that counterfeit goods might be sold on its website. Quite simply, the law demands more specific knowledge as to which items are infringing and which seller is listing those items before requiring eBay to take action.

The result of the application of this legal standard is that Tiffany must ultimately bear the burden of protecting its trademark. Policymakers may yet decide that the law as it stands is inadequate to protect rights owners in light of the increasing scope of Internet commerce and the concomitant rise in potential trademark infringement. Nevertheless, under the law as it currently stands, it does not matter whether eBay or Tiffany could more efficiently bear the burden of policing the eBay website for Tiffany counterfeits—an open question left unresolved by this trial. Instead, the issue is whether eBay continued to provide its website to sellers when eBay knew or had reason to know that those sellers were using the website to traffic in counterfeit Tiffany jewelry. The Court finds that when eBay possessed the requisite knowledge, it took appropriate steps to remove listings and suspend service. Under these circumstances, the Court declines to impose liability for contributory trademark infringement.

The court began its extensive discussion of contributory infringement by applying the second prong of the *Inwood* standard: did eBay "continue to supply" its service despite its knowledge, or reason to know, that counterfeit merchandise was being sold? The court ruled that *Inwood* precluded Tiffany's proposed alternative standard, which would have inquired whether eBay failed to take reasonable precautions to prevent infringement, when eBay could "reasonably anticipate" that some of its sellers would infringe. As an additional threshold matter, the court determined that eBay's services came within the *Inwood* framework.

[T]he Court will look not only to whether eBay provided the necessary marketplace for the counterfeiting (which it clearly did), but further, to whether eBay had direct control over the means of infringement. eBay argues that it lacked such control and indeed, that it is more like an online classified ads service than an online flea market, noting that it is undisputed that eBay never took possession of the items sold via its website, and that eBay could not physically inspect, examine, or authenticate such items. The evidence at trial also demonstrated that eBay has limited control over the listings and advertisements on its website, and that individual sellers have a great deal of latitude in describing the products that are for sale. Nevertheless, in examining all of the facts that were proved at trial, the Court finds by a preponderance of the evidence that eBay exercises sufficient control and monitoring over its website such that it fits squarely within the *Fonavisa* and *Hard Rock Cafe* line of cases.

In reaching this conclusion, the Court first notes that while eBay itself does not sell or possess the items available on its website, eBay retains significant control over the transactions conducted through eBay. By providing the software to set up the listings and store listing information on its servers, eBay supplies the necessary marketplace for the sale of counterfeit goods. eBay takes an active role in supplying customers—namely, registered buyers—to registered sellers, and actively facilitates transactions between them.

Second, eBay has actively promoted the sale of Tiffany jewelry items. eBay advertises merchandise on its own website as well as through other websites, including until 2003, Google and Yahoo!. eBay also actively works with sellers and PowerSellers to help them grow their jewelry business. eBay's seminars, account management programs, and research on most frequently-searched terms all actively contribute to the sale of items on eBay. eBay even told its sellers that Tiffany was one of the "most effective keywords" and had one of the best "Returns on Investment." For example, in an eBay newsletter provided to its top jewelry sellers, in the section entitled, "Planning for Growth: Accelerate Your Sales," eBay advised its top sellers to "us[e] recommended keywords to boost sales," and identified "Tiffany & Co." as one such keyword.

Third, eBay profits from the listing of items and successful completion of sales, through insertion fees and final value fees. eBay also profits by taking an additional percentage of the sales price if the transaction is consummated through PayPal.

Fourth, eBay maintains significant control over the listings on its website. Certain categories of items are entirely barred from the website, including drugs, firearms, and alcohol products. The fraud engine screens listings and removes items that use specific terms in the listing description, for example, "counterfeit" or "fake." Through eBay's User Agreements, users are required to abide by the terms of use, and eBay retains the right to suspend those users who fail to do so.

Finally, to the extent eBay styles itself as a classified ad service, eBay's own witnesses admitted that eBay maintains a classified ad service separate and apart from the eBay listings that are at issue in this action.

Nonetheless, while eBay was providing a service within the *Inwood* framework, the court then held that eBay lacked the requisite knowledge. The court determined that *Inwood* and *Lockheed* required more than "generalized knowledge" that infringers were using its services. The specificity requirement makes demonstration of sufficient knowledge all the more difficult when, as is the case with eBay, not all sellers of Tiffany silver jewelry are purveying counterfeits.

Significantly, Tiffany has not alleged, nor does the evidence support a conclusion, that all of the Tiffany merchandise sold through eBay is counterfeit. Rather, a substantial number of authentic Tiffany goods are sold on eBay, including both new and vintage silver jewelry, sometimes in lots of five or more. As Justice White admonished, the doctrine of contributory trademark infringement should not be used to require defendants to refuse to provide a product or service to those who merely *might* infringe the trademark. *Inwood,* 456 U.S. at 861 (White, J., concurring) (observing that whether a defendant "can anticipate that some illegal substitution will occur to some unspecified extent, and by some unknown [parties], should not by itself be a predicate for contributory liability"). Were Tiffany to prevail on its argument that generalized statements of infringement were sufficient to impute knowledge to eBay of any and all infringing acts, Tiffany's rights in its mark would dramatically expand, potentially stifling legitimate sales of Tiffany goods on eBay. [Citations omitted.] Given the presence of authentic goods on eBay, it therefore cannot be said that generalized knowledge of counterfeiting is sufficient to impute knowledge to eBay of any specific acts of actual infringement.

Tiffany endeavored to show that eBay had the requisite specific knowledge because any seller of "five or more" items was unlikely to be reselling personal jewelry. Rather the allegedly bulk nature of the sales should have alerted eBay to the suspicious character of the site.

Tiffany has failed to present sufficient evidence demonstrating that a seller offering five items or more of Tiffany jewelry is presumptively dealing in counterfeit merchandise. Indeed, Tiffany's own CEO disavowed the importance of the five-or-more rule, calling it a "shorthand solution" and a "compromised effort" to make eBay "do a better job of preventing the sale of Tiffany counterfeit merchandise." As extensively discussed in the Court's Findings of Fact, the precise contours of the "five or more" rule have shifted throughout litigation. Moreover, the evidence at trial demonstrated that the five-item limit is not regularly enforced by Tiffany itself, that lots of more than five identical Tiffany silver jewelry items are available through Tiffany's Corporate Sales Department and international trade accounts, and that lots of five or more pieces of authentic new Tiffany silver jewelry have been made available on eBay.

Accordingly, the record makes clear that not only was Tiffany ambiguous as to the precise contours of its proposed "five-or-more" rule, but that there is little support for the notion that the five-or-more rule presumptively demonstrated the presence of infringing items. eBay was under no obligation to credit the potentially self-serving assertions of a trademark owner, particularly when those assertions—such as the "five-or-more" rule—were unfounded, and when the trademark owner's demands, if met, clearly would have eliminated even legitimate sales on eBay. The doctrine of contributory trademark infringement cannot be used as a sword to cut off resale of authentic Tiffany items.

[Tiffany's contention that eBay had been willfully blind fared no better:]

Tiffany further submits that in order to avoid liability for willful blindness, eBay was obligated to take steps such as conducting its own internal investigation or analyzing its data to prevent further infringement. On this point, it is clear that eBay did not conduct a separate investigation into the extent of counterfeit Tiffany jewelry on its website. eBay did not analyze its data, or research and evaluate the number of "Tiffany" listings removed from its website. Nor did it track the number of sellers suspended because they had posted infringing listings.

Nevertheless, the fact that eBay did not take these additional steps is immaterial, because without specific knowledge or reason to know, eBay is under no affirmative duty to ferret out potential infringement. Willful blindness requires "more than mere negligence or mistake" and does not lie unless the defendant knew of a high probability of illegal conduct and purposefully contrived to avoid learning of it, for example, by failing to inquire further out of fear of the result of the inquiry. [Citation omitted.] Put simply, it cannot be said that eBay purposefully contrived to avoid learning of counterfeiting on its website, or that eBay failed to investigate once it learned of such counterfeiting. To the contrary, in the face of such general awareness, eBay took significant steps to prevent counterfeiting by developing the VeRO Program, which seeks to remove individually infringing listings. Moreover, the record reveals that when eBay became aware, through its VeRO Program, of Tiffany's good-faith belief that a listing was infringing, it investigated and removed that listing from its website.

Were Tiffany to prevail in its argument that eBay was willfully blind, the "reason to know" standard of the *Inwood* test would be inflated into an affirmative duty to take precautions against potential counterfeiters, even when eBay had no specific knowledge of the individual counterfeiters. The law explicitly precludes such an expansion of the "reason to know" standard. [Citations omitted.]

QUESTION

What accounts for the different outcomes in *Vulcan Golf v. Google* and *Tiffany v. eBay*?

C. Statutory Defenses/Incontestability

Page 442. Add the following Question after the Note:
QUESTION

Plaintiff owns an incontestable registration for VAIL for ski resort services. Defendant uses 1–800–SKI-VAIL for marketing services promoting services near Vail, Colorado. In determining the likelihood of confusion between the two marks, should the court presume that plaintiff's mark is strong due to its incontestability or can it also consider the geographic connotation of the term and third party uses in finding that, although protectable, the mark is relatively weak? *See Vail Associates, Inc. v. Vend–Tel–Co., Ltd.*, 516 F.3d 853 (10th Cir. 2008).

Page 449.   Add the following material at the end of Question 1:

What if the signatory of a use declaration is not fluent in English and does not fully comprehend what the declaration means? Does it matter if the attorney who drafts the declaration misunderstands what use the client has communicated that it has made? *See Hachette Filipacchi Presse v. Elle Belle LLC*, 85 U.S.P.Q.2d 1090 (T.T.A.B. 2007) (neither a misunderstanding by client or attorney precludes a finding of fraud; both attorney and client have duty to ensure accuracy of use statement).

Page 449.   Add the following material at the end of Question 2:

Could a use-based applicant amend its application to an intent-to-use application after being opposed on the ground of a fraudulent declaration of use? *See Sinclair Oil Corp. v. Kendrick*, 85 U.S.P.Q.2d 1032 (T.T.A.B. 2007) (an amendment to a 1(b) basis after opposition does not avoid a finding of fraud since the Trademark Office relied on the use-based declaration in approving the mark for publication).

Page 449.   Add Questions 3 and 4:

3.   Is the Board's stringent interpretation of fraud in the *Medinol* line of cases congruent with the requirement of a knowing material misrepresentation or is it in effect a rule of strict liability? If any of the Board's cases were to be appealed, should the Federal Circuit uphold this interpretation? Currently, two *Medinol*-type fraud findings by the Board are on appeal before the Federal Circuit. In *Bose Corp. v. Hexawave, Inc.*, 88 U.S.P.Q.2d 1332 (T.T.A.B. 2007), the Board concluded that Bose's renewal declaration was fraudulent for its WAVE registration because Bose was not using the mark on one of six covered goods, i.e. audio tape recorders and players. The Board rejected Bose's argument that its counsel had a good faith belief that the mark was being used on those goods, although they were no longer being manufactured, because of the transport of repaired goods back to owners. In *Grand Canyon West Ranch LLC v. Hualapai Tribe*, 88 U.S.P.Q.2d 1501 (T.T.A.B. 2008), applicant filed a use-based application for "tours and providing related transportation." In the course of examination, Applicant accepted the Examiner's further specification of "providing related transportation" to "providing transportation of passengers related to recreational travel tours by means of rail, tram, non-motorized vehicles featuring bicycles, and domestic animals." The tribe, when challenged for fraud because it was not actually using these other means of transportation, argued it had unsuccessfully tried to offer horseback rides, bicycle tours and tractor-based tram rides and therefore believed it had "used" the mark. The Board disagreed and found fraud. How should the Federal Circuit decide *Bose* and *Hualapai*?

4. If a registrant files a declaration of use for wines and sparkling wines, but only uses its mark on sparkling wines, would it be guilty of fraud? Why/why not? *See Tri–Star Marketing, LLC v. Nino Franco Spumanti S.R.L.*, 2007 WL 2460996 (T.T.A.B. 2007).

Page 457. Add the following Questions 4, 5 and 6:

4. Where plaintiff has an incontestable registration for LOVE POTION for perfumed essential oils and defendant uses its DESSERT house mark on fragrance products with the phrases "love potion fragrance" or "belly button love potion fragrance" such as shown below, is such use a fair use? *See Dessert Beauty, Inc. v. Fox*, 568 F. Supp.2d 416 (S.D.N.Y. 2008).

5. Is use of the phrase "Ride Hard" by the motorcycle manufacturer Harley Davidson in its advertising and on some promotional merchandise (including T-shirts) that bear a Harley Davidson mark fair use where plaintiff owns the mark RIDE HARD for apparel? *See Bell v. Harley Davidson Motor Co.*, 539 F. Supp.2d 1249 (S.D. Cal. 2008). Does it matter that Harley Davidson has not tried to register RIDE HARD as a mark and that third parties have used the phrase in advertising a variety of businesses?

6. Lettuce Entertain You Enterprises owns a family of LETTUCE marks for restaurant and catering services, although none of its restaurants use LETTUCE in the name of the restaurant. Defendant announced its intention to open a restaurant under the name LETTUCE MIX by placing a sign outside the intended premises. After Lettuce Entertain You brought suit, defendant covered the sign with another sign saying "Let Us Be!" with an image of a head of lettuce. Is this second sign a fair use? *See Lettuce Entertain You Enterprises, Inc. v. Leila Sophia AR, LLC*, 2009 WL 1605917 (E.D. Ill. 2009).

Page 467. Delete *Pro-Football, Inc. v. Harjo* and Questions following that case and substitute the following case, a later appeal in *Harjo*, and Questions below:

Pro Football, Inc. v. Harjo

565 F.3d 880 (D.C. Cir. 2009).

■ TATEL, CIRCUIT JUDGE:

At bottom, this case concerns whether various trademarks related to the Washington Redskins football team disparage Native Americans within the meaning of the Lanham Trademark Act, § 2, 15 U.S.C. § 1052(a). But that question has since been overshadowed by the defense of laches, the basis on which the district court first entered judgment for the Redskins six years ago. We reversed that decision, finding that the district court had misapplied the law of laches to the particular facts of the case. *Pro-Football, Inc. v. Harjo (Harjo II)*, 415 F.3d 44, 50, 367 U.S. App. D.C. 276 (D.C. Cir. 2005). On remand, the district court reconsidered the evidence in light of our instructions and again ruled for the team. *Pro-Football, Inc. v. Harjo (Harjo III)*, 567 F. Supp. 2d 46, 62 (D.D.C. 2008). Now appealing that decision, plaintiffs argue only that the district court improperly assessed evidence of prejudice in applying laches to the facts at issue. Limited to that question, we see no error and affirm.

I.

. . . Appellants, seven Native Americans, filed a 1992 action before the Patent and Trademark Office seeking cancellation of six Redskins trademarks that were, they argued, impermissibly disparaging towards members of their ethnic group. Pro–Football, the Redskins' corporate entity and the owner of the marks, argued to the Trademark Trial and Appeal Board that its long-standing use of the name, combined with plaintiffs' delay in bringing the case, called for application of laches, an equitable defense that applies where there is "(1) lack of diligence by the party against whom the defense is asserted, and (2) prejudice to the party asserting the defense," *Nat'l R.R. Passenger Corp. v. Morgan*, 536 U.S. 101, 121–22, 122 S. Ct. 2061, 153 L. Ed. 2d 106 (2002) (internal quotation marks omitted). The TTAB disagreed, observing that petitioners asserted an interest in preventing "a substantial segment of the population" from being held up "to public ridicule," and that insofar as that interest reached "beyond the personal interest being asserted by the present petitioners," laches was inappropriate. *Harjo v. Pro Football Inc.,* 30 U.S.P.Q. 2d 1828, 1831 (TTAB 1994). Finding on the merits that the marks were indeed disparaging, the TTAB cancelled them, *see Harjo v. Pro Football Inc.,* 50 U.S.P.Q. 2d 1705, 1749 (TTAB 1999), depriving Pro–Football of the ability to pursue infringers.

Pro–Football then exercised its option to dispute this holding by means of a civil action in the United States District Court for the District of Columbia. *See* 15 U.S.C. § 1071(b)(1), (4) (providing choice between district court action and Federal Circuit appeal). The district court sided with Pro–Football on the laches issue, holding that the 25–year delay between the mark's first registration in 1967 and the TTAB filing in 1992 indeed required dismissal of the action. *Pro-Football, Inc. v. Harjo,* 284 F. Supp. 2d 96, 144 (D.D.C. 2003). We reversed. "[L]aches," we said, "attaches only to parties who have unjustifiably delayed," *Harjo II,* 415 F.3d at 49, and the period of unjustifiable delay cannot start before a plaintiff reaches the age of majority, *id. at* 48–49. The youngest plaintiff, Mateo Romero, was only a year old in 1967. Because the correct inquiry would have assessed his delay and the consequent prejudice to Pro–Football only from the day of his eighteenth birthday in December 1984, we remanded the record to the district court to consider, in the first instance, the defense of laches with respect to Romero. *Id.* at 49–50.

On remand in this case, the district court again found the defense of laches persuasive. It held that the seven-year, nine-month "Romero Delay Period" evinced a lack of diligence on Romero's part, *Harjo III,* 567 F. Supp. 2d at 53–56, and following our instructions to consider both trial and economic prejudice, *see Harjo II,* 415 F.3d at 50, it found that that delay harmed Pro–Football, *Harjo III,* 567 F. Supp. 2d at 56–62. Now appealing from that decision, Romero challenges neither the applicability of laches *vel non* nor the district court's finding of unreasonable delay. We thus confine our review to the only question Romero does raise: whether the district court properly found trial and economic prejudice sufficient to support a defense of laches.

II.

... [W]e see no reason to reverse...

The district court relied primarily on two factors in finding trial prejudice: (1) the death of former Redskins president Edward Bennett Williams during the Romero Delay Period; and (2) the delay period's general contribution to the time lapse from the date of registration. *Cf. Harjo,* 50 U.S.P.Q. 2d at 1773–75 (disparagement is analyzed at the time of registration). According to the district court, both factors limited Pro–Football's ability to marshal evidence supporting its mark: Williams had met with Native American leaders close to the time of registration to discuss their views, while the nearly eight years of further delay made it more difficult to obtain any other contemporaneous evidence of public attitudes towards the mark. *See Harjo III,* 567 F. Supp. 2d at 56–58. Romero mainly argues that this "lost evidence" would have had minimal value. He believes that Williams' testimony would have reflected only a narrow set of views on the disparaging nature of the Redskins marks, and that any possibility that 1967 attitudes could have been better surveyed at the time of an earlier suit is outweighed by other overwhelming evidence of disparagement. We needn't cast doubt on Romero's view of the evidence to hold that there was no abuse of discretion. The lost evidence of contemporaneous public opinion is surely not entirely irrelevant, and weighing the prejudice resulting from its loss falls well within the zone of the district court's discretion. In reviewing that assessment, we cannot assume that legally relevant evidence possibly available in an earlier action would have lacked persuasive content.

Nor can we fault the district court's evaluation of economic prejudice. Undisputed record evidence reveals a significant expansion of Redskins merchandising efforts and sizable investment in the mark during the Romero Delay Period. Romero believes this investment is irrelevant absent some evidence that Pro–Football would have acted otherwise—by, say, changing the Redskins name—if Romero had sued earlier. But the district court repeatedly rejected this argument, citing the Federal Circuit's holding in *Bridgestone/Firestone Research, Inc. v. Automobile Club,* 245 F.3d 1359, 1363 (Fed. Cir. 2001), that "[e]conomic prejudice arises from investment in and development of the trademark, and the continued commercial use and economic promotion of a mark over a prolonged period adds weight to the evidence of prejudice." *See Harjo III,* 567 F. Supp. 2d at 59. The court thus thought it sufficient that the team deployed investment capital toward a mark Romero waited too long to attack, whether or not the team could prove that it would necessarily have changed its name or employed a different investment strategy had Romero sued earlier.

This was no abuse of discretion. To be sure, a finding of prejudice requires at least some reliance on the absence of a lawsuit—if Pro–Football would have done exactly the same thing regardless of a more timely complaint, its laches defense devolves into claiming harm not from Romero's tardiness, but from Romero's success on the merits. But in contrast to the defense of estoppel—which requires evidence of specific reliance on a particular plaintiff's silence—laches requires only general evidence of prejudice, which may arise from mere proof of continued investment in the late-attacked mark alone. [Citation omitted] We have thus described as sufficient "a reliance interest resulting from the defendant's continued development of good-will during th[e] period of delay," and treated evidence of continued investment as proof of prejudice sufficient to bar injunctive relief. *NAACP v. NAACP Legal Def. & Educ. Fund, Inc.,* 753 F.2d 131, 137–38, 243 U.S. App. D.C. 313 (D.C. Cir. 1985). Such continued investment was unquestionably present here. The district court thus acted well within our precedent—as well as the precedent of the Federal Circuit, which directly reviews TTAB decisions—in finding economic prejudice on the basis of investments made during the delay period. The lost value of these investments was sufficient evidence of prejudice for the district court to exercise its discretion to apply laches, even absent specific evidence that more productive investments would in fact have resulted from an earlier suit.

In so holding, we stress two factors. First, as the district court correctly noted, the amount of prejudice required in a given case varies with the length of the delay. "If only a short period of time elapses between accrual of the claim and suit, the magnitude of prejudice required before suit would be barred is great; if the delay is lengthy, a lesser showing of prejudice is required." *Gull Airborne Instruments, Inc. v. Weinberger,* 694 F.2d 838, 843, 224 U.S. App. D.C. 272 (D.C. Cir. 1982). This reflects the view that "equity aids the vigilant and not those who slumber on their rights," *NAACP, 753 F.2d at 137,* as well as the fact that evidence of prejudice is among the evidence that can be lost by delay. Eight years is a long time—a delay made only more unreasonable by Romero's acknowledged exposure to the various Redskins trademarks well before reaching the age of majority. *See Harjo III,* 567 F. Supp. 2d at 54–55. The second point follows the first: because laches requires this equitable weighing of both the length of delay and the amount of prejudice, it leaves the district court very broad discretion to take account of the particular facts of particular cases. We have no basis for finding abuse of that discretion where, as here, the claim of error ultimately amounts to nothing more than a different take on hypothetical inquiries into what might have been.

III.

A final issue concerns the trademark of the team's cheerleaders, the "Redskinettes," which Pro–Football first registered in 1990. As to this mark and only this mark, Romero argues that he acted with reasonable diligence by filing his action in 1992, only 29 months from the mark's registration. The district court disagreed, finding even this short delay unreasonable given the relationship between the Redskinettes claim and the other claims on which Romero was already delaying. *See id.* & 54 n.5. This view followed from Romero's own litigation position. He argued to the district court, this Court, and the TTAB that the disparaging nature of the Redskinettes name derives from the disparaging nature of the Redskins name itself. The district court thus saw no reason why Romero, fully aware of both the team's name and the cheerleaders' name and six-years into his delay period on the former, failed to complain immediately about the registration of the Redskinettes.

While Romero delayed considerably less in attacking the Redskinettes mark, the district court did not abuse its discretion by analyzing the reasonableness of this delay in light of the delay in bringing the underlying claims regarding the name of the team itself. The Federal Circuit has at least suggested that a defense of laches as to a recently registered mark may be based on a failure to challenge an earlier, substantially similar mark, *see Lincoln Logs Ltd. v. Lincoln Pre–Cut Log Homes, Inc.,* 971 F.2d 732, 734 (Fed. Cir. 1992), as has the TTAB, *see Copperweld Corp. v. Astralloy–Vulcan Corp.,* 196 U.S.P.Q. 585, 590–91 (TTAB 1977). It is unclear to us how this rule interacts with the requirement to analyze disparagement at the time of registration, since the factual context may well have changed. But in any event and in the context of *this* case, it is difficult to see how it could be inequitable to allow Romero to complain about the Redskins but equitable to allow his complaint about the Redskinettes, particularly because the Redskinettes name had been in use well before the date of registration. Indeed, the registration of the Redskinettes mark reflects perhaps the greatest reliance on the absence of any previous complaints. Thus, without deciding whether Romero could have avoided laches by attacking the Redskinettes mark on the day of registration, we at least see no abuse of discretion in the district court's finding that the 29–month delay evinced a lack of reasonable diligence.

In fact, we think the Redskinettes issue best demonstrates the reasonableness of the district court's approach to this case as a whole. In 1990, six years into the Romero Delay Period, Pro–Football was not only investing in the Redskins mark, but seeking to expand legal protection of related marks, placing greater reliance on the continued validity of its underlying brand name. It would have been bold indeed for the team to have sought to register the Redskinettes under their existing name had the TTAB been considering revocation—or had the TTAB already revoked—the registration of the Redskins mark. We thus think it neither a stretch of imagination nor an abuse of discretion to conclude that Pro–Football might have invested differently in its branding of the Redskins and related entities had Romero acted earlier to place the trademark in doubt. We accordingly have no basis for questioning the district court's determination.

IV.

Deciding only the questions presented, and finding no abuse of discretion in the district court's resolution of them, we affirm.

So ordered.

QUESTIONS

1. What if one of the Native American plaintiffs in *Harjo* had not been born until after 1990 when the REDSKINETTES mark was registered? Would laches have applied in that case? Can a mark always be challenged on the ground of disparagement as long as a member of the allegedly disparaged group was born after the time of the registration?

2. If a trademark owner orders search reports that show a defendant's mark, should that start the period of delay for laches to commence? *See Saul Zaentz Co. v. Wozniak Travel Inc.*, 89 U.S.P.Q.2d 1665 (N.D. Cal. 2008)(defendant's Hobbit Travel business first appeared in Tolkien rights owner's search reports 18 years before suit was brought).

3. In *Internet Specialties West, Inc. v. Milon–DiGiorgio Enterprises, Inc.*, 559 F.3d 985 (9th Cir. 2009), both plaintiff and defendant were internet service providers. Although aware of defendant from 1998, plaintiff did not object until 2005, several months after defendant expanded to offer DSL service. Plaintiff argued that the period of delay for laches should start anew from this expansion. Do you agree or disagree with this position? Additionally, defendant argued it showed prejudice resulting from plaintiff's delay since in the meantime it had built its customer base from 2,000 to 13,000 and had built up goodwill through promoting its services through pay-per-click ads on the internet. Is this a sufficient showing of prejudice? See majority and dissenting opinions.

CHAPTER 7

FALSE DESIGNATION OF ORIGIN

A. SECTION 43(a) OF THE LANHAM ACT AND UNREGISTERED MARKS

Page 480. Add new Question.

QUESTION

In 1999, the musical group Red Hot Chili Peppers released a song titled *"Californication"* on an album of the same name. The album sold 24 million copies, and both song and album were nominated for Grammy awards. The song has remained popular; the album is still available. In 2007, Showtime introduced a new original television series, which it titled *"Californication,"* featuring the sexual adventures of a novelist portrayed by David Duchovny. The series was a success, and Showtime renewed it for the 2008–09 television season, and released the first season's episodes on DVD. Showtime also released a television soundtrack album under the title *"Temptation: Music from the Showtime Series Californication."* The Red Hot Chili Peppers filed suit against Showtime, claiming that Showtime's use of "Californication" as a title for its series, and the use of the word "Californication" in the title of the DVD and soundtrack CD, amount to false designations of origin under § 43(a). How should the court rule? *See Kiedis v. Showtime Networks*, CV 07–8185 DSF (MANx) (C.D. Cal. Feb. 19, 2008).

B. TRADE DRESS

Page 496: Add New Question 3 and the following case.

3. John Raymond Designs sells a line of famed wall art featuring antiqued photographs of Mormon temples like those on the next page. The photos have apparently handwritten descriptions in the upper right hand corner and are framed in heavy dark wood frames. JRD sells its art through its own website and a number of retail distributors, including, until recently, Cultural Hall, a business specializing in décor items for Mormon homes.

Last year, in a dispute over allegedly unpaid bills, JRD canceled its agreement with Cultural Hall. Cultural Hall hired an artist to antique and frame different photographs of the same Mormon temples; these photos also have apparently handwritten identifications and are framed in heavy wooden frames. Cultural Hall sells the framed photos to Costco stores, at fairs and from its website. JRD sues Cultural Hall for trade dress infringement for copying the overall look of its artwork. Is the overall look of JRD's framed wall art trade dress, product design, or some *tertium quid*? *See Framed Wall Art v. PME Holdings*, 2008 WL 5205822 (D. Utah 2008).

Hammerton, Inc v. Heisterman, 2008 WL 2004327 (D. Utah 2008). Hammerton sued its former employee, Heisterman, alleging that defendant was "knocking off" the designs of plaintiff's expensive, handmade lighting fixtures. Heisterman had worked in plaintiff's product development department for two years, before he resigned and founded a competing business. Plaintiff claimed that defendant copied the design of its fixtures from plaintiff's catalog, infringing its trade dress in 50 different fixtures from five different lines. The court granted defendant's motion for summary judgment on the trade dress claim:

> In this case, Defendants are entitled to summary judgment on Plaintiff's trade dress infringement claim because Plaintiff has failed to properly articulate the design elements that comprise its alleged trade dress. Despite two rounds of briefing and a hearing on the Unfair Competition Motion, the Court still does not know what Plaintiff's alleged trade dress or trade dresses look like.
>
> . . .
>
> [I]t appears to the Court that much of the confusion surrounding Plaintiff's trade dress claims stems from a fundamental misunderstanding of the protection afforded under § 43(a) of the Lanham Act. Section 43(a) does not protect manufacturers from having their products copied by competitors. "The Lanham Act does not exist to reward manufacturers for their innovation in creating a particular device; that is the purpose of the patent law and its period of exclusivity."[31] Rather, "the underlying purpose of the Lanham Act . . . is protecting consumers and manufacturers from deceptive representations of affiliation and origin."[32] Accordingly, trade dress protection is directly tied to the combination of specific features (*i.e.*, the trade dress) embedded in a product that identifies the source of the product to the consuming public. Without a careful identification of the combination of design features that comprise the trade dress, and a showing that the trade dress has obtained secondary meaning and is nonfunctional, trade dress law could easily be used to achieve patent-like protection for

---

31. *Traffix Devices, Inc. v. Marketing Displays, Inc.*, 532 U.S. 23, 35 (2001).

32. *Landscape Forms [, Inc. v. Columbia Cascade Co.*, 113 F.3d 373, 381 (2d Cir. 1997))], at 375.

products without regard to the requirements and limitations of patent law.[33] This potential for misuse of trade dress law is of particular concern in product design cases, as "product design almost invariably serves purposes other than source identification."[34] Thus, "courts have exercised particular 'caution' when extending protection to product designs."[35]

In bringing its trade dress infringement claim, Plaintiff seeks to prevent Defendants from "knocking off" its products—relief that is simply not afforded under the Lanham Act.

Page 506. Add the following Question after the *Eco Manufacturing* case.

QUESTION

Plaintiff, who holds an incontestable trademark registration for a circular beach towel, sues defendant for marketing competing round beach towels. Defendant argues that the round shape of the beach towels is functional, and points to ads for plaintiff's towels that say *"Find your spot in the sun without moving your towel around,"* and *"Now when the sun moves, your towel doesn't have to—The round shape eliminates the need to constantly get up and move your towel as the sun moves across the sky. Instead merely reposition yourself."* Defendant insists the ads are mere puffery, since any towel that's large enough will allow sunbathers to reposition themselves without moving their towels. How should the court rule? *See Franek v. WalMart Stores*, 2009 WL 674269 (N.D. Ill. 2009).

Page 515. Add to the end of the Question:

See also Cartier v. Sardell, 294 Fed.Appx. 615 (2d Cir. 2008):

Although the design of the Tank Française does operate to perform a function, the trade dress is not "functional" because there are many alternative designs that could perform the same function. Enforcing Cartier's rights in this design will not inhibit its competitors from being able to compete effectively in the market for luxury watches. The district court did not err in its decision, therefore, that the Tank Française trade dress is not functional.

Page 541. Substitute the following case for *McNeil PPC v. Guardian Drug* and the Question that follows it:

McNeil Nutritionals, LLC v. Heartland Sweeteners, LLC, 511 F.3d 350 (3d Cir. 2007). The producer of Splenda artificial sweetener sued the producer of multiple store brands of artificial sweetener made from sucralose, the principal ingredient in Splenda. Plaintiff argued that defendant's packaging of its store brand sweeteners infringed Splenda's distinctive yellow trade dress. Relying on the reasoning in *Conopco*, the court of

---

33. *See Qualitex Co. v. Jacobson Prods. Co.*, 514 U.S. 159, 164–65 (1995).

34. *Wal–Mart Stores*, 529 U.S. at 213.

35. *Landscape Forms*, 113 F.3d at 380 (quoting *Jeffrey Milstein v. Greger, Lawlor, Roth, Inc.*, 58 F.3d 27, 32 (2d Cir. 1995)).

appeals affirmed the district court's finding that there was no likelihood of confusion for Food Lion and Safeway store brand packaging, in which the name of the stores appeared prominently on the house brand packages:

Applying these principles to the case at bar, we conclude that there was no clear error. First, "Food Lion" and "Safeway" are well-known because they are well-known to the consumers who shop in the stores with those same names. Second, the stores are represented prominently on their respective packages. For example, the Food Lion name and logo in black (a color with virtually no presence on the front of Splenda packages) are displayed in the top-left corner. As importantly, a vertical design element runs through the front of the package, visually dividing it between a dark yellow bar and a light yellow canvas, in a way found on other Food Lion store-brand products. The yellow color aside, these features are far more similar to other Food Lion store-brand packaging features and therefore distinguish themselves from any feature present on the Splenda packages. These distinguishing elements are also found on the Food Lion bag of granular sucralose.

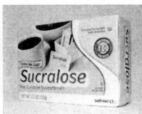

The District Court found additional differences between the Food Lion trade dress and Splenda trade dress. First, the Food Lion product name "Sweet Choice" is shown rather than "Splenda." Second, "Sweet Choice" is positioned at the bottom of the box, rather than at the top. Third, whereas "Sweet Choice" is not surrounded by a white cloud, "Splenda" is. Fourth, missing from the Food Lion packages is the circular element with the slogan "Made From Sugar, Tastes Like Sugar." When combined with the distinguishing use of the Food Lion name and logo, these differences are not minute ones found only upon examination with a microscope . . . .

McNeil argues that the history of color coding in the sweetener industry increases the likelihood of consumer confusion among sucralose-based products. A restaurant consumer, for example, encounters a range of sweeteners organized by packet color: white (and possibly brown) for sugar, pink for saccharin, blue for aspartame, and yellow for Splenda. According to McNeil, these colors have become a "shorthand" by which consumers identify their sweetener of choice. Moreover, there is apparently a history of the manufacturers of Equal and Sweet 'N Low waiting too long to challenge imitators of their respective colors, whereas McNeil has been challenging its imitators since

Splenda's inception. Therefore, McNeil argues that yellow does not signify sucralose; it signifies Splenda.

There are several problems with this argument. . . . .[J]ust because a consumer sees yellow packaging in the sugar aisle does not mean that she believes McNeil or Splenda to be the source, especially because consumers are generally aware of the use of pink and blue by manufacturers other than those of Sweet 'N Low and Equal, respectively. The sugar aisle in a representative grocery store also contains yellow packages of products other than sucralose, including sugar itself. In this factual context, we cannot conclude that whenever any other sucralose producer uses yellow packaging, consumers are likely to associate that product with Splenda.

The court reached the opposite conclusion with respect to the packaging for Giant and Stop & Shop store brands of sucralose sweetener:

In contrast to the products in *Conopco,* the store name and logo are not prominently displayed on the [Giant and Stop & Shop] packaging. Indeed, as already explained, the Food Lion and Safeway packages are in this sense much closer to the *Conopco* packages because a store-specific signature is prominently displayed on them, thereby substantially reducing the degree of similarity and hence the likelihood of confusion. The same simply cannot be said for the [Giant] packages, and the District Court itself so found. To repeat, the District Court may take *Conopco* into account when analyzing the [*Polaroid*] factors, in particular the first . . . factor because . . . ., the more a store's name and/or logo are present around that store's shoppers, the more likely those shoppers will know well that name and/or logo, which in turn may serve to differentiate materially a store-brand packaging that displays them prominently. The District Court may not, however, consider the *Conopco* reasoning as an independent defense that altogether overrides the . . . factors.

The nuanced distinction we make also brings the trade dress infringement issue back to its proper focus: just how similar the trade dresses are.

Editors' Note: On remand, McNeil renewed its motion for a preliminary injunction prohibiting the distribution of sucralose in the Giant and Stop & Shop trade dress. Defendant represented to the court that it had redesigned the packaging of Giant and Stop & Shop sweeteners. It wanted, however, to use up the inventory it had already manufactured. Judge John R. Padova concluded that McNeil was likely to show that its trade dress was distinctive and non-functional and that the Giant and Stop & Shop trade dress posed a likelihood of confusion, and entered an injunction prohibiting use of the original trade dress pending trial. *See McNeil Nutritionals v. Heartland Sweeteners LLC*, 566 F.Supp.2d 378 (E.D. Pa. 2008).

CHAPTER 8

ADVERTISING

B. FALSE REPRESENTATIONS

Page 591. Add new Questions 3 and 4.

3. In 2006, Quizno's sandwich shops launched an ad campaign comparing its PrimeRib Cheesesteak sandwich to Subway restaurant's Subway cheese steak sandwich, depicting the Subway sandwich as having less meat than the Quizno sandwich. One commercial featured a man looking at the Subway and saying "I don't see any meat–oh, there it is." Another showed a man comparing the Quizno and Subway sandwiches by describing them as "meat" and "no meat." Quizno then posted a website at www.meat nomeat.com and announced a "Quiznos v. Subway TV ad challenge." The contest invited consumers to create and upload their own commercials comparing Quizno steak subs to Subway steak subs; the winning commercial would be awarded a $10,000 prize. Throughout the contest, consumer-submitted commercials were available to the public on www.meatnomeat. com. Many of these commercials characterized the Subway steak sandwich as having little or no meat. Subway claims that both the Quizno commercials and the consumer-created commercials are literally false, and has sued Quizno under section 43(a) for false advertising. How should the court rule? See *Doctors Associates v. QIP Holders LLC*, 2008 WL 628263 (D. Conn., filed Oct. 27, 2006).

4. Rose Art manufactures and selling magnetic building block sets, which it advertises as "entertainment for ages 3 to 100." The packages show pictures of elaborate structures, including a sphere, a tower, and an airplane, built from the magnetic blocks. A competing manufacturer sues for false representation, claiming that it is not possible for a child to build the pictured structures from the parts in the building sets. Plaintiff has no consumer survey evidence, but insists the packaging makes representations that are literally false. Rose Art insists that the pictures on the packages are literally true. In support of its motion for summary judgment on the literal falsity claim, Rose Art submits a video to the court showing an expert builder of construction toys putting together each of the structures pictured on its packages. How should the court rule? *See PlastWood SRL v. Rose Art Industries,* 90 U.S.P.Q. 2d (BNA) 1241 (W.D. Wa. 2008).

Page 610.   Add new Question and Note.

3.   Professor Rebecca Tushnet has observed:

> Advertising persistently makes promises that will be nonmisleading or even helpful to some people, while misleading some other group. From a regulatory perspective, it may make sense to bar a claim when more people are misled than helped, or when the number of people misled is of sufficient absolute size regardless of the number helped. False advertising regulations and trademark law generally take the latter tack today.

Rebecca Tushnet, *It Depends on What the Meaning of "False" Is: Falsity and Misleadingness in Commercial Speech Doctrine*, 41 Loyola L.A. L. Rev. 227 (2008). How would limiting relief to cases in which plaintiff could show that more people were misled than informed change the shape of the law? How would plaintiff make such a showing? Would such a change make sense?

FALSE REPRESENTATIONS IN PATENT AND COPYRIGHT CASES AFTER *DASTAR v. 20th CENTURY FOX:*

In *Sybersounds Records v. UAV Corp*, 517 F.3d 1137 (9th Cir. 2008), a producer of karaoke records sued competing karaoke record companies under § 43(a)(1)(B), arguing that they falsely claimed that their recordings were both made with the permission of the copyright owners and 100% fully licensed. Sybersounds also complained that representatives of defendant companies falsely told customers that Sybersounds has failed to obtain the necessary copyright licenses for its karaoke recordings. The former statements, Sybersounds insisted, were misrepresentations made in commercial advertising and promotion about the nature, qualities and characteristics of the competitors' karaoke recordings; the latter statements were misrepresentation about the nature, qualities and characteristics of the recordings sold by Sybersounds. The Court of Appeals for the 9th Circuit dismissed the claim as barred by *Dastar*:

> Following the reasoning in *Dastar*, however, to avoid overlap between the Lanham and Copyright Acts, the nature, characteristics, and qualities of karaoke recordings under the Lanham Act are more properly construed to mean characteristics of the good itself, such as the original song and artist of the karaoke recording, and the quality of its audio and visual effects. Construing the Lanham Act to cover misrepresentations about copyright licensing status as Sybersound urges would allow competitors engaged in the distribution of copyrightable materials to litigate the underlying copyright infringement when they have no standing to do so because they are nonexclusive licensees or third party strangers under copyright law, and we decline to do so.

In *Baden Sports, Inc. v. Molten USA*, 556 F.3d 1300 (Fed Cir. 2009), the owner of a patent for a padded basketball successfully sued the maker of a competing padded basketball for patent infringement. In addition to its patent claim, plaintiff sued for false advertising, arguing that defendant's ads promoting its infringing basketball as "innovative," "proprietary," and "exclusive" falsely represented the nature, qualities and characteristics of defendant's products. Applying 9th Circuit law, the court held that *Dastar* precluded the 43(a)(1)(B) claim:

> Following *Sybersound's* reasoning, we conclude that authorship, like licensing status, is not a nature, characteristic, or quality, as those terms are used in Section 43(a)(1)(B) of the Lanham Act.
>
> Having reached this determination, we now must examine whether Baden's false advertising claims otherwise implicate the nature, characteristics, or qualities of the basketballs. Thus, we must determine whether Baden has alleged anything more than false designation of authorship. We conclude that Baden has not. No physical or functional attributes of the basketballs are implied by Molten's advertisements. "Innovative" only indicates, at most, that its manufacturer created something new, or that the product is new, irrespective of who created it. In essence, Baden's arguments in this case amount to an attempt to avoid the holding in *Dastar* by framing a claim based on false attribution of authorship as a misrepresentation of the nature, characteristics, and qualities of a good.
>
> .   .   .
>
> Baden's claims therefore do not go to the "nature, characteristics, [or] qualities" of the goods, and are therefore not actionable under section 43 (a)(1)(B). To find otherwise, *i.e.*, to allow Baden to proceed with a false advertising claim that is fundamentally about the origin of an idea, is contrary to the Ninth Circuit's interpretation of *Dastar*.

Is the 9th Circuit's broad reading of *Dastar* a sensible one? Does the reasoning of these cases change your answers to either of the Questions on pages 609–10?

Page 611. Insert following *Serbin v. Ziebart*.

Natural Answers v. SmithKline Beecham Corp., 529 F.3d 1325 (11th Cir. 2008). In 2000, Natural Answers introduced HERBAQUIT smoking cessation lozenges, herbal lozenges containing no nicotine, which were advertised as helpful in reducing the urge to smoke. Natural Answers sold HERBAQUIT lozenges in drugstores, and health food stores and over the Internet. Between January of 2000 and March of 2002, customers bought 50,000 packages of HERBAQUIT. In March of 2002, though, Natural Answers discontinued the product. Six months later, defendant launched COMMIT, an FDA-approved nicotine lozenge. Defendant advertised COMMIT as "the first and only stop smoking lozenge." Natural Answers sued for false advertising, claiming that the representation was literally false. The Court of Appeals for the 11th Circuit concluded that plaintiff lacked prudential standing to bring a Lanham Act false advertising claim. Since Natural Answers was no longer selling or promoting HERBAQUIT Lozenges, "it cannot claim to have suffered lost sales, lost market share, or increased promotional costs."

Page 612.   Add new Question after *Ortho Pharmaceutical v. Cosprophar*.

QUESTION

Over the summer, McDonalds ran a series of promotional games to attract customers. It advertised the games heavily, and represented that everyone who entered would have a fair chance to win. The ads gave the odds of winning the top prizes. Without McDonalds' knowledge, the firm it had engaged to operate the games embezzled more than $20,000,000 in prize-winning game pieces. That operator was later caught and convicted, and McDonalds revised its prize security policies in the hope of preventing a recurrence. A group of local Burger King franchisees brought a false advertising claim against McDonalds, arguing that the ads misrepresented customers' chances of winning the contests. McDonalds concedes that the ads were misleading, but argues that the plaintiffs lack prudential standing. How should the court rule? *See Phoenix of Broward v. McDonald's Corporation*, 489 F.3d 1156, (11th Cir. 2007), cert. denied, 128 S.Ct. 1647 (2008).

CHAPTER 9

DILUTION

B. FEDERAL DILUTION

Page 632. Add at the end of the Note:

Editors' Note. When the district court decided the *Moseley* case on remand, the revised dilution statute was in effect for prospective injunctive relief. In deciding that VICTOR'S SECRET and VICTOR'S LITTLE SECRET for the sale of sex toys and adult videos tarnished VICTORIA'S SECRET for lingerie, the court accordingly applied the likelihood of dilution standard set forth in the revised statute. *See V Secret Catalogue, Inc. v. Moseley*, 558 F.Supp.2d 734 (W.D. Ky. 2008).

Page 635. Add additional Question 8:

8. The dilution statute requires that a mark be distinctive (either inherently or through secondary meaning) as well as famous in order to qualify for dilution protection. What if a famous mark is distinctive for some of plaintiff's goods or services but not for defendant's? Should it qualify for dilution protection for goods or services for which it is not distinctive? *See Hormel Foods Corp. v. Spam Arrest, LLC*, 2007 WL 4287254 (T.T.A.B. 2007) (SPAM held distinctive for food and merchandise but generic for unsolicited emails; defendant's SPAM ARREST mark covered software designed to protect against receipt of unwanted email).

Page 635. Insert the following cases and Questions under heading 2. Word Marks:

Nike, Inc. v. Nikepal International, Inc.

84 U.S.P.Q.2d 1521 (E.D. Cal. 2007).

■ BURRELL, JR., J.

. . .

Nike seeks an injunction preventing Nikepal from using the term "Nike" (or any term confusingly similar thereto) alone or as part of any trademark, domain name or business name under which Nikepal offers goods or services in commerce. Nike also seeks a reversal of the TTAB's ruling allowing Nikepal to register the NIKEPAL mark. Nikepal seeks an affirmation of the TTAB's April 21, 2005 order. (TTAB's April 21, 2005 Order ("TTAB Decision").)

Findings of Fact

I. The Parties and their Businesses

A. Nike

[Nike] adopted the NIKE mark to brand its footwear products and in May 1978, the company's name was officially changed to "Nike, Inc." Today, Nike is the largest seller of athletic footwear and apparel in the world. Nike sells around 180 million pairs of shoes annually in the United States alone....

B. Nikepal

Nikepal was incorporated on May 18, 1998 by the company's founder and president, Palminder Sandhu ... Nikepal provides services and products to analytical, environmental, and scientific laboratories. Nikepal's trademark application to the PTO requested registration for: "import and export agencies and wholesale distributorships featuring scientific, chemical, pharmaceutical, biotechnology testing instruments and glassware for laboratory use, electrical instruments, paper products and household products and cooking appliances." Nikepal distributes glass syringes in varying volumes and other laboratory products to testing and power companies and also distributes paper boxes (syringe carrying cases) and nylon valves and caps for use with the syringes....

II. The Parties' Marks

. . .

B. NIKEPAL

. . .

The "Nike" portion of the NIKEPAL mark is pronounced the same way as the NIKE mark is pronounced: with a hard "i" (like bike) in the first syllable and a hard "e" (like in "key") in the second syllable. The articles of incorporation signed by Mr. Sandhu for Nikepal in 1998 display the company name ... with the first word of the company name spelled "NikePal," with a capital "N" and a capital "P."

In addition to using Nikepal as the company name, NIKEPAL appears directly on some of Nikepal's products, including on its syringe products, and on its marketing materials.... Nikepal also uses the NIKEPAL mark in a vanity phone number (1–877–N-I-K-E-P-A-L), on its website, and in its domain names, including nikepal.com, nikepal.biz, nikepal.us, nikepal.tv, nikepal.info, and nikepal.net.

III. Nike's Sales

By the late 1980s, United States sales of NIKE branded products were over one billion dollars per year. Starting in 1991 and through the mid 1990s, sales of NIKE products in the United States were approximately two billion dollars per year, and were above five billion dollars per year by 1997. By 1997, Nike was the largest seller of athletic footwear and apparel in the world. The geographic area of Nike's sales includes the United States and

140 countries throughout the world. Since 1997, Nike has sold over 100,000,000 pairs of NIKE shoes each year.

IV. Advertising and Promotion of the NIKE Mark

Nike has undertaken significant expense to promote the NIKE mark. Nike advertises in various types of media, including traditional print advertising, such as magazines (of both special and general interest), newspapers (of general circulation), leaflets, and billboards. Nike also advertises in electronic media, including radio, television, cable and internet, on sides of buildings, on taxi cabs, and through direct mailings. Nike's television advertisements have run on network channels and have reached national audiences. Nike has also promoted its mark by associating with athletes through endorsement arrangements. By 1991, Nike was spending in excess of one hundred million dollars per year in the United States alone to advertise products bearing the NIKE mark. By 1997, Nike had spent at least $1,567,900,000.00 to promote the NIKE mark in the United States.

V. Notoriety of NIKE

The NIKE mark has been consistently ranked as a top brand in publications that survey the top brands each year. Since at least 1990, Nike has been named one of the top forty (40) brands in the United States based on the EquiTrend and other studies published in BrandWeek and Financial World Magazine.... One story printed in Forbes magazine, reported a survey conducted by Young & Rubicam that ranked the NIKE brand among the top ten (10) in the United States in 1996 with COKE, DISNEY, and HALLMARK.

VI. Evidence of Actual Association

A survey conducted by Phillip Johnson ... ("Mr. Johnson's survey"), ... determined that a significant number of Nikepal's potential laboratory customers actually associated NIKE with NIKEPAL....

... Mr. Johnson used a universe of survey participants randomly selected from lists of companies that ... deposition testimony identified as the sources for Nikepal's current and prospective customers. Mr. Johnson conducted the survey by phone and asked respondents about their perception of a website called nikepal.com. In designing his survey, Mr. Johnson chose one of the ways that the NIKEPAL mark is used in commerce which allowed him to reasonably recreate a purchasing context while obtaining a controlled and accurate measurement....

Once [s]urvey respondents were screened to confirm that they were the persons most responsible for ordering laboratory equipment at their business, they were asked: "What if anything, came to your mind when I first said the word Nikepal?" Many survey respondents who were not actually confused about the source of the Nikepal website nonetheless identified Nike. Mr. Johnson testified that his survey revealed that the vast majority of respondents, 87%, associated Nikepal with Nike; that is, when they encounter the mark NIKEPAL, they think of Nike and/or its offerings....

Conclusions of Law

I.   Dilution

... To prevail on its dilution claim, Nike must prove 1) that its mark was famous as of a date prior to the first use of the NIKEPAL mark and 2) that Nikepal's use of its allegedly diluting mark creates a likelihood of dilution by blurring or tarnishment.

A.   Whether NIKE Was Famous Prior to the First Use of NIKEPAL

A "famous" mark is one that "is widely recognized by the general consuming public of the United States as a designation of source of the goods or services of the mark's owner." 15 U.S.C. § 1125(c)(2)(A).

In determining whether a mark possesses the requisite degree of recognition, the court may consider all relevant factors, including the following:

(i) The duration, extent, and geographic reach of advertising and publicity of the mark, whether advertised or publicized by the owner or third parties.

(ii) The amount, volume, and geographic extent of sales of goods or services offered under the mark.

(iii) The extent of actual recognition of the mark.

(iv) Whether the mark was registered under the Act of March 3, 1881, or the Act of February 20, 1905, or on the principal register.

Since Nikepal's first use of NIKEPAL commenced in May 1998, Nike must show that NIKE was famous before that date.

With regard to the first factor, the evidence clearly establishes that through various combinations of athlete endorsements, television, radio, print media, and billboard placements, NIKE was promoted nationally for more than two decades before 1998. By the 1990s, Nike had spent in excess of a billion dollars for promotion of NIKE products in the United States.

With regard to the second factor, Nike's sales of NIKE products reached the billion dollar per year level in the United States well before May 1998. By 1997, Nike had spent in excess of one billion dollars to promote the NIKE mark in the United States.

Nike also satisfies the third factor, since recognition of the success of NIKE has been recorded by various publications in surveys and articles written prior to May 1998. Since the early 1990s, NIKE has been consistently ranked as a top brand in brand surveys in the United States and the world.... Nikepal counters that only Nike's Swoosh design mark, and not the NIKE mark itself, is famous. However, Mr. Johnson's survey revealed that when participants were exposed solely to the word "Nike" without the Swoosh, the response overwhelmingly indicated recognition of the NIKE mark.

Finally, with regard to the fourth factor, the NIKE mark is registered on the PTO's principal register. Nike owns ten (10) federal registrations for NIKE covering uses prior to 1998 which include retail services, bags, footwear, apparel, heart monitors, electrical items and paper products. Accordingly, the court concludes that NIKE was famous under 15 U.S.C. § 1125(c)(2)(A), prior to Nikepal's first use of the NIKEPAL mark.

B. Likelihood of Dilution by Blurring

The TDRA defines dilution by blurring as an "association arising from the similarity between a mark or trade name and a famous mark that impairs the distinctiveness of the famous mark." 15 U.S.C. § 1125(c)(2)(A).

In determining whether a mark or trade name is likely to cause dilution by blurring, the court may consider all relevant factors, including the following:

(i) The degree of similarity between the mark or trade name and the famous mark.

(ii) The degree of inherent or acquired distinctiveness of the famous mark.

(iii) The extent to which the owner of the famous mark is engaging in substantially exclusive use of the mark.

(iv) The degree of recognition of the famous mark.

(v) Whether the user of the mark or trade name intended to create an association with the famous mark.

(vi) Any actual association between the mark or trade name and the famous mark.

(i) The Degree of Similarity

Marks in a dilution analysis must be "identical" or "nearly identical." *Thane Int'l, Inc. v. Trek Bicycle Corp.*, 305 F.3d 894, 906 (9th Cir. 2002). "For marks to be nearly identical to one another, they 'must be similar enough that a significant segment of the target group of customers sees the two marks as essentially the same.'" *Playboy Enters., Inc. v. Welles*, 279 F.3d 796, 806 n. 41 (9th Cir. 2002)(internal citation omitted).

The parties' marks are nearly identical. The NIKEPAL mark is a composite of the word "Nike" with the term of affinity, "pal." The composite nature of the NIKEPAL mark is evident in the logo selected by the company which clearly features an "N" and a "P." In each case the dominant feature of the mark is the term "Nike." In addition, the term "Nike" in both marks is pronounced identically with an "i" like in "bike" and an "e" like in "key." See *Porsche Cars N. Am., Inc.*, 2000 U.S. Dist. LEXIS 7060, 2000 WL 641209, at *3, (finding that the trademark PORSCHE was diluted by PORCHESOURCE.COM); see also *Jada Toys, Inc.*, 496 F.3d 974, at *4 (concluding "that a reasonable trier of fact could find that the HOT WHEELS and HOT RIGZ marks are nearly identical.").

Further, as shown by Mr. Johnson's survey, the vast majority of the survey respondents, representing a significant segment of Nikepal's target customer group, associate Nike and/or its products and services when they encounter the mark NIKEPAL, thus perceiving the two marks as essentially the same. See *Thane Int'l, Inc.*, 305 F.3d at 906 ("The marks must be of sufficient similarity so that, in the mind of the consumer, the junior mark will conjure an association with the senior.") (citing *Nabisco, Inc. v. PF Brands, 191 F.3d 208 (2d Cir. 1999))*. Accordingly, this factor favors Nike.

(ii) Distinctiveness

... Nikepal does not dispute that NIKE is, at the very least, suggestive. Accordingly, NIKE is inherently distinctive and this factor favors Nike.

(iii) Substantially Exclusive Use

The law does not require that use of the famous mark be absolutely exclusive, but merely "substantially exclusive." [citation omitted]. Therefore, a limited amount of third party use is insufficient to defeat a showing of substantially exclusive use. [citation omitted]

... Nikepal introduced evidence of use of the term "Nike" in the company name "Nike Hydraulics, Inc.," through a bottle jack purchased from the company and a 1958 trademark registration for "Nike" owned by Nike Hydraulics. However, this evidence is insufficient to disprove Nike's claim that its use of NIKE is substantially exclusive. Even Nikepal's witness, Roger Smith, admitted that he had not encountered Nike Hydraulics before hearing that name in connection with this action. Accordingly, the court finds that Nike's use of the NIKE mark is substantially exclusive and this factor therefore favors Nike.[10]

(iv) Degree of Recognition

The degree of recognition of NIKE is quite strong. Millions of NIKE products are sold in the United States annually and the evidence demonstrates that NIKE is readily recognized. This factor therefore favors Nike.

(v) Intent to Create Association

Mr. Sandhu admitted that he was aware of the existence of the NIKE mark before he adopted the company name. Although he testified at trial that he came up with the term Nikepal by opening the dictionary to a random page and essentially finding that word by "fate," his testimony was not credible. Therefore, this factor favors Nike.

(vi) Actual Association

Nikepal registered the domain names nikepal.biz, nikepal.net, nikepal.us, nikepal.info and nikepal.tv. The evidence shows that the domain registrar assigned the domain names an "under construction" page and then associated with that page promotions and advertisement links to a number of web pages that offered NIKE products (or products of Nike's

---

10. Nikepal also introduced evidence that the term "Nike" appears in dictionaries referring to the Greek goddess of victory, that the image of Nike the goddess appeared on some Olympic medals, and that the United States Government named one of its missile programs "Nike." However, Nikepal did not show that these uses were made in commerce in association with the sale or marketing of goods or services as required under the TDRA. (See 15 U.S.C. § 1125(c)(1) (providing that under the TDRA, only "use of a mark or trade name in commerce" is actionable as diluting a famous mark.).)

competitors in the shoe and apparel field). Thus, in the internet context, there is actual association between NIKEPAL and NIKE.

Further, Mr. Johnson's survey also evinced that there is a strong degree of association between NIKEPAL and NIKE. Mr. Johnson's survey showed over 87% of the people in Nikepal's own customer pool associated the stimulus "Nikepal" with NIKE. The survey presents ample proof of association between the marks to support a finding that such exists in the general public. Accordingly, the court finds that there is actual association between the NIKEPAL and NIKE marks and this factor favors Nike.

In conclusion, since the six factors considered in the likelihood of dilution analysis favor Nike, there is a likelihood that NIKE will suffer dilution if Nikepal is allowed to continue its use of NIKEPAL. Accordingly, Nike prevails on its federal and state dilution claims.

. . .

II.   Reversal of TTAB Decision

Finally, Nike seeks reversal of the TTAB's decision denying its opposition to the registration of the NIKEPAL mark. Specifically, the TTAB held there was no likelihood of dilution based on its finding that the parties' marks were not sufficiently similar.

Here, Nike presented new evidence in the form of, *inter alia,* Mr. Johnson's survey showing that the vast majority of the survey respondents, representing a significant segment of Nikepal's target customer group, associate Nike and/or its products and services when they encounter NIKEPAL, thus perceiving the two marks as essentially the same. *See Thane Int'l, Inc.,* 305 F.3d at 906 ("The marks must be of sufficient similarity so that, in the mind of the consumer, the junior mark will conjure an association with the senior.") (citing *Nabisco, Inc.,* 191 F.3d at 208); see also *Playboy Enters., Inc.,* 279 F.3d at 806 n.41 (holding that "[f]or marks to be nearly identical to one another, they 'must be similar enough that a significant segment of the target group of customers sees the two marks as essentially the same.' "). The new evidence submitted by Nike therefore compels a contrary finding on the similarity of the parties' marks.

Accordingly, although the court gives deference to TTAB's fact-finding, the evidence presented by Nike in this action compels reversal of the TTAB's decision dismissing Nike's opposition to the registration of Nikepal's mark.

Therefore, the TTAB ruling is reversed and Nike's request for an order sustaining the opposition to Nikepal's registration for the NIKEPAL mark is granted.

CONCLUSION

For the reasons stated, Nike prevails on its federal and state dilution claims, the decision of the TTAB is reversed, and the opposition to Nikepal's registration of the NIKEPAL mark is sustained. Further, Nikepal is permanently enjoined from using NIKEPAL in connection with the offering of goods or services in commerce, including its use in domain names, on web pages, in printed matter, and on products, and shall cease any such uses of NIKEPAL within sixty (60) days of the date on which this order is filed. Nikepal may continue to use its numeric telephone number, but may not advertise or associate it with the designation "1–877–NIKE-PAL."

QUESTION

Do you agree that "Nike" and "Nikepal" are nearly identical? Is the association survey relied on by the court persuasive evidence that Nikepal's target customer group perceives the two marks as the "essentially the same"? Why/why not?

7–Eleven, Inc. v. Wechsler

83 U.S.P.Q.2d 1715 (T.T.A.B. 2007).

■ BERGSMAN, ADMINISTRATIVE TRADEMARK JUDGE:

Lawrence I. Wechsler filed an intent-to-use application for the mark GULPY, in standard character form, for goods ultimately identified as "portable animal water dishes and animal water containers sold empty."

7–Eleven, Inc. opposed the registration of applicant's mark on the ground of priority of use and likelihood of confusion in accordance with Section 2(d) of the Lanham Act, 15 U.S.C. § 1052(d). Subsequently, opposer amended its Notice of Opposition to include dilution in accordance with Sections 13(a) and 43(c) of the Lanham Act, 15 U.S.C. §§ 1063(a) and 1125(c).

Findings of Fact

Opposer is a convenience store chain with approximately 5,300 stores.... The BIG GULP trademark and other "Gulp" marks are used to identify opposer's fountain drink program. The BIG GULP fountain drink was introduced in 1978. Opposer's "Gulp" fountain drinks include the following products:

1. GULP for the 16 ounce drink;

2. BIG GULP for the 32 ounce drink;

3. SUPER BIG GULP for the 44 ounce drink; and,

4. DOUBLE GULP for the 64–ounce drink.

Opposer continually adds new products to its "Gulp" line (e.g., X–TREME GULP, a 52 ounce insulated, refillable mug, CAR GULP, a mug that fits in a car cup holder), and it has expanded the "Gulp" line of products to include CANDY GULP for candy, GARDEN GULP for salads, and FRUIT GULP for a cup of fruit. Opposer is the owner of nine (9) registered trademarks, including Registration No. 1,110,172 for the mark BIG GULP and Registration No. 1,586,016 for the mark GULP both for "soft drinks for consumption on or off the premises."

... Opposer also participates in national and local promotions with other organizations (e.g., Major League Baseball, NASCAR, the local zoo, etc.) using collector cups in connection with one of the GULP trademarks.

Opposer's sales for its "Gulp" line of fountain drinks have averaged in excess of $180,000,000 per year from 1985 through 2001.

Opposer conducts in-store advertising through backlit signs on the fountain machines or through in-store signs and/or window banners. Through the backlit advertising, opposer advertises promotions, such as collectors' cups, combo meals, etc. Also, opposer advertises nationally on radio and television and through the Internet. Opposer changes its fountain drink advertising programs every 30 to 60 days. The "Big Gulp" trademark is featured on collateral merchandising products such as phone cards, flying discs, and hats.

Opposer has actively sought to place its "Gulp" line of products in movies and television programs. Opposer has had one of its "Gulp" products appear in various movies, inter alia, Reality Bites, American Pie, and Pretty Woman, as well as several television programs.

Opposer has spent millions of dollars in advertising and promoting its "Gulp" line of products since 1983.

In the early 1990's, opposer authorized M/A/R/C Inc., a research company, to conduct a brand recognition study for the BIG GULP trademark. This was not a consumer survey conducted for this legal proceeding.... The study showed that the BIG GULP trademark had an unaided awareness of 73% among consumers in general.

   . . .

Likelihood of Confusion

   . . .

B. The fame or relative strength of opposer's marks.

... We note that fame for likelihood of confusion purposes and for dilution are not the same, and that fame for dilution purposes requires a more stringent showing. *Palm Bay Imports, Inc. v. Veuve Clicquot Ponsardin Maison Fondee En 1772*, 396 F.3d 1369, 73 USPQ2d 1689, 1694 (Fed. Cir. 2005); *Toro Co. v. ToroHead Inc.*, 61 USPQ2d 1164, 1170 (TTAB 2001). Likelihood of confusion fame "varies along a spectrum from very strong to very weak" while dilution fame is an either/or proposition— sufficient fame for dilution either exists or does not exist. *Id. See also Carefirst of Maryland Inc. v. FirstHealth of the Carolinas Inc.*, 77 USPQ2d 1492, 1507 (TTAB 2005)(likelihood of confusion "Fame is relative . . . not absolute"). A mark, therefore, may have acquired sufficient public recognition and renown to be famous for purposes of likelihood of confusion without meeting the more stringent requirement for dilution fame ... In an undated market research study authorized by opposer ... the BIG

GULP trademark had a very high degree of public recognition. The table below summarizes the BIG GULP unaided awareness study.[52]

As a result of this evidence, particularly the market research study, we conclude that opposer's BIG GULP mark when used in connection with fountain soft drinks has a very high degree of public recognition and renown. On the other hand, the evidence does not show any significant public recognition and renown for opposer's GULP trademark or for any other variance of the "Gulp" trademarks....

. . .

F.   The similarity or dissimilarity of the marks

. . .

... "Gulp" is an ordinary word found in the dictionary ... that is suggestive of opposer's fountain drinks (i.e., the manner in which one may swallow opposer's soft drinks or, in the case of BIG GULP, a big swallow) .... GULPY, by contrast, appears to be a coined term, and because it is applied to portable pet water dispensers, it engenders a different commercial impression—perhaps, a playful puppy lapping water or of a pet's name—from opposer's GULP and BIG GULP marks ....

[The Board goes on to conclude that there is no likelihood of confusion]

Dilution

Since we have already determined that only opposer's BIG GULP mark has a high degree of public recognition and renown (i.e., "fame") for purposes of likelihood of confusion, and because the requirements for proving fame for dilution are more stringent than the requirements for proving "fame" for likelihood of confusion, we limit our dilution analysis to opposer's BIG GULP trademark. [citations omitted]

Our dilution analysis ... therefore, requires consideration of the following issues:

1.   Whether BIG GULP is a famous mark;

2.   Whether BIG GULP became famous prior to the filing date of applicant's GULPY trademark application; and,

3.   Whether GULPY is likely to cause dilution by blurring of the distinctiveness of BIG GULP.

52. ... [Q]uestion No. 2 in the questionnaire ... reads as follows: "Some places have developed their own names for items they carry, like Burger King named it's (sic) hamburger The Whopper. When you think of places that sell fountain soft drinks, what names for these fountain drinks can you think of?"

	Total Respondents	Total Respondents 7–Eleven Users	7–Eleven Non–Users
	201	125	76
	%	%	%
Gulp Names (Net)	76	81	67
BIG GULP	73	78	64
SUPER BIG GULP	16	18	12
DOUBLE GULP	2	2	1

A. The fame of opposer's mark.

. . .

. . . In our opinion, BIG GULP has acquired the fame necessary to support a dilution claim as evidenced by extensive media attention, particularly those references identifying the mark as a symbol of American culture, and the market research study evidencing a 73% unaided awareness among all consumers (including non-users of opposer's services).

. . .

B. Opposer's mark became famous prior to the filing date of applicant's application.

. . . In this case, all of the evidence on which we relied to find that BIG GULP is famous predates the filing date of the GULPY trademark application.

C. Dilution by blurring.

Dilution by blurring occurs when a substantial percentage of consumers, upon seeing the junior party's use of a mark on its goods [in this case GULPY used in connection with portable pet water dishes], are immediately reminded of the famous mark [in this case BIG GULP] and associate the junior party's use with the owner of the famous mark, even if they do not believe that the goods come from the famous mark's owner. *Toro Co. v. ToroHead Inc., supra,* 61 USPQ2d at 1183.

The Board may look to all relevant facts in determining whether applicant's GULPY trademark will blur the distinctiveness of opposer's BIG GULP mark. . . .

1. The degree of similarity between the mark or trade name and the famous mark.

For purposes of dilution, a party must prove more than confusing similarity; it must show that the marks are "identical or very substantially similar." *Carefirst of Maryland Inc. v. FirstHealth of the Carolinas Inc., supra,* 77 USPQ2d at 1514, *quoting Toro Co. v. ToroHead, Inc., supra,* 61 USPQ2d at 1183. As the Board explained in *Toro Co. v. ToroHead, Inc.*:

> . . . "To support an action for dilution by blurring, 'the marks must be similar enough that a significant segment of the target group sees the two marks as essentially the same.' " *Luigino's, Inc.,* 170 F.3d at 832, 50 USPQ2d at 1051 (quoting 2 McCarthy on Trademarks and Unfair Competition, § 24:90.1 (4<th> ed. 1998). Therefore, differences between the marks are often significant. . . .

Toro Co. v. ToroHead, Inc., supra, 61 USPQ2d at 1183 (TORO and ToroMR and Design are not substantially similar for dilution purposes).

Because applicant's mark GULPY engenders a different commercial impression than opposer's BIG GULP mark, we do not see these marks as being essentially the same. In discussing likelihood of confusion, we found that GULPY and BIG GULP are not similar. Given that finding of fact, in the context of dilution, we must also find that the marks are not substantially similar. Therefore, the similarity, or in this case, dissimilarity of the marks heavily favors applicant.

2.   The degree of inherent or acquired distinctiveness of the famous mark.

BIG GULP is an inherently distinctive trademark when used in connection with fountain soft drinks. It is suggestive to the extent that it implies that one will drink opposer's products in big swallows. Accordingly, because BIG GULP is suggestive, this is a dilution factor that slightly favors opposer.

3.   The extent to which the owner of the famous mark is engaging in substantially exclusive use of the mark.

While applicant submitted evidence of third-party use of various "Gulp" trademarks, applicant did not introduce any evidence as to the extent of the third-parties' use and promotion of their marks. Without such evidence, we cannot assess whether third-party use has been so widespread as to have had any impact on consumer perceptions. [citations omitted] Accordingly, on this record, we conclude that opposer has made substantially exclusive use of the BIG GULP trademark, and therefore, this dilution factor favors opposer.

4.   The degree of recognition of the famous mark.

. . . [T]he degree of recognition of the famous mark requires us to determine the level of fame acquired by the famous mark. In other words, once the mark is determined to be famous as a prerequisite for dilution protection, we must apply a sliding scale to determine the extent of that protection (i.e., the more famous the mark, the more likely there will be an association between the famous mark and the defendant's mark).

While we have previously found that BIG GULP is a famous mark for dilution purposes, there is insufficient evidence to demonstrate that BIG GULP has acquired an extraordinary degree of recognition relative to other famous marks. Accordingly, we find that this dilution factor is neutral.

5.   Whether the user of the mark or trade name intended to create an association with the famous mark.

Opposer failed to present any evidence demonstrating that applicant intended to create an association with the BIG GULP trademark. In view thereof, this dilution factor favors applicant.

6.   Any actual association between the mark or trade name and the famous mark.

Opposer failed to present any evidence demonstrating that there is any actual association between applicant's GULPY trademark and opposer's BIG GULP trademark. Since we have no evidence on which to conclude that potential customers of applicant's products would make any association between the parties' marks when used on their respective products, this dilution factor favors applicant.

7.   Balancing the factors.

The facts that the marks are not so substantially similar as to support a dilution claim, that there is no evidence demonstrating any association between the parties' marks, and that there is no evidence that applicant intended to create an association with opposer's mark far outweigh the fame, distinctiveness, and substantially exclusive use of the BIG GULP trademark. Based on the record before us, opposer has not demonstrated that the registration of applicant's mark will dilute its BIG GULP trademark.

QUESTIONS

1.   The *Nike* opinion dismisses the importance of dictionary definitions of "Nike" in footnote 10; whereas, the *7–Eleven* opinion highlights the common meaning of "gulp" in finding that "gulpy" presents a different commercial impression. Are these analytical approaches consistent?

2.   The foreign model Twiggy was found to be famous enough in the U.S. to win on a false suggestion of a connection claim against an applicant for the mark TWIGGY for children's clothes. Should she also succeed in a federal dilution claim despite not using her name as a mark in connection with goods or services in the U.S.? *See Hornby v. TJX Companies, Inc.,* *supra* Chapter 4.C.1.c, this Supplement and section 43(c)(1) of the Lanham Act.

Page 635.   Delete the district court opinion in *Louis Vuitton* and Questions thereafter and substitute the 4th Circuit's opinion in that case and Questions as follows:

Louis Vuitton Malletier S.A. v. Haute Diggity Dog, LLC

507 F.3d 252 (4th Cir. 2007).

■ NIEMEYER, J.

Louis Vuitton Malletier S.A., a French corporation located in Paris, that manufactures luxury luggage, handbags, and accessories, commenced this action against Haute Diggity Dog, LLC, a Nevada corporation that manufactures and sells pet products nationally, alleging trademark infringement under 15 U.S.C. § 1114(1)(a), trademark dilution under 15 U.S.C. § 1125(c), copyright infringement under 17 U.S.C. § 501, and related statutory and common law violations. . . .

On cross-motions for summary judgment, the district court concluded that Haute Diggity Dog's "Chewy Vuiton" dog toys were successful parodies of Louis Vuitton Malletier's trademarks, designs, and products, and on that basis, entered judgment in favor of Haute Diggity Dog on all of Louis Vuitton Malletier's claims.

On appeal, we agree with the district court that Haute Diggity Dog's products are not likely to cause confusion with those of Louis Vuitton Malletier and that Louis Vuitton Malletier's copyright was not infringed. On the trademark dilution claim, however, we reject the district court's reasoning but reach the same conclusion through a different analysis. Accordingly, we affirm.

I

. . .

LVM has registered trademarks for "LOUIS VUITTON," in connection with luggage and ladies' handbags (the "LOUIS VUITTON mark"); for a stylized monogram of "LV," in connection with traveling bags and other goods (the "LV mark"); and for a monogram canvas design consisting of a canvas with repetitions of the LV mark along with four-pointed stars, four-pointed stars inset in curved diamonds, and four-pointed flowers inset in circles, in connection with traveling bags and other products (the "Monogram Canvas mark"). In 2002, LVM adopted a brightly-colored version of the Monogram Canvas mark in which the LV mark and the designs were of various colors and the background was white (the "Multicolor design"), created in collaboration with Japanese artist Takashi Murakami.... In 2005, LVM adopted another design consisting of a canvas with repetitions of the LV mark and smiling cherries on a brown background (the "Cherry design").

.. [T]he Multicolor design and the Cherry design attracted immediate and extraordinary media attention and publicity in magazines such as *Vogue, W, Elle, Harper's Bazaar, Us Weekly, Life and Style, Travel & Leisure, People, In Style*, and *Jane*. The press published photographs showing celebrities carrying these handbags, including Jennifer Lopez, Madonna, Eve, Elizabeth Hurley, Carmen Electra, and Anna Kournikova, among others. When the Multicolor design first appeared in 2003, the magazines typically reported, "The Murakami designs for Louis Vuitton, which were the hit of the summer, came with hefty price tags and a long waiting list." *People Magazine* said, "the wait list is in the thousands." The handbags retailed in the range of $995 for a medium handbag to $4500 for a large travel bag....

The original LOUIS VUITTON, LV, and Monogram Canvas marks ... have been used as identifiers of LVM products continuously since 1896.

During the period 2003–2005, LVM spent more than $48 million advertising products using its marks and designs, including more than $4 million for the Multicolor design ... LVM also advertises its products on the Internet through the specific websites www.louisvuitton.com and www.eluxury.com.

Although better known for its handbags and luggage, LVM also markets a limited selection of luxury pet accessories—collars, leashes, and dog carriers—which bear the Monogram Canvas mark and the Multicolor design. These items range in price from approximately $200 to $1600. LVM does not make dog toys.

Haute Diggity Dog, LLC, ... manufactures and sells nationally—primarily through pet stores—a line of pet chew toys and beds whose names parody elegant high-end brands of products such as perfume, cars, shoes, sparkling wine, and handbags. These include—in addition to Chewy Vuiton (LOUIS VUITTON)—Chewnel No. 5 (Chanel No. 5), Furcedes (Mercedes), Jimmy Chew (Jimmy Choo), Dog Perignonn (Dom Perignon), Sniffany & Co. (Tiffany & Co.), and Dogior (Dior). The chew toys and pet beds are plush, made of polyester, and have a shape and design that loosely imitate the signature product of the targeted brand. . . . The dog toys are generally sold for less than $20, although larger versions of some of Haute Diggity Dog's plush dog beds sell for more than $100.

．．．

II

LVM contends first that Haute Diggity Dog's marketing and sale of its "Chewy Vuiton" dog toys infringe its trademarks because the advertising and sale of the "Chewy Vuiton" dog toys is likely to cause confusion. See 15 U.S.C. § 1114(1)(a). . . .

. . . [W]e agree with the district court that the "Chewy Vuiton" dog toys are successful parodies of LVM handbags and the LVM marks and trade dress. . . . First, the pet chew toy is obviously an irreverent, and indeed intentional, representation of an LVM handbag, albeit much smaller and coarser. The dog toy is shaped roughly like a handbag; its name "Chewy Vuiton" sounds like and rhymes with LOUIS VUITTON; its monogram CV mimics LVM's LV mark; the repetitious design clearly imitates the design on the LVM handbag; and the coloring is similar. In short, the dog toy is a small, plush imitation of an LVM handbag carried by women, which invokes the marks and design of the handbag, albeit irreverently and incompletely. No one can doubt that LVM handbags are the target of the imitation by Haute Diggity Dog's "Chewy Vuiton" dog toys.

．．．

. . . [T]he juxtaposition of the similar and dissimilar—the irreverent representation and the idealized image of an LVM handbag—immediately conveys a joking and amusing parody. The furry little "Chewy Vuiton" imitation, as something to be *chewed by a dog*, pokes fun at the elegance and expensiveness of a LOUIS VUITTON handbag, which must *not* be chewed by a dog. The LVM handbag is provided for the most elegant and well-to-do celebrity, to proudly display to the public and the press, whereas the imitation "Chewy Vuiton" "handbag" is designed to mock the celebrity and be used by a dog. The dog toy irreverently presents haute couture as an object for casual canine destruction. The satire is unmistakable. The dog toy is a comment on the rich and famous, on the LOUIS VUITTON name and related marks, and on conspicuous consumption in general. This parody is enhanced by the fact that "Chewy Vuiton" dog toys are sold with similar parodies of other famous and expensive brands—"Chewnel No. 5" targeting "Chanel No. 5"; "Dog Perignonn" targeting "Dom Perignon"; and "Sniffany & Co." targeting "Tiffany & Co."

．．．

[The court concludes that there is no likelihood of confusion]

. . .

III

LVM also contends that Haute Diggity Dog's advertising, sale, and distribution of the "Chewy Vuiton" dog toys dilutes its LOUIS VUITTON, LV, and Monogram Canvas marks, which are famous and distinctive, in violation of the Trademark Dilution Revision Act of 2006 ("TDRA"), 15 U.S.C.A. § 1125(c) (West Supp. 2007).... It also contends that "Chewy Vuiton" dog toys are likely to tarnish LVM's marks because they "pose a choking hazard for some dogs."

. . .

A

We address first LVM's claim for dilution by blurring.

The first three elements of a trademark dilution claim are not at issue in this case. LVM owns famous marks that are distinctive; Haute Diggity Dog has commenced using "Chewy Vuiton," "CV," and designs and colors that are allegedly diluting LVM's marks; and the similarity between Haute Diggity Dog's marks and LVM's marks gives rise to an association between the marks, albeit a parody. The issue for resolution is whether the association between Haute Diggity Dog's marks and LVM's marks is likely to impair the distinctiveness of LVM's famous marks.

In deciding this issue, the district court correctly outlined the six factors to be considered in determining whether dilution by blurring has been shown. *See* 15 U.S.C.A. § 1125(c)(2)(B). But in evaluating the facts of the case, the court did not directly apply those factors it enumerated. It held simply:

> [The famous mark's] strength is not likely to be blurred by a parody dog toy product. Instead of blurring Plaintiff's mark, the success of the parodic use depends upon the continued association with LOUIS VUITTON.

Louis Vuitton Malletier, 464 F. Supp. 2d at 505....

The TDRA prohibits a person from using a junior mark that is likely to dilute (by blurring) the famous mark, and blurring is defined to be an impairment to the famous mark's distinctiveness. "Distinctiveness" in turn refers to the public's recognition that the famous mark identifies a single source of the product using the famous mark.

To determine whether a junior mark is likely to dilute a famous mark through blurring, the TDRA directs the court to consider all factors relevant to the issue, including six factors that are enumerated in the statute: ...

Not every factor will be relevant in every case.... But a trial court must offer a sufficient indication of which factors it has found persuasive and explain why they are persuasive so that the court's decision can be reviewed. The district court did not do this adequately in this case. Nonetheless, after we apply the factors as a matter of law, we reach the same conclusion reached by the district court.

. . . Although the TDRA does provide that fair use is a complete defense and allows that a parody can be considered fair use, it does not extend the fair use defense to parodies used as a trademark. As the statute provides:

> The following shall not be actionable as dilution by blurring or dilution by tarnishment under this subsection:
>
> (A) Any fair use . . . *other than as a designation of source for the person's own goods or services*, including use in connection with . . . parodying. . . .

15 U.S.C.A. § 1125(c)(3)(A)(ii) (emphasis added). Under the statute's plain language, parodying a famous mark is protected by the fair use defense only if the parody is *not* "a designation of source for the person's own goods or services."

The TDRA, however, does not require a court to ignore the existence of a parody that is used as a trademark, and it does not preclude a court from considering parody as part of the circumstances to be considered for determining whether the plaintiff has made out a claim for dilution by blurring. Indeed, the statute permits a court to consider "all relevant factors," including the six factors supplied in § 1125(c)(2)(B).

Thus, it would appear that a defendant's use of a mark as a parody is relevant to the overall question of whether the defendant's use is likely to impair the famous mark's distinctiveness. Moreover, the fact that the defendant uses its marks as a parody is specifically relevant to several of the listed factors. For example, factor *(v)* (whether the defendant intended to create an association with the famous mark) and factor *(vi)* (whether there exists an actual association between the defendant's mark and the famous mark) directly invite inquiries into the defendant's intent in using the parody, the defendant's actual use of the parody, and the effect that its use has on the famous mark. While a parody intentionally creates an association with the famous mark in order to be a parody, it also intentionally communicates, if it is successful, that it is *not* the famous mark, but rather a satire of the famous mark. *See PETA* [*v. Doughney*, 263 F.3d 359 (4th Cir. 2001)], at 366. That the defendant is using its mark as a parody is therefore relevant in the consideration of these statutory factors.

Similarly, factors *(i)*, *(ii)*, and *(iv)*—the degree of similarity between the two marks, the degree of distinctiveness of the famous mark, and its recognizability—are directly implicated by consideration of the fact that the defendant's mark is a successful parody. Indeed, by making the famous mark an object of the parody, a successful parody might actually enhance the famous mark's distinctiveness by making it an icon. The brunt of the joke becomes yet more famous. *See Hormel Foods* [*v. Jim Henson Productions*, 73 F.3d 497 (2d Cir. 1996)], at 506 (observing that a successful parody "tends to increase public identification" of the famous mark with its source); *see also Yankee Publ'g Inc. v. News Am. Publ'g Inc.*, 809 F. Supp. 267, 272–82 (S.D.N.Y. 1992) (suggesting that a sufficiently obvious parody is unlikely to blur the targeted famous mark).

In sum, while a defendant's use of a parody as a mark does not support a "fair use" defense, it may be considered in determining whether the plaintiff-owner of a famous mark has proved its claim that the defendant's use of a parody mark is likely to impair the distinctiveness of the famous mark.

In the case before us, when considering factors *(ii)*, *(iii)*, and *(iv)*, it is readily apparent, indeed conceded by Haute Diggity Dog, that LVM's marks are distinctive, famous, and strong. The LOUIS VUITTON mark is well known and is commonly identified as a brand of the great Parisian fashion house, Louis Vuitton Malletier. So too are its other marks and designs, which are invariably used with the LOUIS VUITTON mark. It may not be too strong to refer to these famous marks as icons of high fashion.

While the establishment of these facts satisfies essential elements of LVM's dilution claim, *see* 15 U.S.C.A. § 1125(c)(1), the facts impose on LVM an increased burden to demonstrate that the distinctiveness of its famous marks is likely to be impaired by a successful parody. Even as Haute Diggity Dog's parody mimics the famous mark, it communicates simultaneously that it is not the famous mark, but is only satirizing it. [citation omitted]. And because the famous mark is particularly strong and distinctive, it becomes more likely that a parody will not impair the distinctiveness of the mark. In short, as Haute Diggity Dog's "Chewy Vuiton" marks are a successful parody, we conclude that they will not blur the distinctiveness of the famous mark as a unique identifier of its source.

It is important to note, however, that this might not be true if the parody is so similar to the famous mark that it likely could be construed as actual use of the famous mark itself. Factor *(i)* directs an inquiry into the "degree of similarity between the junior mark and the famous mark." If Haute Diggity Dog used the actual marks of LVM (as a parody or other-wise), it could dilute LVM's marks by blurring, regardless of whether Haute Diggity Dog's use was confusingly similar, whether it was in compe-tition with LVM, or whether LVM sustained actual injury. *See* 15 U.S.C.A. § 1125(c)(1). Thus, "the use of DUPONT shoes, BUICK aspirin, and KODAK pianos would be actionable" under the TDRA because the unau-thorized use of the famous marks *themselves* on unrelated goods might diminish the capacity of these trademarks to distinctively identify a single source. *Moseley*, 537 U.S. at 431 (quoting H.R. Rep. No. 104–374, at 3 (1995), *as reprinted in* 1995 U.S.C.C.A.N. 1029, 1030). This is true even though a consumer would be unlikely to confuse the manufacturer of KODAK film with the hypothetical producer of KODAK pianos.

But in this case, Haute Diggity Dog mimicked the famous marks; it did not come so close to them as to destroy the success of its parody and, more importantly, to diminish the LVM marks' capacity to identify a single source. Haute Diggity Dog designed a pet chew toy to imitate and suggest, but not *use*, the marks of a high-fashion LOUIS VUITTON handbag. It used "Chewy Vuiton" to mimic "LOUIS VUITTON"; it used "CV" to mimic "LV"; and it adopted *imperfectly* the items of LVM's designs. We conclude that these uses by Haute Diggity Dog were not so similar as to be likely to impair the distinctiveness of LVM's famous marks.

In a similar vein, when considering factors *(v)* and *(vi)*, it becomes apparent that Haute Diggity Dog intentionally associated its marks, but only partially and certainly imperfectly, so as to convey the simultaneous message that it was not in fact a source of LVM products. Rather, as a parody, it separated itself from the LVM marks in order to make fun of them.

In sum, when considering the relevant factors to determine whether blurring is likely to occur in this case, we readily come to the conclusion, as did the district court, that LVM has failed to make out a case of trademark dilution by blurring by failing to establish that the distinctiveness of its marks was likely to be impaired by Haute Diggity Dog's marketing and sale of its "Chewy Vuiton" products.

B

. . . To establish its claim for dilution by tarnishment, LVM must show, in lieu of blurring, that Haute Diggity Dog's use of the "Chewy Vuiton" mark on dog toys harms the reputation of the LOUIS VUITTON mark and LVM's other marks. LVM argues that the possibility that a dog could choke on a "Chewy Vuiton" toy causes this harm. LVM has, however, provided no record support for its assertion . . . .

We agree with the district court that LVM failed to demonstrate a claim for dilution by tarnishment. *See Hormel Foods,* 73 F.3d at 507.

. . .

The judgment of the district court is

AFFIRMED.

QUESTIONS

1. To qualify under the fair use exemption to a dilution claim, a parody cannot be used as a trademark. Review section 1125(c)(3)(C), which also exempts "noncommercial use of a mark." Can a parodic mark qualify as noncommercial use? *See Smith v. Wal–Mart Stores,* 537 F.Supp.2d 1302 (N.D. Ga. 2008)(considered defendant's use of Wal–Queda and Walocaust on t-shirts and stickers as a parody of Wal–Mart) excerpted *infra*, this Supplement, Chapter 12.B.

2. Do you agree that the CHEWY VUITON, CV and design marks shown on the next page are sufficiently dissimilar from the LOUIS VUITTON, LV and design marks shown below so that blurring is not likely? Does it matter that the plaintiff sells LOUIS VUITTON pet products? What if defendant used the same overall design pattern that plaintiff employs except that it used CV in place of the LV in the pattern?

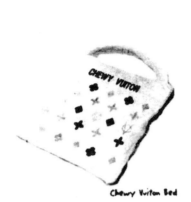

Chewy Vuiton Bed

Page 641.   Delete *Hershey Foods and* substitute the following case:

Consider the truck design below discussed in the following case:

The Hershey Company v. Art Van Furniture, Inc.

2008 WL 4724756 (E.D. Mich. 2008).

■ ROBERTS, DISTRICT COURT JUDGE.

. . . For the reasons stated, the Court GRANTS Plaintiffs' request [for a preliminary injunction], but only with respect to its dilution by blurring claim.

II. BACKGROUND

Plaintiff is a well-known maker of chocolate and confectionery goods, whose products are distributed and sold the world over. Defendant is Michigan's largest furniture retailer, operating 30 stores (all in-state), a website where customers may buy products online, and a fleet of about two dozen trucks for customer deliveries. The issue before the Court concerns Defendant's decoration of its delivery trucks.

On October 10, 2008, Defendant launched an advertising campaign. It posted ten truck decorations on its website and invited visitors to vote for their favorite design. . . .

The first design on the contest page of Defendant's website is an image of a brown sofa emerging from a red and/or burgundy wrapper reminiscent of a candy bar. This "couch bar" is designed to bring to mind a candy or a chocolate bar, with its packaging torn open and mouth-watering contents exposed. Emblazoned across the wrapper are the words "ART VAN," spelled in white, block lettering, and on the bottom left of the wrapper, in smaller type, "Since 1959." On the right side of the image, where the sofa juts from the "candy bar," the torn wrapper has the appearance of crackled and ripped tinfoil. On the left, the same silver-colored foil is visible, protruding beneath the red and white wrapper.

Plaintiff contends that Defendant's design truck is an unauthorized and deliberate infringement of its trademarks and trade dress. Plaintiff claims that its trademark and trade dress packaging include:

1. a rectangular design;

2. silver, stylized lettering;

3. a brownish-maroon colored wrapper;

4. the name "Hershey's;" and

5. silver foil protruding from under the wrapper along the edges of the bar.

.   .   .

III.   ANALYSIS

.   .   .

a.   Strength of Plaintiff's Trade Mark and Trade Dress

.   .   .

Plaintiff states that its trademark and trade dress have appeared on its products in substantially the same form for over a century, to the point that they are immediately recognizable. Defendant counters that Plaintiff's trade dress is famous only if it includes the name "Hershey's;" without it, Defendant contends, Plaintiff's trade dress is much weaker, as the plethora of brown-colored, rectangular-shaped candy bars on the market indicates.

Defendant's argument ignores the fundamental nature of a trade dress. In the language of the Supreme Court, the trade dress of a product is the result of "its total image and overall appearance," not one or more isolated elements of its packaging. *Two Pesos*, 505 U.S. at 765 n.1. Here, the strength of Plaintiff's trade dress comes from the combination of its features and its historical presence in the marketplace, strengthened by decades of advertising.

There is no doubt that Plaintiff's trade dress is both "highly distinctive" and "widely accepted as the hallmark" of Hershey's chocolates; this factor strongly suggests a likelihood of confusion.

. . .

c.   Similarity of the Trademarks or Trade Dresses

. . .

There is no question that Defendant's "couch bar" bears a resemblance to a Hershey's chocolate bar, particularly to Plaintiff's "Special Dark" bar. One feature in particular is identical in both designs: each wrapper is composed of two distinct elements, a silver foil containing the actual product, and a slightly narrower "sleeve" inscribed with the company name. Because the sleeve is not as wide as the product itself, the foil visibly protrudes along the edges of the candy bar.

Other aspects of the "couch bar" also evoke Hershey's candy bars, but in a more subtle way. For instance, the words "HERSHEY'S" and "ART VAN" are both printed in stylized block lettering; however, their font, color and positioning are different: the letters on Plaintiff's iconic chocolate bar are silver and occupy the upper half of the wrapper, whereas Defendant's letters are white and sit squarely in the middle.

One aspect of Defendant's design seems entirely different from Plaintiff's trade dress: Plaintiff's famous bar is wrapped in brown paper, while Defendant's "couch bar" emerges from a sleeve that appears to be burgundy. However, at oral argument, counsel for Plaintiff exhibited its "Special Dark" bar, with a wrapper divided roughly between brown and a similar shade of red or burgundy.

Finally, other similarities are so generic that their impact on the overall analysis is minimal: both designs are indeed, as Plaintiff points out, rectangular in shape, but the relevance of this observation is limited, since most candy bars share this characteristic. Likewise, Defendant's brown-colored sofa evokes chocolate in general, not Plaintiff's chocolate, much less Plaintiff's trademark or trade dress.

[The Court concludes that plaintiff is unlikely to succeed on the merits of its likelihood of confusion claim]

C.   Likelihood of Success on Merits—Federal Dilution Claim

. . .

a.   Famous and Distinctive

. . . As discussed earlier . . . Plaintiff is one of the largest producers of chocolate and confectionery goods, its products are sold around the world and it spends tens of millions of dollars annually to maintain and promote its products. Plaintiff is also protective of its brands and holds hundreds of trademarks, although none specifically covers the trade dress at issue here.

These factors, combined with the iconic status of the classic Hershey's bar, prove that Plaintiff's mark is both famous and distinctive.

. . .

d.   Defendant's use has/has not caused Dilution

. . . Congress enacted the Trademark Dilution Revision Act of 2006, by and large expanding trademark protection under the FDTA. Pub. L. No. 109–312, § 2, 120 Stat. 1730. The updated FDTA identifies six non-exclusive factors for courts to consider when analyzing whether a mark or trade name is likely to cause dilution by blurring.

> 1.   The degree of similarity between the mark or trade name and the famous mark.

> 2.   The degree of inherent or acquired distinctiveness of the famous mark.

> 3.   The extent to which the owner of the famous mark is engaging in substantially exclusive use of the mark.

> 4.   The degree of recognition of the famous mark.

> 5.   Whether the user of the mark or trade name intended to create an association with the famous mark.

> 6.   Any actual association between the mark or trade name and the famous mark.

15 U.S.C. § 1125(c)(2)(B). Under the test established by the FDTA, the Court finds that a likelihood exists that Defendant's design will cause dilution of Plaintiff's mark.

As discussed in the infringement analysis above, the second, third and fourth requirements of § 1125(c)(2)(B) are easily met. The evidence certainly supports an inference that Defendant intended to "create an association" with Plaintiff's mark (fifth factor), but whether such an association has actually been made is unclear (sixth factor). Finally, Defendant's "couch bar" design, with its stylized block lettering, its packaging in two elements, and especially its silver foil visible beneath the wrapper's sleeve, bears an unmistakable resemblance to some of Plaintiff's candy bars (first factor). *See Jada Toys,* 518 F.3d at 635 (denying summary judgment because a reasonable trier of fact could find that two marks, "Hot Wheels" and "Hot Rigz," were "nearly identical" because both contained the word "hot," were accompanied by a flame, and used similar colors).

Plaintiff sustains its burden to show a reasonable likelihood of succeeding on the merits of its dilution by blurring claim.

D.   Parody Defense

. . . Defendant relies heavily on the theory that its "couch bar" is merely a "clever parody" of an actual candy bar, and that the amusing nature of the design diffuses any risk that confused consumers would mistake its source or sponsorship. Defendant emphasizes that this image appears on its website next to nine other "whimsical" pictures, further reinforcing its satirical character. Defendant's reliance on the parody exception is misplaced.

> For trademark purposes, "[a] 'parody' is defined as a simple form of entertainment conveyed by juxtaposing the irreverent representation of the trademark with the idealized image created by the mark's owner." "A parody must convey two simultaneous—and contradictory—messages: that it is the original, but also that it is not the original and is instead a parody." This second message must not only differentiate the alleged parody from the original but must also communicate some articulable element of satire, ridicule, joking, or amusement.

Louis Vuitton Malletier S.A. v. Haute Diggity Dog, LLC, 507 F.3d 252, 260 (4th Cir. 2007) (*quoting People for the Ethical Treatment of Animals v. Doughney,* 263 F.3d 359, 366 (4th Cir. 2001)). In *Louis Vuitton,* the plaintiff sued a maker of pet toys, the names and appearances of which mimicked those of high-end brands. *Id. at 258.* The plaintiff took exception to the defendant's "Chewy Vuiton" line of chew toys, which looked like little furry versions of the plaintiff's elegant handbags, complete with a "CV" symbol instead of the signature "LV." *Id.* The court dismissed the plaintiff's infringement and dilution claims; there was no mistaking the intentional, yet irreverent nature of the defendant's miniature handbags. *Id.* at 260–61.

"It is a matter of common sense that the strength of a famous mark allows consumers immediately to perceive the target of the parody, while simultaneously allowing them to recognize the changes to the mark that make the parody funny or biting." *Id. at 261.* Defendant's "couch bar" may be funny, but it is not biting; its resemblance to Plaintiff's famous trade dress is too muted to poke fun, yet too transparent to evoke a generic candy bar.

An important theme running through *Louis Vuitton* is that, while a parody may be nearly identical to the original in some respects, in others it is so different that no one could possibly mistake it for the real thing. *Id.* Defendant's design is neither similar nor different enough to convey a satirical message.

. . .

IV. CONCLUSION

The Court GRANTS Plaintiff's Motion for Temporary Restraining Order and Preliminary Injunction. Defendant is enjoined from continuing to display the "couch bar" design on its website, and must remove it immediately. Further, because Defendant represented to the Court that it would not display the "couch bar" design on its trucks, pending the outcome of this litigation, the Court does not need to address that part of Plaintiff's request. . . .

Page 642. Delete Questions 1, 2 and 3 and add the following Questions:

1. The *Nike* and *7–Eleven* opinions required that a dilutive word mark be identical or nearly identical to the plaintiff's mark. How similar does trade dress need to be in order to be potentially dilutive? For example, Adidas uses the three-stripe design on footwear, which is registered as shown below. Would a competitor that uses a two or four-stripe design, such as the shoe shown below, be liable for dilution? for likelihood of confusion? *See adidas–America, Inc. v. Payless Shoesource, Inc.,* 546 F.Supp.2d 1029 (D.Or. 2008).

2. The *Art Van* court noted differences in the parties' trade dresses. Why did these differences not preclude a finding of blurring?

3. Did the *Art Van* court persuasively distinguish the CHEWY VUITON parody? *See Louis Vuitton Malletier S.A. v. Haute Diggity Dog, LLC, supra* this Supplement. What did the court mean that Art Van's design "is neither similar nor different enough to convey a satirical message"?

CHAPTER 10

AUTHORS' AND PERFORMERS' RIGHTS

A. AUTHORS' AND PERFORMERS' RIGHTS OF ATTRIBUTION

Page 669.   Add to end of carry-over paragraph:

For decisions applying *Dastar* to rule that § 43(a)(1)(A) of the Lanham Act concerns only tangible goods, and therefore precludes claims alleging misattribution of authorship, see, e.g., *Vogel v. Wolters Kluwer*, 2008 WL 5453835 (M.D.N.C. 2008) (author of contributions to first three editions of textbook alleges fourth and fifth editions incorporated his contributions but without authorship credit to him; claim dismissed on the ground that a false designation of origin under the Lanham Act concerns only the provenance of the physical copies of the books, not authorship; state law unfair competition claims held preempted by the Copyright Act); *Harbour v. Farquhar* 245 Fed.Appx. 582 (9th Cir. 2007) (dismissing claim involving musical compositions included in television programs).

B. RIGHT OF PUBLICITY

Page 718.   Add after ETW Corp v. Jireh:

Facenda v. NFL, 542 F.3d 1007 (3d Cir. 2008). The heirs of the broadcaster John Facenda alleged that the National Football League's incorporation of portions of Facenda's play-by-play into what the court termed a half-hour infomercial promoting an NFL-sponsored videogame, "The Making of Madden NFL '06," falsely conveyed the impression that Facenda's estate endorsed the game. The NFL contended under *Rogers v. Grimaldi*, the unauthorized incorporation of the sound samples of Facenda's voice bore sufficient artistic relevance. The court declined to apply *Rogers*, ruling that the promotional film was commercial speech rather than "artistic expression."

The analysis of *Rogers* has been adopted by three other Courts of Appeals. *See Parks v. LaFace Records*, 329 F.3d 437, 451–52 (6th Cir. 2003) (applying *Rogers* to a song title); *Mattel, Inc. v. MCA Records, Inc.*, 296 F.3d 894, 902 (9th Cir. 2002) (same); *Sugar Busters LLC v. Brennan*, 177 F.3d 258, 269 & n.7 (5th Cir. 1999) (adopting *Rogers* in a case concerning a book title). Soon after announcing the *Rogers* test, the Second Circuit stated that the test is "generally applicable to Lanham Act claims against works of artistic expression, a category that includes parody." *Cliffs Notes, Inc. v. Bantam Doubleday Dell Publ'g Group,* 886 F.2d 490, 495 (2d Cir. 1989) (applying *Rogers* to a parody book cover). But we have identified only one federal appellate case other than *Cliffs Notes* that applies the *Rogers* test to something other than the title of a creative work. *See ETW Corp. v. Jireh Publ'g, Inc.,* 332 F.3d 915, 936–37 (6th Cir. 2003) (applying *Rogers* to a commemorative sports painting of Tiger Woods's victory at the Masters golf tournament in 1997). *But see id.* at 943–49 (Clay, J., dissenting) (declining to endorse the application of *Rogers* in that case and arguing that the majority had applied *Rogers* in a faulty fashion).

The NFL asks us also to adopt *Rogers* and apply it to the use of "The Making of Madden NFL 06." Before considering whether either prong of the *Rogers* test applies, however, we must decide whether the television production is a "work[] of artistic expression," . . .

The Estate contends that the program is commercial speech, and we agree. Our Court has "three factors to consider in deciding whether speech is commercial: (1) is the speech an advertisement; (2) does the speech refer to a specific product or service; and (3) does the speaker have an economic motivation for the speech." [Citation omitted.] This inquiry involves making "a ' "commonsense distinction between speech proposing a commercial transaction . . . and other varieties of speech." ' " [Citation omitted.]

The first factor presents a novel issue, because the program is not a traditional 30–or 60–second television advertisement. But ultimately the question is not close. The Estate's comparison of the program to a late-night, half-hour-long "infomercial" is apt. Like an infomercial, the program focuses on one product, explaining both how it works and the source of its innovations, all in a positive tone. While it does not advertise the game's price, the program did feature a clock at its ending that displayed the number of days until the video game's release for sale. Furthermore, the program was only broadcast eight times in a three-day span immediately before the release of the video game to retail stores—much like an advertisement for an upcoming film. The second factor is easily satisfied because the program's sole subject is Madden NFL 06. The show does not refer to other video games—excepting previous years' versions of "Madden," which the program portrays as antiquated. The third factor is satisfied by NFL's licensing agreement with EA Sports, which gives the NFL a direct financial interest in sales of the video game. Moreover, the video game's general promotion of NFL-branded football provides an additional indirect financial motivation. In this context, we deem "The Making of Madden NFL 06" to be commercial speech.

Although we err on the side of fully protecting speech when confronted with works near the line dividing commercial and noncommercial speech, we do not view "The Making of Madden NFL 06" as close to that boundary. Unlike the film title in *Rogers,* the books in *Cliffs Notes,* or the painting in *ETW,* the work accused of trademark infringement in our case aims to promote another creative work, the video game. Even if *Rogers* should apply beyond titles (an extension undertaken, to our knowledge, in only the two cases mentioned above), we decline to apply it here in a context with that additional degree of separation. Moreover, the artistic and informational messages that the NFL contends the program conveys amount to mere praise for the product, attesting to its realism and popularity. As the District Court noted, "no one in The Making of Madden had a negative thing to say about the game," 488 F. Supp. 2d at 500, unlike news accounts that mentioned various criticisms. This belies any argument that the program has a documentary purpose.

Because we hold that "The Making of Madden NFL 06" is commercial speech rather than artistic expression, we need not reach the issue whether our Court will adopt the *Rogers* test. We acknowledge that commercial speech does receive some First Amendment protection. [Citations omitted.] Yet the Lanham Act customarily avoids violating the First Amendment, in part by enforcing a trademark only when consumers are likely to be misled or confused by the alleged infringer's use. *See id.* at 563 ("[T]here can be no constitutional objection to the suppression of commercial messages that do not accurately inform the public about lawful activity."); *see also* 6 J. Thomas McCarthy, McCarthy on Trademarks and Unfair Competition § 31:142, at 31–229 (4th ed. 1996 & Supp. 2008) (describing the low level of First Amendment protection for misleading speech); Alex Kozinski, *Trademarks Unplugged,* 68 N.Y.U. L. Rev. 960, 973 (1993) ("So long as trademark law limits itself to its traditional role of avoiding confusion in the marketplace, there's little likelihood that free expression will be hindered."). Thus, we reject the NFL's First Amendment defense and proceed to analyze the Estate's false-endorsement claim under trademark law without overlaying the balancing test of *Rogers.*

Applying the Third Circuit's likelihood of confusion factors, the court determined there were material questions of fact to be resolved, and accordingly vacated the lower court's entry of summary judgment for the estate, and remanded for trial.

QUESTION

Rogers and progeny appear to require courts to inquire, first, whether the accused use of the plaintiff's name, likeness or other identifying characteristics, was for the purposes of "artistic expression," and second, if so, whether the use was relevant to that expression. Are judges well-suited to these inquiries? Is there a better alternative?

C. Merchandizing

Page 723.   Add the following to the end of Question 6.

In **C.B.C. Distribution and Marketing, Inc. v. Major League Baseball**, the Eighth Circuit affirmed the grant of summary judgment to CBC v. Major League Baseball Advanced Media, 505 F.3d 818 (8th Cir. 2007), and the Supreme Court denied certiorari on June 2, 2008. The appellate court held a prima facie violation of the Missouri right of publicity, but found the fantasy leagues' use privileged under the First Amendment:

> [I]t is clear that CBC uses baseball players' identities in its fantasy baseball products for purposes of profit, we believe that their identities are being used for commercial advantage and that the players therefore offered sufficient evidence to make out a cause of action for violation of their rights of publicity under Missouri law.
>
> . . .
>
> The Supreme Court has directed that state law rights of publicity must be balanced against first amendment considerations, *see Zacchini v. Scripps–Howard Broad.*, 433 U.S. 562, 97 S. Ct. 2849, 53 L. Ed. 2d 965 (1977), and here we conclude that the former must give way to the latter. First, the information used in CBC's fantasy baseball games is all readily available in the public domain, and it would be strange law that a person would not have a first amendment right to use information that is available to everyone. It is true that CBC's use of the information is meant to provide entertainment, but "[s]peech that entertains, like speech that informs, is protected by the First Amendment because '[t]he line between the informing and the entertaining is too elusive for the protection of that basic right.'" *Cardtoons, L.C. v. Major League Baseball Players Ass'n*, 95 F.3d 959, 969 (10th Cir. 1996) (quoting *Winters v. New York*, 333 U.S. 507, 510, 68 S. Ct. 665, 92 L. Ed. 840 (1948)); *see also Zacchini*, 433 U.S. at 578. We also find no merit in the argument that CBC's use of players' names and information in its fantasy baseball games is not speech at all. We have held that "the pictures, graphic design, concept art, sounds, music, stories, and narrative present in video games" is speech entitled to first amendment protection. *See Interactive Digital Software Ass'n v. St. Louis County, Mo.*, 329 F.3d 954, 957 (8th Cir. 2003). Similarly, here CBC uses the "names, nicknames, likenesses, signatures, pictures, playing records, and/or biographical data of each player" in an interactive form in connection with its fantasy baseball products. This use is no less expressive than the use that was at issue in *Interactive Digital*.
>
> Courts have also recognized the public value of information about the game of baseball and its players, referring to baseball as "the national pastime." *Cardtoons*, 95 F.3d at 972. A California court, in a case where Major League Baseball was itself defending its use of

players' names, likenesses, and information against the players' assert-ed rights of publicity, observed, "Major league baseball is followed by millions of people across this country on a daily basis ... The public has an enduring fascination in the records set by former players and in memorable moments from previous games ... The records and statis-tics remain of interest to the public because they provide context that allows fans to better appreciate (or deprecate) today's performances." *Gionfriddo v. Major League Baseball*, 94 Cal. App. 4th 400, 411, 114 Cal. Rptr. 2d 307 (2001). The Court in *Gionfriddo* concluded that the "recitation and discussion of factual data concerning the athletic performance of [players on Major League Baseball's website] command a substantial public interest, and, therefore, is a form of expression due substantial constitutional protection." *Id*. We find these views persua-sive.

Page 737.   Insert before QUESTION:

Louisiana State University v. Smack Apparel, 550 F.3d 465 (5th Cir. 2008). Smack Apparel sells unauthorized t-shirts in the colors of various college sports teams. The t-shirts do not incorporate University insignia, but the wording on some of the t-shirts alludes in various ways to the colleges and teams whose colors the t-shirts reproduce. The Universi-ties sued Smack, claiming that its t-shirts competed with the Universities' licensed goods and were likely to cause confusion. On appeal from a ruling of liability, Smack contended that the claimed color combination marks were too broad to warrant protection.

There is no dispute in this case that for a significant period of time the Universities have been using their color schemes along with other indicia to identify and distinguish themselves from others. Smack admits in its brief that the Universities' colors are well known among fans "as a shorthand nonverbal visual means of identifying the univer-sities." But according to Smack, the longstanding use of the school colors to adorn licensed products is not the same as public recognition that the school colors identify the Universities as a unique source of goods. We think, however, that the factors for determining secondary meaning and an examination of the context in which the school colors are used and presented in this case support the conclusion that the secondary meaning of the marks is inescapable.

The record shows that the Universities have been using their color combinations since the late 1800s. The color schemes appear on all manner of materials, including brochures, media guides, and alumni materials associated with the Universities. Significantly, each universi-ty features the color schemes on merchandise, especially apparel con-nected with school sports teams, and such prominent display supports a finding of secondary meaning. The record also shows that sales of licensed products combining the color schemes with other references to the Universities annually exceed the tens of millions of dollars. As for advertising, the district court held that the Universities "advertise

items with their school colors in almost every conceivable manner...."
It is not clear from the summary judgment evidence where and how
the Universities advertise their merchandise, but they certainly do use
their color schemes and indicia in numerous promotional materials
aimed at students, faculty, alumni, and the public in general, which
strengthens the conclusion that the color schemes and indicia viewed
in context of wearing apparel also serves as an indicator of the
Universities as the source or sponsor of the apparel. Furthermore, the
district court correctly observed that the school color schemes have
been referenced multiple times in newspapers and magazines and that
the schools also frequently refer to themselves using the colors. The
district court did not specifically refer to any consumer-survey evidence
or direct consumer testimony, but it noted that Smack admitted it had
incorporated the Universities' color schemes into its shirts to refer to
the Universities and call them to the mind of the consumer. Thus,
Smack itself believed that the Universities' color schemes had secondary meaning that could influence consumers, which further supports
the conclusion that there is secondary meaning here. Given the long-
standing use of the color scheme marks and their prominent display on
merchandise, in addition to the well-known nature of the colors as
shorthand for the schools themselves and Smack's intentional use of
the colors and other references, there is no genuine issue of fact that
when viewed in the context of t-shirts or other apparel, the marks at
issue here have acquired the secondary meaning of identifying the
Universities in the minds of consumers as the source or sponsor of the
products rather than identifying the products themselves.

After applying the local factors and finding likelihood of confusion as to
the source, affiliation or sponsorship of the t-shirts, the court addressed
Smack's contention that the colors were "functional" on the ground of
"competitive necessity":

> Smack contends that it will be placed at a significant non-reputa-
> tion-related disadvantage if it "is unable to satisfy consumer demand
> for game day clothing that allows fans to conform to the crowd, or
> satisfy consumer demand for game day clothing that matches other
> items of clothing worn by the consumer." Smack has admitted that the
> colors and indicia on its shirts are designed to call the Universities to
> the mind of the fans, and it acknowledges in its brief that fans
> purchase t-shirts to wear to football games to show the colors of the
> team that the consumer is supporting. In other words, fans desire to
> wear the t-shirts precisely because they show the Universities' marks.
> The Court in *Qualitex* stressed that the focus of functionality is
> "legitimate (non-trademark-related) competition." But here any de-
> mand for Smack's t-shirts is inextricably tied to the Universities'
> trademarks themselves. We agree with the Ninth Circuit that "the fact
> that a trademark is desirable does not, and should not, render it
> unprotectable." Smack's alleged competitive disadvantage in the ability

to sell game day apparel relates solely to an inability to take advantage of the Universities' reputation and the public's desired association with the Universities that its shirts create. This is not an advantage to which it is entitled under the rubric of legitimate competition. We conclude that the district court correctly held that the marks at issue here are nonfunctional.

CHAPTER 11

INTERNET DOMAIN NAMES

B. ANTICYBERSQUATTING CONSUMER PROTECTION ACT

Page 762. Add the following cases after the Note on Section 43(d) and "Gripe Sites."

Utah Lighthouse Ministry v. Foundation for Apologetic Information And Research

527 F.3d 1045 (10th Cir. 2008).

Utah Lighthouse Ministry (UTLM) appeals from a decision of the district court granting Defendants' motion for summary judgment on UTLM's claims of trademark infringement, unfair competition, and cybersquatting.

I. BACKGROUND

A. Facts

Jerald and Sandra Tanner founded UTLM in 1982 to critique the Church of Jesus Christ of Latter-day Saints (LDS Church). In support of its mission, UTLM sells books at both a brick-and-mortar bookstore in Utah and through an online bookstore at the official UTLM website, www.utlm. org.

The Foundation for Apologetic Information and Research (FAIR) is a volunteer organization that responds to criticisms of the LDS Church. FAIR's website also has an online bookstore, and both FAIR and UTLM provide online publications on the subject of the LDS Church. The publications in the two bookstores overlap by thirty titles. Defendant–Appellee Allen Wyatt is the vice president and webmaster for FAIR. In November 2003, Wyatt created a website parodying the UTLM website—the Wyatt website is similar in appearance but has different, though suggestively parallel, content.

The district court's Memorandum Decision and Order describes the design and content of the Wyatt and UTLM websites, and Appellant's appendix includes screen shots of the websites. The design elements are similar, including the image of a lighthouse with black and white barbershop stripes. However, the words "Destroy, Mislead, and Deceive" are written across the stripes on the Wyatt website. Prominent text on the Wyatt website consists of a slight modification of the language located in the same position on the UTLM website. For example, the UTLM website states: "Welcome to the Official Website of the Utah Lighthouse Ministry, founded by Jerald and Sandra Tanner." In comparison, the Wyatt website states: "Welcome to an official website *about* the Utah Lighthouse Ministry, *which was* founded by Jerald and Sandra Tanner." (emphasis added.) The Wyatt website does not have any kind of disclaimer that it is not associated with UTLM.

The Wyatt website contains no advertising and offers no goods or services for sale. The Wyatt website includes sixteen external hyperlinks. Eleven of these hyperlinks point to the website of an organization at Brigham Young University. Three hyperlinks point to articles on the FAIR website that are critical of the Tanners, and another takes viewers directly to the FAIR homepage. The other external hyperlink is to the website of the LDS Church.

Wyatt, through his company Discovery Computing, Inc., registered ten domain names, each of which directed visitors to the Wyatt website. The domain names are combinations of "Utah Lighthouse Ministry," "Sandra Tanner," "Gerald Tanner," "Jerald Tanner," and ".com" and ".org." Wyatt first publicized the Wyatt website to FAIR members in April 2004. Defendants assert that prior to April 2004 only Wyatt had any knowledge of or input into the website.

Wyatt ceased operation of the website and began to transfer the domain names to UTLM in April 2005.

B. Procedural History

UTLM's complaint made six claims for relief: (1) trademark infringement, 15 U.S.C. § 1125(a); (2) unfair competition, *id.;* (3) unfair competition under Utah law, Utah Code Ann. § 13–5a–101 to–103 (2008); (4) trademark dilution, 15 U.S.C. § 1125(c); (5) cybersquatting, *id.* § 1125(d); and (6) trade dress infringement, *id.* § 1125(a). The parties filed cross-motions for summary judgment, and the district court judge denied Plaintiff's motion and granted Defendants' motion on all six counts. UTLM appeals only the district court's ruling on the trademark infringement, unfair competition, and cybersquatting claims. Furthermore, UTLM appeals with regard to only one of its trademarks, UTAH LIGHTHOUSE.

II. DISCUSSION

. . . .

C. Anti–Cybersquatting Protection Act

Congress enacted the Anti–Cybersquatting Protection Act (ACPA), 15 U.S.C. § 1125(d), to address "a new form of piracy on the Internet caused by acts of 'cybersquatting,' which refers to the deliberate, bad-faith, and abusive registration of Internet domain names in violation of the rights of trademark owners." S. Rep. No. 106–140, at 4 (1999). The ACPA provides for liability if a person registers, traffics in, or uses a domain name that is identical or confusingly similar to a distinctive mark, with a bad faith intent to profit from that mark. 15 U.S.C. § 1125(d)(1)(A).

To prevail on the cybersquatting claim, UTLM must show (1) that its trademark, UTAH LIGHTHOUSE, was distinctive at the time of registration of the domain name, (2) that the domain names registered by Wyatt, including utahlighthouse.com and utahlighthouse.org, are identical or confusingly similar to the trademark, and (3) that Wyatt used or registered the domain names with a bad faith intent to profit. The district court ruled that Defendants' conduct did not involve a bad faith intent to profit and on that ground granted Defendants' motion for summary judgment on UTLM's cybersquatting claim. We review this ruling *de novo*.

As discussed in the trademark infringement section above, UTLM did not meet its burden of showing that UTAH LIGHTHOUSE is distinctive. Moreover, UTLM did not submit any evidence to the district court of the distinctiveness of the mark at the time that Wyatt registered the domain names, as required by 15 U.S.C. § 1125(d)(1)(A)(ii)(I). Hence, UTLM failed to meet its burden on the first element.

However, the second element of the cybersquatting claim is easily satisfied, as the domain names utahlighthouse.com and utahlighthouse.org are virtually identical to the trademark with the minor exceptions of spacing between "Utah" and "Lighthouse," and the addition of .com and .org.

As to the third element, UTLM did not demonstrate that Defendants used the domain names with a bad faith intent to profit. The ACPA enumerates nine nonexclusive factors to assist the court in determining whether the use of a trademark involves a bad faith intent to profit. *See* 15 U.S.C. § 1125(d)(1)(B)(i). It is not necessary to evaluate all of the factors because several of the factors readily defeat an inference that the Defendants intended to profit by using domain names similar to UTLM's trademark. The quintessential example of a bad faith intent to profit is when a defendant purchases a domain name very similar to the trademark and then offers to sell the name to the trademark owner at an extortionate price. A defendant could also intend to profit by diverting customers from the website of the trademark owner to the defendant's own website, where those consumers would purchase the defendant's products or services instead of the trademark owner's. Neither of these purposes is evident here.[10]

One factor is the domain name registrant's "bona fide noncommercial or fair use of the mark in a site accessible under the domain name." 15 U.S.C. § 1125(d)(1)(B)(i)(IV). The district court determined that Defendants' use was entirely noncommercial, and a fair use parody, and therefore found that Defendants did not use the mark in bad faith. This is consistent with the reasoning of several other courts that a website that critiques a product and uses the product's trademark as the website's domain name may be a fair use. *See Lucas Nursery & Landscaping, Inc. v.*

---

10. UTLM did proffer evidence that during the time the Wyatt website was posted, the FAIR bookstore sold nine titles that were also offered by the UTLM bookstore. This is at most evidence that FAIR may have incidentally profited, but not that Wyatt intended to profit from the use of UTLM's trademark.

Grosse, 359 F.3d 806, 809 (6th Cir. 2004) (consumer registering domain name "lucasnursery.com" and complaining about nursery's work was not liable under ACPA); TMI, Inc. v. Maxwell, 368 F.3d 433 (5th Cir. 2004) (holding that a website with the purpose of informing other consumers did not create the harm the ACPA intended to eliminate); Mayflower Transit, L.L.C. v. Prince, 314 F. Supp. 2d 362 (D.N.J. 2004) (finding no ACPA liability where Defendant registered "mayflowervanline.com," since the totality of circumstances demonstrated that registrant's motive was to express dissatisfaction in doing business with the mark's owner). Because Wyatt's parody offers an indirect critique and lacks an overt commercial purpose, it is similar to these consumer commentaries, and under the circumstances of this case, constitutes fair use.

Another critical factor is the defendant's intent to divert consumers to a website that "could harm the goodwill represented by the mark, either for commercial gain or with the intent to tarnish or disparage the mark, by creating a likelihood of confusion as to the source, sponsorship, affiliation, or endorsement of the site." 15 U.S.C. § 1125(d)(1)(B)(i)(V). The district court concluded, and we agree, that the Wyatt website created no likelihood of confusion as to its source, or whether it was affiliated with or endorsed by UTLM. In the trademark infringement context, the plaintiff has the burden of proving likelihood of confusion. *Australian Gold,* 436 F.3d at 1238–39. Applying this same burden of proof to the likelihood of confusion in the context of cybersquatting, we conclude that UTLM failed to raise a genuine issue of material fact as to Defendants' intent to cause confusion about the source of the Wyatt website as a means of harming the goodwill of the UTAH LIGHTHOUSE mark.

Our evaluation of the nine statutory factors along with other evidence submitted by UTLM leads us to conclude that Defendants lacked a bad faith intent to profit from the use of UTLM's trademark in several domain names linked with the Wyatt website. In addition, the ACPA contains a "safe harbor" provision, which precludes a finding of bad faith intent if "the court determines that the person believed and had reasonable grounds to believe that the use of the domain name was a fair use or otherwise lawful." 15 U.S.C. § 1125(d)(1)(B)(ii). The district court reasoned that because the Wyatt website was a parody, Defendants could have reasonably believed that use of the domain names was legal. UTLM contends that Defendants lacked such a reasonable belief because they did not contact an attorney to verify the legality of the Wyatt parody. UTLM cites to no authority that an attorney's opinion is necessary to forming a good faith, reasonable belief in this context. We conclude upon *de novo* review that the safe harbor provision applies to Defendants' use.

The district court properly granted summary judgment on UTLM's cybersquatting claim.

The Southern Company v. Dauben, Inc.

2009 WL 1011183 (5th Cir. 2009).

PER CURIAM:

Defendant–Appellant Dauben Inc. appeals the district court's entry of a preliminary injunction barring the company from, among other things, "[r]egistering, transferring, trafficking, using, or maintaining" the domain names sotherncompany.com and southerncopany.com. Plaintiff–Appellee The Southern Company, which holds federal and state trademarks for "SOUTHERN COMPANY" and the domain name southerncompany.com, instituted this action against Dauben Inc. under the Anticybersquatting Consumer Protection Act ("ACPA"), 15 U.S.C. § 1125(d). At the outset of the proceedings, Southern Company filed a motion for a preliminary injunction, which the district court granted in an October 22, 2007 order. Dauben Inc. now challenges the district court's findings that (1) Southern Company was likely to succeed on the merits because Dauben Inc. registered the domain names with a bad faith intent to profit and (2) there existed a substantial threat that Southern Company would suffer irreparable injury without the preliminary injunction. Because the district court conducted an incomplete analysis in its findings of a likelihood of success on the merits and a substantial threat of irreparable injury, we conclude that the district court abused its discretion in granting the preliminary injunction.

I. FACTUAL AND PROCEDURAL BACKGROUND

A. Factual Background

The Southern Company ("Southern") is a Fortune 500 company that provides energy-related services to consumers throughout the southern United States. It holds the federal, incontestable mark "SOUTHERN COMPANY" and is the registrant of the domain name southerncompany.com.

Dauben Inc. ("Dauben"), a Texas corporation, is the listed registrant of nearly 635,000 domain names. The two challenged domain names, sotherncompany.com and southerncopany.com, are linked to a website that only provides pay-per-click advertising—when an Internet user enters either domain name in her browser, she is directed to a webpage that lists links to the websites of paying advertisers. If the user clicks on any of these links, then the advertiser pays a fee to the website. .... The advertising links are related to, among other things, real estate and employment companies in the southern United States. The only connection between this webpage and Southern is that the webpage contains an advertisement link to Georgia Power, a Southern subsidiary.

B. Procedural Background

. . .

... Southern filed the current claim in the United States District Court for the Northern District of Texas on October 5, 2007, alleging that Dauben's "typosquatting" violates ACPA. Simultaneously, Southern filed a motion for preliminary injunction seeking to prevent Dauben's continued use of the domain names. Over Dauben's objections, the district court ...

enjoined Dauben from "[r]egistering, transferring, trafficking, using, or maintaining the registration of the domain names, SOTHERNCOMPA-NY.COM and SOUTHERNCOPANY.COM, or any other domain name that is identical or confusingly similar to any of Plaintiff's SOUTHERN COM-PANY marks."

In response, Dauben filed a motion for reconsideration. In it, Dauben argued that its employment of the domain names constituted a fair use by pointing to ACPA's safe harbor provision, which states: "Bad faith intent . . . shall not be found in any case in which the court determines that the person believed and had reasonable grounds to believe that the use of the domain name was a fair use or otherwise lawful." 15 U.S.C. § 1125(d)(1)(B)(ii). According to Dauben, its use fell within this safe harbor because it employed the words "southern" and "company" in their descriptive sense by providing pay-per-click links to companies located in the South, a use allegedly comparable to a yellow pages phone book. Second, Dauben averred that the district court failed to consider the nine factors listed in 15 U.S.C. § 1125(d)(1)(B)(i) to determine whether Dauben possessed a bad faith intent to profit from the domain names. . . . And third, Dauben asserted that the district court incorrectly presumed the existence of a threat of irreparable injury based on its finding a likelihood of confusion, which in turn was impermissibly based on the court's finding the domain names confusingly similar to Southern's mark. For Southern's part, it countered that Dauben is not making fair use of common or descriptive words because the misspelled "sothern" and "copany" are not actual words. Southern further claimed that a majority of 15 U.S.C. § 1125(d)(1)(B)(i)'s factors support a finding of bad faith. Finally, Southern did not address Dauben's assertion that the district court incorrectly determined that a substantial threat of irreparable injury exists.

In denying Dauben's motion for reconsideration on February 14, 2008, the district court rebuffed all of Dauben's arguments. . . . .

Subsequently, Dauben filed this timely appeal. . . .

II.   DISCUSSION

. . .

B.   The Preliminary Injunction Should Be Vacated

We conclude that the district court abused its discretion by conducting an incomplete analysis of Southern's likelihood to succeed on the merits and of the existence of a substantial threat of irreparable injury to Southern absent the preliminary injunction.

1.   Likelihood of Success on the Merits

. . .

The statute sets forth a nonexhaustive list of nine factors for the court to consider in determining whether a defendant registered a domain name with a bad faith intent to profit. *See* 15 U.S.C. § 1125(d)(1)(B)(i). . . . Additionally, there can be no bad faith intent where ACPA's fair use safe harbor applies: "Bad faith intent described under subparagraph (A) shall not be found in any case in which the court determines that the [defendant] believed and had reasonable grounds to believe that the use of the domain name was a fair use or otherwise lawful." 15 U.S.C. § 1125(d)(1)(B)(ii); *see also E. & J. Gallo Winery v. Spider Webs Ltd.,* 286 F.3d 270, 275 (5th Cir. 2002). Fair use is defined as "a use, otherwise than as a mark, ... of a term or device which is descriptive of and used fairly and in good faith only to describe the goods or services of such party, or their geographic origin." 15 U.S.C. § 1115(b)(4).

. . .

Dauben ... argues that the district court abused its discretion by omitting any consideration of ACPA's fair use provision, which affects the bad faith finding, and we agree. Though ACPA explicitly provides a fair use safe harbor, the district court made no reference to this portion of ACPA in its analysis despite recognizing Dauben's invocations of the defense. ACPA's safe harbor provides a narrow berth for fair use arguments, and, on the merits, Dauben's claims may or may not hold up. *See Virtual Works, Inc.,* 238 F.3d at 270 ("A defendant who acts even partially in bad faith in registering a domain name is not, as a matter of law, entitled to benefit from the Act's safe harbor provision."). Nonetheless, where one is raised, a fair use defense bears on the likelihood of success on the merits. [Citations] By failing to analyze this segment of the law pertinent to the parties' claims, the district court abused its discretion.

Southern asserts that Dauben's fair use argument lacks merit because Dauben offered no evidence of "its business or about its intent in registering" the domain names and because Dauben cannot make a fair use of misspelled variations of SOUTHERN COMPANY. As to the former argument, we are unpersuaded because the district court had before it evidence concerning the content of the websites to which Dauben's domain names linked. As to Southern's latter argument, Dauben's using misspelled variations of "southern" and "company" (that is, "sothern" and "copany") certainly may weaken its fair use argument, but that is a question to be considered in the district court's evaluation of the facts and circumstances surrounding the claim—an evaluation that the court below failed to undertake.

2. Irreparable Injury

Dauben next contends that the district court erred in concluding there exists a substantial threat that Southern will suffer irreparable injury were the preliminary injunction denied. In its order granting the preliminary injunction, the court reasoned that this threat exists because "[e]stablishing a strong likelihood of confusion in the consumer's mind 'almost inevitably establishes irreparable harm' " and because "[Southern]'s evidence establishes the danger of confusion and loss of [Southern]'s good will as a result of consumer confusion." In denying Dauben's motion for reconsideration, the district court described the evidence that led to finding a strong likelihood of confusion:

The Court has already determined that [Dauben]'s utilization of the subject domain names is "identical or confusingly similar to" [Southern]'s mark insofar as the names are actually identical, letter for letter, but for the subtraction of one letter in each domain. The Court does not find it hard to find that a consumer could be confused as to the sponsorship of the Defendant's domain names because of their stark similarity to [Southern]'s domain name, thus causing irreparable harm.

To summarize, the district court found a likelihood of confusion because Dauben's domain names are confusingly similar to Southern's mark and, accordingly, may confuse a consumer as to the sponsorship of the websites linked to by the challenged domain names. This consumer confusion, in turn, threatens irreparable injury to Southern.

The court's determination is flawed for two reasons. First, the likelihood of confusion test in trademark infringement law is different, and more comprehensive, than the test for "confusingly similar" under ACPA. *See N. Light Tech., Inc. v. N. Lights Club,* 236 F.3d 57, 66 n.14 (1st Cir. 2001) ("[T]he likelihood of confusion test of trademark infringement is more comprehensive than the identical or confusingly similar requirement of ACPA, as it requires considering factors beyond the facial similarity of the two marks." (internal quotation marks omitted)); *see also Coca–Cola Co.,*382 F.3d at 783 ("The inquiry under the ACPA is thus narrower than the traditional multifactor likelihood of confusion test for trademark infringement."); *Sporty's Farm,*202 F.3d at 498 n.11 ("We note that 'confusingly similar' is a different standard from the 'likelihood of confusion' standard for trademark infringement. . . .").

Second, the court failed to describe how Dauben's confusingly similar domain names would injure Southern, let alone do so irreparably. Courts making this finding often describe how the content of a defendant's website threatens injury to the plaintiff. *See, e.g., Audi AG v. D'Amato,*469 F.3d 534, 550 (6th Cir. 2006) (stating that without an injunction "Audi would be irreparably harmed by consumers on [defendant]'s site purchasing counterfeit items, instead of those that were lawfully sold by Audi"); *Coca–Cola Co.,* 382 F.3d at 789 ("The district court did not clearly err in finding that plaintiffs would be irreparably harmed by [defendant]'s continued . . . use of the [confusingly similar] domain names to display pictures of dismembered aborted fetuses and by the links to fundraising appeals that did not originate from the plaintiffs."); *Shields,*254 F.3d at 486 (concluding that the district court properly determined that a likelihood of confusion threatened irreparable injury because "[plaintiff] does not want his audience trapped in [Defendant]'s sites" by defendant's practice of "mousetrapping"—the trapping of Internet users in a succession of pop-up advertisements). Here, however, the district court pointed only to the likelihood that a consumer might accidentally come across Dauben's websites when seeking Southern's website, but it made no finding bearing on *how* this navigational miscue might injure Southern. Southern contends that the court properly determined that "[p]laintiff's evidence establishes . . . a significant risk of irreparable injury." However, the court made clear that the only evidence it considered was Dauben's domain names and their similarity to Southern's mark. The court made no finding beyond the text of the domain names—such as the content of Dauben's websites—that suggests Southern may be irreparably harmed. For these two reasons, the district court abused its discretion in its analysis of whether there exists a threat of irreparable injury to Southern.

. . .

III. CONCLUSION

For the above reasons, the district court's order granting the preliminary injunction is VACATED.

QUESTION

On remand, Dauben will have the opportunity to persuade the trial court that its registration and use of the domain names <sotherncompany.com> and <southerncopany.com> is a fair use under section 33(b)(4) because it used the misspelled sothern and copany to represent the words "southern" and "company" in their descriptive sense. Flesh out that argument for Dauben. What's the most persuasive case it can make that it believed and had reasonable grounds to believe that its use was fair under the statute?

Page 765. Add the following case after Ford v. Great Domains.

Vulcan Golf, LLC v. Google, Inc., 552 F.Supp.2d 752 (N.D. Ill. 2008). Vulcan Golf filed a class action complaint against domain name registrars, domain name aggregators, auction sites, and Google, alleging that defendants engaged in a scheme to use deceptive domain names on the Internet to generate billions of advertising dollars at the expense of the plaintiffs. The facts and allegations underlying the lawsuit appear in an earlier excerpt from the case, *supra* this Supplement Chapter 6.B. In addition to its trademark claims, Vulcan argued that defendants were liable under the ACPA claim. The district court refused to dismiss plaintiff's 43(d) claims. Defendants Sedo, Oversee and Google argued that they could not be held liable under the ACPA, because they were neither the registrants nor the owners of any deceptive domain names. The court was unpersuaded:

> The plaintiffs allege that "Defendants taste,[5] register, license, own, traffic in, monetize and/or otherwise utilize and control Deceptive Domains that are identical and/or substantially similar to Lead Plaintiffs.". While the [Complaint] does not specifically allege that Sedo or Oversee registered or owned any of the allegedly deceptive domain

---

5. The [Complaint] defines "domain tasting" as "the practice of domain registrants registering a domain name to assess its profitability for the display of online advertising. Via the tasting procedure, a regis- trant may return a domain name within five days for a full refund. Domain tasters typically return domain names that they project to be unprofitable.".

names, it identifies them as "parking companies." In turn, the [Complaint] defines a "parking company" as "a company that aggregates numerous domain names from individual domain registrants and contracts with an advertising service to license and monetize those domain names." Moreover, the [Complaint] alleges that "[a]fter Oversee/Snapnames takes control of the domain names, Oversee/Snapnames traffics in, monetizes, and/or sells the domain names using an auction system. . . . " It is plausible that these allegations fall under the ACPA's prohibition of "trafficking in," which is defined by the ACPA as engaging in "transactions that include, but are not limited to, sales, purchases, loans, pledges, licenses, exchanges of currency, and any other transfer for consideration or receipt in exchange for consideration," 15 U.S.C. § 1125(d)(1)(E). Thus, the court denies Sedo and Oversee's motion to dismiss the ACPA claim on this ground.

. . .

b.   Google

Google contends that the ACPA cannot apply to it because it does not own or operate any of the allegedly infringing domain names. As noted above and by the parties, the ACPA imposes liability on one who "registers, traffics in, or uses" certain types of domain names. 15 U.S.C. § 1125(d). Google then refers to the statute, which states that "[a] person shall be liable for using a domain name under subparagraph (A) only if that person is the domain registrant or that registrant's authorized licensee," and argues that because the plaintiffs do not allege that Google has registered or is operating any of the allegedly infringing domain names, it cannot be liable under the ACPA. This argument, however, ignores that one can also be liable for, as discussed above, "trafficking in" a domain name. The [Complaint] alleges that Google pays registrants for its use of the purportedly deceptive domain names, provides domain performance reporting, participates in the tasting of domain names, uses semantics technology to analyze the meaning of domain names and select revenue maximizing advertisements and controls and maintains that advertising. Given these allegations, Google's motion to dismiss the ACPA count is denied.

QUESTION

eNom provides domain name registration services and offers customers the opportunity to bid on soon-to-expire domain names under a program it calls "Club Drop." Five days before a domain name registration is due to expire, eNom invites customers to bid on the opportunity to acquire it. eNom then uses proprietary technology to attempt to register the domain name as soon as it becomes available; if it is successful, it allows the winning bidder to register the domain in its own name for the bid amount. A sporting goods store carelessly allows its domain name registration to lapse. eNom registers the domain name under its Club Drop program and conveys it to an unrelated sporting goods store in a different region. The initial owner of the domain name registration sues eNom under the ACPA.

eNom argues that it lacks "bad faith intent to profit" as a matter of law, since it merely registered the domain name on a customer's behalf. How should the court rule? *See Philbrick v. eNom, Inc.*, 593 F.Supp.2d 352 (D.N.H. 2009).

C. ICANN AND THE UNIFORM TRADEMARK DOMAIN NAME DISPUTE RESOLUTION POLICY

Page 792. Insert the following case after *Estate of Frank Gorshin v. Martin.*

Fields for Senate v. Toddles Inc., WIPO Arbitration and Mediation Center Case No. D2006–1510 (March 14, 2007). In 2006, C. Virginia Fields ran for the New York State Senate. John Fisher, a political commentator, registered the domain names <virginafields.com>, <virginiafields.net>, <virginiafields.org> and <virginiafields.info>, and used them to direct Internet users to a website criticizing Ms. Fields:

> The site states, in part:
>
>> "C Virginia Fields would be a terrible State Senator. Keep her in the private sector (or unemployed), where she can't hurt anyone."
>
> The site also states:
>
>> "This website is not associated with, approved by or supported by any candidate (especially C. Virginia Fields), political party or club. It is intended to provide political criticism and satire."

Fields' Senatorial campaign filed a UDRP complaint seeking transfer of the domain names. The panel held that the complainant had failed to establish that it owned trademark rights in the name "Virginia Fields:"

> On the initial question of the ownership of rights, the Complaint is confusing in that it identifies the Complainant as either Fields for Senate, a political campaign committee, or C. Virginia Fields, an individual.
>
> There is no evidence that Fields for Senate owns any rights in the claimed mark. Thus, it appears that the political campaign committee lacks standing to bring this action. A similar result was reached in *Friends of Kathleen Kennedy Townsend v. B.G. Birt*, WIPO Case No. D2002–0451 (2002)(denying relief where action committee lacked rights in individual's name).
>
> As for Ms. Fields' ownership of trademark rights, the record shows that she has been a public figure in New York for many years, has held office, and has received several awards for her service. The Complainant provides no case or other authority to support its position that such use gives rise to ownership of trademark rights in the name. The Respondent in contrast points to authority indicating that the render-

ing of services as a politician is not a sufficient basis for finding trademark rights under the Policy.

For example, The Final Report on the Second WIPO Domain Name Process, dated September 3, 2001, recommended that the Policy should be limited in its protection of personal names to those that have been commercially exploited. Following that Report, a WIPO Panel denied trademark protection to the personal name of a politician in *Kathleen Kennedy Townsend v. B.G. Birt,* WIPO Case No. D2002–0030 (2002). A U.S. Federal Court considering a similar case has also found that use of a name as a politician does not create trademark rights. *Ficker v. Tuohy,* 305 F.Supp.2d 569 (D Md. 2004).

Here, we agree with the Respondent that the Complainant has not established trademark rights in the name C. Virginia Fields. The argument presented is limited to use of the name as a politician. There is no indication that the name has ever been used or advertised as an indication of the source of any goods or services. Although Complainant says there has been "continuous commercial use of C.Virginia Fields mark for over seventeen years," we do not find any evidence of trademark or service mark use of that name in the record. Although there may be circumstances where a political figure uses his or her name in a manner that would establish trademark use, merely using a name as a public figure for seventeen years is not sufficient to establish such rights as are necessary for relief under the Policy.

Accordingly, the Panel concludes that the Complainant has not satisfied the first necessary element of a claim under the Policy. Further, given this conclusion, it is unnecessary to consider the remaining elements of a claim under the Policy, namely, whether or not the Respondent has a legitimate interest in using the domain names for criticism and whether the Respondent registered and used the domain names in bad faith.

Page 803.   Insert the following case after the Questions.

Southern California Regional Rail Authority v. Arkow, WIPO Arbitration and Mediation Center Case No. D2008–0430 (May 12, 2008). The Southern California Regional Rail Authority [SCRRA] operates the Metrolink commuter railway and owns a service mark registration for METROLINK. The authority operates an informational website at "www. metrolinktrains.com. "Robert Arkow, a frequent Metrolink passenger, registered the domain name <metrolinkrider.com>, and put up a website inviting comments on the commuter railway. The website included a disclaimer noting that the site was "NOT an official website of Metrolink or the SCCRA." SCRRA objected to the use of the "metrolink" service mark in his domain name and sent Arkow a cease and desist letter. Arkow then registered the domain name <metrolinksucks.com>. SCCRA filed a UDRP complaint.

The Complainant indisputably has rights in the registered METRO-LINK service mark. The mark is included in its entirety in both Domain Names.

The addition of the generic word "rider" to the first Domain Name, <metrolinkrider.com>, does not avoid confusion. Rather, it tends to increase the likelihood of confusion, since the METROLINK commuter trains carry tens of thousands of riders daily. For purposes of the first element of the Complaint, the disclaimer of affiliation on the Respondent's website associated with this Domain Name does not avoid the initial confusion of an Internet user seeking online information from the Complainant.

The Respondent argues that the second Domain Name, <metrolinksucks.com>, "clearly" reveals by the name itself that it is not affiliated with the Complainant. Numerous Policy decisions (and several judicial precedents in the United States of America, where both parties are located) have addressed the question of whether adding a derogatory word such as "sucks" to a domain name makes it unlikely that Internet users would be confused as to source or affiliation. The American Heritage Dictionary of the English Language (4th ed. 2000) defines "sucks" as a "vulgar slang" term meaning, "to be disgustingly disagreeable or offensive." Merriam–Webster's Online Dictionary ("www.m-w.com") similarly includes the "slang" definition of "sucks" as "to be objectionable or inadequate". Presumably, most organizations would not publish a website with such a self-denigrating domain name, and some UDRP panels have concluded that such a domain name is not, therefore, "confusingly similar" to a mark included in the domain name. See, *e.g., Lockheed Martin Corporation v. Dan Parisi*, WIPO Case No. D2000–1015.

However, it is not self-evident that Internet users would always take notice of the slang word following the trademark in the Domain Name and recognize its negative import. Moreover, as in a number of other Policy proceedings, many Internet users potentially interested in the Complainant's services are not fluent English-speakers. The record establishes that the Complainant's METROLINK system serves ethnically diverse counties in Southern California and attracts tourists and business travelers from around the world. See, *e.g., Wachovia Corporation v. Alton Flanders*, WIPO Case No. D2003–0596; *Koninklijke Philips Electronics N.V. v. In Seo Kim*, WIPO Case No. D2001–1195 (non-native English speakers may not recognize the negative connotations of a pejorative slang term included in a domain name). It is also by no means improbable that a trademark holder would use a domain name with such a suffix wryly, perhaps deliberately seeking an opportunity to communicate with younger or disaffected consumers.

It is for such reasons that most panels have tended to find that a domain name consisting of a trademark and a negative term are "confusingly similar" to the complainant's mark for the threshold purpose of establishing the first element of a UDRP complaint. See, *e.g.* WIPO Overview of WIPO Panel Views on Selected UDRP Questions, paragraph 1.3, and cases cited therein. As the *Wachovia* and *Philips* panels observed, a finding of confusing similarity does not deprive a legitimate protest website from protection under the second and third elements of a Policy complaint.

The Panel concludes, therefore, that both Domain Names are confusingly similar to the Complainant's METROLINK service mark for purposes of the first Policy element.

C. Rights or Legitimate Interests

The Policy, paragraph 4(c), provides a non-exhaustive list of circumstances in which a respondent could demonstrate rights or legitimate interests in a contested domain name. These include one on which the Respondent relies:

> "(iii) you are making a legitimate noncommercial or fair use of the domain name, without intent for commercial gain to misleadingly divert consumers or to tarnish the trademark or service mark at issue."

The Complainant does not contend that the Respondent's website is commercial. Rather, the Complainant argues that while the Respondent may legitimately criticize the Complainant online, it may not use its trademark in the Domain Names, because these mislead the public as to the nature of the associated website.

There is admittedly a split in UDRP decisions as to whether it can be legitimate to use a domain name incorporating a trademark for a noncommercial criticism website. Some panels hold that it is not legitimate to do so; others that it is legitimate only if the domain name clearly conveys protest or criticism. However, panels in proceedings with parties in the United States of America, where judicial decisions tend to support criticism websites against trademark infringement and cybersquatting claims on constitutional First Amendment grounds, have been more likely to find a legitimate interest as long as the use is fair and noncommercial. See WIPO Overview of WIPO Panel Views on Selected UDRP Questions, paragraph 2.4, and cases cited therein.

The Panel is inclined toward the latter view in the present case, as it involves parties in the United States of America and the Respondent unquestionably operates a noncommercial comment and criticism website. Such use could not be considered legitimate, however, if the record indicated that the Respondent selected and used the Domain Names fundamentally in a bad-faith effort to tarnish the Complainant's mark and disrupt its business, as the Complainant asserts. That possibility is better addressed below, in connection with the bad-faith element of the Complaint.

The Complainant advances a different argument against the Respondent's legitimate interest in the second Domain Name, <metrolink-sucks.com>: the Complainant contends that it was registered not for a criticism website but only as a "retaliatory or preemptive measure to any legal proceedings that SCRRA would take'', citing the Respondent's February 11, 2008 letter. This argument is unpersuasive. The Domain Name pointed, at least for a time, to the same comment and criticism website associated with the first Domain Name, <metrolinkrider.com>. The Respondent plausibly claims that he registered the second Domain Name, with a more explicitly critical connotation, as a "fall back" for his website in case the first Domain Name was taken away from him. This does not undercut the legitimacy of using, or planning to use, the second Domain Name for the same or similar website. That appears to be a legitimate use, unless it represents a bad-faith effort to tarnish and disrupt, as discussed below.

D. Registered and Used in Bad Faith

. . . .

The Complainant argues that the first Domain Name, <metrolinkrider.com>, was selected to mislead and divert Internet users. But that name is ambiguous; it might be linked to the Complainant, but it could suggest a different, consumer's perspective. The Respondent denies any intent to mislead Internet users and points out that his website is replete with prominent disclaimers of affiliation. He claims he was motivated by a desire to give METROLINK passengers and employees a forum where they could speak without "censorship", and the contents of his website are consistent with such an intent to distinguish the website emphatically from any affiliation with the Complainant. Some Internet users could be confused initially by this Domain Name, but the Panel is not persuaded on the present record that this is why the Respondent registered and used the Domain Name <metrolinkrider.com> for a comment and criticism website.

The Complainant's inference of bad-faith with respect to the second Domain Name, <metrolinksucks.com> reprises the argument from the second element of the Complaint. This argument is to the effect that since the Domain Name was registered after notice of the Complainant's trademark concerns, it was motivated simply by a desire to frustrate the Complainant's efforts to obtain the transfer of a domain name. The Complainant cites *CBS Broadcasting, Inc., f/k/a CBS, Inc. v. Nabil Z. aghloul*, WIPO Case No. D2004–0988. In that case, however, the panel found that there was no credible evidence that the respondent ever intended to use the domain name for a criticism website. Here, the Domain Name <metrolinksucks.com> was pointed to the Respondent's comment and criticism website for some time, and the Respondent credibly claims he would use the second Domain Name for that website if the first Domain Name became unavailable to him. Thus, the Panel does not find bad-faith established on this theory.

The Complainant contends, finally, that both Domain Names were registered "primarily to disrupt" its business. There is no evidence in the record demonstrating how the handful of diverse comments posted on the Respondent's website have interfered with the Complainant's business. From the record and a perusal of the Respondent's website, it appears rather that the Domain Names were registered for precisely the reason stated by the Respondent–to provide a forum for airing comments about the Complainant's transit service. Many of these comments are critical, but something more than criticism is required to establish illegitimacy and bad-faith for purposes of the Policy. See *La Quinta Worldwide L.L.C. v. Heartland Times LLC, MD Sullivan*, WIPO Case No. D2007–1660. For example, in *Covance, Inc. and Covance Laboratories Ltd. v. The Covance Campaign*, WIPO Case No. D2004–0206, articles and posts on the respondent's protest website threatened to publish the complainants' confidential client lists, encouraged readers to harass the complainants' suppliers, and made defamatory remarks about employees of the complainants. There is no similar evidence here of a concerted attempt to interfere with the Complainant's business. The Panel does not find, therefore, that the Respondent registered the Domain Names "primarily to disrupt" the Complainant's business.

In sum, the Complainant has not met its burden of persuasion to establish the second and third elements of the Complaint with respect to illegitimacy and bad-faith.

Page 806.   Insert the following case after *Deutshe Welle v. Diamondware, Ltd.*

Plan. Net concept Spezialagentur für interactive Kommunikation GmbH v. Yikilmaz, WIPO Arbitration and Mediation Center Case No. D2006–0082 (March 24, 2006). The German Plan.Net, owner of both EU and German trademark registrations, brought a UDRP complaint against Turkish businessman Murat Yikilmaz over the registration of the domain "plan.net." Yikilmaz had registered a number of common English words as domain names, including <intelligence.net>, <dirtbike.com>, <airplane.com>, <matchmakers.com>, <graph.com>. The panel found that the domain name was confusingly similar to Plan Net's registered mark, but that the complainant had failed to prove either that Yikilmaz had no legitimate interests in the domain name or that he had registered and was using the domain name in bad faith. It refused to find reverse domain name hijacking:

B.   Rights or Legitimate Interests

The second factor that the Complainant is required to establish is that the Respondent has no rights or legitimate interests in respect of the domain name.

In view of the difficulty in disproving a negative, the Complainant must adduce sufficient material to raise a *prima facie* case under this factor and then an evidential burden shifts to the Respondent to rebut that *prima facie* case.

The Complainant contends that the Respondent does not have rights or legitimate interests in the domain name as:

(a) the domain name is not derived from the Respondent's name and the Respondent's website does not identify any corporate entity using the name;

(b) the Respondent does not have a Community Trademark for "Plan Net";

(c) the Respondent's website is an arbitrary collection of links for which there is neither necessity nor justification for the use of <plan.net>; and

(d) generally, there does not appear to be any legitimate interest in using the domain name.

The Respondent points out that he is Turkish and based in Turkey. There is no obligation nor need for him to obtain a Community Trademark. The Respondent also contends that the domain name is simply a generic term "plan" with a gTLD. The Respondent notes that a Google search of "PLAN NET" reveals numerous references including use by various companies in the English speaking world which, the Respondent asserts, have no relation to the Complainant. These include an English company, Plan-net Services plc, which provides a range of IT skills and recruitment services and a Canadian company, Plan:Net Ltd, which provides consultancy services in relation to project management. . . . .

The Respondent makes no bones about registering domain names using generic terms and using them to generate commercial revenues, e.g., through "pay per click" advertising. The Respondent argues that, where a domain name consists of a generic term, the first person who registers it in good faith has rights or a legitimate interest in it. In this connection, the Respondent specifically denies any prior knowledge of the Complainant or its trademark. . . .

While a respondent's denial of knowledge of trademark rights often lacks credibility where the trademark is extremely well known or there are other compelling factors to the contrary, that is not this situation. The domain name here consists of a very plain English word plus a gTLD and there is nothing particularly about the Respondent's website that suggests any intention to pass off on the Complainant's rights or business. This is not a case where the Respondent's motives can be impugned solely on the papers.

In these circumstances, the Panel is far from satisfied that a *prima facie* case of the absence of rights or legitimate interests has been made out. Even if it were, the Respondent has sufficiently explained its position. Accordingly, the Panel finds that the Complainant has not established the second requirement under the Policy.

C.   Registered and Used in Bad Faith

The third requirement that the Complainant must demonstrate to succeed is that the domain name has been registered and used in bad faith.

In view of the Panel's conclusion on the second factor, it is not strictly necessary to decide this issue.

For completeness, however, the Panel notes that the Complainant seeks to make out this ground by reference to the number of domain names which the Respondent has registered and which the Complainant contends either have no functioning website or have largely identical content which is said not to be "real content in the sense of manual search results selected by hand". Accordingly, the Complainant invites the Panel to infer that the Respondent has merely registered the domain name with the intention of selling it or to block others from using it.

. . . .

The Respondent, as already noted, freely admits he registers generic terms for the purposes of revenue generation. The problem for the Complainant is that such conduct breaches the Policy only if it is in bad faith and, in the absence of bad faith, the Respondent's conduct is perfectly legitimate. . . .

Here, there is no evidence of bad faith. The Respondent has plausibly in the circumstances of this case and the limited nature of these proceedings as proceedings on the papers denied any foreknowledge of the Complainant's trademark; the domain name consists of a plain English term and the Respondent has not sought to pass off on the Complainant's trademark or business.

Accordingly, the Panel would find that this third requirement under the Policy is also not satisfied.

D. Reverse Domain Name Hijacking

The Respondent seeks a finding of Reverse Domain Name Hijacking against the Complainant under paragraph 15(e) of the Rules. . . .

The mere failure of the Complaint is not sufficient to found a finding under paragraph 15(e) of the Rules; such a finding is intended only for the worst cases where there is bad faith such as malice or dishonesty or some other abuse of process. See e.g. *Jazeera Space Channel TV Station v. AJ Publishing*, WIPO Case No. D2005–0309.

It can be argued that the Complainant ought to have recognised the very speculative nature of the Complaint in the absence of any attempt to pass off on the Complainant's business or otherwise to hold the Complainant to ransom . . . . . While the case is perhaps approaching the borderline, however, the Panel ultimately is not prepared to make such a finding in this case. Here, the Complainant does in fact have a registered Community Trademark. It is entitled to seek to protect that.

CHAPTER 12

TRADEMARKS AS SPEECH

Page 822. **Add the following case after *SFAA v. USOC*.**

Wrenn v. Boy Scouts of America, 89 U.S.P.Q.2d 1039 (N.D. Cal. 2008). When Gregory Wrenn's daughter was denied admission to her twin brother's Cub Scouts troop, the Wrenns decided to start a new non-discriminatory scouting organization under the name "Youthscouts." Wrenn attempted to register YOUTHSCOUTS as a service mark, but the Boy Scouts of America successfully opposed the registration. Wrenn filed a federal court action seeking a declaration that his YOUTHSCOUTS service mark did not infringe any mark owned by the Boy Scouts of America because the term "Scouts" was a generic term for youth-based organizations modeled on the scouting movement of the early 20th century. The court noted that the Boy Scouts of America received a Congressional Charter in 1916, and currently operates under a statutory charter that provides: "The corporation has the exclusive right to use emblems, badges, descriptive or designating marks, and words or phrases the corporation adopts." 36 U.S.C. § 30905. Relying on *SFAA v. USOC*, the court agreed that the Boy Scouts of America "need not demonstrate the likelihood of confusion because it has been granted special protection by Congressional charter." Even without special protection, the court concluded that the mark YOUTHSCOUTS was likely to be confused with BOY SCOUTS, CUB SCOUTS and EAGLE SCOUTS.

B. PARODY

Page 855. **Add the following case after *Anheuser-Busch v. Balducci*.**

Anheuser–Busch v. VIP Products, 2008 WL 4619702 (E.D.Mo. 2008). VIP sold squeaky rubber dog toys designed to parody plaintiff's Budweiser beer bottle under the name "Buttwiper." Anheuser–Busch com-

missioned a survey of adult pet-owners in shopping malls; its expert
reported that 30% of those surveyed believed that Buttwiper toys were sold
with the approval or sponsorship of, or were produced by a company
affiliated with, the maker of Budweiser beer. The survey evidence, plus the
fact that plaintiff sold licensed Budweiser promotional goods including
some pet products, persuaded the court that the case was controlled by
Mutual of Omaha v. Novak and *Anheuser-Busch v. Balducci*, both of which
included surveys finding some degree of consumer confusion. The court
distinguished other parody cases as cases in which courts found no likelihood of confusion. It therefore entered a preliminary injunction barring the
manufacture, distribution, marketing or sale of the Buttwiper dog toy.

Page 855. Insert the following case and question after Question 2:

Smith v. Wal–Mart Stores, 537 F.Supp.2d 1302 (N.D. Ga. 2008).

This action arises from the contention of Defendant Wal–Mart
Stores, Inc. that its registered trademarks "WALMART"; "WAL–
MART"; and "WAL*MART"; its registered word mark "ALWAYS
LOW PRICES. ALWAYS"; and its "well-known smiley face mark"
were infringed by Plaintiff Charles Smith's anti-Wal–Mart merchandise. Smith petitions the Court to declare his activities legal so that he
may resume them without fear of incurring liability for damages; Wal-
Mart counterclaims for an award of ownership of Smith's Wal–Mart-
related domain names, an injunction precluding Smith from making
commercial use of any designation beginning with the prefix "WAL,"
and an award of nominal damages. . . . .

Smith is an avid and vocal critic of Wal–Mart. He believes that
Wal–Mart has a destructive effect on communities, treats workers
badly, and has a damaging influence on the United States as a whole—
an influence so detrimental to the United States and its communities
that Smith likens it to that of the Nazi regime. With the goals of
stimulating discussions about Wal–Mart and getting others of like
mind to join him in expressing strongly negative views about Wal-
Mart, Smith created various designs and slogans that incorporated the
word "Walocaust," a word Smith invented by combining the first three
letters of Wal–Mart's name with the last six letters of the word
"holocaust."

[Smith designed several graphics expressing his anti-Wal–Mart message
and applied his designs to teeshirts and stickers. He sold these items online
via a website at www.walocaust.com. When Wal–Mart objected, Smith
coined the term "Wal–Queda," registered the domain name wal-queda.com,
and designed new stickers and tee-shirts incorporating the term.]

Wal–Mart contends that Smith is a merchant who misappropriated
its trademarks and business reputation in pursuit of illegal profit and
who disingenuously seeks to cloak those activities under the First

Amendment. Smith alleges that Wal–Mart is attempting to misuse trademark laws to censor his criticism of the company. According to Smith, at stake in this case is a person's right to publicly criticize the world's largest retailer—or any other business.

. . . .

Because Smith's arguments with regard to the *Safeway* [likelihood of confusion] factors depend heavily on whether his designs are successful parodies, the Court must first consider whether the contested designs are in fact parodies of Wal–Mart's registered marks. *See Dr. Seuss Enters. v. Penguin Books, Inc.,* 109 F.3d 1394, 1405 (9th Cir. 1997) (noting that the claim that a secondary use is a parody is not a separate defense to a charge of trademark infringement but is instead is considered within the likelihood of confusion analysis); *see also Connick v. Myers,* 461 U.S. 138, 148 n.7 (1983) ("The inquiry into the protected status of speech is one of law, not fact."). For the purposes of trademark analysis, "a parody is defined as a simple form of entertainment conveyed by juxtaposing the irreverent representation of the trademark with the idealized image created by the mark's owner." *Louis Vuitton Malletier v. Haute Diggity Dog, LLC,* 507 F.3d 252, 260 (4th Cir. 2007). To be considered successful, the alleged parody must both call to mind and differentiate itself from the original, and it must "communicate some articulable element of satire, ridicule, joking or amusement." *Id.*

When applying these criteria to the facts of the case, it is clear that Smith's concepts are parodies of the registered Wal–Mart marks. Smith successfully calls Wal–Mart to mind by using either "WAL" or "MART" as part of the concept; by mimicking its fonts and storefront design; by mentioning Bentonville, the location of Wal–Mart's headquarters; or by including various other icons typically associated with Wal–Mart. As Wal–Mart fervently contends, it is obvious that Smith's concepts use Wal–Mart imagery to evoke the company in the mind of his viewers.

It is equally obvious that Smith's concepts are not the "idealized image" of the registered Wal–Mart marks. "Walocaust," "Wal-Qaeda" and "Freedom–Hater–Mart" are not "Wal–Mart." The imagery on Smith's t-shirts includes portraits of Mao Zedong, a United States map with the word "DECEASED" stamped over it, and the slogan "FREE-DOM HATERS ALWAYS."

Finally, the juxtaposition of the similar and dissimilar—the satirical representation and the idealized image of Wal–Mart—conveys a scathing parody. In the "smiley eagle" Walocaust concept, the reference to the Holocaust and the image of the Nazi eagle clutching a smiley face at once portrays and contradicts the benign image that Wal–Mart portrays to the community. In the "SUPPORT OUR TROOPS" Wal–Qaeda concept, Smith transforms all-American "Wal–Mart" into the terrorist group "Wal–Qaeda" and satirically urges the viewer to support Wal–Qaeda's troops, apparently commenting both on what Smith considers to be Wal–Mart's ruthless business tactics and its detrimental impact on the United States. Other concepts juxtapose Wal–Mart's reputation for low prices with a reference to poor store security and the company's family values imagery with the fact that it offers for sale inexpensive alcohol, tobacco and firearms—products known better for destroying families.

The Court thus concludes that Smith's concepts adequately evoke Wal–Mart while maintaining their differentiation, and they convey Smith's satirical commentary; thus, they are successful parodies. *See Louis Vuitton,* 507 F.3d at 261.

The finding that Smith's concepts are parodies does not preclude the likelihood of confusion analysis, however; it merely influences the way the likelihood of confusion factors are applied. *Id.* "[A]n effective parody will actually diminish the likelihood of confusion, while an: ineffective parody does not." *Id.* Because even a parody may constitute trademark infringement if that parody is confusing, the Court will next consider the likelihood of confusion factors. *Id.*

[The court conducted a lengthy likelihood of confusion analysis.]

Evaluating the overall balance of the seven likelihood of confusion factors, the Court finds that Wal–Mart has failed to demonstrate a likelihood that its trademarks ... would be confused with Smith's [Walocaust and Wal–Queda] concepts. In so finding, the Court concludes that factors three (similarity of the marks), five (similarity of sales methods) and six (similarity of advertising methods), weigh in Smith's favor, with particular emphasis on how different the appearance and usage of the marks were and how vastly the parties' advertising methods differed. The Court concludes that factors one (actual confusion), two (strength of the mark), four (similarity of product) and seven (Smith's intent) favor neither party.

In sum, the Court is convinced that no fair-minded jury could find that a reasonable consumer is likely to be confused by the challenged marks. . . . .

[The court then turned to Wal–Mart's dilution by tarnishment claim:]

The Court is convinced that a reasonable juror could only find that Smith primarily intended to express himself with his Walocaust and

Wal–Qaeda concepts and that commercial success was a secondary motive at most. Smith has strongly adverse opinions about Wal–Mart; he believes that it has a destructive effect on communities, treats workers badly and has a damaging influence on the United States as a whole. He invented the term "Walocaust" to encapsulate his feelings about Wal–Mart, and he created his Walocaust designs with the intent of calling attention to his beliefs and cause. He never expected to have any exclusive rights to the word. He created the term "Wal–Qaeda" and designs incorporating it with similar expressive intent. The Court has found those designs to be successful parodies.

Thus, Smith's parodic work is considered noncommercial speech and therefore not subject to Wal–Mart's trademark dilution claims, despite the fact that Smith sold the designs to the public on t-shirts and other novelty merchandise.

QUESTION

Does the test the court employs for "successful parody" differentiate parodic from non-parodic content in a useful way? How would the test have fared on the facts of *Anheuser-Busch v. Balducci* or *Mutual of Omaha v. Novak*? Can you devise a more useful test?

C. TRADEMARKS AS SPEECH

Page 874. Insert before *Rogers v. Grimaldi*:

QUESTION

Professor Tushnet has suggested that the consequences of extending full first amendment protection to commercial speech would be substantial:

> The murky boundary between true and false has significant consequences for commercial speech doctrine. Theorists who believe that commercial speech should be given full First Amendment protection often claim, either explicitly or implicitly, that we need not fear the consequences of such protection for ordinary consumer transactions. A cause of action for fraud, they suggest, is not offensive to the First Amendment, and so the worst abuses of consumers' trust can still be redressed. But the heightened scienter requirement for fraud—as compared to the generally strict liability that exists in trademark and consumer protection law—combined with the inherent flexibility of language means that the promise of continued protection is largely illusory. We cannot have much consumer protection law in a world that treats commercial speech like political speech. Consider, by way of comparison, how much of a constraint libel law imposes on what politicians say about each other.

> We must choose between the difficult line-drawing problems that the commercial speech doctrine creates and the consumer protection objectives served by modern commercial speech regulation. Some will

conclude that the law should treat drug advertisements just like electioneering, but at least the costs of doing so will be clear. My own view is that, though excluding false and misleading commercial speech from constitutional protection has significant costs when legislatures, agencies, or juries make mistakes about what is false, those costs are similar to the harms of other mistaken economic policies. We are better off overall in a system that regulates false and misleading commercial speech without heightened First Amendment scrutiny.

Rebecca Tushnet, *It Depends on What the Meaning of "False" Is: Falsity and Misleadingness in Commercial Speech Doctrine*, 41 Loyola L.A. L. Rev. 227 (2008)(footnotes omitted). Do you agree? Can you articulate a middle ground?

Page 874. Delete *Parks v. La Face Records* and the QUESTIONS following it on pages 874–885, and substitute the following material:

Parks v. LaFace Records, 329 F.3d 437 (6th Cir. 2003). Rosa Parks sued hip hop duo Outkast over the song titled "Rosa Parks." The song did not refer directly to Parks, but included the following lyric: "*Ah ha, hush that fuss / Everybody move to the back of the bus / Do you wanna bump and slump with us / We the type of people make the club get crunk.*" Outkast argued that the *Rogers v. Grimaldi* test insulated it from liability. The Court of Appeals for the Sixth Circuit disagreed:

> The *Rogers* court made an important point which clearly applies in this case. The court said, "poetic license is not without limits. The purchaser of a book, like the purchaser of a can of peas, has a right not to be misled as to the source of the product." *Rogers*, 875 F.2d at 997. The same is also true regarding the content of a song. The purchaser of a song titled *Rosa Parks* has a right not to be misled regarding the content of that song. While the expressive element of titles admittedly requires more protection than the labeling of ordinary commercial products, "[a] misleading title with no artistic relevance cannot be sufficiently justified by a free expression interest," *id.* at 999, and the use of such a title, as in the present case, could be found to constitute a violation of the Lanham Act. Including the phrase "move to the back of the bus" in the lyrics of this song, in our opinion, does not justify, as a matter of law, the appropriation of Rosa Parks' name for the title to the song, and the fact that the phrase is repeated ten times or fifty times does not affect the question of the relevancy of the title to the lyrics. . . .

> While Defendants' lyrics contain profanity and a great deal of "explicit" language (together with a parental warning), they contain absolutely nothing that could conceivably, by any stretch of the imagination, be considered, explicitly or implicitly, a reference to courage, to sacrifice, to the civil rights movement or to any other quality with which Rosa Parks is identified. If the requirement of "relevance" is to have any meaning at all, it would not be unreasonable to conclude that the title *Rosa Parks* is not relevant to the content of the song in

question. The use of this woman's name unquestionably was a good marketing tool—*Rosa Parks* was likely to sell far more recordings than *Back of the Bus*—but its use could be found by a reasonable finder of fact to be a flagrant deception on the public regarding the actual content of this song and the creation of an impression that Rosa Parks, who had approved the use of her name in connection with the *Tribute* album, had also approved or sponsored the use of her name on Defendants' composition.

E.S.S. Entertainment 2000, Inc. v. Rock Star Videos, Inc.

547 F.3d 1095 (9th Cir. 2008).

■ O'SCANNLAIN, CIRCUIT JUDGE:

We must decide whether a producer of a video game in the "Grand Theft Auto" series has a defense under the First Amendment against a claim of trademark infringement.

I

A

Rockstar Games, Inc. ("Rockstar"), a wholly owned subsidiary of Take–Two Interactive Software, Inc., manufactures and distributes the Grand Theft Auto series of video games (the "Series"), including Grand Theft Auto: San Andreas ("San Andreas" or the "Game"). The Series is known for an irreverent and sometimes crass brand of humor, gratuitous violence and sex, and overall seediness.

Each game in the Series takes place in one or more dystopic, cartoonish cities modeled after actual American urban areas. The games always include a disclaimer stating that the locations depicted are fictional. Players control the game's protagonist, trying to complete various "missions" on a video screen. The plot advances with each mission accomplished until the player, having passed through thousands of cartoon-style places along the way, wins the game.

Consistent with the tone of the Series, San Andreas allows a player to experience a version of West Coast "gangster" culture. The Game takes place in the virtual cities of "Los Santos," "San Fierro," and "Las Venturas," based on Los Angeles, San Francisco, and Las Vegas, respectively.

Los Santos, of course, mimics the look and feel of actual Los Angeles neighborhoods. Instead of "Hollywood," "Santa Monica," "Venice Beach," and "Compton," Los Santos contains "Vinewood," "Santa Maria," "Verona Beach," and "Ganton." Rockstar has populated these areas with virtual liquor stores, ammunition dealers, casinos, pawn shops, tattoo parlors, bars, and strip clubs. The brand names, business names, and other aspects of the locations have been changed to fit the irreverent "Los Santos" tone. Not especially saintly, Los Santos is complete with gangs who roam streets inhabited by prostitutes and drug pushers while random gunfire punctuates the soundtrack.

To generate their vision for Los Santos, some of the artists who drew it visited Los Angeles to take reference photographs. The artists took pictures of businesses, streets, and other places in Los Angeles that they thought evoked the San Andreas theme. They then returned home (to Scotland) to draw Los Santos, changing the images from the photographs as necessary to fit into the fictional world of Los Santos and San Andreas. According to Nikolas Taylor ("Taylor"), the Lead Map Artist for Los Santos, he and other artists did not seek to "re-creat[e] a realistic depiction of Los Angeles; rather, [they] were creating 'Los Santos,' a fictional city that lampooned the seedy underbelly of Los Angeles and the people, business and places [that] comprise it." One neighborhood in the fictional city is "East Los Santos," the Game's version of East Los Angeles. East Los Santos contains variations on the businesses and architecture of the real thing, including a virtual, cartoon-style strip club known as the "Pig Pen."

B

ESS Entertainment 2000, Inc. ("ESS"), operates a strip club, which features females dancing nude, on the eastern edge of downtown Los Angeles under the name Play Pen Gentlemen's Club ("Play Pen"). ESS claims that Rockstar's depiction of an East Los Santos strip club called the Pig Pen infringes its trademark and trade dress associated with the Play Pen.

The Play Pen's "logo" consists of the words "the Play Pen" (and the lower-and upper-case letters forming those words) and the phrase "Totally Nude" displayed in a publicly available font, with a silhouette of a nude female dancer inside the stem of the first "P." Apparently, ESS has no physical master or precise template for its logo. Different artists draw the nude silhouette in Play Pen's logo anew for each representation, although any final drawing must be acceptable to Play Pen's owners. There are several different versions of the silhouette, and some advertisements and signs for the Play Pen do not contain the nude silhouettes.

Although the artists took some inspiration from their photographs of the Play Pen, it seems they used photographs of other East Los Angeles locations to design other aspects of the Pig Pen. The Pig Pen building in Los Santos, for instance, lacks certain characteristics of the Play Pen building such as a stone facade, a valet stand, large plants and gold columns around the entrance, and a six-foot black iron fence around the parking lot. The Play Pen also has a red, white, and blue pole sign near the premises, which includes a trio of nude silhouettes above the logo and a separate "Totally Nude" sign below. The Pig Pen does not.

C

On April 22, 2005, ESS filed the underlying trademark violation action in district court against Rockstar. ESS asserted four claims: (1) trade dress infringement and unfair competition under section 43(a) of the Lanham

Act, 15 U.S.C. § 1125(a); (2) trademark infringement under California Business and Professions Code § 14320; (3) unfair competition under California Business and Professions Code §§ 17200 et seq.; and (4) unfair competition under California common law. The heart of ESS's complaint is that Rockstar has used Play Pen's distinctive logo and trade dress without its authorization and has created a likelihood of confusion among consumers as to whether ESS has endorsed, or is associated with, the video depiction.

In response, Rockstar moved for summary judgment on all of ESS's claims, arguing that the affirmative defenses of nominative fair use and the First Amendment protected it against liability. It also argued that its use of ESS's intellectual property did not infringe ESS's trademark by creating a "likelihood of confusion."

Although the district court rejected Rockstar's nominative fair use defense, it granted summary judgment based on the First Amendment defense. The district court did not address the merits of the trademark claim because its finding that Rockstar had a defense against liability made such analysis unnecessary.

II

Rockstar argues that, regardless of whether it infringed ESS's trademark under the Lanham Act or related California law, it is entitled to two defenses: one under the nominative fair use doctrine and one under the First Amendment. [The court held that "Since Rockstar did not use the trademarked logo to describe ESS's strip club, the district court correctly held that the nominative fair use defense does not apply in this case."]

B

Rockstar's second defense asks us to consider the intersection of trademark law and the First Amendment. The road is well traveled. We have adopted the Second Circuit's approach from *Rogers v. Grimaldi*, which "requires courts to construe the Lanham Act 'to apply to artistic works only where the public interest in avoiding consumer confusion *outweighs* the public interest in free expression.' " *Walking Mountain*, 353 F.3d at 807 (emphasis in original) (quoting *Rogers v. Grimaldi*, 875 F.2d 994, 999 (2d Cir. 1989)). The specific test contains two prongs. An artistic work's use of a trademark that otherwise would violate the Lanham Act is not actionable " 'unless the [use of the mark] has no artistic relevance to the underlying work whatsoever, or, if it has some artistic relevance, unless [it] explicitly misleads as to the source or the content of the work.' " *Mattel, Inc. v. MCA Records, Inc.*, 296 F.3d 894, 902 (9th Cir. 2002) (quoting *Rogers*, 875 F.2d at 999). Although this test traditionally applies to uses of a trademark in the title of an artistic work, there is no principled reason why it ought not also apply to the use of a trademark in the body of the work. *See Walking Mountain*, 353 F.3d at 809 n.17 (implying that it would be acceptable to apply the *Rogers* test to non-titular trade dress claim). The parties do not dispute such an extension of the doctrine.

1

We first adopted the *Rogers* test in *MCA Records*, a case which is instructive for that reason. *MCA Records*, 296 F.3d at 902 ("We agree with the Second Circuit's analysis and adopt the *Rogers* standard as our own."). In *MCA Records*, the maker of the iconic "Barbie" dolls sued MCA for trademark infringement in the title of a song the record company had released, called "Barbie Girl." *Id.* at 899–900. The song was a commentary "about Barbie and the values ... she [supposedly] represents." *Id.* at 902. Applying Rogers, the court held that the First Amendment protected the record company. The first prong was straightforward. Because the song was about Barbie, "the use of Barbie in the song title clearly is relevant to the underlying work." *Id.; see also Walking Mountain*, 353 F.3d at 807 (holding that use of Barbie doll in photographic parody was relevant to the underlying work).

Moving to the second prong, we made an important point. "The *only* indication," we observed, "that Mattel might be associated with the song is the use of Barbie in the title; if this were enough to satisfy this prong of the *Rogers* test, it would render *Rogers* a nullity." *MCA Records*, 296 F.2d at 902 (emphasis in original). This makes good sense. After all, a trademark infringement claim presupposes a use of the mark. If that necessary element in every trademark case vitiated a First Amendment defense, the First Amendment would provide no defense at all.

2

Keeping *MCA Records* and related cases in mind, we now turn to the matter before us. ESS concedes that the Game is artistic and that therefore the *Rogers* test applies. However, ESS argues both that the incorporation of the Pig Pen into the Game has no artistic relevance and that it is explicitly misleading. It rests its argument on two observations: (1) the Game is not "about" ESS's Play Pen club the way that "Barbie Girl" was "about" the Barbie doll in *MCA Records*; and (2) also unlike the Barbie case, where the trademark and trade dress at issue was a cultural icon (Barbie), the Play Pen is not a cultural icon.

ESS's objections, though factually accurate, miss the point. Under *MCA Records* and the cases that followed it, only the use of a trademark with " '*no* artistic relevance to the underlying work *whatsoever*' " does not merit First Amendment protection. *Id.* (emphasis added) (quoting *Rogers*, 875 F.2d at 999). In other words, the level of relevance merely must be above zero. It is true that the Game is not "about" the Play Pen the way that Barbie Girl was about Barbie. But, given the low threshold the Game must surmount, that fact is hardly dispositive. It is also true that Play Pen has little cultural significance, but the same could be said about most of the individual establishments in East Los Angeles. Like most urban neighborhoods, its distinctiveness lies in its "look and feel," not in particular destinations as in a downtown or tourist district. And that neighborhood, with all that characterizes it, is relevant to Rockstar's artistic goal, which is to develop a cartoon-style parody of East Los Angeles. Possibly the only way, and certainly a reasonable way, to do that is to recreate a critical mass of the businesses and buildings that constitute it. In this context, we conclude that to include a strip club that is similar in look and feel to the Play Pen does indeed have at least "some artistic relevance." *See id.*

3

ESS also argues that Rockstar's use of the Pig Pen " 'explicitly misleads as to the source or the content of the work.' " *Id.* (quoting *Rogers*, 875 F.2d at 999). This prong of the test points directly at the purpose of trademark law, namely to "avoid confusion in the marketplace by allowing a trademark owner to prevent others from duping consumers into buying a product they mistakenly believe is sponsored by the trademark owner." *Walking Mountain*, 353 F.3d at 806 (internal quotation marks and alteration omitted). The relevant question, therefore, is whether the Game would confuse its players into thinking that the Play Pen is somehow behind the Pig Pen or that it sponsors Rockstar's product. In answering that question, we keep in mind our observation in *MCA Records* that the mere use of a trademark alone cannot suffice to make such use explicitly misleading. *See MCA Records*, 296 F.3d at 902.

Both San Andreas and the Play Pen offer a form of lowbrow entertainment; besides this general similarity, they have nothing in common. The San Andreas Game is not complementary to the Play Pen; video games and strip clubs do not go together like a horse and carriage or, perish the thought, love and marriage. Nothing indicates that the buying public would reasonably have believed that ESS produced the video game or, for that matter, that Rockstar operated a strip club. A player can enter the virtual strip club in Los Santos, but ESS has provided no evidence that the setting is anything but generic. It also seems far-fetched that someone playing San Andreas would think ESS had provided whatever expertise, support, or unique strip-club knowledge it possesses to the production of the game. After all, the Game does not revolve around running or patronizing a strip club. Whatever one can do at the Pig Pen seems quite incidental to the overall story of the Game. A reasonable consumer would not think a company that owns one strip club in East Los Angeles, which is not well known to the public at large, also produces a technologically sophisticated video game like San Andreas.

Undeterred, ESS also argues that, because players are free to ignore the storyline and spend as much time as they want at the Pig Pen, the Pig Pen can be considered a significant part of the Game, leading to confusion. But fans can spend all nine innings of a baseball game at the hot dog stand; that hardly makes Dodger Stadium a butcher's shop. In other words, the chance to attend a virtual strip club is unambiguously *not* the main selling point of the Game.

III

Considering all of the foregoing, we conclude that Rockstar's modification of ESS's trademark is not explicitly misleading and is thus protected by the First Amendment. Since the First Amendment defense applies equally to ESS's state law claims as to its Lanham Act claim, the district court properly dismissed the entire case on Rockstar's motion for summary judgment.

AFFIRMED.

QUESTIONS

1. How would it have changed the court's analysis if the Pig Pen had been named the "Play Pen," or if it had looked more like plaintiff's site, or both? Wouldn't the game version of the strip club still pass the test of non-zero artistic relevance?

2. Marketers of consumer products commonly pay for product placement in videogames. In 2005, the sportswear and shoe manufacturer Puma paid Activision to dress the characters in *True Crime New York City* in Puma® brand clothing and sneakers. In 2008, Barack Obama's presidential campaign purchased virtual billboard space in *Burnout Paradise* for the Xbox 360. Video game players might reasonably conclude that if a product shows up in a videogame, the producer has purchased the opportunity. How would you advise a producer who wants to keep tight control on its product image to respond to an unlicensed videogame appearance? If a particularly violent serial killer in an M-rated blood-and-guts videogame should be depicted swigging a Bud Lite® after every grisly murder, how should Anheuser–Busch respond?

3. Should the *Rogers* test be applied in the same way to videogames as to movies? How about series television? Bravo Television's reality show *Top Chef* challenges chefs to cook gourmet meals in a series of competitive elimination challenges, until the final remaining chef claims the title "Top Chef." Commonly, a given contest features a particular commercial setting or ingredient. Some episodes have revolved around named high-end restaurants; others have required contestants to cook something yummy using Quaker® Oats or Baileys' Irish Cream® Liqueur. If the show's producers choose to use a branded ingredient whose producer declines to pay for placement, may they go ahead without permission? In the summer of 2009, NBC announced that it had signed a deal with Subway® restaurants to make Subway® an integral presence in its adventure series, *Chuck*. As such deals become more common, won't viewers naturally assume that a product that makes repeated appearances in a television series or film is there because its producer paid for them? If a different network airs an episode of a hospital drama in which multitudes come down with food poisoning after eating at a local Subway® restaurant, should Subway have any recourse?

4. In *Trademark: Champion of Free Speech*, 27 Colum. J. L. & Arts 187 (2004), Judge Pierre Leval suggests that courts have been too willing to invoke the First Amendment without first determining whether their cases present a real likelihood of consumer confusion. The trademark law, he argues, incorporates strong protection for free expression by limiting the scope of the trademark owner's right to control the unauthorized use of its mark:

When lawsuits pit claims of exclusive trademark right against interests of free expression, courts should not run unnecessarily to the Constitution. The governing statutes charge the courts with a delegated duty to seek the answers first in the complex, intelligently balanced terms of the trademark laws themselves. Those terms are designed to balance the needs of merchants for identification as the provider of goods with the needs of society for free communication and discussion. Where the terms of the trademark law adequately protect an accused infringer's use as falling outside the scope of the trademark owner's exclusive right, the court has no need to seek answers in the First Amendment.

Recall the cases you have read so far in which courts excused the unauthorized use of a mark on grounds informed by First Amendment considerations. Would any of these cases, in your view, have reached a different result if the courts had concentrated on limiting doctrines intrinsic to trademark law rather than relying on the First Amendment? Now recall the cases in which courts have refused to recognize any constitutional limit on trademark rights. Did those cases reflect the nuanced understanding of the "intelligently balanced terms of the trademark laws" that Judge Leval invokes?

CHAPTER 13

REMEDIES

Page 916.   Delete Question 2 and renumber Questions 3 and 4 as 2 and 3.

Page 917.   Insert the following case excerpt after the Questions:

The *Nova Wines, Inc.* decision states that a finding of likely confusion ordinarily leads to a presumption of irreparable harm. Some courts have questioned routine application of this presumption in the wake of the Supreme Court's decision in *eBay Inc. v. MercExchange, LLC,* 547 U.S. 388 (2006), involving a patent infringement claim. For example, the Eleventh Circuit in **North American Medical Corp. v. Axiom Worldwide, Inc.,** 522 F.3d 1211 (11th Cir. 2008), stated:

> Even though we hold that NAM and Adagen have established a substantial likelihood of success on the merits of their trademark infringement and false advertising claims, we must still evaluate whether NAM and Adagen have demonstrated, with respect to each claim, that they will suffer irreparable harm in the absence of an injunction. In reaching its conclusion that NAM and Adagen satisfied this element of the preliminary injunction test, the district court relied on two presumptions, one regarding the infringement claims and one regarding the false advertising claims. For the reasons that follow, we vacate the preliminary injunction with respect to both the trademark claims and the false advertising claims.

> . . . .

> . . . [O]ur prior cases do extend a presumption of irreparable harm once a plaintiff establishes a likelihood of success on the merits of a trademark infringement claim. Our circuit has acknowledged as much on several occasions. [citations omitted]

> Nonetheless, . . . a recent U.S. Supreme Court case calls into question whether courts may presume irreparable harm merely because a plaintiff in an intellectual property case has demonstrated a likelihood of success on the merits. *See generally eBay Inc. v. MercExchange, L.L.C.,* 547 U.S. 388, 126 S. Ct. 1837, 164 L. Ed. 2d 641 (2006). In *eBay,* the district court denied the plaintiff's motion for permanent injunctive relief. In so doing, the district court "appeared to adopt certain expansive principles suggesting that injunctive relief could not issue in a broad swath of cases." *Id.* at 393, 126 S. Ct. at 1840. On appeal, the Federal Circuit reversed the denial of injunctive relief, articulating a categorical rule that permanent injunctions shall issue once infringement is established. The Supreme Court reversed the

Federal Circuit and admonished both the district and appellate courts for applying categorical rules to the grant or denial of injunctive relief. The Court stressed that the Patent Act indicates "that injunctive relief 'may' issue only 'in accordance with the principles of equity.'" *Id.* at 393, 126 S. Ct. at 1839. Because the Court concluded "that neither court below correctly applied the traditional four-factor framework that governs the award of injunctive relief, [it] vacated the judgment of the Court of Appeals, so that the District Court may apply that framework in the first instance." *Id.* at 394, 126 S. Ct. at 1841. The Supreme Court held that while "the decision whether to grant or deny injunctive relief rests within the equitable discretion of the district courts, . . . such discretion must be exercised consistent with traditional principles of equity, in patent disputes no less than in other cases governed by such standards." *Id.*

Although *eBay* dealt with the Patent Act and with permanent injunctive relief, a strong case can be made that *eBay's* holding necessarily extends to the grant of preliminary injunctions under the Lanham Act. Similar to the Patent Act, the Lanham Act grants federal courts the "power to grant injunctions, according to the principles of equity and upon such terms as the court may deem reasonable." 15 U.S.C. § 1116(a) (2006). Furthermore, no obvious distinction exists between permanent and preliminary injunctive relief to suggest that *eBay* should not apply to the latter. Because the language of the Lanham Act—granting federal courts the power to grant injunctions "according to the principles of equity and upon such terms as the court may deem reasonable"—is so similar to the language of the Patent Act, we conclude that the Supreme Court's *eBay* case is applicable to the instant case.

However, we decline to express any further opinion with respect to the effect of *eBay* on this case. For example, we decline to decide whether the district court was correct in its holding that the nature of the trademark infringement gives rise to a presumption of irreparable injury. In other words, we decline to address whether such a presumption is the equivalent of the categorical rules rejected by the Court in *eBay* for several reasons. First, the briefing on appeal has been entirely inadequate in this regard. Second, the district court has not addressed the effect of *eBay*. Finally, the district court may well conclude on remand that it can readily reach an appropriate decision by fully applying *eBay* without the benefit of a presumption of irreparable injury, or it may well decide that the particular circumstances of the instant case bear substantial parallels to previous cases such that a presumption of irreparable injury is an appropriate exercise of its discretion in light of the historical traditions. *See eBay,* 547 U.S. at 394–97, 126 S. Ct. at 1841–43 (concurring opinions of Chief Justice Roberts and Justice Kennedy, representing the views of seven Justices). Accordingly, we also vacate the preliminary injunction as it applies to the trademark infringement claim, and remand to the district court for further proceedings not inconsistent with this opinion, and with *eBay.*

On remand, is the district court free to apply a presumption of irreparable harm based on a finding of a likelihood of confusion?

B.   MONETARY RELIEF

Page 943.   Add Question 5 as follows:

5.   Section 1117(a) provides that in "assessing profits the plaintiff shall be required to prove defendant's sales only; defendant must prove all elements of cost or deduction claimed." Is it legitimate for a plaintiff to prove a defendant's gross sales of all products via defendant's tax returns or does a plaintiff need to prove gross sales of the infringing items? *See Venture Tape Corp. v. McGills Glass Warehouse*, 540 F.3d 56 (1st Cir. 2008), *cert. denied*, 129 S.Ct. 1622 (2009).

C.   TRADEMARK COUNTERFEITING

Page 971.   Insert the following Question before *Torkington*:
QUESTION

In order to be considered counterfeit, a mark must be identical or "substantially indistinguishable" from the registered mark. Under this standard, would COLDATE for toothpaste be a counterfeit of COLGATE for toothpaste? *See Colgate–Palmolive Co. v. J.M.D. All–Star Import and Export Inc.*, 486 F.Supp.2d 286 (S.D.N.Y. 2007).

Page 981.   Insert additional Question 3.

3.   The *El Greco* decision cited in *Hunting World* found that, although originally ordered by the plaintiff, the shoes sold by the defendant were not "genuine" because they had not been inspected by plaintiff and thus did not satisfy plaintiff's quality control procedures. If a manufacturer sells its health supplement only to health care providers and approved retailers who agree not to sell the products over the internet or to the general public except through licensed pharmacies and health clinics, would the product be considered "genuine" if a doctor acquired the supplement from third parties and sold it over the internet without any consultation? *See Standard Process, Inc. v. Dr. Banks*, 554 F.Supp.2d 866 (E.D.Wis.2008).

Page 984.   Insert following case excerpt and Question after *Chanel*:

Lorillard Tobacco Co., Inc. v. A & E Oil, Inc.

503 F.3d 588 (7th Cir. 2007).

■ MANION, CIRCUIT J.

[After finding that the defendants were selling counterfeit cigarettes, the Court addressed the question whether the defendants had knowledge that the cigarettes were counterfeit as a matter of law and thus were liable for attorney's fees absent extenuating circumstances.]

... To prove knowledge of the counterfeiting, Lorillard was not required to prove the defendants' actual knowledge; knowledge includes a willful blindness or a failure to investigate because one "was afraid of what the inquiry would yield." *Louis Vuitton v. Lee*, 875 F.2d 584, 590 (7th Cir. 1989). If willful blindness occurs, an award of attorneys' fees is required by the statutory language absent extenuating circumstances. 15 U.S.C. § 1117(b) ("the court shall ... enter judgment ... with a reasonable attorney's fee."); *see also Hard Rock Cafe Licensing v. Concession Servs., Inc.*, 955 F.2d 1143, 1151 ("Willful blindness is sufficient to trigger the mandatory provisions of subsection b." (citing *Lee*, 875 F.2d at 590)).

... After thoroughly reviewing the record, we find that the evidence demonstrates that the defendants acted with knowledge or willful blindness. Notably, the defendants do not contest on appeal the counterfeit nature of the cigarettes recovered from the station. *See* Def.-App. Br. at 8 ("Lorillard seized nine counterfeit Newport cigarette[ ] [packs] from the A & E mini-mart.... Each of the nine packets apparently bore fake tax-stamps."). Furthermore, the tax stamps on the counterfeit cigarettes were noticeably fraudulent. *Cf. Lee*, 875 F.2d at 590 (finding willfulness when shop owner failed to consider that "expensive brand-name goods [are] unlikely to display ... poor workmanship, to be lined with purple vinyl, and to be sold by itinerant peddlers at bargain-basement prices."). Kuruvilla.... [w]hile stocking the cigarettes, ... checks for the tax stamps and examines each pack "every time," explaining that "before I put them in the counter, I—when I open up a carton, I do" check. Yet somehow he "never noticed" any discrepancies in the counterfeit tax stamps, notwithstanding the obviousness of the counterfeit. Later, however, in an affidavit submitted in opposition to the summary judgment motion, Kuruvilla denies checking tax stamps "most of the time," thus contradicting his deposition testimony. A defendant, however, cannot create " 'sham' issues of fact with affidavits that contradict their prior depositions." *Ineichen v. Ameritech*, 410 F.3d 956, 963 (7th Cir. 2005) (internal quotation and citation omitted). Kuruvilla's attempt to create such a sham issue negates his feigned ignorance.

The record contains other contradictory evidence. For example, when Kuruvilla spoke with his brother, Kurian, about the seizure of the three packs of cigarettes, Kurian told Kuruvilla about the source of two of the packs. Specifically, one pack came from a customer returning a pack of bad-tasting cigarettes, and a second pack from Kurian testing a pack from the stock that likewise tasted "terrible." Kuruvilla, however, contradicted his brother and testified subsequently in a deposition that the cigarette packs belonged to Kurian personally. Kuruvilla attempted to retract his damaging deposition testimony by stating in the affidavit submitted in opposition to the summary judgment motion that "[t]he three open packs of cigarettes

... were stale cigarettes returned by customers." Again, this statement merely creates a sham issue of fact, since the defendants do not contest on appeal that the seized cigarettes were counterfeits, not just stale.

    . . .

There is simply no evidence in the record to support defendants' claims of an innocent source for the counterfeit cigarettes. Furthermore, the defendants fail to present any evidence to counter Lorillard's evidence that the counterfeit cigarettes came from U.S.A. Cigarettes, a supplier connected to counterfeit cigarettes. Although the defendants denied in depositions ever purchasing cigarettes from U.S.A. Cigarettes, they admit that they could have done so. In fact, they acknowledge that they did purchase other products from this company whose name makes it an obvious source for cigarettes. One check written by A & E to U.S.A. Cigarettes bears the endorsement of Amin Arba, an alias for Amin Umar, who ... is a known source for counterfeit cigarettes. Umar would drive a green van around to various gas stations selling counterfeit cigarettes ... and, it can be reasonably inferred, receiving checks made out to U.S.A. Cigarettes. Many other checks to U.S.A. Cigarettes from other retailers also bear Umar's endorsement. In other related investigations and lawsuits, Lorillard has linked Umar specifically to sales of Newport counterfeit cigarettes. Joseph, the co-owner of A & E, also does business with U.S.A. Cigarettes at his other gas stations and, although Joseph denies ever speaking to Umar, Umar's telephone records indicate that he placed a call to Joseph's telephone number once. Finally, A & E's conduct during discovery suggests that it knew about the counterfeit cigarettes. Notably, A & E did not produce the checks written to U.S.A. Cigarettes until July 2004, after A & E had inaccurately represented to the district court that Lorillard already possessed "all business records in Defendant's possession." The district court found that "the individual Defendants in this case were less than forthcoming with Lorillard at the discovery stage of the litigation ... stalled ... and only cooperated after they were held in default."

    . . .

When reviewing an appeal from summary judgment, we recognize that, in determining whether a defendant acted with willful blindness to counterfeit products, "[a]s a general rule, a party's state of mind (such as knowledge or intent) is a question of fact for the factfinder, to be determined after trial." *Chanel, Inc. v. Italian Activewear of Florida, Inc.*, 931 F.2d 1472, 1476 (11th Cir. 1991) [citations omitted] However, "we are not constrained to accept denials supported by a mere scintilla of evidence. Such bare denials—for example, where the defendant's alleged ignorance amounts to willful blindness, or where the owner's claims of ignorance are 'inconsistent with the uncontested facts'—are insufficient to create a genuine triable issue ." *United States v. 16328 S. 43rd E. Ave., Bixby, Tulsa County, Okla.*, 275 F.3d 1281, 1285 (10th Cir. 2002) (affirming grant of summary judgment to United States in a forfeiture case based on legal conclusion that facts showed the defendant knew of and consented to criminal activities on property).

Similarly, in this case defendants must do more than baldly deny the reasonable inferences and facts presented by Lorillard to avoid the conclusion that they knowingly sold counterfeit cigarettes. [citation omitted] Yet we reiterate that defendants offer no plausible explanation for the presence of the counterfeit cigarettes, the failure to notice the tax stamps when checked, implausible denials of knowledge of known counterfeit trafficker Umar and U.S.A. Cigarettes, and questionable discovery practices. As we have noted in the summary judgment context, "neither presenting a scintilla of evidence, . . . nor the mere existence of some alleged factual dispute between the parties or some metaphysical doubt as to the material facts, is sufficient to oppose a motion for summary judgment. . . . The party must supply evidence sufficient to allow a jury to render a verdict in his favor." *Van Diest Supply Co. v. Shelby County State Bank*, 425 F.3d 437, 439 (7th Cir. 2005) (internal quotation and citation omitted). The defendants have failed to do so. Accordingly, the district court did not err as a matter of law in determining that defendants knowingly sold counterfeit cigarettes and, therefore, the mandatory award for attorneys' fees under 15 U.S.C. § 1117(b) applied.

QUESTION

Both the *Chanel* and *Lorillard* decisions involved summary judgment motions but came out differently on willful blindness. Are they consistent?

Page 985.   Add Question 3:

3.   What factors should a court consider in awarding statutory damages in lieu of actual damages in a case of counterfeiting? Is knowledge or "willful blindness" about the counterfeit nature required? *See Diane Von Furstenberg Studio v. Snyder*, 2007 WL 3143690 (E.D. Va. 2007).

D.   BORDER CONTROL MEASURES

Page 1002.   Number the Question as 1 and insert additional Question 2 as follows:

2.   Would differences in the warranties offered for gray market auto parts sold to auto dealers be a "material" difference so as to make such goods infringing? Does it matter that the auto dealers are aware of the warranty differences? Should post-sale confusion of the dealers' customers be considered in determining materiality? *See Kia Motors America, Inc. v. Autoworks Distributing*, 90 U.S.P.Q.2d 1598 (D. Minn. 2009).

APPENDIX A

Lanham Trademark Act of 1946, as Amended and Codified in Chapter 22 of Title 15 of the United States Code

NOTE: The headings used for sections and subsections or paragraphs in the following reprint of the Act are not part of the Act but have been added for convenience. Prior trademark statutes may be found in Title 15, Chapter 3, of the U.S. Code and in the Statutes at Large. The present Act forms Chapter 22 of Title 15 of the U.S. Code. Lanham Act section numbers appear at the beginning of each section, followed by the U.S. Code cite in parentheses.

CHAPTER 22—TRADEMARKS

SUBCHAPTER I—THE PRINCIPAL REGISTER

SUBCHAPTER IV—THE MADRID PROTOCOL

SUBCHAPTER I—THE PRINCIPAL REGISTER

§ 1   (15 U.S.C. § 1051). Application for registration; verification

(a) Application for use of trademark

(1) The owner of a trademark used in commerce may request registration of its trademark on the principal register hereby established by paying the prescribed fee and filing in the Patent and Trademark Office an application and a verified statement, in such form as may be prescribed by the Director, and such number of specimens or facsimiles of the mark as used as may be required by the Director.

(2) The application shall include specification of the applicant's domicile and citizenship, the date of the applicant's first use of the mark, the date of the applicant's first use of the mark in commerce, the goods in connection with which the mark is used, and a drawing of the mark.

(3) The statement shall be verified by the applicant and specify that—

(A) the person making the verification believes that he or she, or the juristic person in whose behalf he or she makes the verification, to be the owner of the mark sought to be registered;

(B) to the best of the verifier's knowledge and belief, the facts recited in the application are accurate;

(C) the mark is in use in commerce; and

(D) to the best of the verifier's knowledge and belief, no other person has the right to use such mark in commerce either in the identical form thereof or in such near resemblance thereto as to be likely, when used on or in connection with the goods of such other person, to cause confusion, or to cause mistake, or to deceive, except that, in the case of every application claiming concurrent use, the applicant shall—

(i) state exceptions to the claim of exclusive use; and

(ii) shall 1 specify, to the extent of the verifier's knowledge—

(I) any concurrent use by others;

(II) the goods on or in connection with which and the areas in which each concurrent use exists;

(III) the periods of each use; and

(IV) the goods and area for which the applicant desires registration.

(4) The applicant shall comply with such rules or regulations as may be prescribed by the Director. The Director shall promulgate rules prescribing the requirements for the application and for obtaining a filing date herein.

(b) Application for bona fide intention to use trademark

(1) A person who has a bona fide intention, under circumstances showing the good faith of such person, to use a trademark in commerce may request registration of its trademark on the principal register hereby established by paying the prescribed fee and filing in the Patent and Trademark Office an application and a verified statement, in such form as may be prescribed by the Director.

(2) The application shall include specification of the applicant's domicile and citizenship, the goods in connection with which the applicant has a bona fide intention to use the mark, and a drawing of the mark.

(3) The statement shall be verified by the applicant and specify—

(A) that the person making the verification believes that he or she, or the juristic person in whose behalf he or she makes the verification, to be entitled to use the mark in commerce;

(B) the applicant's bona fide intention to use the mark in commerce;

(C) that, to the best of the verifier's knowledge and belief, the facts recited in the application are accurate; and

(D) that, to the best of the verifier's knowledge and belief, no other person has the right to use such mark in commerce either in the identical form thereof or in such near resemblance thereto as to be likely, when used on or in connection with the goods of such other person, to cause confusion, or to cause mistake, or to deceive. Except for applications filed pursuant to section 1126 of this title, no mark shall be registered until the applicant has met the requirements of subsections (c) and (d) of this section.

(4) The applicant shall comply with such rules or regulations as may be prescribed by the Director. The Director shall promulgate rules prescribing the requirements for the application and for obtaining a filing date herein.

(c) Amendment of application under subsection (b) to conform to requirements of subsection (a)

At any time during examination of an application filed under subsection (b) of this section, an applicant who has made use of the mark in commerce may claim the benefits of such use for purposes of this chapter, by amending his or her application to bring it into conformity with the requirements of subsection (a) of this section.

(d) Verified statement that trademark is used in commerce

(1) Within six months after the date on which the notice of allowance with respect to a mark is issued under section 1063(b)(2) of this title to an applicant under subsection (b) of this section, the applicant shall file in the Patent and Trademark Office, together with such number of specimens or facsimiles of the mark as used in commerce as may be required by the Director and payment of the prescribed fee, a verified statement that the mark is in use in commerce and specifying the date of the applicant's first use of the mark in commerce and those goods or services specified in the notice of allowance on or in connection with which the mark is used in commerce. Subject to examination and acceptance of the statement of use, the mark shall be registered in the Patent and Trademark Office, a certificate of registration shall be issued for those goods or services recited in the statement of use for which the mark is entitled to registration, and notice of registration shall be published in the Official Gazette of the Patent and Trademark Office. Such examination may include an examination of the factors set forth in subsections (a) through (e) of section 1052 of this title. The notice of registration shall specify the goods or services for which the mark is registered.

(2) The Director shall extend, for one additional 6–month period, the time for filing the statement of use under paragraph (1), upon written request of the applicant before the expiration of the 6–month period provided in paragraph (1). In addition to an extension under the preceding sentence, the Director may, upon a showing of good cause by the applicant, further extend the time for filing the statement of use under paragraph (1) for periods aggregating not more than 24 months, pursuant to written request of the applicant made before the expiration of the last extension granted under this paragraph. Any request for an extension under this paragraph shall be accompanied by a verified statement that the applicant has a continued bona fide intention to use the mark in commerce and specifying those goods or services identified in the notice of allowance on or in connection with which the applicant has a continued bona fide intention to use the mark in commerce. Any request for an extension under this paragraph

shall be accompanied by payment of the prescribed fee. The Director shall issue regulations setting forth guidelines for determining what constitutes good cause for purposes of this paragraph.

(3) The Director shall notify any applicant who files a statement of use of the acceptance or refusal thereof and, if the statement of use is refused, the reasons for the refusal. An applicant may amend the statement of use.

(4) The failure to timely file a verified statement of use under paragraph (1) or an extension request under paragraph (2) shall result in abandonment of the application, unless it can be shown to the satisfaction of the Director that the delay in responding was unintentional, in which case the time for filing may be extended, but for a period not to exceed the period specified in paragraphs (1) and (2) for filing a statement of use.

(e) Designation of resident for service of process and notices

If the applicant is not domiciled in the United States the applicant may designate, by a document filed in the United States Patent and Trademark Office, the name and address of a person resident in the United States on whom may be served notices or process in proceedings affecting the mark. Such notices or process may be served upon the person so designated by leaving with that person or mailing to that person a copy thereof at the address specified in the last designation so filed. If the person so designated cannot be found at the address given in the last designation, or if the registrant does not designate by a document filed in the United States Patent and Trademark Office the name and address of a person resident in the United States on whom may be served notices or process in proceedings affecting the mark, such notices or process may be served on the Director.

§ 2 (15 U.S.C. § 1052). Trademarks registrable on principal register; concurrent registration

No trademark by which the goods of the applicant may be distinguished from the goods of others shall be refused registration on the principal register on account of its nature unless it—

(a) Consists of or comprises immoral, deceptive, or scandalous matter; or matter which may disparage or falsely suggest a connection with persons, living or dead, institutions, beliefs, or national symbols, or bring them into contempt, or disrepute; or a geographical indication which, when used on or in connection with wines or spirits, identifies a place other than the origin of the goods and is first used on or in connection with wines or spirits by the applicant on or after one year after the date on which the WTO Agreement (as defined in section 3501(9) of title 19) enters into force with respect to the United States.

(b) Consists of or comprises the flag or coat of arms or other insignia of the United States, or of any State or municipality, or of any foreign nation, or any simulation thereof.

(c) Consists of or comprises a name, portrait, or signature identifying a particular living individual except by his written consent, or the name, signature, or portrait of a deceased President of the United States during the life of his widow, if any, except by the written consent of the widow.

(d) Consists of or comprises a mark which so resembles a mark registered in the Patent and Trademark Office, or a mark or trade name previously used in the United States by another and not abandoned, as to be likely, when used on or in connection with the goods of the applicant, to cause confusion, or to cause mistake, or to deceive: *Provided*, That if the Director determines that confusion, mistake, or deception is not likely to result from the continued use by more than one person of the same or similar marks under conditions and limitations as to the mode or place of use of the marks or the goods on or in connection with which such marks are used, concurrent registrations may be issued to such persons when they have become entitled to use such marks as a result of their concurrent lawful use in commerce prior to (1) the earliest of the filing dates of the applications pending or of any registration issued under this chapter; (2) July 5, 1947, in the case of registrations previously issued under the Act of March 3, 1881, or February 20, 1905, and continuing in full force and effect on that date; or (3) July 5, 1947, in the case of applications filed under the Act of February 20, 1905, and registered after July 5, 1947. Use prior to the filing date of any pending application or a registration shall not be required when the owner of such application or registration consents to the grant of a concurrent registration to the applicant. Concurrent registrations may also be issued by the Director when a court of competent jurisdiction has finally determined that more than one person is entitled to use the same or similar marks in commerce. In issuing concurrent registrations, the Director shall prescribe conditions and limitations as to the mode or place of use of the mark or the goods on or in connection with which such mark is registered to the respective persons.

(e) Consists of a mark which (1) when used on or in connection with the goods of the applicant is merely descriptive or deceptively misdescriptive of them, (2) when used on or in connection with the goods of the applicant is primarily geographically descriptive of them, except as indications of regional origin may be registrable under section 1054 of this title, (3) when used on or in connection with the goods of the applicant is primarily geographically deceptively misdescriptive of them, (4) is primarily merely a surname, or (5) comprises any matter that, as a whole, is functional.

(f) Except as expressly excluded in subsections (a), (b), (c), (d), (e)(3), and (e)(5) of this section, nothing in this chapter shall prevent the registration of a mark used by the applicant which has become distinctive of the applicant's goods in commerce. The Director may accept as prima facie evidence that the mark has become distinctive, as used on or in connection with the applicant's goods in commerce, proof of substantially exclusive and continuous use thereof as a mark by the applicant in commerce for the five years before the date on which the claim of distinctiveness is made. Nothing in this section shall prevent the registration of a mark which, when used on or in connection with the goods of the applicant, is primarily geographically deceptively misdescriptive of them, and which became distinctive of the applicant's goods in commerce before December 8, 1993.

A mark which would be likely to cause dilution by blurring or dilution by tarnishment under section 1125(c) [§ 43(c)] of this title, may be refused registration only pursuant to a proceeding brought under section 1063 [§ 13] of this title. A registration for a mark which would be likely to cause dilution by blurring or dilution by tarnishment under section 1125(c) of this title, may be canceled pursuant to a proceeding brought under either section 1064 [§ 14] of this title or section 1092 [§ 19] of this title.

§ 3 (15 U.S.C. § 1053). Service marks registrable

Subject to the provisions relating to the registration of trademarks, so far as they are applicable, service marks shall be registrable, in the same manner and with the same effect as are trademarks, and when registered they shall be entitled to the protection provided in this chapter in the case of trademarks. Applications and procedure under this section shall conform as nearly as practicable to those prescribed for the registration of trademarks.

§ 4 (15 U.S.C. § 1054). Collective marks and certification marks registrable

Subject to the provisions relating to the registration of trademarks, so far as they are applicable, collective and certification marks, including indications of regional origin, shall be registrable under this chapter, in the same manner and with the same effect as are trademarks, by persons, and nations, States, municipalities, and the like, exercising legitimate control over the use of the marks sought to be registered, even though not possessing an industrial or commercial establishment, and when registered they shall be entitled to the protection provided in this chapter in the case of trademarks, except in the case of certification marks when used so as to represent falsely that the owner or a user thereof makes or sells the goods or performs the services on or in connection with which such mark is used. Applications and procedure under this section shall conform as nearly as practicable to those prescribed for the registration of trademarks.

§ 5 (15 U.S.C. § 1055). Use by related companies affecting validity and registration

Where a registered mark or a mark sought to be registered is or may be used legitimately by related companies, such use shall inure to the benefit of the registrant or applicant for registration, and such use shall not affect the validity of such mark or of its registration, provided such mark is not used in such manner as to deceive the public. If first use of a mark by a person is controlled by the registrant or applicant for registration of the mark with respect to the nature and quality of the goods or services, such first use shall inure to the benefit of the registrant or applicant, as the case may be.

§ 6 (15 U.S.C. § 1056). Disclaimer of unregistrable matter

(a) Compulsory and voluntary disclaimers

The Director may require the applicant to disclaim an unregistrable component of a mark otherwise registrable. An applicant may voluntarily disclaim a component of a mark sought to be registered.

(b) Prejudice of rights

No disclaimer, including those made under subsection (e) of section 1057 of this title, shall prejudice or affect the applicant's or registrant's rights then existing or thereafter arising in the disclaimed matter, or his right of registration on another application if the disclaimed matter be or shall have become distinctive of his goods or services.

§ 7 (15 U.S.C. § 1057). Certificates of registration

(a) Issuance and form

Certificates of registration of marks registered upon the principal register shall be issued in the name of the United States of America, under the seal of the Patent and Trademark Office, and shall be signed by the Director or have his signature placed thereon, and a record thereof shall be kept in the Patent and Trademark Office. The registration shall reproduce the mark, and state that the mark is registered on the principal register under this chapter, the date of the first use of the mark, the date of the first use of the mark in commerce, the particular goods or services for which it is registered, the number and date of the registration, the term thereof, the date on which the application for registration was received in the Patent and Trademark Office, and any conditions and limitations that may be imposed in the registration.

(b) Certificate as prima facie evidence

A certificate of registration of a mark upon the principal register provided by this chapter shall be prima facie evidence of the validity of the registered mark and of the registration of the mark, of the registrant's ownership of the mark, and of the registrant's exclusive right to use the registered mark in commerce on or in connection with the goods or services specified in the certificate, subject to any conditions or limitations stated in the certificate.

(c) Application to register mark considered constructive use

Contingent on the registration of a mark on the principal register provided by this chapter, the filing of the application to register such mark shall constitute constructive use of the mark, conferring a right of priority, nationwide in effect, on or in connection with the goods or services specified in the registration against any other person except for a person whose mark has not been abandoned and who, prior to such filing—

(1) has used the mark;

(2) has filed an application to register the mark which is pending or has resulted in registration of the mark; or

(3) has filed a foreign application to register the mark on the basis of which he or she has acquired a right of priority, and timely files an application under section 1126(d) of this title to register the mark which is pending or has resulted in registration of the mark.

(d) Issuance to assignee

A certificate of registration of a mark may be issued to the assignee of the applicant, but the assignment must first be recorded in the Patent and Trademark Office. In case of change of ownership the Director shall, at the request of the owner and upon a proper showing and the payment of the prescribed fee, issue to such assignee a new certificate of registration of the said mark in the name of such assignee, and for the unexpired part of the original period.

(e) Surrender, cancellation, or amendment by registrant

Upon application of the registrant the Director may permit any registration to be surrendered for cancellation, and upon cancellation appropriate entry shall be made in the records of the Patent and Trademark Office. Upon application of the registrant and payment of the prescribed fee, the Director for good cause may permit any registration to be amended or to be disclaimed in part: *Provided*, That the amendment or disclaimer does not alter materially the character of the mark. Appropriate entry shall be made in the records of the Patent and Trademark Office and upon the certificate of registration or, if said certificate is lost or destroyed, upon a certified copy thereof.

(f) Copies of Patent and Trademark Office records as evidence

Copies of any records, books, papers, or drawings belonging to the Patent and Trademark Office relating to marks, and copies of registrations, when authenticated by the seal of the

Patent and Trademark Office and certified by the Director, or in his name by an employee of the Office duly designated by the Director, shall be evidence in all cases wherein the originals would be evidence; and any person making application therefor and paying the prescribed fee shall have such copies.

(g) Correction of Patent and Trademark Office mistake

Whenever a material mistake in a registration, incurred through the fault of the Patent and Trademark Office, is clearly disclosed by the records of the Office a certificate stating the fact and nature of such mistake, shall be issued without charge and recorded and a printed copy thereof shall be attached to each printed copy of the registration certificate and such corrected registration shall thereafter have the same effect as if the same had been originally issued in such corrected form, or in the discretion of the Director a new certificate of registration may be issued without charge. All certificates of correction heretofore issued in accordance with the rules of the Patent and Trademark Office and the registrations to which they are attached shall have the same force and effect as if such certificates and their issue had been specifically authorized by statute.

(h) Correction of applicant's mistake

Whenever a mistake has been made in a registration and a showing has been made that such mistake occurred in good faith through the fault of the applicant, the Director is authorized to issue a certificate of correction or, in his discretion, a new certificate upon the payment of the prescribed fee: *Provided*, That the correction does not involve such changes in the registration as to require republication of the mark.

§ 8 (15 U.S.C. § 1058). Duration

(a) In general

Each registration shall remain in force for 10 years, except that the registration of any mark shall be canceled by the Director for failure to comply with the provisions of subsection (b) of this section, upon the expiration of the following time periods, as applicable:

(1) For registrations issued pursuant to the provisions of this chapter, at the end of 6 years following the date of registration.

(2) For registrations published under the provisions of section 1062(c) [§ 12] of this title, at the end of 6 years following the date of publication under such section.

(3) For all registrations, at the end of each successive 10–year period following the date of registration.

(b) Affidavit of continuing use

During the 1–year period immediately preceding the end of the applicable time period set forth in subsection (a) of this section, the owner of the registration shall pay the prescribed fee and file in the Patent and Trademark Office—

(1) an affidavit setting forth those goods or services recited in the registration on or in connection with which the mark is in use in commerce and such number of specimens or facsimiles showing current use of the mark as may be required by the Director; or

(2) an affidavit setting forth those goods or services recited in the registration on or in connection with which the mark is not in use in commerce and showing that any such nonuse is due to special circumstances which excuse such nonuse and is not due to any intention to abandon the mark.

(c) Grace period for submissions; deficiency

(1) The owner of the registration may make the submissions required under this section within a grace period of 6 months after the end of the applicable time period set forth in subsection (a) of this section. Such submission is required to be accompanied by a surcharge prescribed by the Director.

(2) If any submission filed under this section is deficient, the deficiency may be corrected after the statutory time period and within the time prescribed after notification of the deficiency. Such submission is required to be accompanied by a surcharge prescribed by the Director.

(d) Notice of affidavit requirement

Special notice of the requirement for affidavits under this section shall be attached to each certificate of registration and notice of publication under section 1062(c) [§ 12(c)] of this title.

(e) Notification of acceptance or refusal of affidavits

The Director shall notify any owner who files of the affidavits required by this section of the Commissioner's* acceptance or refusal thereof and, in the case of a refusal, the reasons therefor.

(f) Designation of resident for service of process and notices

If the registrant is not domiciled in the United States, the registrant may designate, by a document filed in the United States Patent and Trademark Office, the name and address of a person resident in the United States on whom may be served notices or process in proceedings affecting the mark. Such notices or process may be served upon the person so designated by leaving with that person or mailing to that person a copy thereof at the address specified in the last designation so filed. If the person so designated cannot be found at the address given in the last designation, or if the registrant does not designate by a document filed in the United States Patent and Trademark Office the name and address of a person resident in the United States on whom may be served notices or process in proceedings affecting the mark, such notices or process may be served on the Director.

§ 9 (15 U.S.C. § 1059). Renewal of registration

(a) Period of renewal; time for renewal

Subject to the provisions of section 1058 of this title, each registration may be renewed for periods of 10 years at the end of each successive 10–year period following the date of registration upon payment of the prescribed fee

---

* [Editors' note: "Commissioner's" should be "Director's." As originally enacted, the Lanham Act vested authority over trademark registration in the Commissioner of Patents. In 1999, Congress enacted the Patent and Trademark Office Efficiency Act, Pub. L. 106–113, 113 Stat. 1501A–572, which created the position of "Undersecretary of Commerce for Intellectual Property and Director of the United States Patent and Trademark Office." The law also substituted the word "Director" for "Commissioner" wherever it appeared in the Lanham Act.]

and the filing of a written application, in such form as may be prescribed by the Director. Such application may be made at any time within 1 year before the end of each successive 10–year period for which the registration was issued or renewed, or it may be made within a grace period of 6 months after the end of each successive 10–year period, upon payment of a fee and surcharge prescribed therefor. If any application filed under this section is deficient, the deficiency may be corrected within the time prescribed after notification of the deficiency, upon payment of a surcharge prescribed therefor.

(b) Notification of refusal of renewal

If the Director refuses to renew the registration, the Director shall notify the registrant of the Commissioner's** refusal and the reasons therefor.

(c) Designation of resident for service of process and notices

If the registrant is not domiciled in the United States the registrant may designate, by a document filed in the United States Patent and Trademark Office, the name and address of a person resident in the United States on whom may be served notices or process in proceedings affecting the mark. Such notices or process may be served upon the person so designated by leaving with that person or mailing to that person a copy thereof at the address specified in the last designation so filed. If the person so designated cannot be found at the address given in the last designation, or if the registrant does not designate by a document filed in the United States Patent and Trademark Office the name and address of a person resident in the United States on whom may be served notices or process in proceedings affecting the mark, such notices or process may be served on the Director.

§ 10 (15 U.S.C. § 1060). Assignment

(a)(1) A registered mark or a mark for which an application to register has been filed shall be assignable with the good will of the business in which the mark is used, or with that part of the good will of the business connected with the use of and symbolized by the mark. Notwithstanding the preceding sentence, no application to register a mark under section 1051(b) of this title shall be assignable prior to the filing of an amendment under section 1051(c) of this title to bring the application into conformity with section 1051(a) of this title or the filing of the verified statement of use under section 1051(d) of this title, except for an assignment to a successor to the business of the applicant, or portion thereof, to which the mark pertains, if that business is ongoing and existing.

(2) In any assignment authorized by this section, it shall not be necessary to include the good will of the business connected with the use of and symbolized by any other mark used in the business or by the name or style under which the business is conducted.

** [Editors' note: "Commissioner's" should be "Director's." See *supra* note *.]

(3) Assignments shall be by instruments in writing duly executed. Acknowledgment shall be prima facie evidence of the execution of an assignment, and when the prescribed information reporting the assignment is recorded in the United States Patent and Trademark Office, the record shall be prima facie evidence of execution.

(4) An assignment shall be void against any subsequent purchaser for valuable consideration without notice, unless the prescribed information reporting the assignment is recorded in the United States Patent and Trademark Office within 3 months after the date of the assignment or prior to the subsequent purchase.

(5) The United States Patent and Trademark Office shall maintain a record of information on assignments, in such form as may be prescribed by the Director.

(b) An assignee not domiciled in the United States may designate by a document filed in the United States Patent and Trademark Office the name and address of a person resident in the United States on whom may be served notices or process in proceedings affecting the mark. Such notices or process may be served upon the person so designated by leaving with that person or mailing to that person a copy thereof at the address specified in the last designation so filed. If the person so designated cannot be found at the address given in the last designation, or if the assignee does not designate by a document filed in the United States Patent and Trademark Office the name and address of a person resident in the United States on whom may be served notices or process in proceedings affecting the mark, such notices or process may be served upon the Director.

§ 11   (15 U.S.C. § 1061). Execution of acknowledgments and verifications

Acknowledgments and verifications required under this chapter may be made before any person within the United States authorized by law to administer oaths, or, when made in a foreign country, before any diplomatic or consular officer of the United States or before any official authorized to administer oaths in the foreign country concerned whose authority is proved by a certificate of a diplomatic or consular officer of the United States, or apostille of an official designated by a foreign country which, by treaty or convention, accords like effect to apostilles of designated officials in the United States, and shall be valid if they comply with the laws of the state or country where made.

§ 12   (15 U.S.C. § 1062). Publication

(a) Examination and publication

Upon the filing of an application for registration and payment of the prescribed fee, the Director shall refer the application to the examiner in charge of the registration of marks, who shall cause an examination to be made and, if on such examination it shall appear that the applicant is entitled to registration, or would be entitled to registration upon the acceptance of the statement of use required by section 1051(d) of this title, the Director shall cause the mark to be published in the Official Gazette of the Patent and Trademark Office: *Provided*, That in the case of an applicant claiming concurrent use, or in the case of an application to be placed in an interference as provided for in section 1066 of this title the mark, if otherwise registrable, may be published subject to the determination of the rights of the parties to such proceedings.

(b) Refusal of registration; amendment of application; abandonment

If the applicant is found not entitled to registration, the examiner shall advise the applicant thereof and of the reasons therefor. The applicant shall have a period of six months in which to reply or amend his application, which shall then be reexamined. This procedure may be repeated until (1) the examiner finally refuses registration of the mark or (2) the applicant fails for a period of six months to reply or amend or appeal, whereupon the application shall be deemed to have been abandoned, unless it can be shown to the satisfaction of the Director that the delay in responding was unintentional, whereupon such time may be extended.

(c) Republication of marks registered under prior acts

A registrant of a mark registered under the provisions of the Act of March 3, 1881, or the Act of February 20, 1905, may, at any time prior to the expiration of the registration thereof, upon the payment of the prescribed fee file with the Director an affidavit setting forth those goods stated in the registration on which said mark is in use in commerce and that the registrant claims the benefits of this chapter for said mark. The Director shall publish notice thereof with a reproduction of said mark in the Official Gazette, and notify the registrant of such publication and of the requirement for the affidavit of use or nonuse as provided for in subsection (b) of section 1058 of this title. Marks published under this subsection shall not be subject to the provisions of section 1063 of this title.

§ 13   (15 U.S.C. § 1063). Opposition to registration

(a) Any person who believes that he would be damaged by the registration of a mark upon the principal register, including the registration of any mark which would be likely to cause dilution by blurring or dilution by tarnishment under section 1125(c) [§ 43(c)] of this title, may, upon payment of the prescribed fee, file an opposition in the Patent and Trademark Office, stating the grounds therefor, within thirty days after the publication under subsection (a) of section 1062 [§ 12] of this title of the mark sought to be registered. Upon written request prior to the expiration of the thirty-day period, the time for filing opposition shall be extended for an additional thirty days, and further extensions of time for filing opposition may be granted by the Director for good cause when requested prior to the expiration of an extension. The Director shall notify the applicant of each extension of the time for filing opposition. An opposition may be amended under such conditions as may be prescribed by the Director.

(b) Unless registration is successfully opposed—

(1) a mark entitled to registration on the principal register based on an application filed under section 1051(a) [§ 1(a)] of this title or pursuant to section 1126 [§ 44] of this title shall be registered in the Patent and Trademark Office, a certificate of registration shall be issued, and notice of the registration shall be published in the Official Gazette of the Patent and Trademark Office; or

(2) a notice of allowance shall be issued to the applicant if the applicant applied for registration under section 1051(b) [§ 1(b)] of this title.

§ 14   (15 U.S.C. § 1064). Cancellation of registration

A petition to cancel a registration of a mark, stating the grounds relied upon, may, upon payment of the prescribed fee, be filed as follows by any person who believes that he is or will be damaged, including as a result of a likelihood of dilution by blurring or dilution by tarnishment under section 1125(c) [§ 43(c)] of this title, by the registration of a mark on the principal register established by this chapter, or under the Act of March 3, 1881, or the Act of February 20, 1905:

(1) Within five years from the date of the registration of the mark under this chapter.

(2) Within five years from the date of publication under section 1062(c) [§ 12(c)] of this title of a mark registered under the Act of March 3, 1881, or the Act of February 20, 1905.

(3) At any time if the registered mark becomes the generic name for the goods or services, or a portion thereof, for which it is registered, or is functional, or has been abandoned, or its registration was obtained fraudulently or contrary to the provisions of section 1054 [§ 4] of this title or of subsection (a), (b), or (c) of section 1052 [§ 2] of this title for a registration under this chapter, or contrary to similar prohibitory provisions of such prior Acts for a registration under such Acts, or if the registered mark is being used by, or with the permission of, the registrant so as to misrepresent the source of the goods or services on or in connection with which the mark is used. If the registered mark becomes the generic name for less than all of the goods or services for which it is registered, a petition to cancel the registration for only those goods or services may be filed. A registered mark shall not be deemed to be the generic name of goods or services solely because such mark is also used as a name of or to identify a unique product or service. The primary significance of the registered mark to the relevant public rather than purchaser motivation shall be the test for determining whether the registered mark has become the generic name of goods or services on or in connection with which it has been used.

(4) At any time if the mark is registered under the Act of March 3, 1881, or the Act of February 20, 1905, and has not been published under the provisions of subsection (c) of section 1062 of this title.

(5) At any time in the case of a certification mark on the ground that the registrant

(A) does not control, or is not able legitimately to exercise control over, the use of such mark, or

(B) engages in the production or marketing of any goods or services to which the certification mark is applied, or

(C) permits the use of the certification mark for purposes other than to certify, or

(D) discriminately refuses to certify or to continue to certify the goods or services of any person who maintains the standards or conditions which such mark certifies:

Provided, That the Federal Trade Commission may apply to cancel on the grounds specified in paragraphs (3) and (5) of this section any mark registered on the principal register established by this chapter, and the prescribed fee shall not be required. Nothing in paragraph (5) shall be deemed to prohibit the registrant from using its certification mark in advertising or promoting recognition of the certification program or of the goods or services meeting the certification standards of the registrant. Such uses of the certification mark shall not be grounds for cancellation under paragraph (5), so long as the registrant does not itself produce, manufacture, or sell any of the certified goods or services to which its identical certification mark is applied.

§ 15 (15 U.S.C. § 1065). Incontestability of right to use mark under certain conditions

Except on a ground for which application to cancel may be filed at any time under paragraphs (3) and (5) of section 1064 [§ 14] of this title, and except to the extent, if any, to which the use of a mark registered on the principal register infringes a valid right acquired under the law of any State or Territory by use of a mark or trade name continuing from a date prior to the date of registration under this chapter of such registered mark, the right of the registrant to use such registered mark in commerce for the goods or services on or in connection with which such registered mark has been in continuous use for five consecutive years subsequent to the date of such registration and is still in use in commerce, shall be incontestable: *Provided*, That—

(1) there has been no final decision adverse to registrant's claim of ownership of such mark for such goods or services, or to registrant's right to register the same or to keep the same on the register; and

(2) there is no proceeding involving said rights pending in the Patent and Trademark Office or in a court and not finally disposed of; and

(3) an affidavit is filed with the Director within one year after the expiration of any such five-year period setting forth those goods or services stated in the registration on or in connection with which such mark has been in continuous use for such five consecutive years and is

still in use in commerce, and other matters specified in paragraphs (1) and (2) of this section; and

(4) no incontestable right shall be acquired in a mark which is the generic name for the goods or services or a portion thereof, for which it is registered.

Subject to the conditions above specified in this section, the incontestable right with reference to a mark registered under this chapter shall apply to a mark registered under the Act of March 3, 1881, or the Act of February 20, 1905, upon the filing of the required affidavit with the Director within one year after the expiration of any period of five consecutive years after the date of publication of a mark under the provisions of subsection (c) of section 1062 [§ 12] of this title. The Director shall notify any registrant who files the above-prescribed affidavit of the filing thereof.

§ 16   (15 U.S.C. § 1066). Interference; declaration by Director

Upon petition showing extraordinary circumstances, the Director may declare that an interference exists when application is made for the registration of a mark which so resembles a mark previously registered by another, or for the registration of which another has previously made application, as to be likely when used on or in connection with the goods or services of the applicant to cause confusion or mistake or to deceive. No interference shall be declared between an application and the registration of a mark the right to the use of which has become incontestable.

§ 17   (15 U.S.C. § 1067). Interference, opposition, and proceedings for concurrent use registration or for cancellation; notice; Trademark Trial and Appeal Board

(a) In every case of interference, opposition to registration, application to register as a lawful concurrent user, or application to cancel the registration of a mark, the Director shall give notice to all parties and shall direct a Trademark Trial and Appeal Board to determine and decide the respective rights of registration.

(b) The Trademark Trial and Appeal Board shall include the Director, the Commissioner for Patents, the Commissioner for Trademarks, and administrative trademark judges who are appointed by the Director.

§ 18   (15 U.S.C. § 1068). Action of Director in interference, opposition, and proceedings for concurrent use registration or for cancellation

In such proceedings the Director may refuse to register the opposed mark, may cancel the registration, in whole or in part, may modify the application or registration by limiting the goods or services specified therein, may otherwise restrict or rectify with respect to the register the registration of a registered mark, may refuse to register any or all of several interfering marks, or may register the mark or marks for the person or persons entitled thereto, as the rights of the parties under this chapter may be established in the proceedings: *Provided*, That in the case of the registration of any mark based on concurrent use, the Director shall determine and fix the conditions and limitations provided for in subsection (d) of section 1052 of this title. However, no final judgment shall be entered in favor of an applicant under section 1051(b) of this title before the mark is registered, if such applicant cannot prevail without establishing constructive use pursuant to section 1057(c) of this title.

§ 19   (15 U.S.C. § 1069). Application of equitable principles in inter partes proceedings

In all inter partes proceedings equitable principles of laches, estoppel, and acquiescence, where applicable may be considered and applied.

§ 20   (15 U.S.C. § 1070). Appeals to Trademark Trial and Appeal Board from decisions of examiners

An appeal may be taken to the Trademark Trial and Appeal Board from any final decision of the examiner in charge of the registration of marks upon the payment of the prescribed fee.

§ 21   (15 U.S.C. § 1071). Appeal to courts

(a) Persons entitled to appeal; United States Court of Appeals for the Federal Circuit; waiver of civil action; election of civil action by adverse party; procedure

(1) An applicant for registration of a mark, party to an interference proceeding, party to an opposition proceeding, party to an application to register as a lawful concurrent user, party to a cancellation proceeding, a registrant who has filed an affidavit as provided in section 1058 of this title, or an applicant for renewal, who is dissatisfied with the decision of the Director or Trademark Trial and Appeal Board, may appeal to the United States Court of Appeals for the Federal Circuit thereby waiving his right to proceed under subsection (b) of this section: *Provided*, That such appeal shall be dismissed if any adverse party to the proceeding, other than the Director, shall, within twenty days after the appellant has filed notice of appeal according to paragraph (2) of this subsection, files notice with the Director that he elects to have all further proceedings conducted as provided in subsection (b) of this section. Thereupon the appellant shall have thirty days thereafter within which to file a civil action under subsection (b) of this section, in default of which the decision appealed from shall govern the further proceedings in the case.

(2) When an appeal is taken to the United States Court of Appeals for the Federal Circuit, the appellant shall file in the Patent and Trademark Office a written notice of appeal directed to the Director, within such time after the date of the decision from which the appeal is taken as the Director prescribes, but in no case less than 60 days after that date.

(3) The Director shall transmit to the United States Court of Appeals for the Federal Circuit a certified list of the documents comprising the record in the Patent and Trademark Office. The court may request that the Director forward the original or certified copies of such documents during pendency of the appeal. In an ex parte case, the Director shall submit to that court a brief explaining the grounds for the decision of the Patent and Trademark Office, addressing all the issues involved in the appeal. The court shall, before hearing an appeal, give notice of the time and place of the hearing to the Director and the parties in the appeal.

(4) The United States Court of Appeals for the Federal Circuit shall review the decision from which the appeal is taken on the record before the Patent and Trademark Office. Upon its determination the court shall issue its mandate and opinion to the Director, which shall be entered of record in the Patent and Trademark Office and shall govern the further proceedings in the case. However, no final judgment shall be entered in favor of an applicant under section 1051(b) [§ 1(b)] of this title before the mark is registered, if such applicant cannot prevail without establishing constructive use pursuant to section 1057(c) [§ 7(c)] of this title.

(b) Civil action; persons entitled to; jurisdiction of court; status of Director; procedure

(1) Whenever a person authorized by subsection (a) of this section to appeal to the United States Court of Appeals for the Federal Circuit is dissatisfied with the decision of the Director or Trademark Trial and Appeal Board, said person may, unless appeal has been taken to said United States Court of Appeals for the Federal Circuit, have remedy by a civil action if commenced within such time after such decision, not less than sixty days, as the Director appoints or as provided in subsection (a) of this section. The court may adjudge that an applicant is entitled to a registration upon the application involved, that a registration involved should be canceled, or such other matter as the issues in the proceeding require, as the facts in the case may appear. Such adjudication shall authorize the Director to take any necessary action, upon compliance with the requirements of law. However, no final judgment shall be entered in favor of an applicant under section 1051(b) [§ 1(b)] of this title before the mark is registered, if such applicant cannot prevail without establishing constructive use pursuant to section 1057(c) [§ 7(c)] of this title.

(2) The Director shall not be made a party to an inter partes proceeding under this subsection, but he shall be notified of the filing of the complaint by the clerk of the court in which it is filed and shall have the right to intervene in the action.

(3) In any case where there is no adverse party, a copy of the complaint shall be served on the Director, and, unless the court finds the expenses to be unreasonable, all the expenses of the proceeding

shall be paid by the party bringing the case, whether the final decision is in favor of such party or not. In suits brought hereunder, the record in the Patent and Trademark Office shall be admitted on motion of any party, upon such terms and conditions as to costs, expenses, and the further cross-examination of the witnesses as the court imposes, without prejudice to the right of any party to take further testimony. The testimony and exhibits of the record in the Patent and Trademark Office, when admitted, shall have the same effect as if originally taken and produced in the suit.

(4) Where there is an adverse party, such suit may be instituted against the party in interest as shown by the records of the Patent and Trademark Office at the time of the decision complained of, but any party in interest may become a party to the action. If there be adverse parties residing in a plurality of districts not embraced within the same State, or an adverse party residing in a foreign country, the United States District Court for the District of Columbia shall have jurisdiction and may issue summons against the adverse parties directed to the marshal of any district in which any adverse party resides. Summons against adverse parties residing in foreign countries may be served by publication or otherwise as the court directs.

§ 22 (15 U.S.C. § 1072). Registration as constructive notice of claim of ownership

Registration of a mark on the principal register provided by this chapter or under the Act of March 3, 1881, or the Act of February 20, 1905, shall be constructive notice of the registrant's claim of ownership thereof.

SUBCHAPTER II—THE SUPPLEMENTAL REGISTER

§ 23 (15 U.S.C. § 1091). Supplemental register

(a) Marks registerable

In addition to the principal register, the Director shall keep a continuation of the register provided in paragraph (b) of section 1 of the Act of March 19, 1920, entitled "An Act to give effect to certain provisions of the convention for the protection of trademarks and commercial names, made and signed in the city of Buenos Aires, in the Argentine Republic, August 20, 1910, and for other purposes", to be called the supplemental register. All marks capable of distinguishing applicant's goods or services and not registrable on the principal register provided in this chapter, except those declared to be unregistrable under subsections (a), (b), (c), (d), and (e)(3) of section 1052 [§ 2] of this title, which are in lawful use in commerce by the owner thereof, on or in connection with any goods or services may be registered on the supplemental register upon the payment of the prescribed fee and compliance with the provisions of subsections (a) and (e) of section 1051 [§ 1] of this title so far as they are applicable. Nothing in this section shall prevent the registration on the supplemental register of a mark, capable of distinguishing the applicant's goods or services and not registrable on the principal register under this chapter, that is declared to be unregistrable under section 1052(e)(3) [§ 2(e)(3)] of this title, if such mark has been in lawful use in commerce by the owner thereof, on or in connection with any goods or services, since before December 8, 1993.

(b) Application and proceedings for registration

Upon the filing of an application for registration on the supplemental register and payment of the prescribed fee the Director shall refer the application to the examiner in charge of the registration of marks, who shall cause an examination to be made and if on such examination it shall appear that the applicant is entitled to registration, the registration shall be granted. If the applicant is found not entitled to registration the provisions of subsection (b) of section 1062 [§ 12] of this title shall apply.

(c) Nature of mark

For the purposes of registration on the supplemental register, a mark may consist of any trademark, symbol, label, package, configuration of goods, name, word, slogan, phrase, surname, geographical name, numeral, device, any matter that as a whole is not functional, or any combination of any of the foregoing, but such mark must be capable of distinguishing the applicant's goods or services.

§ 24   (15 U.S.C. § 1092). Publication; not subject to opposition; cancellation

Marks for the supplemental register shall not be published for or be subject to opposition, but shall be published on registration in the Official Gazette of the Patent and Trademark Office. Whenever any person believes that such person is or will be damaged by the registration of a mark on the supplemental register—

(1) for which the effective filing date is after the date on which such person's mark became famous and which would be likely to cause dilution by blurring or dilution by tarnishment under section 1125(c) [§ 43(c)] of this title; or

(2) on grounds other than dilution by blurring or dilution by tarnishment, such person may at any time, upon payment of the prescribed fee and the filing of a petition stating the ground therefor, apply to the Director to cancel such registration. The Director shall refer such application to the Trademark Trial and Appeal Board which shall give notice thereof to the registrant. If it is found after a hearing before the Board that the registrant is not entitled to registration, or that the mark has been abandoned, the registration shall be canceled by the Director. However, no final judgment shall be entered in favor of an applicant under section 1051(b) [§ 1(b)] of this title before the mark is registered, if such applicant cannot prevail without establishing constructive use pursuant to section 1057(c) [§ 7(c)] of this title.

§ 25   (15 U.S.C. § 1093). Registration certificates for marks on principal and supplemental registers to be different

The certificates of registration for marks registered on the supplemental register shall be conspicuously different from certificates issued for marks registered on the principal register.

§ 26 (15 U.S.C. § 1094). Provisions of chapter applicable to registrations on supplemental register

The provisions of this chapter shall govern so far as applicable applications for registration and registrations on the supplemental register as well as those on the principal register, but applications for and registrations on the supplemental register shall not be subject to or receive the advantages of sections 1051(b), 1052(e), 1052(f), 1057(b), 1057(c), 1062(a), 1063 to 1068, inclusive, 1072, 1115 and 1124 [§§ 1(b), 2(e), 2(f), 7 (b), 7(c), 12(a), 13–18, 22, 33, 42] of this title.

§ 27 (15 U.S.C. § 1095). Registration on principal register not precluded

Registration of a mark on the supplemental register, or under the Act of March 19, 1920, shall not preclude registration by the registrant on the principal register established by this chapter. Registration of a mark on the supplemental register shall not constitute an admission that the mark has not acquired distinctiveness.

§ 28 (15 U.S.C. § 1096). Registration on supplemental register not used to stop importations

Registration on the supplemental register or under the Act of March 19, 1920, shall not be filed in the Department of the Treasury or be used to stop importations.

SUBCHAPTER III—GENERAL PROVISIONS

§ 29 (15 U.S.C. § 1111). Notice of registration; display with mark; recovery of profits and damages in infringement suit

Notwithstanding the provisions of section 1072 [§ 22] of this title, a registrant of a mark registered in the Patent and Trademark Office, may give notice that his mark is registered by displaying with the mark the words "Registered in U.S. Patent and Trademark Office" or "Reg. U.S. Pat. & Tm. Off." or the letter R enclosed within a circle, thus ®; and in any suit for infringement under this chapter by such a registrant failing to give such notice of registration, no profits and no damages shall be recovered under the provisions of this chapter unless the defendant had actual notice of the registration.

§ 30 (15 U.S.C. § 1112). Classification of goods and services; registration in plurality of classes

The Director may establish a classification of goods and services, for convenience of Patent and Trademark Office administration, but not to limit or extend the applicant's or registrant's rights. The applicant may apply to register a mark for any or all of the goods or services on or in connection with which he or she is using or has a bona fide intention to use the mark in commerce: *Provided,* That if the Director by regulation permits the filing of an application for the registration of a mark for goods or services which fall within a plurality of classes, a fee equaling the sum of the fees for filing an application in each class shall be paid, and the Director may issue a single certificate of registration for such mark.

§ 31 (15 U.S.C. § 1113). Fees

(a) Applications; services; materials

The Director shall establish fees for the filing and processing of an application for the registration of a trademark or other mark and for all other services performed by and materials furnished by the Patent and Trademark Office related to trademarks and other marks. Fees established under this subsection may be adjusted by the Director once each year to reflect, in the aggregate, any fluctuations during the preceding 12 months in the Consumer Price Index, as determined by the Secretary of Labor. Changes of less than 1 percent may be ignored. No fee established under this section shall take effect until at least 30 days after notice of the fee has been published in the Federal Register and in the Official Gazette of the Patent and Trademark Office.

(b) Waiver; Indian products

The Director may waive the payment of any fee for any service or material related to trademarks or other marks in connection with an occasional request made by a department or agency of the Government, or any officer thereof. The Indian Arts and Crafts Board will not be charged any fee to register Government trademarks of genuineness and quality for Indian products or for products of particular Indian tribes and groups.

§ 32 (15 U.S.C. § 1114). Remedies; infringement; innocent infringement by printers and publishers

(1) Any person who shall, without the consent of the registrant—

(a) use in commerce any reproduction, counterfeit, copy, or colorable imitation of a registered mark in connection with the sale, offering for sale, distribution, or advertising of any goods or services on or in connection with which such use is likely to cause confusion, or to cause mistake, or to deceive; or

(b) reproduce, counterfeit, copy, or colorably imitate a registered mark and apply such reproduction, counterfeit, copy, or colorable imitation to labels, signs, prints, packages, wrappers, receptacles or advertisements intended to be used in commerce upon or in connection with the sale, offering for sale, distribution, or advertising of goods or services on or in connection with which such use is likely to cause confusion, or to cause mistake, or to deceive,

shall be liable in a civil action by the registrant for the remedies hereinafter provided. Under subsection (b) hereof, the registrant shall not be entitled to recover profits or damages unless the acts have been committed with knowledge that such imitation is intended to be used to cause confusion, or to cause mistake, or to deceive.

As used in this paragraph, the term "any person" includes the United States, all agencies and instrumentalities thereof, and all individuals, firms, corporations, or other persons acting for the United States and with the authorization and consent of the United States, and any State, any instrumentality of a State, and any officer or employee of a State or instrumentality of a State acting in his or her official capacity. The United States, all agencies and instrumentalities thereof, and all individuals, firms, corporations, other persons acting for the United States and with the authorization and consent of the United States, and any State, and any such instrumentality, officer, or employee, shall be subject to the provisions of this chapter in the same manner and to the same extent as any nongovernmental entity.

(2) Notwithstanding any other provision of this chapter, the remedies given to the owner of a right infringed under this chapter or to a person bringing an action under section 1125 [§ 43] (a) or (d) of this title shall be limited as follows:

(A) Where an infringer or violator is engaged solely in the business of printing the mark or violating matter for others and establishes that he or she was an innocent infringer or innocent violator, the owner of the right infringed or person bringing the action under section 1125(a) of this title shall be entitled as against such infringer or violator only to an injunction against future printing.

(B) Where the infringement or violation complained of is contained in or is part of paid advertising matter in a newspaper, magazine, or other similar periodical or in an electronic communication as defined in section 2510(12) of title 18, the remedies of the owner of the right infringed or person bringing the action under section 1125(a) of this title as against the publisher or distributor of such newspaper, magazine, or other similar periodical or electronic communication shall be limited to an injunction against the presentation of such advertising matter in future issues of such newspapers, magazines, or other similar periodicals or in future transmissions of such electronic communications. The limitations of this subparagraph shall apply only to innocent infringers and innocent violators.

(C) Injunctive relief shall not be available to the owner of the right infringed or person bringing the action under section 1125(a) of this title with respect to an issue of a newspaper, magazine, or other similar periodical or an electronic communication containing infringing matter or violating matter where restraining the dissemination of such infringing matter or violating matter in any particular issue of such periodical or in an electronic communication would delay the delivery of such issue or transmission of such electronic communication after the regular time for such delivery or transmission, and such delay would be due to the method by which publication and distribution of such periodical or transmission of such electronic communication is customarily conducted in accordance with sound business practice, and not due to any method or device adopted to evade this section or to prevent or delay the issuance of an injunction or restraining order with respect to such infringing matter or violating matter.

(D)(i)(I) A domain name registrar, a domain name registry, or other domain name registration authority that takes any action described under clause (ii) affecting a domain name shall not be liable for monetary relief or, except as provided in subclause (II), for injunctive relief, to any person for such action, regardless of whether the domain name is finally determined to infringe or dilute the mark.

(II) A domain name registrar, domain name registry, or other domain name registration authority described in subclause (I) may be subject to injunctive relief only if such registrar, registry, or other registration authority has—

(aa) not expeditiously deposited with a court, in which an action has been filed regarding the disposition of the domain name, documents sufficient for the court to establish the court's control and authority regarding the disposition of the registration and use of the domain name;

(bb) transferred, suspended, or otherwise modified the domain name during the pendency of the action, except upon order of the court; or

(cc) willfully failed to comply with any such court order.

(ii) An action referred to under clause (i)(I) is any action of refusing to register, removing from registration, transferring, temporarily disabling, or permanently canceling a domain name—

(I) in compliance with a court order under section 1125(d) of this title; or

(II) in the implementation of a reasonable policy by such registrar, registry, or authority prohibiting the registration of a domain name that is identical to, confusingly similar to, or dilutive of another's mark.

(iii) A domain name registrar, a domain name registry, or other domain name registration authority shall not be liable for damages under this section for the registration or maintenance of a domain name for another absent a showing of bad faith intent to profit from such registration or maintenance of the domain name.

(iv) If a registrar, registry, or other registration authority takes an action described under clause (ii) based on a knowing and material misrepresentation by any other person that a domain name is identical to, confusingly similar to, or dilutive of a mark, the person making the knowing and material misrepresentation shall be liable for any damages, including costs and attorney's fees, incurred by the domain name registrant as a result of such action. The court may also grant injunctive relief to the domain name registrant, including the reactivation of the domain name or the transfer of the domain name to the domain name registrant.

(v) A domain name registrant whose domain name has been suspended, disabled, or transferred under a policy described under clause (ii)(II) may, upon notice to the mark owner, file a civil action to establish that the registration or use of the domain name by such registrant is not unlawful under this chapter. The court may grant injunctive relief to the domain name registrant, including the reactivation of the domain name or transfer of the domain name to the domain name registrant.

(E) As used in this paragraph—

(i) the term "violator" means a person who violates section 1125(a) [§ 43(a)] of this title; and

(ii) the term "violating matter" means matter that is the subject of a violation under section 1125(a) of this title.

(3)(A) Any person who engages in the conduct described in paragraph (11) of section 110 of title 17 and who complies with the requirements set forth in that paragraph is not liable on account of such conduct for a violation of any right under this chapter. This subparagraph does not preclude liability, nor shall it be construed to restrict the defenses or limitations on rights granted under this chapter, of a person for conduct not described in paragraph (11) of section 110 of title 17, even if that person also engages in conduct described in paragraph (11) of section 110 of such title.

(B) A manufacturer, licensee, or licensor of technology that enables the making of limited portions of audio or video content of a motion picture imperceptible as described in subparagraph (A) is not liable on account of such manufacture or license for a violation of any right under this chapter, if such manufacturer, licensee, or licensor ensures that the technology provides a clear and conspicuous notice at the beginning of each performance that the performance of the motion picture is altered from the performance intended by the director or copyright holder of the motion picture. The limitations on liability in subparagraph (A) and this subparagraph shall not apply to a manufacturer, licensee, or licensor of technology that fails to comply with this paragraph.

(C) The requirement under subparagraph (B) to provide notice shall apply only with respect to technology manufactured after the end of the 180–day period beginning on April 27, 2005.

(D) Any failure by a manufacturer, licensee, or licensor of technology to qualify for the exemption under subparagraphs (A) and (B) shall not be construed to create an inference that any such party that engages in conduct described in paragraph (11) of section 110 of title 17 is liable for trademark infringement by reason of such conduct.

§ 33 (15 U.S.C. § 1115). Registration on principal register as evidence of exclusive right to use mark; defenses

(a) Evidentiary value; defenses

Any registration issued under the Act of March 3, 1881, or the Act of February 20, 1905, or of a mark registered on the principal register provided by this chapter and owned by a party to an action shall be admissible in evidence and shall be prima facie evidence of the validity of the registered mark and of the registration of the mark, of the registrant's ownership of the mark, and of the registrant's exclusive right to use the registered mark in commerce on or in connection with the goods or services specified in the registration subject to any conditions or limitations stated therein, but shall not preclude another person from proving any legal or equitable defense or defect, including those set forth in subsection (b) of this section, which might have been asserted if such mark had not been registered.

(b) Incontestability; defenses

To the extent that the right to use the registered mark has become incontestable under

. . .

section 1065 of this title, the registration shall be conclusive evidence of the validity of the registered mark and of the registration of the mark, of the registrant's ownership of the mark, and of the registrant's exclusive right to use the registered mark in commerce. Such conclusive evidence shall relate to the exclusive right to use the mark on or in connection with the goods or services specified in the affidavit filed under the provisions of section 1065 [§ 15] of this title, or in the renewal application filed under the provisions of section 1059 [§ 9] of this title if the goods or services specified in the renewal are fewer in number, subject to any conditions or limitations in the registration or in such affidavit or renewal application. Such conclusive evidence of the right to use the registered mark shall be subject to proof of infringement as defined in section 1114 [§ 32] of this title, and shall be subject to the following defenses or defects:

> (1) That the registration or the incontestable right to use the mark was obtained fraudulently; or
>
> (2) That the mark has been abandoned by the registrant; or
>
> (3) That the registered mark is being used by or with the permission of the registrant or a person in privity with the registrant, so as to misrepresent the source of the goods or services on or in connection with which the mark is used; or
>
> (4) That the use of the name, term, or device charged to be an infringement is a use, otherwise than as a mark, of the party's individual name in his own business, or of the individual name of anyone in privity with such party, or of a term or device which is

descriptive of and used fairly and in good faith only to describe the goods or services of such party, or their geographic origin; or

(5) That the mark whose use by a party is charged as an infringement was adopted without knowledge of the registrant's prior use and has been continuously used by such party or those in privity with him from a date prior to (A) the date of constructive use of the mark established pursuant to section 1057(c) [§ 7(c)] of this title, (B) the registration of the mark under this chapter if the application for registration is filed before the effective date of the Trademark Law Revision Act of 1988, or (C) publication of the registered mark under subsection (c) of section 1062 [§ 12] of this title: *Provided, however*, That this defense or defect shall apply only for the area in which such continuous prior use is proved; or

(6) That the mark whose use is charged as an infringement was registered and used prior to the registration under this chapter or publication under subsection (c) of section 1062 of this title of the registered mark of the registrant, and not abandoned: *Provided, however*, That this defense or defect shall apply only for the area in which the mark was used prior to such registration or such publication of the registrant's mark; or

(7) That the mark has been or is being used to violate the antitrust laws of the United States; or

(8) That the mark is functional; or

(9) That equitable principles, including laches, estoppel, and acquiescence, are applicable.

§ 34   (15 U.S.C. § 1116). Injunctive relief

(a) Jurisdiction; service

The several courts vested with jurisdiction of civil actions arising under this chapter shall have power to grant injunctions, according to the principles of equity and upon such terms as the court may deem reasonable, to prevent the violation of any right of the registrant of a mark registered in the Patent and Trademark Office or to prevent a violation under subsection (a), (c), or (d) of section 1125 [§ 43] of this title. Any such injunction may include a provision directing the defendant to file with the court and serve on the plaintiff within thirty days after the service on the defendant of such injunction, or such extended period as the court may direct, a report in writing under oath setting forth in detail the manner and form in which the defendant has complied with the injunction. Any such injunction granted upon hearing, after notice to the defendant, by any district court of the United States, may be served on the parties against whom such injunction is granted anywhere in the United States where they may be found, and shall be operative and may be enforced by proceedings to punish for contempt, or otherwise, by the court by which such injunction was granted, or by any other United States district court in whose jurisdiction the defendant may be found.

(b) Transfer of certified copies of court papers

The said courts shall have jurisdiction to enforce said injunction, as provided in this chapter, as fully as if the injunction had been granted by the district court in which it is sought to be enforced. The clerk of the court or judge granting the injunction shall, when required to do so by the court before which application to enforce said injunction is made, transfer without delay to said court a certified copy of all papers on file in his office upon which said injunction was granted.

(c) Notice to Director

It shall be the duty of the clerks of such courts within one month after the filing of any action, suit, or proceeding involving a mark registered under the provisions of this chapter to give notice thereof in writing to the Director setting forth in order so far as known the names and addresses of the litigants and the designating number or numbers of the registration or registrations upon which the action, suit, or proceeding has been brought, and in the event any other registration be subsequently included in the action, suit, or proceeding by amendment, answer, or other pleading, the clerk shall give like notice thereof to the Director, and within one month after the judgment is entered or an appeal is taken the clerk of the court shall give notice thereof to the Director, and it shall be the duty of the Director on receipt of such notice forthwith to endorse the same upon the file wrapper of the said registration or registrations and to incorporate the same as a part of the contents of said file wrapper.

(d) Civil actions arising out of use of counterfeit marks

(1)(A) In the case of a civil action arising under section 1114(1)(a) [§ 32(1)(a)] of this title or section 220506 of title 36 with respect to a violation that consists of using a counterfeit mark in connection with the sale, offering for sale, or distribution of goods or services, the court may, upon ex parte application, grant an order under subsection (a) of this section pursuant to this subsection providing for the seizure of goods and counterfeit marks involved in such violation and the means of making such marks, and records documenting the manufacture, sale, or receipt of things involved in such violation.

(B) As used in this subsection the term "counterfeit mark" means—

(i) a counterfeit of a mark that is registered on the principal register in the United States Patent and Trademark Office for such goods or services sold, offered for sale, or distributed and that is in use, whether or not the person against whom relief is sought knew such mark was so registered; or

(ii) a spurious designation that is identical with, or substantially indistinguishable from, a designation as to which the remedies of this chapter are made available by reason of section 220506 of title 36;

but such term does not include any mark or designation used on or in connection with goods or services of which the manufacture or producer was, at the time of the manufacture or production in question authorized to use the mark or designation for the type of goods or services so manufactured or produced, by the holder of the right to use such mark or designation.

(2) The court shall not receive an application under this subsection unless the applicant has given such notice of the application as is reasonable under the circumstances to the United States attorney for the judicial district in which such order is sought. Such attorney may participate in the proceedings arising under such application if such proceedings may affect evidence of an offense against the United States. The court may deny such application if the court determines that the public interest in a potential prosecution so requires.

(3) The application for an order under this subsection shall—

(A) be based on an affidavit or the verified complaint establishing facts sufficient to support the findings of fact and conclusions of law required for such order; and

(B) contain the additional information required by paragraph (5) of this subsection to be set forth in such order.

(4) The court shall not grant such an application unless—

(A) the person obtaining an order under this subsection provides the security determined adequate by the court for the payment of such damages as any person may be entitled to recover as a result of a wrongful seizure or wrongful attempted seizure under this subsection; and

(B) the court finds that it clearly appears from specific facts that—

(i) an order other than an ex parte seizure order is not adequate to achieve the purposes of section 1114 [§ 32] of this title;

(ii) the applicant has not publicized the requested seizure;

(iii) the applicant is likely to succeed in showing that the person against whom seizure would be ordered used a counterfeit mark in connection with the sale, offering for sale, or distribution of goods or services;

(iv) an immediate and irreparable injury will occur if such seizure is not ordered;

(v) the matter to be seized will be located at the place identified in the application;

(vi) the harm to the applicant of denying the application outweighs the harm to the legitimate interests of the person against whom seizure would be ordered of granting the application; and

(vii) the person against whom seizure would be ordered, or persons acting in concert with such person, would destroy, move, hide, or otherwise make such matter inaccessible to the court, if the applicant were to proceed on notice to such person.

(5) An order under this subsection shall set forth—

(A) the findings of fact and conclusions of law required for the order;

(B) a particular description of the matter to be seized, and a description of each place at which such matter is to be seized;

(C) the time period, which shall end not later than seven days after the date on which such order is issued, during which the seizure is to be made;

(D) the amount of security required to be provided under this subsection; and

(E) a date for the hearing required under paragraph (10) of this subsection.

(6) The court shall take appropriate action to protect the person against whom an order under this subsection is directed from publicity, by or at the behest of the plaintiff, about such order and any seizure under such order.

(7) Any materials seized under this subsection shall be taken into the custody of the court. The court shall enter an appropriate protective order with respect to discovery by the applicant of any records that have been seized. The protective order shall provide for appropriate procedures to assure that confidential information contained in such records is not improperly disclosed to the applicant.

(8) An order under this subsection, together with the supporting documents, shall be sealed until the person against whom the order is directed has an opportunity to contest such order,except that any person against whom such order is issued shall have access to such order and supporting documents after the seizure has been carried out.

(9) The court shall order that service of a copy of the order under this subsection shall be made by a Federal law enforcement officer (such as a United States marshal or an officer or agent of the United States Customs Service, Secret Service, Federal Bureau of Investigation, or Post Office) or may be made by a State or local law enforcement officer, who, upon making service, shall carry out the seizure under the order. The court shall issue orders, when appropriate, to protect the defendant from undue damage from the disclosure of trade secrets or other confidential information during the course of the seizure, including, when appropriate, orders restricting the access of the applicant (or any agent or employee of the applicant) to such secrets or information.

(10)

(A) The court shall hold a hearing, unless waived by all the parties, on the date set by the court in the order of seizure. That date shall be not sooner than ten days after the order is issued and not later than fifteen days after the order is issued, unless the applicant for the order shows good cause for another date or unless the party against whom such order is directed consents to another date for such hearing. At such hearing the party obtaining the order shall have the burden to prove that the facts supporting findings of fact and conclusions of law necessary to support such order are still in effect. If that party fails to meet that burden, the seizure order shall be dissolved or modified appropriately.

(B) In connection with a hearing under this paragraph, the court may make such orders modifying the time limits for discovery under the Rules of Civil Procedure as may be necessary to prevent the frustration of the purposes of such hearing.

(11) A person who suffers damage by reason of a wrongful seizure under this subsection has a cause of action against the applicant for the order under which such seizure was made, and shall be entitled to recover such relief as may be appropriate, including damages for lost profits, cost of materials, loss of good will, and punitive damages in instances where the seizure was sought in bad faith, and, unless the court finds extenuating circumstances, to recover a reasonable attorney's fee. The court in its discretion may award prejudgment interest on relief recovered under this paragraph, at an annual interest rate established under section 6621(a)(2) of title 26, commencing on the date of service of the claimant's pleading setting forth the claim under this paragraph and ending on the date such recovery is granted, or for such shorter time as the court deems appropriate.

§ 35   (15 U.S.C. § 1117). Recovery for violation of rights

(a) Profits; damages and costs; attorney fees

When a violation of any right of the registrant of a mark registered in the Patent and Trademark Office, a violation under section 1125 [§ 43] (a) or (d) of this title, or a willful violation under section 1125(c) of this title, shall have been established in any civil action arising under this chapter, the plaintiff shall be entitled, subject to the provisions of sections 1111 [§ 29] and 1114 [§ 32] of this title, and subject to the principles of equity, to recover (1) defendant's profits, (2) any damages sustained by the plaintiff, and (3) the costs of the action. The court shall assess such profits and damages or cause the same to be assessed under its direction. In assessing profits the plaintiff shall be required to prove defendant's sales only; defendant must prove all elements of cost or deduction claimed. In assessing damages the court may enter judgment, according to the circumstances of the case, for any sum above the amount found as actual damages, not exceeding three times such amount. If the court shall find that the amount of the recovery based on profits is either inadequate or excessive the court may in its discretion enter judgment for such sum as the court shall find to be just, according to the circumstances of the case. Such sum in either of the above circumstances shall constitute compensation and not a penalty. The court in exceptional cases may award reasonable attorney fees to the prevailing party.

(b) Treble damages for use of counterfeit mark

In assessing damages under subsection (a) of this section, the court shall, unless the court finds extenuating circumstances, enter judgment for three times such profits or damages, whichever is greater, together with a reasonable attorney's fee, in the case of any violation of section 1114(1)(a) [§ 32(1)(a)] of this title or section 220506 of title 36 that consists of intentionally using a mark or designation, knowing such mark or designation is a counterfeit mark (as defined in section 1116(d) [§ 34(d)] of this title), in connection with the sale, offering for sale, or distribution of goods or services. In such cases, the court may in its discretion award prejudgment interest on such amount at an annual interest rate established under section 6621(a)(2) of title 26, commencing on the date of the service of the claimant's pleadings setting forth the claim for such entry and ending on the date such entry is made, or for such shorter time as the court deems appropriate.

(c) Statutory damages for use of counterfeit marks

In a case involving the use of a counterfeit mark (as defined in section 1116(d) [§ 34] of this title) in connection with the sale, offering for sale, or distribution of goods or services, the plaintiff may elect, at any time before final judgment is rendered by the trial court, to recover, instead of actual damages and profits under subsection (a) of this section, an award of statutory damages for any such use in connection with the sale, offering for sale, or distribution of goods or services in the amount of—

(1) not less than $500 or more than $100,000 per counterfeit mark per type of goods or services sold, offered for sale, or distributed, as the court considers just; or

(2) if the court finds that the use of the counterfeit mark was willful, not more than $1,000,000 per counterfeit mark per type of goods or services sold, offered for sale, or distributed, as the court considers just.

(d) Statutory damages for violation of section 1125(d)(1) [§ 45(d)(1)]

In a case involving a violation of section 1125(d)(1) of this title, the plaintiff may elect, at any time before final judgment is rendered by the trial court, to recover, instead of actual damages and profits, an award of statutory damages in the amount of not less than $1,000 and not more than $100,000 per domain name, as the court considers just.

(e) Rebuttable presumption of willful violation

In the case of a violation referred to in this section, it shall be a rebuttable presumption that the violation is willful for purposes of determining relief if the violator, or a person acting in concert with the violator, knowingly provided or knowingly caused to be provided materially false contact information to a domain name registrar, domain name registry, or other domain name registration authority in registering, maintaining, or renewing a domain name used in connection with the violation. Nothing in this subsection limits what may be considered a willful violation under this section.

§ 36 (15 U.S.C. § 1118). Destruction of infringing articles

In any action arising under this chapter, in which a violation of any right of the registrant of a mark registered in the Patent and Trademark Office, a violation under section 1125(a) [§ 43(a)] of this title, or a willful violation under section 1125(c) of this title, shall have been established, the court may order that all labels, signs, prints, packages, wrappers, receptacles, and advertisements in the possession of the defendant, bearing the registered mark or, in the case of a violation of section 1125(a) of this title or a willful violation under section 1125(c) of this title, the word, term, name, symbol, device, combination thereof, designation, description, or representation that is the subject of the violation, or any reproduction, counterfeit, copy, or colorable imitation thereof, and all plates, molds, matrices, and other means of making the same, shall be delivered up and destroyed. The party seeking an order under this section for destruction of articles seized under section 1116(d) [§ 34(d)] of this title shall give ten days' notice to the United States attorney for the judicial district in which such order is sought (unless good cause is shown for lesser notice) and such United States attorney may, if such destruction may affect evidence of an offense against the United States, seek a hearing on such destruction or participate in any hearing otherwise to be held with respect to such destruction.

§ 37 (15 U.S.C. § 1119). Power of court over registration

In any action involving a registered mark the court may determine the right to registration, order the cancelation of registrations, in whole or in part, restore canceled registrations, and otherwise rectify the register with respect to the registrations of any party to the action. Decrees and orders shall be certified by the court to the Director, who shall make appropriate entry upon the records of the Patent and Trademark Office, and shall be controlled thereby.

§ 38 (15 U.S.C. § 1120). Civil liability for false or fraudulent registration

Any person who shall procure registration in the Patent and Trademark Office of a mark by a false or fraudulent declaration or representation, oral or in writing, or by any false means, shall be liable in a civil action by any person injured thereby for any damages sustained in consequence thereof.

§ 39 (15 U.S.C. § 1121). Jurisdiction of Federal courts; State and local requirements that registered trademarks be altered or displayed differently; prohibition

(a) The district and territorial courts of the United States shall have original jurisdiction and the courts of appeal of the United States (other than the United States Court of Appeals for the Federal Circuit) shall have appellate jurisdiction, of all actions arising under this chapter, without regard to the amount in controversy or to diversity or lack of diversity of the citizenship of the parties.

(b) No State or other jurisdiction of the United States or any political subdivision or any agency thereof may require alteration of a registered mark, or require that additional trademarks, service marks, trade names, or corporate names that may be associated with or incorporated into the registered mark be displayed in the mark in a manner differing from the display of such additional trademarks, service marks, trade names, or corporate names contemplated by the registered mark as exhibited in the certificate of registration issued by the United States Patent and Trademark Office.

§ 40 (15 U.S.C. § 1122). Liability of United States and States, and instrumentalities and officials thereof

(a) Waiver of sovereign immunity by the United States

The United States, all agencies and instrumentalities thereof, and all individuals, firms, corporations, other persons acting for the United States and with the authorization and consent of the United States, shall not be immune from suit in Federal or State court by any person, including any governmental or nongovernmental entity, for any violation under this chapter.

(b) Waiver of sovereign immunity by States

Any State, instrumentality of a State or any officer or employee of a State or instrumentality of a State acting in his or her official capacity, shall not be immune, under the eleventh amendment of the Constitution of the United States or under any other doctrine of sovereign immunity, from suit in Federal court by any person, including any governmental or nongovernmental entity for any violation under this chapter.

(c) Remedies

In a suit described in subsection (a) or (b) of this section for a violation described therein, remedies (including remedies both at law and in equity) are available for the violation to the same extent as such remedies are available for such a violation in a suit against any person other than the United States or any agency or instrumentality thereof, or any individual, firm, corporation, or other person acting for the United States and with authorization and consent of the United States, or a State, instrumentality of a State, or officer or employee of a State or instrumentality of a State acting in his or her official capacity. Such remedies include injunctive relief under section 1116 [§ 34] of this title, actual damages, profits, costs and attorney's fees under section 1117 [§ 35] of this title, destruction of infringing articles under section 1118 [§ 36] of this title, the remedies provided for under sections 1114 [§ 32], 1119 [§ 37], 1120 [§ 38], 1124

[§ 42] and 1125 [§ 43] of this title, and for any other remedies provided under this chapter.

§ 41 (15 U.S.C. § 1123). Rules and regulations for conduct of proceedings in Patent and Trademark Office

The Director shall make rules and regulations, not inconsistent with law, for the conduct of proceedings in the Patent and Trademark Office under this chapter.

§ 42 (15 U.S.C. § 1124). Importation of goods bearing infringing marks or names forbidden

Except as provided in subsection (d) of section 1526 of title 19, no article of imported merchandise which shall copy or simulate the name of any domestic manufacture, or manufacturer, or trader, or of any manufacturer or trader located in any foreign country which, by treaty, convention, or law affords similar privileges to citizens of the United States, or which shall copy or simulate a trademark registered in accordance with the provisions of this chapter or shall bear a name or mark calculated to induce the public to believe that the article is manufactured in the United States, or that it is manufactured in any foreign country or locality other than the country or locality in which it is in fact manufactured, shall be admitted to entry at any customhouse of the United States; and, in order to aid the officers of the customs in enforcing this prohibition, any domestic manufacturer or trader, and any foreign manufacturer or trader, who is entitled under the provisions of a treaty, convention, declaration, or agreement between the United States and any foreign country to the advantages afforded by law to citizens of the United States in respect to trademarks and commercial names, may require his name and residence, and the name of the locality in which his goods are manufactured, and a copy of the certificate of registration of his trademark, issued in accordance with the provisions of this chapter, to be recorded in books which shall be kept for this purpose in the Department of the Treasury, under such regulations as the Secretary of the Treasury shall prescribe, and may furnish to the Department facsimiles of his name, the name of the locality in which his goods are manufactured, or of his registered trademark, and thereupon the Secretary of the Treasury shall cause one or more copies of the same to be transmitted to each collector or other proper officer of customs.

§ 43 (15 U.S.C. § 1125). False designations of origin, false descriptions, and dilution forbidden

(a) Civil action

(1) Any person who, on or in connection with any goods or services, or any container for goods, uses in commerce any word, term, name, symbol, or device, or any combination thereof, or any false designation of origin, false or misleading description of fact, or false or misleading representation of fact, which—

(A) is likely to cause confusion, or to cause mistake, or to deceive as to the affiliation, connection, or association of such person with another person, or as to the origin, sponsorship, or approval of his or her goods, services, or commercial activities by another person, or

(B) in commercial advertising or promotion, misrepresents the nature, characteristics, qualities, or geographic origin of his or her or another person's goods, services, or commercial activities,

shall be liable in a civil action by any person who believes that he or she is or is likely to be damaged by such act.

(2) As used in this subsection, the term "any person" includes any State, instrumentality of a State or employee of a State or instrumentality of a State acting in his or her official capacity. Any State, and any such instrumentality, officer, or employee, shall be subject to the provisions of this chapter in the same manner and to the same extent as any nongovernmental entity.

(3) In a civil action for trade dress infringement under this chapter for trade dress not registered on the principal register, the person who asserts trade dress protection has the burden of proving that the matter sought to be protected is not functional.

(b) Importation

Any goods marked or labeled in contravention of the provisions of this section shall not be imported into the United States or admitted to entry at any customhouse of the United States. The owner, importer, or consignee of goods refused entry at any customhouse under this section may have any recourse by protest or appeal that is given under the customs revenue laws or may have the remedy given by this chapter in cases involving goods refused entry or seized.

(c) Dilution by blurring; dilution by tarnishment

(1) Injunctive relief

Subject to the principles of equity, the owner of a famous mark that is distinctive, inherently or through acquired distinctiveness, shall be entitled to an injunction against another person who, at any time after the owner's mark has become famous, commences use of a mark or trade name in commerce that is likely to cause dilution by blurring or dilution by tarnishment of the famous mark, regardless of the presence or absence of actual or likely confusion, of competition, or of actual economic injury.

(2) Definitions

(A) For purposes of paragraph (1), a mark is famous if it is widely recognized by the general consuming public of the United States as a designation of source of the goods or services of the mark's owner. In determining whether a mark possesses the requisite degree of recognition, the court may consider all relevant factors, including the following:

(i) The duration, extent, and geographic reach of advertising and publicity of the mark, whether advertised or publicized by the owner or third parties.

(ii) The amount, volume, and geographic extent of sales of goods or services offered under the mark.

(iii) The extent of actual recognition of the mark.

(iv) Whether the mark was registered under the Act of March 3, 1881, or the Act of February 20, 1905, or on the principal register.

(B) For purposes of paragraph (1), "dilution by blurring" is association arising from the similarity between a mark or trade name and a famous mark that impairs the distinctiveness of the famous mark. In determining whether a mark or trade name is likely to cause dilution by blurring, the court may consider all relevant factors, including the following:

(i) The degree of similarity between the mark or trade name and the famous mark.

(ii) The degree of inherent or acquired distinctiveness of the famous mark.

(iii) The extent to which the owner of the famous mark is engaging in substantially exclusive use of the mark.

(iv) The degree of recognition of the famous mark.

(v) Whether the user of the mark or trade name intended to create an association with the famous mark.

(vi) Any actual association between the mark or trade name and the famous mark.

(C) For purposes of paragraph (1), "dilution by tarnishment" is association arising from the similarity between a mark or trade name and a famous mark that harms the reputation of the famous mark.

(3) Exclusions

The following shall not be actionable as dilution by blurring or dilution by tarnishment under this subsection:

(A) Any fair use, including a nominative or descriptive fair use, or facilitation of such fair use, of a famous mark by another person other than as a designation of source for the person's own goods or services, including use in connection with—

(i) advertising or promotion that permits consumers to compare goods or services; or

(ii) identifying and parodying, criticizing, or commenting upon the famous mark owner or the goods or services of the famous mark owner.

(B) All forms of news reporting and news commentary.

(C) Any noncommercial use of a mark.

(4) Burden of proof

In a civil action for trade dress dilution under this chapter for trade dress not registered on the principal register, the person who asserts trade dress protection has the burden of proving that—

(A) the claimed trade dress, taken as a whole, is not functional and is famous; and

(B) if the claimed trade dress includes any mark or marks registered on the principal register, the unregistered matter, taken as a whole, is famous separate and apart from any fame of such registered marks.

(5) Additional remedies

In an action brought under this subsection, the owner of the famous mark shall be entitled to injunctive relief as set forth in section 1116 [§ 34] of this title. The owner of the famous mark shall also be entitled to the remedies set forth in sections 1117(a) [§ 35(a)] and 1118 [§ 36] of this title, subject to the discretion of the court and the principles of equity if—

(A) the mark or trade name that is likely to cause dilution by blurring or dilution by tarnishment was first used in commerce by the person against whom the injunction is sought after October 6, 2006; and

(B) in a claim arising under this subsection—

(i) by reason of dilution by blurring, the person against whom the injunction is sought willfully intended to trade on the recognition of the famous mark; or

(ii) by reason of dilution by tarnishment, the person against whom the injunction is sought willfully intended to harm the reputation of the famous mark.

(6) Ownership of valid registration a complete bar to action

The ownership by a person of a valid registration under the Act of March 3, 1881, or the Act of February 20, 1905, or on the principal register under this chapter shall be a complete bar to an action against that person, with respect to that mark, that—

(A)(i) is brought by another person under the common law or a statute of a State; and

(ii) seeks to prevent dilution by blurring or dilution by tarnishment; or

(B) asserts any claim of actual or likely damage or harm to the distinctiveness or reputation of a mark, label, or form of advertisement.

(7) Savings clause

Nothing in this subsection shall be construed to impair, modify, or supersede the applicability of the patent laws of the United States.

(d) Cyberpiracy prevention

(1)(A) A person shall be liable in a civil action by the owner of a mark, including a personal name which is protected as a mark under this section, if, without regard to the goods or services of the parties, that person—

(i) has a bad faith intent to profit from that mark, including a personal name which is protected as a mark under this section; and

(ii) registers, traffics in, or uses a domain name that—

(I) in the case of a mark that is distinctive at the time of registration of the domain name, is identical or confusingly similar to that mark;

(II) in the case of a famous mark that is famous at the time of registration of the domain name, is identical or confusingly similar to or dilutive of that mark; or

(III) is a trademark, word, or name protected by reason of section 706 of title 18 or section 220506 of title 36.

(B)(i) In determining whether a person has a bad faith intent described under subparagraph (A), a court may consider factors such as, but not limited to—

(I) the trademark or other intellectual property rights of the person, if any, in the domain name;

(II) the extent to which the domain name consists of the legal name of the person or a name that is otherwise commonly used to identify that person;

(III) the person's prior use, if any, of the domain name in connection with the bona fide offering of any goods or services;

(IV) the person's bona fide noncommercial or fair use of the mark in a site accessible under the domain name;

(V) the person's intent to divert consumers from the mark owner's online location to a site accessible under the domain name that could harm the goodwill represented by the mark, either for commercial gain or with the intent to tarnish or disparage the mark, by creating a likelihood of confusion as to the source, sponsorship, affiliation, or endorsement of the site;

(VI) the person's offer to transfer, sell, or otherwise assign the domain name to the mark owner or any third party for financial gain without having used, or having an intent to use, the domain name in the bona fide offering of any goods or services, or the person's prior conduct indicating a pattern of such conduct;

(VII) the person's provision of material and misleading false contact information when applying for the registration of the domain name, the person's intentional failure to maintain accurate contact information, or the person's prior conduct indicating a pattern of such conduct;

(VIII) the person's registration or acquisition of multiple domain names which the person knows are identical or confusingly similar to marks of others that are distinctive at the time of registration of such domain names, or dilutive of famous marks of others that are famous at the time of registration of such domain names, without regard to the goods or services of the parties; and

(IX) the extent to which the mark incorporated in the person's domain name registration is or is not distinctive and famous within the meaning of subsection (c).

(ii) Bad faith intent described under subparagraph (A) shall not be found in any case in which the court determines that the person believed and had reasonable grounds to believe that the use of the domain name was a fair use or otherwise lawful.

(C) In any civil action involving the registration, trafficking, or use of a domain name under this paragraph, a court may order the forfeiture or cancellation of the domain name or the transfer of the domain name to the owner of the mark.

(D) A person shall be liable for using a domain name under subparagraph (A) only if that person is the domain name registrant or that registrant's authorized licensee.

(E) As used in this paragraph, the term "traffics in" refers to transactions that include, but are not limited to, sales, purchases, loans, pledges, licenses, exchanges of currency, and any other transfer for consideration or receipt in exchange for consideration.

(2)(A) The owner of a mark may file an in rem civil action against a domain name in the judicial district in which the domain name registrar, domain name registry, or other domain name authority that registered or assigned the domain name is located if—

(i) the domain name violates any right of the owner of a mark registered in the Patent and Trademark Office, or protected under subsection (a) or (c) of this section; and

(ii) the court finds that the owner—

(I) is not able to obtain in personam jurisdiction over a person who would have been a defendant in a civil action under paragraph (1); or

(II) through due diligence was not able to find a person who would have been a defendant in a civil action under paragraph (1) by—

(aa) sending a notice of the alleged violation and intent to proceed under this paragraph to the registrant of the domain name at the postal and e-mail address provided by the registrant to the registrar; and

(bb) publishing notice of the action as the court may direct promptly after filing the action.

(B) The actions under subparagraph (A)(ii) shall constitute service of process.

(C) In an in rem action under this paragraph, a domain name shall be deemed to have its situs in the judicial district in which—

(i) the domain name registrar, registry, or other domain name authority that registered or assigned the domain name is located; or

(ii) documents sufficient to establish control and authority regarding the disposition of the registration and use of the domain name are deposited with the court.

(D)(i) The remedies in an in rem action under this paragraph shall be limited to a court order for the forfeiture or cancellation of the domain name or the transfer of the domain name to the owner of the mark. Upon receipt of written notification of a filed, stamped copy of a complaint filed by the owner of a mark in a United States district court under this paragraph, the domain name registrar, domain name registry, or other domain name authority shall—

(I) expeditiously deposit with the court documents sufficient to establish the court's control and authority regarding the disposition of the registration and use of the domain name to the court; and

(II) not transfer, suspend, or otherwise modify the domain name during the pendency of the action, except upon order of the court.

(ii) The domain name registrar or registry or other domain name authority shall not be liable for injunctive or monetary relief under this paragraph except in the case of bad faith or reckless disregard, which includes a willful failure to comply with any such court order.

(3) The civil action established under paragraph (1) and the in rem action established under paragraph (2), and any remedy available under either such action, shall be in addition to any other civil action or remedy otherwise applicable.

(4) The in rem jurisdiction established under paragraph (2) shall be in addition to any other jurisdiction that otherwise exists, whether in rem or in personam.

§ 44   (15 U.S.C. § 1126). International conventions

(a) Register of marks communicated by international bureaus

The Director shall keep a register of all marks communicated to him by the international bureaus provided for by the conventions for the protection of industrial property, trademarks, trade and commercial names, and the repression of unfair competition to which the United States is or may become a party, and upon the payment of the fees required by such conventions and the fees required in this chapter may place the marks so communicated upon such register. This register shall show a facsimile of the mark or trade or commercial name; the name, citizenship, and address of the registrant; the number, date, and place of the first registration of the mark, including the dates on which application for such registration was filed and granted and the term of such registration; a list of goods or services to which the mark is applied as shown by the registration in the country of origin, and such other data as may be useful concerning the mark. This register shall be a continuation of the register provided in section 1(a) of the Act of March 19, 1920.

(b) Benefits of section to persons whose country of origin is party to convention or treaty

Any person whose country of origin is a party to any convention or treaty relating to trademarks, trade or commercial names, or the repression of unfair competition, to which the United States is also a party, or extends reciprocal rights to nationals of the United States by law, shall be entitled to the benefits of this section under the conditions expressed herein to the extent necessary to give effect to any provision of such convention, treaty or reciprocal law, in addition to the rights to which any owner of a mark is otherwise entitled by this chapter.

(c) Prior registration in country of origin; country of origin defined

No registration of a mark in the United States by a person described in subsection (b) of this section shall be granted until such mark has been registered in the country of origin of the applicant, unless the applicant alleges use in commerce. For the purposes of this section, the country of origin of the applicant is the country in which he has a bona fide and effective industrial or commercial establishment, or if he has not such an establishment the country in which he is domiciled, or if he has not a domicile in any of the countries described in subsection (b) of this section, the country of which he is a national.

(d) Right of priority

An application for registration of a mark under section 1051 [§ 1], 1053 [§ 3], 1054 [§ 4], or 1091 [§ 23] of this title or under subsection (e) of this section, filed by a person described in subsection (b) of this section who has previously duly filed an application for registration of the same mark in one of the countries described in subsection (b) of this section shall be accorded the same force and effect as would be accorded to the same application if filed in the United States on the same date on which the application was first filed in such foreign country: *Provided*, That—

> (1) the application in the United States is filed within six months from the date on which the application was first filed in the foreign country;

> (2) the application conforms as nearly as practicable to the requirements of this chapter, including a statement that the applicant has a bona fide intention to use the mark in commerce;

> (3) the rights acquired by third parties before the date of the filing of the first application in the foreign country shall in no way be affected by a registration obtained on an application filed under this subsection;

> (4) nothing in this subsection shall entitle the owner of a registration granted under this section to sue for acts committed prior to the date on which his mark was registered in this country unless the registration is based on use in commerce.

In like manner and subject to the same conditions and requirements, the right provided in this section may be based upon a subsequent regularly filed application in the same foreign country, instead of the first filed foreign application: *Provided*, That any foreign application filed prior to such subsequent application has been withdrawn, abandoned, or otherwise disposed of, without having been laid open to public inspection and without leaving any rights outstanding, and has not served, nor thereafter shall serve, as a basis for claiming a right of priority.

(e) Registration on principal or supplemental register; copy of foreign registration

A mark duly registered in the country of origin of the foreign applicant may be registered on the principal register if eligible, otherwise on the supplemental register in this chapter provided. Such applicant shall submit, within such time period as may be prescribed by the Director, a true copy, a photocopy, a certification, or a certified copy of the registration in the country of origin of the applicant. The application must state the applicant's bona fide intention to use the mark in commerce, but use in commerce shall not be required prior to registration.

(f) Domestic registration independent of foreign registration

The registration of a mark under the provisions of subsections (c), (d), and (e) of this section by a person described in subsection (b) of this section shall be independent of the registration in the country of origin and the duration, validity, or transfer in the United States of such registration shall be governed by the provisions of this chapter.

(g) Trade or commercial names of foreign nationals protected without registration

Trade names or commercial names of persons described in subsection (b) of this section shall be protected without the obligation of filing or registration whether or not they form parts of marks.

(h) Protection of foreign nationals against unfair competition

Any person designated in subsection (b) of this section as entitled to the benefits and subject to the provisions of this chapter shall be entitled to effective protection against unfair competition, and the remedies provided in this chapter for infringement of marks shall be available so far as they may be appropriate in repressing acts of unfair competition.

(i) Citizens or residents of United States entitled to benefits of section

Citizens or residents of the United States shall have the same benefits as are granted by this section to persons described in subsection (b) of this section.

§ 45 (15 U.S.C. § 1127). Construction and definitions; intent of chapter

In the construction of this chapter, unless the contrary is plainly apparent from the context—

United States. The United States includes and embraces all territory which is under its jurisdiction and control.

Commerce. The word "commerce" means all commerce which may lawfully be regulated by Congress.

Principal Register. The term "principal register" refers to the register provided for by sections 1051 [§ 1] to 1072 [§ 22] of this title, and the term "supplemental register" refers to the register provided for by sections 1091 [§ 23] to 1096 [§ 28] of this title.

Person. The term "person" and any other word or term used to designate the applicant or other entitled to a benefit or privilege or rendered liable under the provisions of this chapter includes a juristic person as well as a natural person. The term "juristic person" includes a firm, corporation, union, association, or other organization capable of suing and being sued in a court of law.

The term "person" also includes the United States, any agency or instrumentality thereof, or any individual, firm, or corporation acting for the United States and with the authorization and consent of the United States. The United States, any agency or instrumentality thereof, and any individual, firm, or corporation acting for the United States and with the authorization and consent of the United States, shall be subject to the provisions of this chapter in the same manner and to the same extent as any nongovernmental entity.

The term "person" also includes any State, any instrumentality of a State, and any officer or employee of a State or instrumentality of a State acting in his or her official capacity. Any State, and any such instrumentality, officer, or employee, shall be subject to the provisions of this chapter in the same manner and to the same extent as any nongovernmental entity.

Applicant, registrant. The terms "applicant" and "registrant" embrace the legal representatives, predecessors, successors and assigns of such applicant or registrant.

Director. The term "Director" means the Under Secretary of Commerce for Intellectual Property and Director of the United States Patent and Trademark Office.

Related Company. The term "related company" means any person whose use of a mark is controlled by the owner of the mark with respect to the nature and quality of the goods or services on or in connection with which the mark is used.

Trade name, commercial name. The terms "trade name" and "commercial name" mean any name used by a person to identify his or her business or vocation.

Trademark. The term "trademark" includes any word, name, symbol, or device, or any combination thereof—

  (1) used by a person, or

  (2) which a person has a bona fide intention to use in commerce and applies to register on the principal register established by this chapter,

to identify and distinguish his or her goods, including a unique product, from those manufactured or sold by others and to indicate the source of the goods, even if that source is unknown.

Service mark. The term "service mark" means any word, name, symbol, or device, or any combination thereof—

  (1) used by a person, or

  (2) which a person has a bona fide intention to use in commerce and applies to register on the principal register established by this chapter,

to identify and distinguish the services of one person, including a unique service, from the services of others and to indicate the source of the services, even if that source is unknown. Titles, character names, and other distinctive features of radio or television programs may be registered as service marks notwithstanding that they, or the programs, may advertise the goods of the sponsor.

Certification mark. The term "certification mark" means any word, name, symbol, or device, or any combination thereof—

    (1) used by a person other than its owner, or

    (2) which its owner has a bona fide intention to permit a person other than the owner to use in commerce and files an application to register on the principal register established by this chapter, to certify regional or other origin, material, mode of manufacture, quality, accuracy, or other characteristics of such person's goods or services or that the work or labor on the goods or services was performed by members of a union or other organization.

Collective mark. The term "collective mark" means a trademark or service mark—

    (1) used by the members of a cooperative, an association, or other collective group or organization, or

    (2) which such cooperative, association, or other collective group or organization has a bona fide intention to use in commerce and applies to register on the principal register established by this chapter, and includes marks indicating membership in a union, an association, or other organization.

Mark. The term "mark" includes any trademark, service mark, collective mark, or certification mark.

Use in commerce. The term "use in commerce" means the bona fide use of a mark in the ordinary course of trade, and not made merely to reserve a right in a mark. For purposes of this chapter, a mark shall be deemed to be in use in commerce—

    (1) on goods when—

        (A) it is placed in any manner on the goods or their containers or the displays associated therewith or on the tags or labels affixed thereto, or if the nature of the goods makes such placement impracticable, then on documents associated with the goods or their sale, and

        (B) the goods are sold or transported in commerce, and

    (2) on services when it is used or displayed in the sale or advertising of services and the services are rendered in commerce, or the services are rendered in more than one State or in the United States and a foreign country and the person rendering the services is engaged in commerce in connection with the services.

Abandonment. A mark shall be deemed to be "abandoned" if either of the following occurs:

(1) When its use has been discontinued with intent not to resume such use. Intent not to resume may be inferred from circumstances. Nonuse for 3 consecutive years shall be prima facie evidence of abandonment. "Use" of a mark means the bona fide use of such mark made in the ordinary course of trade, and not made merely to reserve a right in a mark.

(2) When any course of conduct of the owner, including acts of omission as well as commission, causes the mark to become the generic name for the goods or services on or in connection with which it is used or otherwise to lose its significance as a mark. Purchaser motivation shall not be a test for determining abandonment under this paragraph.

Colorable imitation. The term "colorable imitation" includes any mark which so resembles a registered mark as to be likely to cause confusion or mistake or to deceive.

Registered mark. The term "registered mark" means a mark registered in the United States Patent and Trademark Office under this chapter or under the Act of March 3, 1881, or the Act of February 20, 1905, or the Act of March 19, 1920. The phrase "marks registered in the Patent and Trademark Office" means registered marks.

Prior Acts. The term "Act of March 3, 1881", "Act of February 20, 1905", or "Act of March 19, 1920", means the respective Act as amended.

Counterfeit. A "counterfeit" is a spurious mark which is identical with, or substantially indistinguishable from, a registered mark.

Domain name. The term "domain name" means any alphanumeric designation which is registered with or assigned by any domain name registrar, domain name registry, or other domain name registration authority as part of an electronic address on the Internet.

Internet. The term "Internet" has the meaning given that term in section 230(f)(1) of title 47.

Singular and plural. Words used in the singular include the plural and vice versa.

Intent of Act. The intent of this chapter is to regulate commerce within the control of Congress by making actionable the deceptive and misleading use of marks in such commerce; to protect registered marks used in such commerce from interference by State, or territorial legislation; to protect persons engaged in such commerce against unfair competition; to prevent fraud and deception in such commerce by the use of reproductions, copies, counterfeits, or colorable imitations of registered marks; and to provide rights and remedies stipulated by treaties and conventions respecting trademarks, trade names, and unfair competition entered into between the United States and foreign nations.

15 U.S.C. § 1129.   Cyberpiracy protections for individuals***

(1) In general

(A) Civil liability

Any person who registers a domain name that consists of the name of another living person, or a name substantially and confusingly similar thereto, without that person's consent, with the specific intent to profit from such name by selling the domain name for financial gain to that person or any third party, shall be liable in a civil action by such person.

(B) Exception

A person who in good faith registers a domain name consisting of the name of another living person, or a name substantially and confusingly similar thereto, shall not be liable under this paragraph if such name is used in, affiliated with, or related to a work of authorship protected under title 17, including a work made for hire as defined in section 101 of title 17, and if the person registering the domain name is the copyright owner or licensee of the work, the person intends to sell the domain name in conjunction with the lawful exploitation of the work, and such registration is not prohibited by a contract between the registrant and the named person. The exception under this subparagraph shall apply only to a civil action brought under paragraph (1) and shall in no manner limit the protections afforded under the Trademark Act of 1946 (15 U.S.C. 1051 et seq.) or other provision of Federal or State law.

(2) Remedies

In any civil action brought under paragraph (1), a court may award injunctive relief, including the forfeiture or cancellation of the domain name or the transfer of the domain name to the plaintiff. The court may also, in its discretion, award costs and attorneys fees to the prevailing party.

(3) Definition

In this section, the term "domain name" has the meaning given that term in section 45 of the Trademark Act of 1946 (15 U.S.C. 1127).

(4) Effective date

This section shall apply to domain names registered on or after November 29, 1999.

SUBCHAPTER IV—THE MADRID PROTOCOL

§ 60   (15 U.S.C. § 1141). Definitions

In this subchapter:

*** [Editors note: Section 1129 was enacted as part of the *Anticybersquatting Consumer Protection Act*, rather than as an amendment to the Lanham Act. *See* Casebook, Chapter 11.]

(1) Basic application

The term "basic application" means the application for the registration of a mark that has been filed with an Office of a Contracting Party and that constitutes the basis for an application for the international registration of that mark.

(2) Basic registration

The term "basic registration" means the registration of a mark that has been granted by an Office of a Contracting Party and that constitutes the basis for an application for the international registration of that mark.

(3) Contracting Party

The term "Contracting Party" means any country or inter-governmental organization that is a party to the Madrid Protocol.

(4) Date of recordal

The term "date of recordal" means the date on which a request for extension of protection, filed after an international registration is granted, is recorded on the International Register.

(5) Declaration of bona fide intention to use the mark in commerce

The term "declaration of bona fide intention to use the mark in commerce" means a declaration that is signed by the applicant for, or holder of, an international registration who is seeking extension of protection of a mark to the United States and that contains a statement that—

(A) the applicant or holder has a bona fide intention to use the mark in commerce;

(B) the person making the declaration believes himself or herself, or the firm, corporation, or association in whose behalf he or she makes the declaration, to be entitled to use the mark in commerce; and

(C) no other person, firm, corporation, or association, to the best of his or her knowledge and belief, has the right to use such mark in commerce either in the identical form of the mark or in such near resemblance to the mark as to be likely, when used on or in connection with the goods of such other person, firm, corporation, or association, to cause confusion, mistake, or deception.

(6) Extension of protection

The term "extension of protection" means the protection resulting from an international registration that extends to the United States at the request of the holder of the international registration, in accordance with the Madrid Protocol.

(7) Holder of an international registration

A "holder" of an international registration is the natural or juristic person in whose name the international registration is recorded on the International Register.

(8) International application

The term "international application" means an application for international registration that is filed under the Madrid Protocol.

(9) International Bureau

The term "International Bureau" means the International Bureau of the World Intellectual Property Organization.

(10) International Register

The term "International Register" means the official collection of data concerning international registrations maintained by the International Bureau that the Madrid Protocol or its implementing regulations require or permit to be recorded.

(11) International registration

The term "international registration" means the registration of a mark granted under the Madrid Protocol.

(12) International registration date

The term "international registration date" means the date assigned to the international registration by the International Bureau.

(13) Madrid Protocol

The term "Madrid Protocol" means the Protocol Relating to the Madrid Agreement Concerning the International Registration of Marks, adopted at Madrid, Spain, on June 27, 1989.

(14) Notification of refusal

The term "notification of refusal" means the notice sent by the United States Patent and Trademark Office to the International Bureau declaring that an extension of protection cannot be granted.

(15) Office of a Contracting Party

The term "Office of a Contracting Party" means—

(A) the office, or governmental entity, of a Contracting Party that is responsible for the registration of marks; or

(B) the common office, or governmental entity, of more than 1 Contracting Party that is responsible for the registration of marks and is so recognized by the International Bureau.

(16) Office of origin

The term "office of origin" means the Office of a Contracting Party with which a basic application was filed or by which a basic registration was granted.

(17) Opposition period

The term "opposition period" means the time allowed for filing an opposition in the United States Patent and Trademark Office, including any extension of time granted under section 1063 of this title.

§ 61 (15 U.S.C. § 1141a). International applications based on United States applications or registrations

(a) In general

The owner of a basic application pending before the United States Patent and Trademark Office, or the owner of a basic registration granted by the United States Patent and Trademark Office may file an international application by submitting to the United States Patent and Trademark Office a written application in such form, together with such fees, as may be prescribed by the Director.

(b) Qualified owners

A qualified owner, under subsection (a) of this section, shall—

(1) be a national of the United States;

(2) be domiciled in the United States; or

(3) have a real and effective industrial or commercial establishment in the United States.

§ 62 (15 U.S.C. § 1141b). Certification of the international application

(a) Certification procedure

Upon the filing of an application for international registration and payment of the prescribed fees, the Director shall examine the international application for the purpose of certifying that the information contained in the international application corresponds to the information contained in the basic application or basic registration at the time of the certification.

(b) Transmittal

Upon examination and certification of the international application, the Director shall transmit the international application to the International Bureau.

§ 63 (15 U.S.C. § 1141c). Restriction, abandonment, cancellation, or expiration of a basic application or basic registration

With respect to an international application transmitted to the International Bureau under section 1141b [§ 62] of this title, the Director shall notify the International Bureau whenever the basic application or basic registration which is the basis for the international application has been restricted, abandoned, or canceled, or has expired, with respect to some or all of the goods and services listed in the international registration—

(1) within 5 years after the international registration date; or

(2) more than 5 years after the international registration date if the restriction, abandonment, or cancellation of the basic application or basic registration resulted from an action that began before the end of that 5–year period.

§ 64 (15 U.S.C. § 1141d). Request for extension of protection subsequent to international registration

The holder of an international registration that is based upon a basic application filed with the United States Patent and Trademark Office or a basic registration granted by the Patent and Trademark Office may request an extension of protection of its international registration by filing such a request—

(1) directly with the International Bureau; or

(2) with the United States Patent and Trademark Office for transmittal to the International Bureau, if the request is in such form, and contains such transmittal fee, as may be prescribed by the Director.

§ 65 (15 U.S.C. § 1141e). Extension of protection of an international registration to the United States under the Madrid Protocol

(a) In general

Subject to the provisions of section 1141h [§ 68] of this title, the holder of an international registration shall be entitled to the benefits of extension of protection of that international registration to the United States to the extent necessary to give effect to any provision of the Madrid Protocol.

(b) If the United States is office of origin

Where the United States Patent and Trademark Office is the office of origin for a trademark application or registration, any international registration based on such application or registration cannot be used to obtain the benefits of the Madrid Protocol in the United States.

§ 66 (15 U.S.C. § 1141f). Effect of filing a request for extension of protection of an international registration to the United States

(a) Requirement for request for extension of protection

A request for extension of protection of an international registration to the United States that the International Bureau transmits to the United States Patent and Trademark Office shall be deemed to be properly filed in the United States if such request, when received by the International Bureau, has attached to it a declaration of bona fide intention to use the mark in commerce that is verified by the applicant for, or holder of, the international registration.

(b) Effect of proper filing

Unless extension of protection is refused under section 1141h [§ 68] of this title, the proper filing of the request for extension of protection under subsection (a) of this section shall constitute constructive use of the mark, conferring the same rights as those specified in section 1057(c) [§ 7(c)] of this title, as of the earliest of the following:

(1) The international registration date, if the request for extension of protection was filed in the international application.

(2) The date of recordal of the request for extension of protection, if the request for extension of protection was made after the international registration date.

(3) The date of priority claimed pursuant to section 1141g [§ 67] of this title.

§ 67 (15 U.S.C. § 1141g). Right of priority for request for extension of protection to the United States

The holder of an international registration with a request for an extension of protection to the United States shall be entitled to claim a date of priority based on a right of priority within the meaning of Article 4 of the Paris Convention for the Protection of Industrial Property if—

(1) the request for extension of protection contains a claim of priority; and

(2) the date of international registration or the date of the recordal of the request for extension of protection to the United States is not later than 6 months after the date of the first regular national filing (within the meaning of Article 4(A)(3) of the Paris Convention for the Protection of Industrial Property) or a subsequent application (within the meaning of Article 4(C)(4) of the Paris Convention for the Protection of Industrial Property).

§ 68 (15 U.S.C. § 1141h). Examination of and opposition to request for extension of protection; notification of refusal

(a) Examination and opposition

(1) A request for extension of protection described in section 1141f(a) [§ 66(a)] of this title shall be examined as an application for registration on the Principal Register under this chapter, and if on such examination it appears that the applicant is entitled to extension of protection under this subchapter, the Director shall cause the mark to be published in the Official Gazette of the United States Patent and Trademark Office.

(2) Subject to the provisions of subsection (c) of this section, a request for extension of protection under this subchapter shall be subject to opposition under section 1063 [§ 13] of this title.

(3) Extension of protection shall not be refused on the ground that the mark has not been used in commerce.

(4) Extension of protection shall be refused to any mark not registrable on the Principal Register.

(b) Notification of refusal

If, a request for extension of protection is refused under subsection (a) of this section, the Director shall declare in a notification of refusal (as provided in subsection (c) of this section) that the extension of protection cannot be granted, together with a statement of all grounds on which the refusal was based.

(c) Notice to International Bureau

(1) Within 18 months after the date on which the International Bureau transmits to the Patent and Trademark Office a notification of a request for extension of protection, the Director shall transmit to the International Bureau any of the following that applies to such request:

(A) A notification of refusal based on an examination of the request for extension of protection.

(B) A notification of refusal based on the filing of an opposition to the request.

(C) A notification of the possibility that an opposition to the request may be filed after the end of that 18–month period.

(2) If the Director has sent a notification of the possibility of opposition under paragraph (1)(C), the Director shall, if applicable, transmit to the International Bureau a notification of refusal on the basis of the opposition, together with a statement of all the grounds for the opposition, within 7 months after the beginning of the opposition period or within 1 month after the end of the opposition period, whichever is earlier.

(3) If a notification of refusal of a request for extension of protection is transmitted under paragraph (1) or (2), no grounds for refusal of such request other than those set forth in such notification may be transmitted to the International Bureau by the Director after the expiration of the time periods set forth in paragraph (1) or (2), as the case may be.

(4) If a notification specified in paragraph (1) or (2) is not sent to the International Bureau within the time period set forth in such paragraph, with respect to a request for extension of protection, the request for extension of protection shall not be refused and the Director shall issue a certificate of extension of protection pursuant to the request.

(d) Designation of agent for service of process

In responding to a notification of refusal with respect to a mark, the holder of the international registration of the mark may designate, by a document filed in the United States Patent and Trademark Office, the name and address of a person residing in the United States on whom notices or process in proceedings affecting the mark may be served. Such notices or process may be served upon the person designated by leaving with that person, or mailing to that person, a copy thereof at the address specified in the last designation filed. If the person designated cannot be found at the address given in the last designation, or if the holder does not designate by a document filed in the United States Patent and Trademark Office the name and address of a person residing in the United States for service of notices or process in proceedings affecting the mark, the notice or process may be served on the Director.

§ 69 (15 U.S.C. § 1141i). Effect of extension of protection

(a) Issuance of extension of protection

Unless a request for extension of protection is refused under section 1141h [§ 68] of this title, the Director shall issue a certificate of extension of protection pursuant to the request and shall cause notice of such certificate of extension of protection to be published in the Official Gazette of the United States Patent and Trademark Office.

(b) Effect of extension of protection

From the date on which a certificate of extension of protection is issued under subsection (a) of this section—

(1) such extension of protection shall have the same effect and validity as a registration on the Principal Register; and

(2) the holder of the international registration shall have the same rights and remedies as the owner of a registration on the Principal Register.

§ 70 (15 U.S.C. § 1141j). Dependence of extension of protection to the United States on the underlying international registration

(a) Effect of cancellation of international registration

If the International Bureau notifies the United States Patent and Trademark Office of the cancellation of an international registration with respect to some or all of the goods and services listed in the international registration, the Director shall cancel any extension of protection to the United States with respect to such goods and services as of the date on which the international registration was canceled.

(b) Effect of failure to renew international registration

If the International Bureau does not renew an international registration, the corresponding extension of protection to the United States shall cease to be valid as of the date of the expiration of the international registration.

(c) Transformation of an extension of protection into a United States application

The holder of an international registration canceled in whole or in part by the International Bureau at the request of the office of origin, under article

6(4) of the Madrid Protocol, may file an application, under section 1051 [§ 1] or 1126 [§ 44] of this title, for the registration of the same mark for any of the goods and services to which the cancellation applies that were covered by an extension of protection to the United States based on that international registration. Such an application shall be treated as if it had been filed on the international registration date or the date of recordal of the request for extension of protection with the International Bureau, whichever date applies, and, if the extension of protection enjoyed priority under section 1141g [§ 67] of this title, shall enjoy the same priority. Such an application shall be entitled to the benefits conferred by this subsection only if the application is filed not later than 3 months after the date on which the international registration was canceled, in whole or in part, and only if the application complies with all the requirements of this chapter which apply to any application filed pursuant to section 1051 [§ 1] or 1126 [§ 44] of this title.

§ 71   (15 U.S.C. § 1141k). Affidavits and fees

(a) Required affidavits and fees

An extension of protection for which a certificate of extension of protection has been issued under section 1141i [§ 69] of this title shall remain in force for the term of the international registration upon which it is based, except that the extension of protection of any mark shall be canceled by the Director—

(1) at the end of the 6–year period beginning on the date on which the certificate of extension of protection was issued by the Director, unless within the 1–year period preceding the expiration of that 6–year period the holder of the international registration files in the Patent and Trademark Office an affidavit under subsection (b) of this section together with a fee prescribed by the Director; and

(2) at the end of the 10–year period beginning on the date on which the certificate of extension of protection was issued by the Director, and at the end of each 10–year period thereafter, unless—

(A) within the 6–month period preceding the expiration of such 10–year period the holder of the international registration files in the United States Patent and Trademark Office an affidavit under subsection (b) of this section together with a fee prescribed by the Director; or

(B) within 3 months after the expiration of such 10–year period, the holder of the international registration files in the Patent and Trademark Office an affidavit under subsection (b) of this section together with the fee described in subparagraph (A) and the surcharge prescribed by the Director.

(b) Contents of affidavit

The affidavit referred to in subsection (a) of this section shall set forth those goods or services recited in the extension of protection on or in connection with which the mark is in use in commerce and the holder of the international registration shall attach to the affidavit a specimen or facsimile showing the current use of the mark in commerce, or shall set forth that any nonuse is due to special circumstances which excuse such nonuse and is not due to any intention to abandon the mark. Special notice of the requirement for such affidavit shall be attached to each certificate of extension of protection.

(c) Notification

The Director shall notify the holder of the international registration who files 1 of the affidavits of the Director's acceptance or refusal thereof and, in case of a refusal, the reasons therefor.

(d) Service of notice or process

The holder of the international registration of the mark may designate, by a document filed in the United States Patent and Trademark Office, the name and address of a person residing in the United States on whom notices or process in proceedings affecting the mark may be served. Such notices or process may be served upon the person so designated by leaving with that person, or mailing to that person, a copy thereof at the address specified in the last designation so filed. If the person designated cannot be found at the address given in the last designation, or if the holder does not designate by a document filed in the United States Patent and Trademark Office the name and address of a person residing in the United States for service of notices or process in proceedings affecting the mark, the notice or process may be served on the Director.

§ 72 (15 U.S.C. § 1141*l*). Assignment of an extension of protection

An extension of protection may be assigned, together with the goodwill associated with the mark, only to a person who is a national of, is domiciled in, or has a bona fide and effective industrial or commercial establishment either in a country that is a Contracting Party or in a country that is a member of an intergovernmental organization that is a Contracting Party.

§ 73 (15 U.S.C. § 1141m). Incontestability

The period of continuous use prescribed under section 1065 [§ 15] of this title for a mark covered by an extension of protection issued under this subchapter may begin no earlier than the date on which the Director issues the certificate of the extension of protection under section 1141i [§ 69] of this title, except as provided in section 1141n [§ 74] of this title.

§ 74 (15 U.S.C. § 1141n). Rights of extension of protection

When a United States registration and a subsequently issued certificate of extension of protection to the United States are owned by the same person, identify the same mark, and list the same goods or services, the extension of protection shall have the same rights that accrued to the registration prior to issuance of the certificate of extension of protection.

APPENDIX B

RESTATEMENT OF THE LAW (THIRD) OF UNFAIR COMPETITION, §§ 1, 9, 13, 16–17, 20–27

Note: The sections below are reprinted with the permission of the American Law Institute. Copyright © 1995 by the American Law Institute.

Topic 3. Infringement of Rights

§ 1. General Principles

One who causes harm to the commercial relations of another by engaging in a business or trade is not subject to liability to the other for such harm unless:

(a) the harm results from acts or practices of the actor actionable by the other under the rules of this Restatement relating to:

(1) deceptive marketing, as specified in Chapter Two;

(2) infringement of trademarks and other indicia of identification, as specified in Chapter Three;

(3) appropriation of intangible trade values including trade secrets and the right of publicity, as specified in Chapter Four;

or from other acts or practices of the actor determined to be actionable as an unfair method of competition, taking into account the nature of the conduct and its likely effect on both the person seeking relief and the public; or

(b) the acts or practices of the actor are actionable by the other under federal or state statutes, international agreements, or general principles of common law apart from those considered in this Restatement.

§ 9. Definitions of Trademark and Service Mark

A trademark is a word, name, symbol, device, or other designation, or a combination of such designations, that is distinctive of a person's goods or services and that is used in a manner that identifies those goods or services and distinguishes them from the goods or services of others. A service mark is a trademark that is used in connection with services.

§ 13. Distinctiveness; Secondary Meaning

A word name, symbol, device, or other designation, or a combination of such designations, is "distinctive" under the rules stated in §§ 9–12 if:

(a) the designation is "inherently distinctive," in that, because of the nature of the designation and the context in which it is used, prospective purchasers are likely to perceive it as a designation that, in the case of a trademark, identifies goods or services produced or sponsored by a particular person, whether known or anonymous, or in the case of a trade name, identifies the business or other enterprise of a particular person, whether known or anonymous, or in the case of a collective mark, identifies members of the collective group or goods or services produced or sponsored by members, or in the case of a certification mark, identifies the certified goods or services; or

(b) the designation, although not "inherently distinctive," has become distinctive, in that, as a result of its use, prospective purchasers have come to perceive it as a designation that identifies goods, services, businesses, or members in the manner described in Subsection (a). Such acquired distinctiveness is commonly referred to as "secondary meaning."

§ 16. Configurations of Packaging and Products: Trade Dress and Product Designs

The design of elements that constitute the appearance or image of goods or services as presented to prospective purchasers, including the design of packaging, labels, containers, displays, decor, or the design of a product, a product feature, or a combination of product features, is eligible for protection as a mark under the rules stated in this Chapter if:

(a) the design is distinctive under the rule stated in § 13; and

(b) the design is not functional under the rule stated in § 17.

§ 17. Functional Designs

A design is "functional" for purposes of the rule stated in § 16 if the design affords benefits in the manufacturing, marketing, or use of the goods or services with which the design is used, apart from any benefits attributable to the design's significance as an indication of source, that are important to effective competition by others and that are not practically available through the use of alternative designs.

§ 20. Standard of Infringement

(1) One is subject to liability for infringement of another's trademark, trade name, collective mark, or certification mark if the other's use has priority under the rules stated in § 19 and in identifying the actor's business or marketing the actor's goods or services the actor uses a designation that causes a likelihood of confusion

(a) that the actor's business is the business of the other or is associated or otherwise connected with the other; or

(b) that the goods or services marketed by the actor are produced, sponsored, certified, or approved by the other; or

(c) that the goods or services marketed by the other are produced, sponsored, certified, or approved by the actor.

(2) One is also subject to liability for infringement of another's collective membership mark if the other's use has priority under the rules stated in § 19 and the actor uses a designation that causes a likelihood of confusion that the actor is a member of or otherwise associated with the collective group.

§ 21. Proof of Likelihood of Confusion—Market Factors

Whether an actor's use of a designation causes a likelihood of confusion with the use of a trademark, trade name, collective mark, or certification mark by another under the rule stated in § 20 is determined by a consideration of all the circumstances involved in the marketing of the respective goods or services or the operation of the respective businesses. In making that determination the following market factors, among others, may be important:

(a) the degree of similarity between the respective designations, including a comparison of

(i) the overall impression created by the designations as they are used in marketing the respective goods or services or in identifying the respective businesses;

(ii) the pronunciation of the designations;

(iii) the translation of foreign words contained in the designations;

(iv) the verbal translation of pictures, illustrations, or designs contained in the designations;

(v) the suggestions, connotations, or meanings of the designations;

(b) the degree of similarity in the marketing methods and channels of distribution used for the respective goods or services;

(c) the characteristics of the prospective purchasers of the goods or services and the degree of care they are likely to exercise in making purchasing decisions;

(d) the degree of distinctiveness of the other's designation;

(e) when the goods, services, or business of the actor differ in kind from those of the other, the likelihood that the actor's prospective purchasers would expect a person in the position of the other to expand its marketing or sponsorship into the product, service, or business market of the actor;

(f) when the actor and the other sell their goods or services or carry on their businesses in different geographic markets, the extent to which the other's designation is identified with the other in the geographic market of the actor.

§ 22. Proof of Likelihood of Confusion—Intent of the Actor

(1) A likelihood of confusion may be inferred from proof that the actor used a designation resembling another's trademark, trade name, collective mark, or certification mark with the intent to cause confusion or to deceive.

(2) A likelihood of confusion should not be inferred from proof that the actor intentionally copied the other's designation if the actor acted in good faith under circumstances that do not otherwise indicate an intent to cause confusion or to deceive.

§ 23. Proof of Likelihood of Confusion— Evidence of Actual Confusion

(1) A likelihood of confusion may be inferred from proof of actual confusion.

(2) An absence of likelihood of confusion may be inferred from the absence of proof of actual confusion if the actor and the other have made significant use of their respective designations in the same geographic market for a substantial period of time, and any resulting confusion would ordinarily be manifested by provable facts.

§ 24. Use of Another's Trademark on Genuine Goods

One is not subject to liability under the rule stated in § 20 for using another's trademark, trade name, collective mark, or certification mark in marketing genuine goods or services the source, sponsorship, or certification of which is accurately identified by the mark unless:

(a) the other uses a different mark for different types or grades of goods or services and the actor markets one of the types or grades under a mark used for another type or grade; or

(b) the actor markets under the mark the genuine goods of the other that have been repaired, reconditioned, altered, or used, or genuine services that do not conform to the standards imposed by the other, and the actor's use of the mark causes a likelihood of confusion that the goods are new or unaltered or that the repair, reconditioning, or alteration was performed, authorized, or certified by the other, or that the services as performed conform to the other's standards.

§ 25. Liability Without Proof of Confusion— Dilution and Tarnishment

(1) One may be subject to liability under the law of trademarks for the use of a designation that resembles the trademark, trade name, collective mark, or certification mark of another without proof of a likelihood of confusion only under an applicable antidilution statute. An actor is subject to liability under an antidilution statute if the actor uses such a designation in a manner that is likely to associate the other's mark with the goods, services, or business of the actor and:

(a) the other's mark is highly distinctive and the association of the mark with the actor's goods, services, or business is likely to cause a reduction in that distinctiveness; or

(b) the association of the other's mark with the actor's goods, services, or business, or the nature of the actor's use, is likely to cause prospective purchasers to associate the actor's and the other's goods, services, businesses, or marks in a manner that disparages the other's goods, services, or business or tarnishes the images associated with the other's mark.

(2) One who uses a designation that resembles the trademark, trade name, collective mark, or certification mark of another, not in a manner that is likely to associate the other's mark with the goods, services, or business of the actor, but rather to comment on, criticize, ridicule, parody, or disparage the other or the other's goods, services, business, or mark, is subject to liability without proof of a likelihood of confusion only if the actor's conduct meets the requirements of a cause of action for defamation, invasion of privacy, or injurious falsehood.

§ 26. Contributory Infringement by Printers, Publishers, and Other Suppliers

(1) One who, on behalf of a third person, reproduces or imitates the trademark, trade name, collective mark, or certification mark of another on goods, labels, packaging, advertisements, or other materials that are used by the third person in a manner that subjects the third person to liability to the other for infringement under the rule stated in § 20 is subject to liability to that other for contributory infringement.

(2) If an actor subject to contributory liability under the rule stated in Subsection (1) acted without knowledge that the reproduction or imitation

was intended by the third person to confuse or deceive, the actor is subject only to appropriate injunctive relief.

§ 27. Contributory Infringement by Manufacturers and Distributors

One who markets goods or services to a third person who further markets the goods or services in a manner that subjects the third person to liability to another for infringement under the rule stated in § 20 is subject to liability to that other for contributory infringement if:

(a) the actor intentionally induces the third person to engage in the infringing conduct; or

(b) the actor fails to take reasonable precautions against the occurrence of the third person's infringing conduct in circumstances in which the infringing conduct can be reasonably anticipated.

Trademark Manual of Examining Procedure (5th Edition 2007) (Excerpts)

Editor's note: The Full Trademark manual of Examining Procedure is available online at the USPTO website. See http://tess2.uspto.gov/tmdb/ tmep/.

CHAPTER 1200: SUBSTANTIVE EXAMINATION OF APPLICATIONS

1202 Use of Subject Matter as Trademark

In an application under § 1 of the Act, the examining attorney must determine whether the subject matter for which registration is sought is used as a trademark by reviewing all evidence (*e.g.*, the specimens of use and any promotional material) of record in the application. *See In re Safariland Hunting Corp.*, 24 USPQ2d 1380 (TTAB 1992) (examining attorney should look primarily to specimens to determine whether a designation would be perceived as a source indicator, but may also consider other evidence, if there is other evidence of record).

Not everything that a party adopts and uses with the intent that it function as a trademark necessarily achieves this goal or is legally capable of doing so, and not everything that is recognized or associated with a party is necessarily a registrable trademark. As the Court of Customs and Patent Appeals observed in *In re Standard Oil Co.*, 275 F.2d 945, 947, 125 USPQ 227, 229 (C.C.P.A. 1960):

> The Trademark Act is not an act to register words but to register trademarks. Before there can be registrability, there must be a trademark (or a service mark) and, unless words have been so used, they cannot qualify for registration. Words are not registrable *merely* because they do not happen to be descriptive of the goods or services with which they are associated.

Sections 1 and 2 of the Trademark Act, 15 U.S.C. §§ 1051 and 1052, require that the subject matter presented for registration be a "trademark." Section 45 of the Act, 15 U.S.C. § 1127, defines that term as follows:

> The term "trademark" includes any word, name, symbol, or device, or any combination thereof—

(1) used by a person, or

(2) which a person has a bona fide intention to use in commerce and applies to register on the principal register established by this Act,

to identify and distinguish his or her goods, including a unique product, from those manufactured or sold by others and to indicate the source of the goods, even if that source is unknown.

Thus, §§ 1, 2 and 45 of the Trademark Act, 15 U.S.C. §§ 1051, 1052, and 1127, provide the statutory basis for refusal to register on the Principal Register subject matter that, due to its inherent nature or the manner in which it is used, does not function as a mark to identify and distinguish the applicant's goods. The statutory basis for refusal of registration on the Supplemental Register of matter that does not function as a trademark because it does not fit within the statutory definition of a trademark is §§ 23 and 45, 15 U.S.C. §§ 1091 and 1127.

When the examining attorney refuses registration on the ground that the subject matter is not used as a trademark, the examining attorney should explain the specific reason for the conclusion that the subject matter is not used as a trademark. *See* TMEP §§ 1202.01 *et seq.* for a discussion of situations in which it may be appropriate, depending on the circumstances, for the examining attorney to refuse registration on the ground that the asserted trademark does not function as a trademark, *e.g.,* TMEP §§ 1202.01 (trade names), 1202.02(a) *et seq.* (functionality), 1202.03 (ornamentation), 1202.04 (informational matter), 1202.05 (color marks), 1202.06 (goods in trade), 1202.07 (columns or sections of publications), 1202.08 (title of single creative work), 1202.09 (names of artists and authors), 1202.10 (model or grade designations), 1202.11 (background designs and shapes), 1202.12 (varietal and cultivar names).

The presence of the letters "SM" or "TM" cannot transform an otherwise unregistrable designation into a mark. *In re Remington Products Inc.,* 3 USPQ2d 1714 (TTAB 1987); *In re Anchor Hocking Corp.,* 223 USPQ 85 (TTAB 1984); *In re Minnetonka, Inc.,* 212 USPQ 772 (TTAB 1981).

The issue of whether a designation functions as a mark is tied to use of the mark, as evidenced by the specimen. Therefore, generally, no refusal will be issued in an intent-to-use application under § 1(b) of the Trademark Act, 15 U.S.C. § 1051(b), until the applicant has submitted a specimen(s) with an allegation of use under § 1(c) or § 1(d) of the Trademark Act, 15 U.S.C. § 1051(c) or (d). However, in a § 1(b) application for which no specimen has been submitted, if the examining attorney anticipates that a refusal will be made on the ground that the matter presented for registration does not function as a mark, the potential refusal should be brought to the applicant's attention in the first action issued by the Office. This is done strictly as a courtesy. If information regarding this possible ground for refusal is not provided to the applicant before the allegation of use is filed, the Office is not precluded from refusing registration on this basis.

See TMEP §§ 1301.02 *et seq.* regarding use of subject matter as a service mark; TMEP §§ 1302 through 1304 *et seq.* regarding use of subject matter as a collective mark; and TMEP §§ 1306 *et seq.* regarding use of subject matter as a certification mark.

1202.02   Registration of Trade Dress

1202.02(a)   Functionality

1202.02(a)(ii)   Purpose of Functionality Doctrine

The functionality doctrine, which prohibits registration of functional product features, is intended to encourage legitimate competition by maintaining the proper balance between trademark law and patent law. As the Supreme Court explained, in *Qualitex Co. v. Jacobson Products Co., Inc.,* 514 U.S. 159, 164, 34 USPQ2d 1161, 1163 (1995):

> The functionality doctrine prevents trademark law, which seeks to promote competition by protecting a firm's reputation, from instead inhibiting legitimate competition by allowing a producer to control a useful product feature. It is the province of patent law, not trademark law, to encourage invention by granting inventors a monopoly over new product designs or functions for a limited time, 35 U.S.C. §§ 154, 173, after which competitors are free to use the innovation. If a product's functional features could be used as trademarks, however, a monopoly over such features could be obtained without regard to whether they qualify as patents and could be extended forever (because trademarks may be renewed in perpetuity).

In other words, the functionality doctrine ensures that protection for utilitarian product features be properly sought through a limited-duration utility patent, and not through the potentially unlimited protection of a trademark registration. Upon expiration of a utility patent, the invention covered by the patent enters the public domain, and the functional features disclosed in the patent may then be copied by others—thus encouraging advances in product design and manufacture. In *TrafFix Devices, Inc. v. Marketing Displays, Inc.,* 532 U.S. 23, 34–35, 58 USPQ2d 1001, 1007 (2001), the Supreme Court reiterated this rationale, also noting that the functionality doctrine is not affected by evidence of acquired distinctiveness.

Thus, even where the evidence establishes that consumers have come to associate a functional product feature with a single source, trademark protection will not be granted in light of the public policy reasons just stated. *Id.*

1202.02(a)(iii) Background and Definitions

1202.02(a)(iii)(A)   Functionality

Functional matter cannot be protected as trade dress or a trademark. 15 U.S.C. §§ 1052(e)(5) and (f), 1091(c), 1064(3), and 1115(b). A feature is functional as a matter of law if it is "essential to the use or purpose of the product or if it affects the cost or quality of the product." *TrafFix Devices, Inc. v. Marketing Displays, Inc.*, 532 U.S. 23, 33, 58 USPQ2d 1001, 1006 (2001); *Qualitex Co. v. Jacobson Products Co., Inc.*, 514 U.S. 159, 165, 34 USPQ2d 1161, 1163–64 (1995); *Inwood Laboratories, Inc. v. Ives Laboratories, Inc.*, 456 U.S. 844, 850, 214 USPQ 1, 4 n.10 (1982).

While some courts had developed a definition of functionality that focused solely on "competitive need"–thus finding a particular product feature functional only if competitors needed to copy that design in order to compete effectively–the Supreme Court held that this "was incorrect as a comprehensive definition" of functionality. *TrafFix*, 532 U.S. at 33, 58 USPQ2d at 1006. The Court emphasized that where a product feature meets the traditional functionality definition–that is, it is essential to the use or purpose of the product or affects its cost or quality–then the feature is functional, regardless of the availability to competitors of other alternatives. *Id.*; *see also Valu Engineering, Inc. v. Rexnord Corp.*, 278 F.3d 1268, 1277, 61 USPQ2d 1422, 1428 (Fed. Cir. 2002) ("Rather, we conclude that the [*TrafFix*] Court merely noted that once a product feature is found functional based on other considerations there is no need to consider the availability of alternative designs, because the feature cannot be given trade dress protection merely because there are alternative designs available" (footnote omitted).)

However, since the preservation of competition is an important policy underlying the functionality doctrine, competitive need, although not determinative, remains a significant consideration in functionality determinations. *Valu Engineering*, 278 F.3d at 1276, 61 USPQ2d at 1427.

The determination that a proposed mark is functional constitutes, for public policy reasons, an absolute bar to registration on either the Principal Register or the Supplemental Register, regardless of evidence showing that the proposed mark has acquired distinctiveness. *TrafFix*, 532 U.S. at 29, 58 USPQ2d at 1006. *See also In re Controls Corp. of America*, 46 USPQ2d 1308, 1311 (TTAB 1998).

See TMEP §§ 1202.02(a)(v) *et seq.* regarding evidentiary considerations pertaining to functionality refusals.

1202.15 Sound Marks

A sound mark identifies and distinguishes a product or service through audio rather than visual means. Examples of sound marks include: (1) a series of tones or musical notes, with or without words; and (2) wording accompanied by music. For a discussion of the criteria for registration of sound marks, *see In re General Electric Broadcasting Co., Inc.*, 199 USPQ 560 (TTAB 1978).

Detailed Description of the Mark Required. The requirement for a drawing does not apply to sound marks. Instead, the applicant must submit a detailed description of the mark. 37 C.F.R. § 2.52(e). If the sound mark includes words or lyrics, they should be included in the description. *See* TMEP § 807.09.

Audio or Video Reproduction of the Mark. To supplement and clarify the description, the applicant should also submit an audio or video reproduction of any sound mark sought to be registered. 37 C.F.R. § 2.61(b). This reproduction should contain only the mark itself; it is not meant to be a specimen.

For paper filings, reproductions of sound marks may be submitted on compact discs ("CDs"), digital video discs ("DVDs"), audiotapes, or videotapes. *See* TMEP § 904.03(d). The applicant should indicate that the reproduction of the mark contained on the disc or tape is meant to supplement the mark description.

For TEAS filings, the reproductions must be in an electronic file, in .wav, .mp3, .mpg, or .avi format. However, TEAS does not permit direct attachment of these types of electronic files. Therefore, the electronic reproduction must be sent after the TEAS document is transmitted, as an attachment to an e-mail message directed to TEAS@uspto.gov, with clear instructions that the electronic reproduction should be associated with "the application filed under Serial No. <specify>" as a supplement to the mark description.

Specimen. The specimen is not the same as the reproduction required to supplement and clarify the description of the mark. *See* TMEP § 807.09. To show that the sound mark actually identifies and distinguishes the goods/services and indicates their source, the specimen should contain a sufficient portion of the audio or video content to show how the mark is used on or in connection with the goods/services.

For paper filings, specimens for sound marks may be submitted on audio CDs, DVDs, audiotapes or videotapes. For TEAS filings, the specimen must be in an electronic file, in .wav, .mp3, .mpg, or .avi format. When filing an application, allegation of use, response to an Office action, or § 8 affidavit through TEAS, an audio or video reproduction file cannot be sent as an attachment. Therefore, the Office has developed a special procedure for handling these files. The electronic specimen must be sent after the TEAS document is transmitted, as an attachment to an e-mail message directed to TEAS@uspto.gov, with clear instructions that the electronic specimen should be associated with "the application/registration filed under Serial No./Registration No. <specify>."

For any filing where a specimen is required, the TEAS form only validates if there is an attachment in the specimen field. Therefore, in conjunction with the workaround identified above, the applicant should create a .jpg or .pdf file that states that an electronic specimen has been sent to TEAS@ uspto.gov, and attach the .jpg or .pdf file to the TEAS document in the specimen field.

If the mark comprises music or words set to music, the applicant may also be required to submit the musical score sheet music to supplement and clarify the description of the mark. *See* TMEP § 807.09.

Checklist. To expedite examination, when filing a sound mark application, the applicant should submit:

- An indication that the application is for a "NON–VISUAL MARK." *See* TMEP § 807.09;

- A detailed description of the mark, including any words or lyrics;

- An audio or video reproduction of the mark, to supplement the description. *See* TMEP § 807.09;

- In an application under § 1, a separate audio or video reproduction, as a specimen, showing how the mark is used on or in connection with the goods/services. In a § 1(b) application, the specimen must be submitted with the allegation of use. *See* TMEP § 904.03(f); and

- If the mark comprises music or words set to music, the applicant should generally submit the musical score sheet music. *See* TMEP § 807.09.

1203.03   Matter which May Disparage, Falsely Suggest a Connection, or Bring into Contempt or Disrepute

Section 2(a) of the Trademark Act, 15 U.S.C. § 1052(a), bars the registration on either the Principal or the Supplemental Register of a designation that consists of or comprises matter which, with regard to persons, institutions, beliefs, or national symbols, does any of the following: (1) disparages them, (2) falsely suggests a connection with them, (3) brings them into contempt, or (4) brings them into disrepute.

Section 2(a) is distinctly different from § 2(d), 15 U.S.C. § 1052(d), for which the relevant test is likelihood of confusion. In *University of Notre Dame du Lac v. J.C. Gourmet Food Imports Co., Inc.,* 703 F.2d 1372, 1375–76, 217 USPQ 505, 508–09 (Fed. Cir. 1983), *aff'g* 213 USPQ 594 (TTAB 1982), the Court of Appeals for the Federal Circuit noted as follows:

> A reading of the legislative history with respect to what became § 2(a) shows that the drafters were concerned with protecting the name of an individual or institution which was not a technical "trademark" or "trade name" upon which an objection could be made under § 2(d)....

> Although not articulated as such, it appears that the drafters sought by § 2(a) to embrace concepts of the right to privacy, an area of the law then in an embryonic state (footnote omitted). Our review of case law discloses that the elements of a claim of invasion of one's privacy have emerged as distinctly different from those of trademark or trade name infringement. There may be no likelihood of such confusion as to the source of goods even under a theory of "sponsorship" or "endorsement," and, nevertheless, one's right of privacy, or the related right of publicity, may be violated.

The right to privacy protects a party's control over the use of its identity or "persona." A party acquires a protectible interest in a name or equivalent designation under § 2(a) where the name or designation is unmistakably associated with, and points uniquely to, that party's personality or "persona." A party's interest in a name or designation does not depend upon adoption and use as a technical trademark or trade name. *University of Notre Dame du Lac v. J.C. Gourmet Food Imports Co., Inc.*, 703 F.2d at 1376–77, 217 USPQ at 509; *Buffett v. Chi–Chi's, Inc.*, 226 USPQ 428, 429 (TTAB 1985).

See TMEP §§ 1203.03(c) and 1203.03(d) regarding disparagement, bringing into contempt and bringing into disrepute, and TMEP §§ 1203.03(e) and 1203.03(f) regarding false suggestion of a connection.

See Carson v. Here's Johnny Portable Toilets, Inc., 698 F.2d 831, 218 USPQ 1 (6th Cir. 1983), concerning the various forms of identity which have been protected under the rights of privacy and publicity.

1203.03(b)   "National Symbols" Defined

A "national symbol" is subject matter of unique and special significance that, because of its meaning, appearance and/or sound, immediately suggests or refers to the country for which it stands. *In re Consolidated Foods Corp.*, 187 USPQ 63 (TTAB 1975) (noted national symbols include the bald eagle, Statue of Liberty, American flag, Presidential symbol, designation "Uncle Sam" and the unique human representation thereof, and the heraldry and shield designs used in governmental offices). National symbols include the symbols of foreign countries as well as those of the United States. *In re Anti–Communist World Freedom Congress, Inc.*, 161 USPQ 304 (TTAB 1969).

The Trademark Act does not prohibit registration of marks comprising national symbols; it only prohibits registration of matter that may disparage national symbols, falsely suggest a connection with them, or hold them up to contempt or disrepute. *Liberty Mutual Insurance Co. v. Liberty Insurance Co. of Texas*, 185 F. Supp. 895, 908, 127 USPQ 312, 323 (E.D. Ark. 1960) (marks comprising portion of the Statue of Liberty found not to disparage, bring into contempt or disrepute, or falsely suggest a connection with the Statue of Liberty or the United States government, the Court "[a]ssuming without deciding" that the statue is a national symbol).

Designations have been held to be national symbols within the meaning of § 2(a) in the following cases: *In re Anti–Communist World Freedom Congress, Inc.*, 161 USPQ 304 (TTAB 1969) (representation of a hammer and sickle held to be a national symbol of the Union of Soviet Socialist Republics (U.S.S.R.)); *In re National Collection & Credit Control, Inc.*, 152 USPQ 200, 201 n.2 (TTAB 1966) ("The American or bald eagle with wings extended is a well-known national symbol or emblem of the United States"); *In re Teasdale Packing Co., Inc.*, 137 USPQ 482 (TTAB 1963) (U.S. AQUA and design held unregistrable under § 2(a) on the ground that purchasers of applicant's canned drinking water would be misled into assuming approval or sponsorship by the United States government in view of the nature of the mark, including a red, white and blue shield design, and the nature of the goods, the Board noting a program for stocking emergency supplies of water in fallout shelters and the setting of standards for drinking water by United States government agencies).

Designations have been held not to be national symbols in the following cases: *W. H. Snyder and Sons, Inc. v. Ladd*, 227 F. Supp. 185, 140 USPQ 647 (D.D.C. 1964) (HOUSE OF WINDSOR held not to be a national symbol of England, but merely the name of its present reigning family); *NASA v. Bully Hill Vineyards, Inc.*, 3 USPQ2d 1671 (TTAB 1987) (SPACE SHUT-TLE found not to constitute a national symbol on the evidence of record, the Board also finding "shuttle" to be a generic term for a space vehicle or system); *Jacobs v. International Multifoods Corp.*, 211 USPQ 165, 170–71 (TTAB 1981), *aff'd on other grounds*, 668 F.2d 1234, 212 USPQ 641 (C.C.P.A. 1982) ("[H]istorical events such as the 'BOSTON TEA PARTY' ..., although undoubtedly associated with the American heritage, do not take on that unique and special significance of a 'national symbol' designed to be equated with and associated with a particular country."); *In re General Mills, Inc.*, 169 USPQ 244 (TTAB 1971) (UNION JACK, which applicant was using on packages of frozen fish marked "English cut cod" and in its restaurant near representations of the British national flag, found not to suggest a particular country, the Board noting that it could consider only the matter for which registration was sought); *In re Horwitt*, 125 USPQ 145, 146 (TTAB 1960) (U.S. HEALTH CLUB found registrable for vitamin tablets. "Considering both the nature of the mark and the goods, it is concluded that the purchasing public would not be likely to mistakenly assume that the United States Government is operating a health club, that it is distributing vitamins, or that it has approved applicant's goods.")

The name of a country is not a national symbol within the meaning of § 2(a) of the Trademark Act, *In re Sweden Freezer Mfg. Co.*, 159 USPQ 246, 248–249 (TTAB 1968), nor does use of the name of a country as a mark, by itself, amount to deception, disparagement, or a "false connection" under § 2(a). *In re Fortune Star Products Corp.*, 217 USPQ 277 (TTAB 1982).

The acronyms for, and names of, government agencies and bureaus are not considered to be national symbols. *Consolidated Foods Corp.*, 187 USPQ at 64 (OSS, acronym for the Office of Strategic Services, held not to be a national symbol, but merely to designate a particular (and long defunct) government agency, the Board contrasting national symbols with names and acronyms of government agencies: " 'National symbols' ... are more enduring in time, ... and immediately conjure up the image of the country as a whole. Symbols of a country take on a special meaning and significance and are not so numerous as to dilute the special meaning and significance that each has.")

"National symbols" cannot be equated with the "insignia" of nations. As noted in *Liberty Mutual Insurance Co.,* 185 F. Supp. at 908, 127 USPQ at 323:

> The Act ... does not put national symbols on a par with the flag, coat of arms, or other insignia of the United States, which may not in any event be made the subject matter of a trade or service mark. With regard to national symbols the statute provides merely that they shall not be disparaged or held up to contempt or disrepute, and shall not be used as falsely to suggest a connection between the holder of the mark and the symbol.

See TMEP § 1204 regarding insignia.

While the prohibition of § 2(a) against the registration of matter that may disparage or falsely suggest a connection with national symbols, or bring them into contempt or disrepute, may not be applicable to a particular designation, many names, acronyms, titles, terms, and symbols are protected by other statutes or rules. *See* TMEP § 1205.01.

1203.03(c) Disparagement, Bringing into Contempt and Bringing into Disrepute

Section 2(a) prohibits the registration of a mark that consists of or comprises matter that may disparage, or bring into contempt or disrepute, persons, institutions, beliefs or national symbols. *See* TMEP § 1203.03(a) regarding persons, and TMEP § 1203.03(b) regarding national symbols.

In sustaining an opposition on this ground, the Trademark Trial and Appeal Board stated as follows:

> Disparagement is essentially a violation of one's right of privacy—the right to be "let alone" from contempt or ridicule. See, *Carson v. Here's Johnny Portable Toilets, Inc.,* 698 F.2d 831, 218 USPQ 1 (6th Cir. 1983). It has been defined as the publication of a statement which the publisher intends to be understood, or which the recipient reasonably should understand, as tending "to cast doubt upon the quality of another's land, chattels, or intangible things." RESTATEMENT (SECOND) OF TORTS § 629 (1977). The two elements of such a claim are (1) that the communication reasonably would be understood as referring to the plaintiff; and (2) that the communication is disparaging, that is, would be considered offensive or objectionable by a reasonable person of ordinary sensibilities. *Id.* (citations omitted).

Greyhound Corp. v. Both Worlds Inc., 6 USPQ2d 1635, 1639 (TTAB 1988).

The Board applies a two-part test in determining whether a proposed mark is disparaging:

> (1) What is the likely meaning of the matter in question, taking into account not only dictionary definitions, but also the relationship of the matter to the other elements in the mark, the nature of the goods or

services, and the manner in which the mark is used in the marketplace in connection with the goods or services; and

(2) If that meaning is found to refer to identifiable persons, institutions, beliefs or national symbols, whether that meaning may be disparaging to a substantial composite of the referenced group.

See In re Squaw Valley Development Co., 80 USPQ2d 1264 (TTAB 2006); *Order Sons of Italy in America v. The Memphis Mafia, Inc.*, 52 USPQ2d 1364 (TTAB 1999); *Harjo v. Pro–Football Inc.*, 50 USPQ2d 1705 (TTAB 1999), *rev'd on other grounds*, 284 F. Supp. 2d 96, 68 USPQ2d 1225 (D.D.C. 2003), *remanded*, 415 F.3d 44, 75 USPQ2d 1525 (D.C. Cir. 2005).

The question of disparagement must be considered in relation to the goods or services identified in the application. In *Squaw Valley*, the terms SQUAW and SQUAW ONE were found to be disparaging when used in connection with clothing in Class 25 and retail store services in the field of sporting goods and equipment and clothing in Class 35, because the likely meaning of "Squaw" is an American Indian woman or wife, and the examining attorney's evidence established *prima facie* that a substantial composite of Native Americans would consider the term to be offensive. However, these terms were found not to be disparaging when used in connection with ski-related equipment in Class 28, because the likely meaning of "Squaw" in relation to these goods was deemed to be applicant's Squaw Valley ski resort.

In an *ex parte* case, the examining attorney must make a *prima facie* showing that a substantial composite of the referenced group would find the proposed mark, as used on or in connection with the relevant goods or services, to be disparaging. This shifts the burden to applicant to rebut the examining attorney's showing. *Squaw Valley*.

1203.03(d) Disparagement, Bringing into Contempt and Bringing into Disrepute: Case References

See In re Squaw Valley Development Co., 80 USPQ2d 1264 (TTAB 2006) (SQUAW and SQUAW ONE found to be disparaging when used in connection with clothing in Class 25 and retail store services in the field of sporting goods and equipment and clothing in Class 35, because the likely meaning of quaw in relation to these goods/services is an American Indian woman or wife, and the examining attorney evidence established *prima facie* that a substantial composite of Native Americans would consider the term to be offensive; however, these terms were found not to be disparaging when used in connection with ski-related equipment in Class 28, because the likely meaning of quaw in relation to these goods was deemed to be applicant's Squaw Valley ski resort); *Boswell v. Mavety Media Group Ltd.*, 52 USPQ2d 1600 (TTAB 1999) (BLACK TAIL used on adult entertainment magazines, found not to be disparaging of women in general, or African–American women in particular, nor to bring those groups into contempt or disrepute); *Order Sons of Italy in America v. Memphis Mafia Inc.*, 52 USPQ2d 1364 (TTAB 1999) (THE MEMPHIS MAFIA for entertainment services found not to be matter that disparages Italian–Americans or bring them into contempt or disrepute); *In re In Over Our Heads Inc.*, 16 USPQ2d 1653, 1654 (TTAB 1990) (MOONIES and design incorporating a "buttocks caricature," for dolls whose pants can be dropped, held not to be disparaging matter that is unregistrable under § 2(a), the Board finding that the mark "would, when used on a doll, most likely be perceived as indicating that the doll 'moons,' and would not be perceived as referencing members of The Unification Church."); *Greyhound Corp. v. Both Worlds Inc.*, 6 USPQ2d 1635, 1639–40 (TTAB 1988) (design of dog defecating, for clothing, held to disparage, and bring into contempt or disrepute, opposer's running dog symbol, the Board finding the evidence of record "sufficient to show prima facie that this design [the running dog symbol] is, in effect, an alter ego of opposer which points uniquely and unmistakably to opposer's persona."); *In re Anti–Communist World Freedom Congress, Inc.*, 161 USPQ 304 (TTAB 1969) (design of an "X" superimposed over a hammer and sickle held to disparage, and hold in contempt and disrepute, a national symbol of the U.S.S.R.).

1203.03(e)   False Suggestion of a Connection

Section 2(a) prohibits the registration of a mark that consists of or comprises matter that may falsely suggest a connection with persons, institutions, beliefs or national symbols. *See* TMEP § 1203.03(a) regarding persons, TMEP § 1203.03(b) regarding national symbols, and TMEP § 1203.03 for information about the legislative history of § 2(a).

To establish that a proposed mark falsely suggest a connection with a person or an institution, it must be shown that: (1) the mark is the same as, or a close approximation of, the name or identity of a person or institution; (2) the mark would be recognized as such, in that it points uniquely and unmistakably to that person or institution; (3) the person or institution named by the mark is not connected with the activities performed by applicant under the mark; and (4) the fame or reputation of the person or institution is such that, when the mark is used with the applicant's goods or services, a connection with the person or institution would be presumed. *In re White*, 73 USPQ2d 1713 (TTAB 2004); *In re Nuclear Research Corp.*, 16 USPQ2d 1316, 1317 (TTAB 1990); *Buffett v. Chi–Chi's, Inc.*, 226 USPQ 428, 429 (TTAB 1985); *In re Cotter & Co.*, 228 USPQ 202, 204 (TTAB 1985).

In *In re Sloppy Joe's International Inc.*, 43 USPQ2d 1350, 1353–34 (TTAB 1997), the Trademark Trial and Appeal Board held that Ernest Hemingway's friendship with the original owner of applicant's bar, his frequenting the bar and his use of the back room as an office is not the kind of "connection" contemplated by § 2(a). Rather, a commercial connection, such as an ownership interest or commercial endorsement or sponsorship of applicant's services would be necessary to entitle the applicant to registration.

If it is unclear whether the person or institution is connected with the goods sold or services performed by the applicant, the examining attorney should make an explicit inquiry under 37 C.F.R. § 2.61(b).

A refusal on this basis requires, by implication, that the person or institution with which a connection is falsely suggested must be the prior user. *In re Nuclear Research Corp.*, 16 USPQ2d at 1317; *In re Mohawk Air Services Inc.*, 196 USPQ 851, 854–55 (TTAB 1977).

Intent to identify a party or trade on its goodwill is not a required element of a § 2(a) claim of false suggestion of an association with such party. *S & L Acquisition Co. v. Helene Arpels, Inc.*, 9 USPQ2d 1221, 1224 (TTAB 1987); *Consolidated Natural Gas Co. v. CNG Fuel Systems, Ltd.*, 228 USPQ 752, 754 (TTAB 1985). However, evidence of such an intent could be highly persuasive that the public would make the intended false association. *University of Notre Dame du Lac v. J.C. Gourmet Food Imports Co., Inc.*, 703 F.2d 1372, 1377, 217 USPQ 505, 509 (Fed. Cir. 1983), *aff'g* 213 USPQ 594 (TTAB 1982).

1203.03(f)   False Suggestion of a Connection: Case References

See University of Notre Dame du Lac v. J.C. Gourmet Food Imports Co., Inc., 703 F.2d 1372, 1377, 217 USPQ 505, 509 (Fed. Cir. 1983), *aff'g* 213 USPQ 594 (TTAB 1982) (NOTRE DAME and design, for cheese, held not to falsely suggest a connection with the University of Notre Dame. "As the board noted, 'Notre Dame' is not a name solely associated with the University. It serves to identify a famous and sacred religious figure and is used in the names of churches dedicated to Notre Dame, such as the Cathedral of Notre Dame in Paris, France. Thus it cannot be said that the only 'person' which the name possibly identifies is the University and that the mere use of NOTRE DAME by another appropriates its identity."); *In re Sauer*, 27 USPQ2d 1073 (TTAB 1993), *aff'd*, 26 F.3d 140 (Fed. Cir. 1994) (registration of BO BALL for oblong shaped leather ball with white stitching properly refused under § 2(a), since use of "Bo" would be recognized by purchasers as reference to football and baseball player Bo Jackson, and there was no connection between Jackson and applicant); *In re White*, 80 USPQ2d 1654 (TTAB 2006) (Board affirmed refusal of MO-HAWK for cigarettes under § 2(a), on the ground that it would falsely suggest a connection with the federally recognized tribe the St. Regis Band of Mohawk Indians of New York); *In re White*, 73 USPQ2d 1713 (TTAB 2004) (APACHE, used for cigarettes, falsely suggests a connection with the nine federally recognized Apache tribes); *In re Los Angeles Police Revolver and Athletic Club, Inc.*, 69 USPQ2d 1630 (TTAB 2004) (slogan TO PRO-TECT AND TO SERVE, used by applicant Los Angeles Police Revolver and Athletic Club, Inc., does not *falsely* suggest a connection with the Los Angeles Police Department, where evidence showed an actual longstanding commercial connection, publicly acknowledged and endorsed by both parties); *In re Urbano*, 51 USPQ2d 1776 (TTAB 1999) (SYDNEY 2000, used for advertising and business services and communication services, falsely suggests connection with Olympic Games, since general public would recognize phrase as referring unambiguously to Olympic Games to be held in Sydney, Australia, in 2000; entire organization that comprises Olympic games qualifies as "institution."); *In re North American Free Trade Association,* 43 USPQ2d 1282 (TTAB 1997) (NAFTA, used on "promotion of trade and investment" services, falsely suggests connection with North American Free Trade Agreement; NAFTA qualifies as institution because it encompasses treaty, supplemental agreements, and various commissions, committees and offices created by those documents); *In re Sloppy Joe's International Inc.,* 43 USPQ2d 1350 (TTAB 1997) (use of mark SLOPPY JOE'S, with design that includes portrait of Ernest Hemingway, falsely suggests connection with deceased writer); *Internet Inc. v. Corporation for National Research Initiatives,* 38 USPQ2d 1435 (TTAB 1996) (cancellation petitioners failed to state claim for relief where they have not alleged, and cannot reasonably allege, that the term INTERNET points uniquely and unmistakably to their own identity or persona); *Ritz Hotel Ltd. v. Ritz Closet Seat Corp.,* 17 USPQ2d 1466, 1471 (TTAB 1990) (RIT–Z in stylized form, for toilet seats, held not to falsely suggest a connection with opposer, the Board observing that there was "no evidence of record directed to showing a connection of applicant's mark with opposer corporation, The Ritz Hotel Limited"); *In re Nuclear Research Corp.,* 16 USPQ2d 1316 (TTAB 1990) (NRC and design, for radiation and chemical agent monitors, electronic testers and nuclear gauges, held not to falsely suggest a connection with the U.S. Nuclear Regulatory Commission in view of applicant's use of NRC long prior to the inception of that agency); *NASA v. Bully Hill Vineyards, Inc.,* 3 USPQ2d 1671, 1676 (TTAB 1987) (opposition to the registration of SPACE SHUTTLE for wines dismissed, the Board finding "shuttle" to be a generic term for a space vehicle or system. "Where a name claimed to be appropriated does not point uniquely and unmistakably to that party's personality or 'persona,' there can be no false suggestion."); *Board of Trustees of University of Alabama v. BAMA–Werke Curt Baumann,* 231 USPQ 408 (TTAB 1986) (petition to cancel registration of BAMA, for shoes, slippers, stockings, socks and insoles, granted, the Board finding that the evidence of record indicated that BAMA points uniquely to the University of Alabama and thus falsely suggests a connection with the University); *In re Cotter & Co.,* 228 USPQ 202 (TTAB 1985) (WEST-POINT, for shotguns and rifles, held to falsely suggest a connection with an institution, the United States Military Academy). For examples of findings of false suggestion of a connection prior to the decision of the Court of Appeals for the Federal Circuit in *Notre Dame, supra, see In re U.S. Bicentennial Society,* 197 USPQ 905 (TTAB 1978) (U.S. BICENTENNIAL SOCIETY, for ceremonial swords, held to falsely suggest a connection with the American Revolution Bicentennial Commission and the United States government); *In re National Intelligence Academy,* 190 USPQ 570 (TTAB 1976) (NATIONAL INTELLIGENCE ACADEMY, for educational and instructional services in intelligence gathering for law enforcement officers, held to falsely suggest a connection with the United States government).

1204 Refusal on Basis of Flag, Coat of Arms or Other Insignia of United States, State or Municipality, or Foreign Nation

Extract from 15 U.S.C. § 1052. No trademark by which the goods of the applicant may be distinguished from the goods of others shall be refused registration on the principal register on account of its nature unless it ... (b) Consists of or comprises the flag or coat of arms or other insignia of the United States, or of any State or municipality, or of any foreign nation, or any simulation thereof.

Section 2(b) of the Trademark Act, 15 U.S.C. § 1052(b), bars the registration on either the Principal Register or the Supplemental Register of marks that consist of or comprise (whether consisting solely of, or having incorporated in them) the flag, coat of arms, or other insignia of the United States, of any state or municipality, or of any foreign nation. Section 2(b) also bars the registration of marks that consist of or comprise any simulation of such symbols.

Section 2(b) differs from the provision of § 2(a) regarding national symbols (*see* TMEP § 1203.03(b)) in that § 2(b) requires no additional element, such as disparagement or a false suggestion of a connection, to preclude registration.

Flags and coats of arms are specific designs formally adopted to serve as emblems of governmental authority. The wording "other insignia" should not be interpreted broadly, but should be considered to include only those emblems and devices that also represent such authority and that are of the same general class and character as flags and coats of arms. The Trademark Trial and Appeal Board has construed the statutory language as follows:

> [T]he wording "or other insignia of the United States" must be restricted in its application to insignia of the same general class as "the flag or coats of arms" of the United States. Since both the flag and coat of arms are emblems of national authority it seems evident that other insignia of national authority such as the Great Seal of the United States, the Presidential Seal, and seals of government departments would be equally prohibited registration under Section 2(b). On the other hand, it appears equally evident that department insignia which are merely used to identify a service or facility of the Government are not insignia of national authority and that they therefore do not fall within the general prohibitions of this section of the Statute.

In re U.S. Department of the Interior, 142 USPQ 506, 507 (TTAB 1964) (logo comprising the words "NATIONAL PARK SERVICE" and "Department of the Interior," with depiction of trees, mountains and a buffalo, surrounded by an arrowhead design, held not to be an insignia of the United States).

Letters that merely identify people and things associated with a particular agency or department of the United States government, instead of representing the authority of the government or the nation as a whole, are generally not considered to be "insignia of the United States" within the meaning of § 2(b). The Board, in dismissing an opposition to the registration of "USMC" in a stylized presentation, for prostheses, fracture braces and orthopedic components, discussed the meaning of "insignia" under § 2(b), as follows:

> The letters "USMC" are nothing like a flag or coat of arms. These types of insignia are pictorial in nature, they can be described, but cannot be pronounced. Even if the letters could be construed to be an insignia, opposer has not shown that they would be seen as an insignia of the United States.

U.S. Navy v. U.S. Mfg. Co., 2 USPQ2d 1254, 1256 (TTAB 1987). As a result of the enactment of Public Law 98–525 on October 19, 1984, the initials, seal and emblem of the United States Marine Corps are "deemed to be insignia of the United States," under 10 U.S.C. § 7881, pertaining to unauthorized use of Marine Corps insignia. However, "USMC" was not so protected when the applicant began using its stylized version of those letters as a mark. In view of the provision in Public Law 98–525 that the amendments adding Chapter 663 (10 U.S.C. § 7881) shall not affect rights that vested before the date of its enactment, the majority of the Board found that enactment of the law did not adversely affect the mark's registrability, stating that "opposer has not shown that applicant's mark was an insignia of the United States prior to the law making it one, or that the law effectively bars registration to applicant." *Id.* at 1260. (*See* TMEP § 1205.01 regarding subject matter that is protected by statute.)

See also Liberty Mutual Insurance Co. v. Liberty Insurance Co. of Texas, 185 F. Supp. 895, 908, 127 USPQ 312, 323 (E.D. Ark. 1960) ("That the Statue of Liberty is not a part of the 'insignia of the United States' is too clear to require discussion.")

As stated above, marks that consist of or comprise any simulation of the flag, coat of arms, or other insignia of the United States, of any state or municipality, or of any foreign nation are also unregistrable under § 2(b). "Simulation," as contemplated by § 2(b), refers to "something that gives the appearance or effect or has the characteristics of an original item." *In re Waltham Watch Co.*, 179 USPQ 59, 60 (TTAB 1973) (mark consisting of wording and the design of a globe and six flags for watches found registrable, the Board stating, "[A]lthough the flags depicted in applicant's mark incorporate common elements of flag designs such as horizontal or vertical lines, crosses or stars, they are readily distinguishable from any of the flags of the nations alluded to by the examiner. In fact, applicant's mark would be regarded as nothing more than a conglomeration of nondescript flags utilized to symbolize the significance of the globe design and the slogan 'TIMING THE WORLD' appearing thereon.") Whether a mark comprises a simulation must be determined from a visual comparison of the mark vis-à-vis replicas of the flag, coat of arms or other insignia in question. *Id.*

The determination of whether a proposed mark consists of or comprises a flag, coat of arms or other insignia must be made "without a careful analysis and side-by-side comparison." *In re Advance Industrial Security, Inc.*, 194 USPQ 344, 346 (TTAB 1977) (ADVANCE SECURITY and design consisting of an eagle on a triangular shield, in gold and brown, for detective and investigative services and providing security systems and services, found registrable, the Board stating, "When the mark of the applicant and the Coat of Arms or Great Seal of the United States are compared in their entireties, it is adjudged that applicant's mark does not consist of or comprise the Coat of Arms of the United States or any simulation thereof. . . .") The public should be considered to retain only a general or overall, rather than specific, recollection of the various elements or characteristics of design marks. *Id.*

The incorporation in a mark of individual or distorted features that are merely suggestive of flags, coats of arms or other insignia does not bar registration under § 2(b). *See Knorr–Nahrmittel A.G. v. Havland International, Inc.*, 206 USPQ 827, 833 (TTAB 1980) (While applicant originally may have intended to include the flags of the Scandinavian countries in the mark, NOR–KING and design, "[a]ll that the record reflects is that the mark contains a representation of certain flags, but not the flag or flags of any particular nation." Opposer's cause of action under § 2(b) found to be without merit; opposition sustained on other grounds); *In re National Van Lines, Inc.*, 123 USPQ 510 (TTAB 1959) (mark comprising words and the design of a shield with vertical stripes held registrable, the Board finding the design to be readily distinguishable from the shield of the Great Seal of the United States and, therefore, not a simulation of the seal or any portion thereof); *In re American Box Board Co.*, 123 USPQ 508 (TTAB 1959) (design mark comprising an eagle and shield held registrable, the Board finding that it did not involve a simulation of the Great Seal of the United States because the eagle and shield of applicant's mark differed substantially from those on the seal in both appearance and manner of display).

See TMEP §§ 1205 *et seq.* regarding matter that is protected by statute or by Article 6*ter* of the Paris Convention.

To overcome a refusal under § 2(a) or § 2(b), deletion of the unregistrable matter is sometimes permitted. *See* TMEP § 807.14(a) regarding removal of matter from drawings.

1206 Refusal on Basis of Name, Portrait or Signature of Particular Living Individual or Deceased U.S. President Without Consent

Extract from 15 U.S.C. § 1052. No trademark by which the goods of the applicant may be distinguished from the goods of others shall be refused registration on the principal register on account of its nature unless it . . . (c) Consists of or comprises a name, portrait, or signature identifying a particular living individual except by his written consent, or the name, signature, or portrait of a deceased President of the United States during the life of his widow, if any, except by the written consent of the widow.

Section 2(c) of the Trademark Act, 15 U.S.C. § 1052(c), bars the registration of a mark that consists of or comprises (whether consisting solely of, or having incorporated in the mark) a name, portrait or signature that identifies a particular living individual, or a deceased United States president during the life of his widow, except by the written consent of the individual or the president's widow.

Section 2(c) absolutely bars the registration of these marks on either the Principal Register or the Supplemental Register.

The purpose of requiring the consent of a living individual to the registration of his or her name, signature or portrait is to protect rights of privacy and publicity that living persons have in the designations that identify them. *University of Notre Dame du Lac v. J.C. Gourmet Food Imports Co., Inc.*, 703 F.2d 1372, 1376, 217 USPQ 505, 509 (Fed. Cir. 1983), *aff'g* 213 USPQ 594 (TTAB 1982); *Canovas v. Venezia 80 S.R.L.*, 220 USPQ 660, 661 (TTAB 1983). *See* TMEP § 1203.03 for a discussion of the right to control the use of one's identity, which underlies part of § 2(a) as well as § 2(c).

See TMEP § 813 regarding when it is necessary for an examining attorney to inquire of the applicant as to whether a name, signature or portrait in a mark identifies a particular living individual, and regarding the entry of pertinent statements in the record for printing in the *Official Gazette* and on a registration certificate.

1206.01   Name, Portrait or Signature

Section 2(c) explicitly pertains to any name, portrait or signature that identifies a particular living individual, or a deceased president of the United States during the life of the president's widow.

To identify a particular living individual, a name does not have to be the person's full name. *See Ross v. Analytical Technology Inc.*, 51 USPQ2d 1269 (TTAB 1999) (registration of opposer's surname without consent prohibited by § 2(c), where the record showed that because of opposer's reputation as an inventor in the field of electrochemical analysis, the relevant public would associate the goods so marked with opposer); *In re Steak and Ale Restaurants of America, Inc.*, 185 USPQ 447 (TTAB 1975) (PRINCE CHARLES found to identify a particular living individual whose consent was not of record); *Laub v. Industrial Development Laboratories, Inc.*, 121 USPQ 595 (TTAB 1959) (LAUB, for flowmeters, found to identify the holder of a patent for flowmeters, whose written consent was not of record); *Reed v. Bakers Engineering & Equipment Co.*, 100 USPQ 196, 199 (PO Ex. Ch. 1954) (registration of REED REEL OVEN, for ovens, held to be barred by § 2(c) without written consent of the designer and builder of the ovens, Paul N. Reed. " 'Name' in § 2(c) is not restricted to the full name of an individual but refers to any name regardless of whether it is a full name, or a surname or given name, or even a nickname, which identifies a particular living individual . . ."). *Cf. Société Civile Des Domaines, Dourthe Frères v. S.A. Consortium Vinicole De Bordeaux Et De La*

Gironde, 6 USPQ2d 1205, 1209 (TTAB 1988) ("Section 2(c) does not apply to surnames except in those cases where a particular individual is known by a surname alone.")

Cases involving portraits include *In re McKee Baking Co.*, 218 USPQ 287 (TTAB 1983) (mark comprising a sign on which the portrait of a young girl appears below the words LITTLE DEBBIE); *In re Masucci*, 179 USPQ 829 (TTAB 1973) (mark comprising name and portrait of a deceased president of the United States, President Eisenhower); *Garden v. Parfumerie Rigaud, Inc.*, 34 USPQ 30 (Comm'r Pats. 1937) (marks comprising name and portrait of Mary Garden).

1206.02   Particular Living Individual or Deceased U.S. President

Section 2(c) applies to marks that comprise matter that identify living individuals; it does not apply to marks that comprise matter that identifies deceased persons, except for a deceased president of the United States during the life of the president's widow. *See McGraw–Edison Co. v. Thomas Edison Life Insurance Co.*, 160 USPQ 685 (TTAB 1969), *vacated on other grounds*, 162 USPQ 372 (N.D. Ill. 1969) (opposition to the registration of THOMAS EDISON dismissed, the Board finding § 2(c) inapplicable, as the particular individual whom the name identifies is deceased); *In re Masucci*, 179 USPQ 829 (TTAB 1973) (affirming refusal to register mark consisting of the name EISENHOWER, a portrait of President Dwight D. Eisenhower and the words PRESIDENT EISENHOWER REGISTERED PLATINUM MEDALLION #13, for greeting cards, on the ground that the mark comprises the name, signature or portrait of a deceased United States president without the written consent of his widow, under § 2(c)).

The fact that a name appearing in a mark may actually be the name of more than one person does not negate the requirement for a written consent to registration, if the mark identifies, to the relevant public, a particular living individual or deceased United States president whose spouse is living. *In re Steak and Ale Restaurants of America, Inc.*, 185 USPQ 447 (TTAB 1975) (affirming refusal to register PRINCE CHARLES, for meat, in the absence of consent to register by Prince Charles, a member of the English royal family. "Even accepting the existence of more than one living 'Prince Charles,' it does not follow that each is not a particular living individual.")

If it appears that a name, portrait or signature in a mark may identify a particular living individual but in fact the applicant devised the matter as fanciful, or believes it to be fanciful, a statement to that effect should be placed in the record. If appropriate, the statement that a name, portrait or signature does not identify a particular living individual will be printed in the *Official Gazette* and on the registration certificate. *See* TMEP § 813. Additional relevant circumstances should also be explained. For example, if the matter identifies a certain character in literature, or a deceased historical person, then a statement of these facts in the record may be helpful; however, this information should not be printed in the *Official Gazette* or on a registration certificate.

Although a mark may have been devised to be fanciful or arbitrary and not to identify a particular living individual, it nevertheless may name or otherwise identify one or more living individuals. Whether a consent to registration is required depends on whether the public would recognize and understand the mark as identifying the person. Therefore, if the person is not generally known, or well known in the field relating to the relevant goods or services, it may be that the mark would not constitute the identification of a particular person under § 2(c), and consent would not be required. The Trademark Trial and Appeal Board noted as follows in *Martin v. Carter Hawley Hale Stores, Inc.*, 206 USPQ 931, 933 (TTAB 1979):

> [Section] 2(c) was not designed to protect every person from having a name which is similar or identical to his or her name registered as a trademark. Such a scope of protection would practically preclude the registration of a trademark consisting of a name since in most cases there would be someone somewhere who is known by the name and who might be expected to protest its registration. Rather, the Statute was intended to protect one who, for valid reasons, could expect to suffer damage from another's trademark use of his name. That is, it is more than likely that any trademark which is comprised of a given name and surname will, in fact, be the name of a real person. But that coincidence, in and of itself, does not give rise to damage to that individual in the absence of other factors from which it may be determined that the particular individual bearing the name in question will be associated with the mark as used on the goods, either because that person is so well known that the public would reasonably assume the connection or because the individual is publicly connected with the business in which the mark is used.

In *Martin*, the Board held that § 2(c) did not prohibit registration of NEIL MARTIN for men's shirts, where the individual, although well known in his own professional and social circles, failed to establish that he was so famous as to be recognized by the public in general or that he is or ever was connected with the clothing field.

In *Krause v. Krause Publications, Inc.*, 76 USPQ2d 1904 (TTAB 2005), evidence was found sufficient to establish that the cancellation petitioner was publicly connected with the fields of numismatics, car collecting and publishing, such that a connection between petitioner and the mark KRAUSE PUBLICATIONS would be presumed by people who have an interest in these fields. Thus, the mark was unregistrable for magazines featuring antique automobiles and numismatics, conducting trade shows and award programs featuring coins, and other related goods and services. However, the mark was found registrable for "entertainment services in the nature of competitions and awards in the field of cutlery," because petitioner had not demonstrated that he was publicly connected with the field of cutlery, or that he is so well known by the general public that a connection between petitioner and the mark would be presumed with respect to these services. *See also Ross v. Analytical Technology Inc.*, 51 USPQ2d 1269 (TTAB 1999) (evidence found sufficient to establish that opposer Dr. James Ross was publicly connected with the electrochemical analysis equipment field and that use of the name ROSS in connection with equipment in that field would lead to the assumption that opposer was in some way associated with the goods); *In re Sauer,* 27 USPQ2d 1073 (TTAB 1993), *aff'd per curiam,* 26 F.3d 140 (Fed. Cir. 1994) (BO, the recognized nickname of professional football and baseball star Bo Jackson, found to be so well known by the general public that use of the name BO in connection with sports balls would lead to the assumption that he was in some way associated with the goods or with applicant's business); *Fanta v. Coca–Cola Co.*, 140 USPQ 674 (TTAB 1964) (dismissing a petition to cancel registrations of FANTA for soft drinks and syrup concentrate, the Board noting no use by the petitioner, Robert D. Fanta, of his name in connection with the sale of soft drinks, nor any indication that petitioner had attained recognition in that field); *Brand v. Fairchester Packing Co.*, 84 USPQ 97 (Comm'r Pats. 1950) (affirming dismissal of a petition to cancel the registration of ARNOLD BRAND, for fresh tomatoes, the Commissioner finding nothing in the record to indicate that the mark identified the petitioner, Arnold Brand, an attorney specializing in patent and trademark matters, with the tomato business, or that use of the mark would lead the public to make such a connection).

To support a refusal under § 2(c) as to a particular class in an application, it is not necessary to demonstrate that the individual is publicly connected with all the goods or services listed in the class. It is enough to show that the individual is publicly connected with at least some of the goods/services in the class. *Krause, supra.*

1210.08 Wines and Spirits

Section 2(a) of the Trademark Act, 15 U.S.C. § 1052(a), prohibits the registration of a designation that consists of or comprises "a geographical indication which, when used on or in connection with wines or spirits, identifies a place other than the origin of the goods and is first used on or in connection with wines or spirits by the applicant on or after [January 1, 1996]." This provision was added by the Uruguay Round Agreements Act, implementing the Trade–Related Intellectual Property ("TRIPs") portions of the General Agreement on Tariffs and Trade ("GATT"). This provision does not apply to geographic indications that were first used in commerce on or in connection with wines or spirits prior to January 1, 1996.

The term "spirits" refers to "a strong distilled alcoholic liquor" (*e.g.,* gin, rum, vodka, whiskey, brandy). *Random House Webster's Unabridged Dictionary* 1839 (2nd ed. 1998). This provision does not apply to designations used on or in connection with beer, nor does it apply to goods that are not wines or spirits, but are partially composed of wines or spirits (*e.g.,* wine vinegar; wine sauces; wine jelly; rum balls; bourbon chicken).

This provision of § 2(a) applies if the applicant's identification of goods: (1) specifically includes wines or spirits; or (2) describes the goods using broad terms that could include wines or spirits (*e.g.,* alcoholic beverages).

Section 2(a) is an absolute bar to the registration of these geographical designations on either the Principal Register or the Supplemental Register. Neither a disclaimer of the geographical designation nor a claim that it has acquired distinctiveness under § 2(f) can obviate a § 2(a) refusal if the mark consists of or comprises a geographical indication that identifies a place other than the origin of the wines or spirits.

See TMEP § 1210.08(a) regarding geographical indications used on wines and spirits that do not originate in the named place, TMEP § 1210.08(b) regarding geographical indications used on wines and spirits that originate in the named place, and TMEP § 1210.08(c) regarding geographical indications that are generic for wines and spirits.

1210.09   Geographic Certification Marks

Under certain circumstances the name of the place from which goods or services originate may function as a certification mark. When geographic terms are used to certify regional origin (*e.g.* "Idaho" used to certify that potatoes are grown in Idaho), registration of certification marks should not be refused and, in applications to register composite certification marks, disclaimers of these geographic terms should *not* be required on the ground of geographical descriptiveness. *See* TMEP §§ 1306.02 *et seq.* concerning procedures for registration of certification marks that certify regional origin.

When a geographical term used in a composite certification mark is not used to certify regional origin (*e.g.,* "California" used to certify that fruit is organically grown), appropriate refusals pursuant to §§ 2(e)(2), 2(e)(3) or 2(a) should be made.

1211   Refusal on Basis of Surname

Extract from 15 U.S.C. § 1052. No trademark by which the goods of the applicant may be distinguished from the goods of others shall be refused registration on the principal register on account of its nature unless it ... (e) Consists of a mark which ... (4) is primarily merely a surname.

Under § 2(e)(4) of the Trademark Act, 15 U.S.C. § 1052(e)(4), a mark that is primarily merely a surname is not registrable on the Principal Register absent a showing of acquired distinctiveness under § 2(f), 15 U.S.C. § 1052(f). *See* TMEP §§ 1212 *et seq.* regarding acquired distinctiveness. Formerly § 2(e)(3) of the Act, this section was designated § 2(e)(4) when the NAFTA Implementation Act took effect on January 1, 1994. A mark that is primarily merely a surname may be registrable on the Supplemental Register in an application under § 1 or § 44 of the Trademark Act.

The Trademark Act, in § 2(e)(4), reflects the common law that exclusive rights in a surname *per se* cannot be established without evidence of long and exclusive use that changes its significance to the public from that of a surname to that of a mark for particular goods or services. The common law also recognizes that surnames are shared by more than one individual, each of whom may have an interest in using his surname in business; and, by the requirement for evidence of distinctiveness, the law, in effect, delays appropriation of exclusive rights in the name. *In re Etablissements Darty et Fils,* 759 F.2d 15, 17, 225 USPQ 652, 653 (Fed. Cir. 1985).

The question of whether a mark is primarily merely a surname depends on the mark's *primary* significance to the purchasing public. *See, e.g., Ex parte Rivera Watch Corp.*, 106 USPQ 145, 149 (Comm'r Pats. 1955). Each case must be decided on its own facts, based upon the evidence in the record.

1211.01 "Primarily Merely a Surname"

The legislative history of the Trademark Act of 1946 indicates that the word "primarily" was added to the existing statutory language "merely" with the intent to exclude registration of names such as "Johnson" or "Jones," but not registration of names such as "Cotton" or "King" which, while surnames, have a primary significance other than as a surname. *See Sears, Roebuck & Co. v. Watson,* 204 F.2d 32, 33–34, 96 USPQ 360, 362 (D.C. Cir. 1953), *cert. denied,* 346 U.S. 829, 99 USPQ 491 (1953); *Ex parte Rivera Watch Corp.*, 106 USPQ 145, 149 (Comm'r Pats. 1955).

The question of whether a term is primarily merely a surname depends on the primary, not the secondary, significance to the purchasing public. The Trademark Trial and Appeal Board has identified five factors to be considered in making this determination:

(1) whether the surname is rare (*see* TMEP § 1211.01(a)(v));

(2) whether the term is the surname of anyone connected with the applicant (*see* TMEP § 1211.02(b)(iii));

(3) whether the term has any recognized meaning other than as a surname (*see* TMEP §§ 1211.01(a) *et seq.*);

(4) whether it has the "look and feel" of a surname (*see* TMEP § 1211.01(a)(vi)); and

(5) whether the stylization of lettering is distinctive enough to create a separate commercial impression (*see* TMEP § 1211.01(b)(ii)).

In re Benthin Management GmbH, 37 USPQ2d 1332, 1333–1334 (TTAB 1995).

1211.01(a) Non–Surname Significance

Often a word will have a meaning or significance in addition to its significance as a surname. The examining attorney must determine the primary meaning of the term to the public.

1211.01(a)(i) Ordinary Language Meaning

If there is a readily recognized meaning of a term, apart from its surname significance, such that the primary significance of the term is not that of a surname, registration should be granted on the Principal Register without evidence of acquired distinctiveness. *See In re Isabella Fiore, LLC*, 75 USPQ2d 1564 (TTAB 2005) (FIORE is not primarily merely a surname where it is also the Italian translation of the English word "flower" and the non-surname meaning is not obscure); *In re United Distillers plc*, 56 USPQ2d 1220 (TTAB 2000) (the relatively rare surname HACKLER held not primarily merely a surname, in light of dictionary meaning); *Fisher Radio Corp. v. Bird Electronic Corp.*, 162 USPQ 265 (TTAB 1969) (BIRD held not primarily merely a surname despite surname significance); *In re Hunt Electronics Co.*, 155 USPQ 606 (TTAB 1967) (HUNT held not primarily merely a surname despite surname significance). However, this does not mean that an applicant only has to uncover a non-surname meaning of the proposed mark to obviate a refusal under § 2(e)(4). *See In re Nelson Souto Major Piquet*, 5 USPQ2d 1367, 1368 (TTAB 1987) (N. PIQUET (stylized) held primarily merely a surname despite significance of the term "piquet" as "the name of a relatively obscure card game").

1211.01(a)(ii) Phonetic Equivalent of Term With Ordinary Language Meaning

A term may be primarily merely a surname even if it is the phonetic equivalent of a word that has an ordinary meaning (*e.g.*, Byrne/burn; Knott/not or knot; Chappell/chapel). *See In re Pickett Hotel Co.*, 229 USPQ 760 (TTAB 1986) (PICKETT SUITE HOTEL held primarily merely a surname despite applicant's argument that PICKETT is the phonetic equivalent of the word "picket"). *Cf. In re Monotype Corp. PLC*, 14 USPQ2d 1070, 1071 (TTAB 1989) (CALISTO held not primarily merely a surname, the Board characterizing the telephone directory evidence of surname significance as "minimal" and in noting the mythological significance of the name "Callisto," stating that it is common knowledge that there are variations in the rendering of mythological names transliterated from the Greek alphabet (distinguishing *In re Pickett Hotel Co., supra*)). Similarly, the fact that a word that has surname significance is also a hybrid or derivative of another word having ordinary language meaning is insufficient to overcome the surname significance unless the perception of non-surname significance would displace the primary surname import of the word. *See In re Etablissements Darty et Fils*, 759 F.2d 15, 225 USPQ 652 (Fed. Cir. 1985) (DARTY held primarily merely a surname despite applicant's argument that the mark is a play on the word "dart"); *In re Petrin Corp.*, 231 USPQ 902 (TTAB 1986) (PETRIN held primarily merely a surname despite applicant's argument that the mark represents an abbreviation of "petroleum" and "insulation").

1211.01(a)(iii) Geographical Significance

A term with surname significance may not be primarily merely a surname if that term also has a well-known geographical meaning. *In re Colt Industries Operating Corp.*, 195 USPQ 75 (TTAB 1977) (FAIRBANKS held not primarily merely a surname because the geographical significance of the mark was determined to be just as dominant as its surname significance). However, the fact that a term is shown to have some minor significance as a geographical term will not dissipate its primary significance as a surname. *In re Hamilton Pharmaceuticals Ltd.*, 27 USPQ2d 1939, 1943 (TTAB 1993) (HAMILTON held primarily merely a surname).

1211.01(a)(iv) Historical Place or Person

A term with surname significance may not be primarily merely a surname if that term also identifies a historical place or person. *See Lucien Piccard Watch Corp. v. Since 1868 Crescent Corp.*, 314 F. Supp. 329, 165 USPQ 459 (S.D.N.Y. 1970) (DA VINCI found not primarily merely a surname because it primarily connotes Leonardo Da Vinci); *In re Pyro–Spectaculars, Inc.*, 63 USPQ2d 2022, 2024 (TTAB 2002) (SOUSA for fireworks and production of events and shows featuring pyrotechnics held not primarily merely a surname, where the evidence showed present day recognition and continuing fame of John Philip Sousa as a composer of patriotic music, and the applicant's goods and services were of a nature that "would be associated by potential purchasers with patriotic events such as the Fourth of July, patriotic figures, and patriotic music"); *Michael S. Sachs Inc. v. Cordon Art, B.V.*, 56 USPQ2d 1132 (TTAB 2000) (primary significance of M. C. ESCHER is that of famous deceased Dutch artist). *Cf. In re Pickett Hotel Co.*, 229 USPQ 760 (TTAB 1986) (PICKETT SUITE HOTEL held primarily merely a surname despite applicant's evidence that PICKETT was the name of a famous Civil War general); *In re Champion International Corp.*, 229 USPQ 550 (TTAB 1985) (McKINLEY held primarily merely a surname despite being the name of a deceased president).

Evidence that that an individual is famous in a particular field does not necessarily establish that he or she is a historical figure. *In re Thermo LabSystems Inc.*, 85 USPQ2d 1285 (TTAB 2007) (WATSON held primarily merely a surname). Furthermore, the Board has held that a surname that would be evocative of numerous individuals, rather than one particular historical individual, does not qualify as a historical name and is merely a surname of numerous individuals with varying degree of historical significance. *Id.*

1211.01(a)(v) Rare Surnames

The rarity of a surname is a factor to be considered in determining whether a term is primarily merely a surname. *In re Benthin Management GmbH*, 37 USPQ2d 1332 (TTAB 1995) (the fact that BENTHIN was a rare surname found to be a factor weighing against a finding that the term would be perceived as primarily merely a surname); *In re Sava Research Corp.*, 32 USPQ2d 1380 (TTAB 1994) (SAVA not primarily merely a surname, where there was evidence that the term had other meaning, no evidence that the term was the surname of anyone connected with applicant, and the term's use as a surname was very rare); *In re Garan Inc.*, 3 USPQ2d 1537 (TTAB 1987) (GARAN held not primarily merely a surname). However, the fact that a surname is rare does not *per se* preclude a finding that a term is primarily merely a surname. Even a rare surname may be held primarily merely a surname if its primary significance to purchasers is that of a surname. *See In re Etablissements Darty et Fils*, 759 F.2d 15, 225 USPQ 652 (Fed. Cir. 1985) (DARTY held primarily merely a surname); *In re Rebo High Definition Studio Inc.*, 15 USPQ2d 1314 (TTAB 1990) (REBO held primarily merely a surname); *In re Pohang Iron & Steel Co., Ltd.*, 230 USPQ 79 (TTAB 1986) (POSTEN held primarily merely a surname). Regardless of the rarity of the surname, the test is whether the primary significance of the term to the purchasing public is that of a surname.

An issue to be considered in determining how rarely a term is used is the media attention or publicity accorded to public personalities who have the surname. A surname rarely appearing in birth records may nonetheless appear more routinely in news reports, so as to be broadly exposed to the general public. *In re Gregory*, 70 USPQ2d 1792 (TTAB 2004).

. . .

1211.01(b)(vii)   Surname Combined With Domain Name

A surname combined with a top-level domain name (*e.g.*, JOHNSON.COM) is primarily merely a surname under § 2(e)(4). *See* TMEP § 1215.03.

1211.02   Evidence Relating to Surname Refusal
1211.02(a)   Evidentiary Burden—Generally

The burden is initially on the examining attorney to establish a *prima facie* case that a mark is primarily merely a surname. The burden then shifts to the applicant to rebut this showing. *In re Petrin Corp.*, 231 USPQ 902 (TTAB 1986). The evidence submitted by the examining attorney was found insufficient to establish a *prima facie* case in the following decisions: *In re Kahan & Weisz Jewelry Mfg. Corp.*, 508 F.2d 831, 184 USPQ 421 (C.C.P.A. 1975); *In re BDH Two Inc.*, 26 USPQ2d 1556 (TTAB 1993); *In re Raivico*, 9 USPQ2d 2006 (TTAB 1988); *In re Garan Inc.*, 3 USPQ2d 1537 (TTAB 1987).

There is no rule as to the kind or amount of evidence necessary to make out a *prima facie* showing that a term is primarily merely a surname. This question must be resolved on a case-by-case basis. *See, e.g., In re Monotype Corp. PLC*, 14 USPQ2d 1070 (TTAB 1989); *In re Pohang Iron & Steel Co., Ltd.*, 230 USPQ 79 (TTAB 1986). The entire record is examined to determine the surname significance of a term. The following are examples of evidence that may be relevant: telephone directory listings; excerpted articles from computerized research databases; evidence in the record that the term is a surname; the manner of use on specimens; dictionary definitions of the term and evidence from dictionaries showing no definition of the term. The quantum of evidence that is persuasive in finding surname significance in one case may be insufficient in another because of the differences in the names themselves. *See In re Etablissements Darty et Fils*, 759 F.2d 15, 17, 225 USPQ 652, 653 (Fed. Cir. 1985).

. . .

See TMEP §§ 710 *et seq.* and 1211.02(b) *et seq.* for additional information about evidence.

CHAPTER 1300: EXAMINATION OF DIFFERENT TYPES OF MARKS

The Trademark Act of 1946 provides for registration of trademarks, service marks, collective trademarks and service marks, collective membership marks and certification marks. 15 U.S.C. §§ 1051, 1053, and 1054. The language of this Manual is generally directed to trademarks. Procedures for trademarks usually apply to other types of marks, unless otherwise stated. This chapter is devoted to special circumstances relating to service marks, collective marks, collective membership marks, and certification marks.

1301   Service Marks

Section 45 of the Trademark Act, 15 U.S.C. § 1127, defines "service mark" as follows:

> The term "service mark" means any word, name, symbol, or device, or any combination thereof—
>
> (1) used by a person, or
>
> (2) which a person has a bona fide intention to use in commerce and applies to register on the principal register established by this Act,
>
> to identify and distinguish the services of one person, including a unique service, from the services of others and to indicate the source of the services, even if that source is unknown. Titles, character names, and other distinctive features of radio or television programs may be registered as service marks notwithstanding that they, or the programs, may advertise the goods of the sponsor.

Therefore, to be registrable as a service mark, the asserted mark must function both to *identify* the services recited in the application *and distinguish* them from the services of others, and to *indicate the source of* the recited services, even if that source is unknown. The activities recited in the identification must constitute services as contemplated by the Trademark Act. *See* TMEP §§ 1301.01 *et seq.*

If a proposed mark does not function as a service mark for the services recited or if the applicant is not rendering a registrable service, the statutory basis for refusal of registration on the Principal Register is §§ 1, 3 and 45 of the Trademark Act, 15 U.S.C. §§ 1051, 1053 and 1127.

See TMEP § 1303 concerning collective service marks.

1301.01   What Is a Service

A service mark can only be registered for activities that constitute services as contemplated by the Trademark Act. 15 U.S.C. §§ 1051, 1053 and 1127. The Trademark Act defines the term "service mark," but it does not define what constitutes a service. Many activities are obviously services (*e.g.,* dry cleaning, banking, shoe repairing, transportation, and house painting).

1301.01(a)   Criteria for Determining What Constitutes a Service

The following criteria have evolved for determining what constitutes a service: (1) a service must be a real activity; (2) a service must be performed to the order of, or for the benefit of, someone other than the applicant; and (3) the activity performed must be qualitatively different from anything necessarily done in connection with the sale of the applicant's goods or the performance of another service. *In re Canadian Pacific Limited*, 754 F.2d 992, 224 USPQ 971 (Fed. Cir. 1985); *In re Betz Paperchem, Inc.*, 222 USPQ 89 (TTAB 1984); *In re Integrated Resources, Inc.*, 218 USPQ 829 (TTAB 1983); *In re Landmark Communications, Inc.*, 204 USPQ 692 (TTAB 1979).

1301.01(a)(i)   Performance of a Real Activity

A service must be a real activity. A mere idea or concept, *e.g.*, an idea for an accounting organizational format or a recipe for a baked item, is not a service. Similarly, a system, process or method is not a service. *In re Universal Oil Products Co.*, 476 F.2d 653, 177 USPQ 456 (C.C.P.A. 1973); *In re Citibank, N.A.*, 225 USPQ 612 (TTAB 1985); *In re Scientific Methods, Inc.*, 201 USPQ 917 (TTAB 1979); *In re McCormick & Company, Inc.*, 179 USPQ 317 (TTAB 1973). *See* TMEP § 1301.02(e) regarding marks that identify a system or process.

The commercial context must be considered in determining whether a real service is being performed. For example, at one time the activities of grocery stores, department stores, and similar retail stores were not considered to be services. However, it is now recognized that gathering various products together, making a place available for purchasers to select goods, and providing any other necessary means for consummating purchases constitutes the performance of a service.

1301.01(a)(ii)   For the Benefit of Others

To be a service, an activity must be primarily for the benefit of someone other than the applicant. While an advertising agency provides a service when it promotes the goods or services of its clients, a company that promotes the sale of its own goods or services is doing so for its own benefit rather than rendering a service for others. *In re Reichhold Chemicals, Inc.*, 167 USPQ 376 (TTAB 1970). *See* TMEP § 1301.01(b)(i). Similarly, a company that sets up a personnel department to employ workers for itself is merely facilitating the conduct of its own business, while a company whose business is to recruit and place workers for other companies is performing employment agency services.

The controlling question is who *primarily* benefits from the activity for which registration is sought. If the activity is done primarily for the benefit of others, the fact that applicant derives an incidental benefit is not fatal. *In re Venture Lending Associates*, 226 USPQ 285 (TTAB 1985). On the other hand, if the activity primarily benefits applicant, it is not a registrable service even if others derive an incidental benefit. *In re Dr. Pepper Co.*,

836 F.2d 508, 5 USPQ2d 1207 (Fed. Cir. 1987) (contest promoting applicant's goods not a service, even though benefits accrue to winners of contest); *In re Alaska Northwest Publishing Co.*, 212 USPQ 316 (TTAB 1981).

Collecting information for the purpose of publishing one's own periodical is not a service, because it is done primarily for applicant's benefit rather than for the benefit of others. *See* TMEP § 1301.01(b)(iii).

Offering shares of one's own stock for investment is not a service, because these are routine corporate activities that primarily benefit the applicant. *See* TMEP § 1301.01(b)(iv). On the other hand, offering a retirement income plan to applicant's employees was found to be a service, because it primarily benefits the employees. *American International Reinsurance Co., Inc. v. Airco, Inc.*, 570 F.2d 941, 197 USPQ 69 (C.C.P.A. 1978), *cert. denied* 439 U.S. 866, 200 USPQ 64 (1978).

Licensing intangible property has been recognized as a separate service, analogous to leasing or renting tangible property, that primarily benefits the licensee. *In re Universal Press Syndicate*, 229 USPQ 638 (TTAB 1986).

1301.01(a)(iii) Sufficiently Distinct from Activities Involved in Sale of Goods or Performance of Other Services

In determining whether an activity is sufficiently separate from an applicant's principal activity to constitute a service, the examining attorney should first ascertain what is the applicant's principal activity under the mark in question (*i.e.*, the sale of a service or the sale of a tangible product). The examining attorney must then determine whether the activity identified in the application is in any material way a different kind of economic activity than what any provider of that particular product or service normally provides. *In re Landmark Communications, Inc.*, 204 USPQ 692, 695 (TTAB 1979).

For example, operating a grocery store is clearly a service. Bagging groceries for customers is not considered a separately registrable service, because this activity is normally provided to and expected by grocery store customers, and is therefore merely ancillary to the primary service.

Providing general information or instructions as to the purpose and uses of applicant's goods is merely incidental to the sale of goods, not a separate consulting service. *See* TMEP § 1301.01(b)(v).

Conducting a contest to promote the sale of one's own goods or services is usually not considered a service, because it is an ordinary and routine promotional activity. *See* TMEP § 1301.01(b)(i).

While the repair of the goods of others is a recognized service, an applicant's guarantee of repair of its own goods does not normally constitute a separate service because that activity is ancillary to and normally expected in the trade. *See* TMEP § 1301.01(b)(ii).

However, the fact that an activity is ancillary to a principal service or to the sale of goods does not in itself mean that it is not a separately registrable service. The statute makes no distinction between primary, incidental or ancillary services. *In re Universal Press Syndicate,* 229 USPQ 638 (TTAB 1986) (licensing cartoon character found to be a separate service that was not merely incidental or necessary to larger business of magazine and newspaper cartoon strip); *In re Betz Paperchem, Inc.,* 222 USPQ 89 (TTAB 1984) (chemical manufacturer's feed, delivery and storage of liquid chemical products held to constitute separate service, because applicant's activities extend beyond routine sale of chemicals); *In re Congoleum Corp.,* 222 USPQ 452 (TTAB 1984) (awarding prizes to retailers for purchasing applicant's goods from distributors held to be sufficiently separate from the sale of goods to constitute a service rendered to distributors, because it confers a benefit on distributors that is not normally expected by distributors in the relevant industry); *In re C.I.T. Financial Corp.,* 201 USPQ 124 (TTAB 1978) (computerized financial data processing services rendered to applicant's loan customers held to be a registrable service, since it provides benefits that were not previously available, and is separate and distinct from the primary service of making consumer loans); *In re U.S. Home Corp. of Texas,* 199 USPQ 698 (TTAB 1978) (planning and laying out residential communities for others was found to be a service, because it goes above and beyond what the average individual would do in constructing and selling a home on a piece of land that he or she has purchased); *In re John Breuner Co.,* 136 USPQ 94 (TTAB 1963) (credit services provided by a retail store constitute a separate service, since extension of credit is neither mandatory nor required in the operation of a retail establishment).

The fact that the activities are offered only to purchasers of the applicant's primary product or service does not necessarily mean that the activity is not a service. *In re Otis Engineering Corp.,* 217 USPQ 278 (TTAB 1982) (quality control and quality assurance services held to constitute a registrable service even though the services were limited to applicant's own equipment); *In re John Breuner Co., supra* (credit services offered only to customers of applicant's retail store found to be a service).

The fact that the services for which registration is sought are offered to a different class of purchasers than the purchasers of applicant's primary product or service is also a factor to be considered. *In re Forbes Inc.,* 31 USPQ2d 1315 (TTAB 1994); *In re Home Builders Association of Greenville,* 18 USPQ2d 1313 (TTAB 1990).

Another factor to be considered in determining whether an activity is a registrable service is the use of a mark different from the mark used on or in connection with the applicant's principal product or service. *See In re Mitsubishi Motor Sales of America Inc.,* 11 USPQ2d 1312 (TTAB 1989); *In re Universal Press Syndicate, supra*; *In re Congoleum Corp., supra*; *In re C.I.T. Financial Corp., supra*. However, an activity that is normally expected or routinely done in connection with sale of a product or another service is not a registrable service even if it is identified by a different mark. *In re Dr. Pepper Co.*, 836 F.2d 508, 5 USPQ2d 1207 (Fed. Cir. 1987); *In re Television Digest, Inc.*, 169 USPQ 505 (TTAB 1971). Moreover, the mark identifying the ancillary service does not have to be different from the mark identifying the applicant's goods or primary service. *Ex parte Handmacher–Vogel, Inc.*, 98 USPQ 413 (Comm'r Pats. 1953).

1301.01(b)   Whether Particular Activities Constitute "Services"

1301.01(b)(i)   Contests and Promotional Activities

It is well settled that the promotion of one's own goods is not a service. *In re Radio Corp. of America*, 205 F.2d 180, 98 USPQ 157 (C.C.P.A. 1953) (record manufacturer who prepares radio programs primarily designed to advertise and sell records is not rendering service); *In re SCM Corp.*, 209 USPQ 278 (TTAB 1980) (supplying merchandising aids and store displays to retailers does not constitute separate service); *Ex parte Wembley, Inc.*, 111 USPQ 386 (Comm'r Pats. 1956) (national advertising program designed to sell manufacturer's goods to ultimate purchasers is not service to wholesalers and retailers, because national product advertising is normally expected of manufacturers of nationally distributed products, and is done in furtherance of the sale of the advertised products).

However, an activity that goes above and beyond what is normally expected of a manufacturer in the relevant industry may be a registrable service, even if it also serves to promote the applicant's primary product or service. *In re U.S. Tobacco Co.*, 1 USPQ2d 1502 (TTAB 1986) (tobacco company's participating in auto race held to constitute an entertainment service, because participating in an auto race is not an activity that a seller of tobacco normally does); *In re Heavenly Creations, Inc.*, 168 USPQ 317 (TTAB 1971) (applicant's free hairstyling instructional parties found to be a service separate from the applicant's sale of wigs, because it goes beyond what a seller of wigs would normally do in promoting its goods); *Ex parte Handmacher–Vogel, Inc.*, 98 USPQ 413 (Comm'r Pats. 1953) (clothing manufacturer's conducting women's golf tournaments held to be a service, because it is not an activity normally expected in promoting the sale of women's clothing).

Conducting a contest to promote the sale of one's own goods is usually not considered a service, even though benefits may accrue to the winners of the contest. Such a contest is usually ancillary to the sale of goods or services, and is nothing more than a device to advertise the applicant's products. *In re Dr. Pepper Co.*, 836 F.2d 508, 5 USPQ2d 1207 (Fed. Cir. 1987); *In re Loew's Theatres, Inc.*, 179 USPQ 126 (TTAB 1973); *In re Johnson Publishing Co., Inc.*, 130 USPQ 185 (TTAB 1961). However, a contest that serves to promote the sale of the applicant's goods may be registrable if it operates in a way that confers a benefit unrelated to the sale of the goods, and the benefit is not one that is normally expected of a manufacturer in that field. *In re Congoleum Corp.*, 222 USPQ 452 (TTAB 1984).

A mark identifying a beauty contest is registrable either as a promotional service, rendered by the organizer of the contest to the businesses or groups that sponsor the contest, or as an entertainment service. *In re Miss American Teen–Ager, Inc.,* 137 USPQ 82 (TTAB 1963). *See* TMEP § 1402.11.

See TMEP § 1301.01(b)(iii) regarding the providing of advertising space in a periodical.

1301.01(b)(ii)   Warranty or Guarantee of Repair

While the repair of the goods of others is a recognized service, an applicant's guarantee of repair of its own goods does not normally constitute a separate service because that activity is ancillary to and normally expected in the trade. *In re Orion Research Inc.,* 669 F.2d 689, 205 USPQ 688 (C.C.P.A. 1980) (guarantee of repair or replacement of applicant's goods that is not separately offered, promoted or charged for is not a service); *In re Lenox, Inc.,* 228 USPQ 966 (TTAB 1986) (lifetime warranty that is not separately offered, promoted or charged for is not a service). However, a warranty that is offered or charged for separately from the goods, or is sufficiently above and beyond what is normally expected in the industry may constitute a service. *In re Mitsubishi Motor Sales of America, Inc.,* 11 USPQ2d 1312 (TTAB 1989) (comprehensive automobile vehicle preparation, sales and service program held to be a service, where applicant's package included features that were unique and would not normally be expected in the industry); *In re Sun Valley Waterbeds Inc.,* 7 USPQ2d 1825 (TTAB 1988) (retailer's extended warranty for goods manufactured by others held to be a service, where the warranty is considerably more extensive than that offered by others); *In re Otis Engineering Corp.,* 217 USPQ 278 (TTAB 1982) (non-mandatory quality control and quality assurance services held to constitute a registrable service even though the services were limited to applicant's own equipment, where the services were separately charged for, the goods were offered for sale without services, and the services were not merely a time limited manufacturer's guarantee).

1301.01(b)(iii)   Publishing One's Own Periodical

The publication of one's own periodical is not a service, because it is done primarily for applicant's own benefit and not for the benefit of others. *In re Billfish International Corp.,* 229 USPQ 152 (TTAB 1986) (activities of collecting, distributing and soliciting information relating to billfishing tournaments for a periodical publication not a separate service, because these are necessary preliminary activities that a publisher must perform prior to publication and sale of goods); *In re Alaska Northwest Publishing Co.,* 212 USPQ 316 (TTAB 1981) (title of magazine section not registrable for magazine publishing services, because the activities and operations associated with designing, producing and promoting applicant's own product are ancillary activities that would be expected by purchasers and readers of any magazine); *In re Landmark Communications, Inc.,* 204

USPQ 692 (TTAB 1979) (title of newspaper section not registrable as service mark for educational or entertainment service, because collected articles, stories, reports, comics, advertising and illustrations are indispensable components of newspapers without which newspapers would not be sold); *In re Television Digest, Inc.*, 169 USPQ 505 (TTAB 1971) (calculating advertising rates for a trade publication not a registrable service, because this is an integral part of the production or operation of any publication).

However, providing advertising space in one's own periodical may be a registrable service, if the advertising activities are sufficiently separate from the applicant's publishing activities. *In re Forbes Inc.*, 31 USPQ2d 1315 (TTAB 1994) ("providing advertising space in a periodical" held to be a registrable service, where the advertising services were rendered to a different segment of the public under a different mark than the mark used to identify applicant's magazines); *In re Home Builders Association of Greenville*, 18 USPQ2d 1313 (TTAB 1990) (real estate advertising services rendered by soliciting advertisements and publishing a guide comprising the advertisements of others held to be a registrable service, where advertising was found to be the applicant's primary activity, and the customers who received the publication were not same as those to whom the advertising services were rendered).

1301.01(b)(iv)   Soliciting Investors

Offering shares of one's own stock for investment and reinvestment, and publication of reports to one's own shareholders, are not services, because these are routine corporate activities that primarily benefit the applicant. *In re Canadian Pacific Ltd.*, 754 F.2d 992, 224 USPQ 971 (Fed. Cir. 1985). Similarly, soliciting investors in applicant's own partnership is not a registrable service. *In re Integrated Resources, Inc.*, 218 USPQ 829 (TTAB 1983) (syndicating investment partnerships did not constitute a service within the meaning of the Trademark Act, because there was no evidence that the applicant was in the business of syndicating the investment partnerships of others; rather, the applicant partnership was engaged only in syndication of interests in its own organization). On the other hand, investing the funds of others is a registrable service that primarily benefits others. *In re Venture Lending Associates*, 226 USPQ 285 (TTAB 1985) (investment of funds of institutional investors and providing capital for management found to be a registrable service).

In *Canadian Pacific*, 224 USPQ at 974, the court noted that since shareholders are owners of the corporation, an applicant who offers a reinvestment plan to its stockholders is essentially offering the plan to itself and not to a segment of the buying public. The court distinguished *American International Reinsurance Co., Inc. v. Airco, Inc.*, 570 F.2d 941, 197 USPQ 69 (C.C.P.A. 1978), *cert. denied* 439 U.S. 866, 200 USPQ 64 (1978), in which offering an optional retirement plan to applicant's employees was found to be a registrable service that primarily benefits the employees.

1301.01(b)(v)   Informational Services
Ancillary to the Sale of Goods

Providing general information or instructions as to the purpose and uses of applicant's goods is merely incidental to the sale of goods, not a separate consulting service. *In re Moore Business Forms Inc.*, 24 USPQ2d 1638 (TTAB 1992) (paper manufacturer who rates the recycled content and recyclability of its own products is merely providing information about its goods, not rendering a service to others); *In re Reichhold Chemicals, Inc.*, 167 USPQ 376 (TTAB 1970) ("promoting the sale and use of chemicals" is not a registrable service, where applicant is merely providing "technical bulletins" that contain information about its own products); *Ex parte Armco Steel Corp.*, 102 USPQ 124 (Comm'r Pats. 1954) (analyzing the needs of customers is not registrable as a consulting service, because it is an ordinary activity that is normally expected of a manufacturer selling goods); *Ex parte Elwell–Parker Electric Co.*, 93 USPQ 229 (Comm'r Pats. 1952) (providing incidental instructions on the efficient use of applicant's goods not a service). However, an applicant's free hairstyling instructional "parties" were found to be a service, because conducting parties goes beyond what a seller of wigs would normally do in promoting its goods. *In re Heavenly Creations, Inc.*, 168 USPQ 317 (TTAB 1971).

1301.02   What Is a Service Mark

Not every word, combination of words, or other designation used in the sale or advertising of services is registrable as a service mark. To function as a service mark, the asserted mark must be used in a way that identifies and distinguishes the source of the services recited in the application. Even if it is clear that the applicant is rendering a service (*see* TMEP §§ 1301.01 *et seq.*), the record must show that the asserted mark actually identifies and distinguishes the source of the service recited in the application. *In re Advertising and Marketing Development Inc.*, 821 F.2d 614, 2 USPQ2d 2010 (Fed. Cir. 1987) (stationery specimens showed use of THE NOW GENERATION as a mark for applicant's advertising or promotional services as well as to identify a licensed advertising campaign, where the recited services were specified in a byline appearing immediately beneath the mark).

The fact that the proposed mark appears in an advertisement or brochure in which the services are advertised does not in itself show use as a mark. The record must show that there is a direct association between the mark and the service. *See In re Universal Oil Products Co.*, 476 F.2d 653, 177 USPQ 456 (C.C.P.A. 1973) (term that identifies only a process does not function as a service mark, even where services are advertised in the same specimen brochure in which the name of the process is used); *In re Duratech Industries Inc.*, 13 USPQ2d 2052 (TTAB 1989) (term used on bumper sticker with no reference to the services does not function as a mark); *Peopleware Systems, Inc. v. Peopleware, Inc.*, 226 USPQ 320 (TTAB 1985) (term PEOPLEWARE used within a byline on calling card specimen does not constitute service mark usage of term, even if specimen elsewhere shows that applicant provides the recited services); *In re J.F. Pritchard & Co. and Kobe Steel, Ltd.,* 201 USPQ 951 (TTAB 1979) (proposed mark used only to identify a liquefaction process in brochure advertising the services does not function as a mark, because there is no direct association between mark and offering of services). *See* TMEP § 1301.04(b).

The question of whether a designation functions as a mark that identifies and distinguishes the recited services is determined by examining the specimen(s) and any other evidence in the record that shows how the designation is used. *In re Morganroth,* 208 USPQ 284 (TTAB 1980); *In re Republic of Austria Spanische Reitschule,* 197 USPQ 494 (TTAB 1977). It is the perception of the ordinary customer that determines whether the asserted mark functions as a service mark, not the applicant's intent, hope or expectation that it do so. *In re Standard Oil Co.,* 275 F.2d 945, 125 USPQ 227 (C.C.P.A. 1960). Factors that the examining attorney should consider in determining whether the asserted mark is used as a service mark include whether wording is physically separate from textual matter, whether a term is displayed in capital letters or enclosed in quotation marks, and the manner in which a term is used in relation to other material on the specimen.

While a service mark does not have to be displayed in any particular size or degree of prominence, it must be used in a way that makes a commercial impression separate and apart from the other elements of the advertising matter or other material upon which it is used, such that the designation will be recognized by prospective purchasers as a source identifier. *In re C.R. Anthony Co.,* 3 USPQ2d 1894 (TTAB 1987); *In re Post Properties, Inc.,* 227 USPQ 334 (TTAB 1985). The proposed mark must not blend so well with other matter on specimens that it is difficult or impossible to discern what the mark is. *In re McDonald's Corp.,* 229 USPQ 555 (TTAB 1985); *In re Royal Viking Line A/S,* 216 USPQ 795 (TTAB 1982); *In re Republic of Austria Spanische Reitschule, supra; Ex parte National Geographic Society,* 83 USPQ 260 (Comm'r Pats. 1949). On the other hand, the fact that the proposed mark is prominently displayed does not in and of itself make it registrable, if it is not used in a manner that would be perceived by consumers as an indicator of source. *In re Wakefern Food Corp.,* 222 USPQ 76 (TTAB 1984). The important question is not how readily a mark will be noticed but whether, when noticed, it will be understood as identifying and indicating the origin of the services. *In re Singer Mfg. Co.,* 255 F.2d 939, 118 USPQ 310 (C.C.P.A. 1958).

The presence of the "SM" symbol is not dispositive of the issue of whether matter sought to be registered is used as a service mark. *In re British Caledonian Airways Ltd.,* 218 USPQ 737 (TTAB 1983).

See TMEP § 1301.02(a) for further information about matter that does not function as a service mark. *See* TMEP §§ 1301.01 *et seq.* regarding what constitutes a service. *See* TMEP §§ 1301.04 *et seq.* regarding service mark specimens.

1301.02(a)   Matter That Does Not Function as a Service Mark

To function as a service mark, a designation must be used in a manner that would be perceived by purchasers as identifying and distinguishing the source of the services recited in the application.

Use of a designation or slogan to convey advertising or promotional information, rather than to identify and indicate the source of the services, is not service mark use. *See In re Standard Oil Co.*, 275 F.2d 945, 125 USPQ 227 (C.C.P.A. 1960) (GUARANTEED STARTING found to be ordinary words that convey information about the services, not a service mark for the services of "winterizing" motor vehicles); *In re Melville Corp.*, 228 USPQ 970 (TTAB 1986) (BRAND NAMES FOR LESS found to be informational phrase that does not function as a mark for retail store services); *In re Brock Residence Inns, Inc.*, 222 USPQ 920 (TTAB 1984) (FOR A DAY, A WEEK, A MONTH OR MORE so highly descriptive and informational in nature that purchasers would be unlikely to perceive it as an indicator of the source of hotel services); *In re Wakefern Food Corp.*, 222 USPQ 76 (TTAB 1984) (WHY PAY MORE found to be a common commercial phrase that does not serve to identify grocery store services); *In re Gilbert Eiseman, P.C.*, 220 USPQ 89 (TTAB 1983) (IN ONE DAY not used as source identifier but merely as a component of advertising matter that conveyed a characteristic of applicant's plastic surgery services); *In re European–American Bank & Trust Co.*, 201 USPQ 788 (TTAB 1979) (slogan THINK ABOUT IT found to be an informational or instructional phrase that would not be perceived as a mark for banking services); *In re Restonic Corp.*, 189 USPQ 248 (TTAB 1975) (phrase used merely to advertise goods manufactured and sold by applicant's franchisees does not serve to identify franchising services). *Cf. In re Post Properties, Inc.*, 227 USPQ 334 (TTAB 1985) (the designation QUALITY SHOWS, set off from text of advertising copy in extremely large typeface and reiterated at the conclusion of the narrative portion of the ad, held to be a registrable service mark for applicant's real estate management and leasing services, because it was used in a way that made a commercial impression separate from that of the other elements of advertising material upon which it was used, such that the designation would be recognized by prospective customers as a source identifier). *See also* TMEP § 1202.04 regarding informational matter that does not function as a trademark.

A term that is used only to identify a product, device or instrument sold or used in the performance of a service rather than to identify the service itself does not function as a service mark. *See In re Moody's Investors Service Inc.*, 13 USPQ2d 2043 (TTAB 1989) ("Aaa," as used on the specimens, found to identify the applicant's ratings instead of its rating services); *In re Niagara Frontier Services, Inc.*, 221 USPQ 284 (TTAB 1983) (WE MAKE IT, YOU BAKE IT only identifies pizza, and does not function as a service mark to identify grocery store services); *In re British Caledonian Airways Ltd.*, 218 USPQ 737 (TTAB 1983) (term that identifies a seat in the first class section of an airplane does not function as mark for air transportation services); *In re Editel Productions, Inc.*, 189 USPQ 111

(TTAB 1975) (MINI–MOBILE identifies only a vehicle used in rendering services and does not serve to identify the production of television video-tapes for others); *In re Oscar Mayer & Co. Inc.*, 171 USPQ 571 (TTAB 1971) (WIENERMOBILE does not function as mark for advertising and promoting the sale of wieners, where it is used only to identify a vehicle used in rendering claimed services).

Similarly, a term that only identifies a process, style, method, or system used in rendering the services is not registrable as a service mark unless it is also used to identify and distinguish the service. *See* TMEP § 1301.02(e) and cases cited therein.

A term that only identifies a menu item does not function as a mark for restaurant services. *In re El Torito Restaurants, Inc.*, 9 USPQ2d 2002 (TTAB 1988).

The name or design of a character or person does not function as a service mark unless it identifies and distinguishes the services in addition to identifying the character or person. *See* TMEP § 1301.02(b) and cases cited therein.

A term used only as a trade name is not registrable as a service mark. *See In re Signal Companies, Inc.*, 228 USPQ 956 (TTAB 1986) (journal advertisement submitted as specimen showed use of ONE OF THE SIGNAL COMPANIES merely as an informational slogan, where words appeared only in small, subdued typeface underneath the address and telephone number of applicant's subsidiary). *See* TMEP § 1202.01 for additional information about matter used solely as a trade name.

Matter that is merely ornamental in nature does not function as a service mark. *See In re Tad's Wholesale, Inc.*, 132 USPQ 648 (TTAB 1962) (wallpaper design not registrable as a service mark for restaurant services). *See* TMEP § 1202.03 *et seq.* for additional information about ornamentation.

See TMEP § 1202.02(a)(vii) regarding functionality and service marks, and TMEP § 1202.02(b)(ii) regarding trade dress.

1301.02(b)   Names of Characters or Personal Names as Service Marks

Under 15 U.S.C. § 1127, a name or design of a character does not function as a service mark unless it identifies and distinguishes services in addition to identifying the character. If the name or design is used only to identify the character, it is not registrable as a service mark. *In re Hechinger Investment Co. of Delaware Inc.*, 24 USPQ2d 1053 (TTAB 1991) (design of dog appearing in advertisement does not function as mark for retail hardware and housewares services); *In re McDonald's Corp.*, 229 USPQ 555 (TTAB 1985) (APPLE PIE TREE does not function as mark for restaurant services, where the specimens show use of mark only to identify one character in a procession of characters); *In re Whataburger Systems,*

Inc., 209 USPQ 429 (TTAB 1980) (design of zoo animal character distributed to restaurant customers in the form of an iron-on patch not used in a manner that would be perceived as an indicator of source); *In re Burger King Corp.,* 183 USPQ 698 (TTAB 1974) (fanciful design of king does not serve to identify and distinguish restaurant services). See TMEP § 1202.10 regarding the registrability of the names and designs of characters in creative works.

Similarly, personal names (actual names and pseudonyms) of individuals or groups function as marks only if they identify and distinguish the services recited and not merely the individual or group. *In re Mancino,* 219 USPQ 1047 (TTAB 1983) (holding that BOOM BOOM would be viewed by the public solely as applicant's professional boxing nickname and not as an identifier of the service of conducting professional boxing exhibitions); *In re Lee Trevino Enterprises, Inc.,* 182 USPQ 253 (TTAB 1974) (LEE TREVINO used merely to identify a famous professional golfer rather than as a mark to identify and distinguish any services rendered by him); *In re Generation Gap Products, Inc.,* 170 USPQ 423 (TTAB 1971) (GORDON ROSE used only to identify a particular individual and not as a service mark to identify the services of a singing group).

The name of a character or person *is* registrable as a service mark if the record shows that it is used in a manner that would be perceived by purchasers as identifying the services in addition to the character or person. *In re Florida Cypress Gardens Inc.,* 208 USPQ 288 (TTAB 1980) (name CORKY THE CLOWN used on handbills found to function as a mark to identify live performances by a clown, where the mark was used to identify not just the character but also the act or entertainment service performed by the character); *In re Carson,* 197 USPQ 554 (TTAB 1977) (individual's name held to function as mark, where specimens showed use of the name in conjunction with a reference to services and information as to the location and times of performances, costs of tickets, and places where tickets could be purchased); *In re Ames,* 160 USPQ 214 (TTAB 1968) (name of musical group functions as mark, where name was used on advertisements that prominently featured a photograph of the group and gave the name, address and telephone number of the group's booking agent); *In re Folk,* 160 USPQ 213 (TTAB 1968) (THE LOLLIPOP PRINCESS functions as a service mark for entertainment services, namely, telling children's stories by radio broadcasting and personal appearances).

See TMEP §§ 1202.09(a) et seq. regarding the registrability of the names and pseudonyms of authors and performing artists, and TMEP § 1202.09(b) regarding the registrability of the names of artists used on original works of art.

1301.02(c) Three–Dimensional Service Marks

The three-dimensional configuration of a building is registrable as a service mark only if it is used in such a way that it is or could be perceived as a mark. Evidence of use might include menus or letterhead that shows promotion of the building's design, or configuration, as a mark. *See In re Lean–To Barbecue, Inc.*, 172 USPQ 151 (TTAB 1971); *In re Master Kleens of America, Inc.*, 171 USPQ 438 (TTAB 1971); *In re Griffs of America, Inc.*, 157 USPQ 592 (TTAB 1968). *Cf. Fotomat Corp. v. Cochran*, 437 F. Supp. 1231, 194 USPQ 128 (D. Kan. 1977); *Fotomat Corp. v. Photo Drive–Thru, Inc.*, 425 F. Supp. 693, 193 USPQ 342 (D.N.J. 1977).

A three-dimensional costume design may function as a mark for entertainment services. *See In re Red Robin Enterprises, Inc.*, 222 USPQ 911 (TTAB 1984).

Generally, a photograph is a proper specimen of use for a three-dimensional mark. However, photographs of a building are not sufficient to show use of the building design as a mark for services performed in the building if they only show the building in which the services are performed. The specimen must show that the proposed mark is used in a way that would be perceived as a mark.

See 37 C.F.R. § 2.52(b)(2) and TMEP § 807.10 regarding drawings of three-dimensional marks.

When examining a three-dimensional mark, the examining attorney must determine whether the proposed mark is inherently distinctive. *See* TMEP § 1202.02(b)(ii).

1301.02(d) Titles of Radio and Television Programs

The title of a continuing series of presentations (*e.g.*, a television or movie "series," a series of live performances, or a continuing radio program), may constitute a mark for either entertainment services or educational services. However, the title of a single creative work, that is, the title of one episode or event presented as one program, does not function as a service mark. *In re Posthuma*, 45 USPQ2d 2011 (TTAB 1998) (term that identifies title of a play not registrable as service mark for entertainment services). The record must show that the matter sought to be registered is more than the title of one presentation, performance or recording.

Specimens that show use of a service mark in relation to television programs or a movie series may be in the nature of a photograph of the video or film frame when the mark is used in the program.

Service marks in the nature of titles of entertainment programs may be owned by the producer of the show, by the broadcasting system or station, or by the author or creator of the show, depending upon the circumstances.

Normally, an applicant's statement that the applicant owns the mark is sufficient; the examining attorney should not inquire about ownership unless information in the record clearly contradicts the applicant's verified statement that it is the owner of the mark.

1301.02(e)   Process, System or Method

A term that only identifies a process, style, method, system, or the like is not registrable as a service mark. A system or process is only a way of doing something, not a service. The name of a system or process does not become a service mark unless it is also used to identify and distinguish the service. *In re Universal Oil Products Co.*, 476 F.2d 653, 177 USPQ 456 (C.C.P.A. 1973) (term not registrable as service mark where the specimen shows use of the term only as the name of a process, even though applicant is in the business of rendering services generally and the services are advertised in the same specimen brochure in which the name of the process is used); *In re Hughes Aircraft Co.*, 222 USPQ 263 (TTAB 1984) (term does not function as service mark where it only identifies a photochemical process used in rendering service); *In re Turbine Metal Technology, Inc.*, 219 USPQ 1132 (TTAB 1983) (term that merely identifies a coating material does not function as mark for repair and reconstruction services); *In re Vsesoyuzny Ordena Trudovogo Krasnogo Znameni Nauchoissledovatelsky Gorno–Metal-lurgichesky Institut Tsvetnykh Mettalov "Vnitsvetmet"*, 219 USPQ 69 (TTAB 1983) (KIVCET identifies only a process and plant configuration, not engineering services); *In re Scientific Methods, Inc.*, 201 USPQ 917 (TTAB 1979) (term that merely identifies educational technique does not function as mark to identify educational services); *In re J.F. Pritchard & Co. and Kobe Steel, Ltd.*, 201 USPQ 951 (TTAB 1979) (term used only to identify liquefaction process does not function as mark to identify design and engineering services); *In re Produits Chimiques Ugine Kuhlmann Societe Anonyme*, 190 USPQ 305 (TTAB 1976) (term that merely identifies a process used in rendering the service does not function as service mark); *In re Lurgi Gesellschaft Fur Mineraloltechnik m.b.H.*, 175 USPQ 736 (TTAB 1972) (term that merely identifies process for recovery of high purity aromatics from hydrocarbon mixtures does not function as service mark for consulting, designing and construction services); *Ex parte Phillips Petroleum Co.*, 100 USPQ 25 (Comm'r Pats. 1953) (although used in advertising of applicant's engineering services, CYCLOVERSION was only used in the advertisements to identify a catalytic treating and conversion process).

If the term is used to identify *both* the process *and* the services rendered by means of the process, the designation may be registrable as a service mark. *See Liqwacon Corp. v. Browning–Ferris Industries, Inc.*, 203 USPQ 305 (TTAB 1979), in which the Board found that the mark LIQWACON identified both a waste treatment and disposal service and a chemical solidification process.

The name of a system or process is registrable only if (1) the applicant is performing a service (*see* TMEP §§ 1301.01 *et seq.*), and (2) the designation identifies and indicates the source of the service. In determining eligibility for registration, the examining attorney must carefully review the specimens, together with any other information in the record, to see how the applicant uses the proposed mark. The mere advertising of the recited services in a brochure that refers to the process does not establish that a designation functions as a service mark; there must be some association between the offer of services and the matter sought to be registered. *In re Universal Oil Products Co.*, *supra*; *In re J.F. Pritchard & Co.*, *supra*.

Uniform Domain Name Dispute Resolution Policy

(As Approved by ICANN on October 24, 1999)

1. Purpose. This Uniform Domain Name Dispute Resolution Policy (the "Policy") has been adopted by the Internet Corporation for Assigned Names and Numbers ("ICANN"), is incorporated by reference into your Registration Agreement, and sets forth the terms and conditions in connection with a dispute between you and any party other than us (the registrar) over the registration and use of an Internet domain name registered by you. Proceedings under Paragraph 4 of this Policy will be conducted according to the Rules for Uniform Domain Name Dispute Resolution Policy (the "Rules of Procedure"), which are available at www.icann.org/udrp/udrp–rules–24oct99.htm, and the selected administrative-dispute-resolution service provider's supplemental rules.

2. Your Representations. By applying to register a domain name, or by asking us to maintain or renew a domain name registration, you hereby represent and warrant to us that (a) the statements that you made in your Registration Agreement are complete and accurate; (b) to your knowledge, the registration of the domain name will not infringe upon or otherwise violate the rights of any third party; (c) you are not registering the domain name for an unlawful purpose; and (d) you will not knowingly use the domain name in violation of any applicable laws or regulations. It is your responsibility to determine whether your domain name registration infringes or violates someone else's rights.

3. Cancellations, Transfers, and Changes. We will cancel, transfer or otherwise make changes to domain name registrations under the following circumstances:

(a) subject to the provisions of Paragraph 8, our receipt of written or appropriate electronic instructions from you or your authorized agent to take such action;

(b) our receipt of an order from a court or arbitral tribunal, in each case of competent jurisdiction, requiring such action; and/or

(c) our receipt of a decision of an Administrative Panel requiring such action in any administrative proceeding to which you were a party and which was conducted under this Policy or a later version of this Policy adopted by ICANN. (See Paragraph 4(i) and (k) below.)

We may also cancel, transfer or otherwise make changes to a domain name registration in accordance with the terms of your Registration Agreement or other legal requirements.

4. Mandatory Administrative Proceeding. This Paragraph sets forth the type of disputes for which you are required to submit to a mandatory administrative proceeding. These proceedings will be conducted before one of the administrative-dispute-resolution service providers listed at www. icann.org/udrp/approved-providers.htm. (each, a "Provider").

(a) **Applicable Disputes**. You are required to submit to a mandatory administrative proceeding in the event that a third party (a "complainant") asserts to the applicable Provider, in compliance with the Rules of Procedure, that

(i) your domain name is identical or confusingly similar to a trademark or service mark in which the complainant has rights; and

(ii) you have no rights or legitimate interests in respect of the domain name; and

(iii) your domain name has been registered and is being used in bad faith.

In the administrative proceeding, the complainant must prove that each of these three elements are present.

(b) **Evidence of Registration and Use in Bad Faith**. For the purposes of Paragraph 4 (a) (iii), the following circumstances, in particular but without limitation, if found by the Panel to be present, shall be evidence of the registration and use of a domain name in bad faith:

(i) circumstances indicating that you have registered or you have acquired the domain name primarily for the purpose of selling, renting, or otherwise transferring the domain name registration to the complainant who is the owner of the trademark or service mark or to a competitor of that complainant, for valuable consideration in excess of your documented out-of-pocket costs directly related to the domain name; or

(ii) you have registered the domain name in order to prevent the owner of the trademark or service mark from reflecting the mark in a corresponding domain name, provided that you have engaged in a pattern of such conduct; or

(iii) you have registered the domain name primarily for the purpose of disrupting the business of a competitor; or

(iv) by using the domain name, you have intentionally attempted to attract, for commercial gain, Internet users to your web site or other on-line location, by creating a likelihood of confusion with the complainant's mark as to the source, sponsorship, affiliation, or endorsement of your web site or location or of a product or service on your web site or location.

(c) How to Demonstrate Your Rights to and Legitimate Interests in the Domain Name in Responding to a Complaint. When you receive a complaint, you should refer to Paragraph 5 of the Rules of Procedure in determining how your response should be prepared. Any of the following circumstances, in particular but without limitation, if found by the Panel to be proved based on its evaluation of all evidence presented, shall demonstrate your rights or legitimate interests to the domain name for purposes of Paragraph 4(a)(ii):

(i) before any notice to you of the dispute, your use of, or demonstrable preparations to use, the domain name or a name corresponding to the domain name in connection with a bona fide offering of goods or services; or

(ii) you (as an individual, business, or other organization) have been commonly known by the domain name, even if you have acquired no trademark or service mark rights; or

(iii) you are making a legitimate noncommercial or fair use of the domain name, without intent for commercial gain to misleadingly divert consumers or to tarnish the trademark or service mark at issue.

(d) Selection of Provider. The complainant shall select the Provider from among those approved by ICANN by submitting the complaint to that Provider. The selected Provider will administer the proceeding, except in cases of consolidation as described in Paragraph 4(f).

(e) Initiation of Proceeding and Process and Appointment of Administrative Panel. The Rules of Procedure state the process for initiating and conducting a proceeding and for appointing the panel that will decide the dispute (the "Administrative Panel").

(f) Consolidation. In the event of multiple disputes between you and a complainant, either you or the complainant may petition to consolidate the disputes before a single Administrative Panel. This petition shall be made to the first Administrative Panel appointed to hear a pending dispute between the parties. This Administrative Panel may consolidate before it any or all such disputes in its sole discretion, provided that the disputes being consolidated are governed by this Policy or a later version of this Policy adopted by ICANN.

(g) Fees. All fees charged by a Provider in connection with any dispute before an Administrative Panel pursuant to this Policy shall be paid by the complainant, except in cases where you elect to expand the Administrative Panel from one to three panelists as provided in Paragraph 5(b)(iv) of the Rules of Procedure, in which case all fees will be split evenly by you and the complainant.

(h) Our Involvement in Administrative Proceedings. We do not, and will not, participate in the administration or conduct of any proceeding before an Administrative Panel. In addition, we will not be liable as a result of any decisions rendered by the Administrative Panel.

(i) Remedies. The remedies available to a complainant pursuant to any proceeding before an Administrative Panel shall be limited to requiring the cancellation of your domain name or the transfer of your domain name registration to the complainant.

(j) Notification and Publication. The Provider shall notify us of any decision made by an Administrative Panel with respect to a domain name you have registered with us. All decisions under this Policy will be published in full over the Internet, except when an Administrative Panel determines in an exceptional case to redact portions of its decision.

(k) Availability of Court Proceedings. The mandatory administrative proceeding requirements set forth in Paragraph 4 shall not prevent either you or the complainant from submitting the dispute to a court of competent jurisdiction for independent resolution before such mandatory administrative proceeding is commenced or after such proceeding is concluded. If an Administrative Panel decides that your domain name registration should be canceled or transferred, we will wait ten (10) business days (as observed in the location of our principal office) after we are informed by the applicable Provider of the Administrative Panel's decision before implementing that decision. We will then implement the decision unless we have received from you during that ten (10) business day period official documentation (such as a copy of a complaint, file-stamped by the clerk of the court) that you have commenced a lawsuit against the complainant in a jurisdiction to which the complainant has submitted under Paragraph 3(b)(xiii) of the Rules of Procedure. (In general, that jurisdiction is either the location of our principal office or of your address as shown in our Whois database. See Paragraphs 1 and 3(b)(xiii) of the Rules of Procedure for details.) If we receive such documentation within the ten (10) business day period, we will not implement the Administrative Panel's decision, and we will take no further action, until we receive (i) evidence satisfactory to us of a resolution between the parties; (ii) evidence satisfactory to us that your lawsuit has been dismissed or withdrawn; or (iii) a copy of an order from such court dismissing your lawsuit or ordering that you do not have the right to continue to use your domain name.

5. All Other Disputes and Litigation. All other disputes between you and any party other than us regarding your domain name registration that are not brought pursuant to the mandatory administrative proceeding provisions of Paragraph 4 shall be resolved between you and such other party through any court, arbitration or other proceeding that may be available.

6. Our Involvement in Disputes. We will not participate in any way in any dispute between you and any party other than us regarding the registration and use of your domain name. You shall not name us as a party or otherwise include us in any such proceeding. In the event that we are named as a party in any such proceeding, we reserve the right to raise any and all defenses deemed appropriate, and to take any other action necessary to defend ourselves.

7. Maintaining the Status Quo. We will not cancel, transfer, activate, deactivate, or otherwise change the status of any domain name registration under this Policy except as provided in Paragraph 3 above.

8. Transfers During a Dispute.

(a) Transfers of a Domain Name to a New Holder. You may not transfer your domain name registration to another holder (i) during a pending administrative proceeding brought pursuant to Paragraph 4 or for a period of fifteen (15) business days (as observed in the location of our principal place of business) after such proceeding is concluded; or (ii) during a pending court proceeding or arbitration commenced regarding your domain name unless the party to whom the domain name registration is being transferred agrees, in writing, to be bound by the decision of the court or arbitrator. We reserve the right to cancel any transfer of a domain name registration to another holder that is made in violation of this subparagraph.

(b) Changing Registrars. You may not transfer your domain name registration to another registrar during a pending administrative proceeding brought pursuant to Paragraph 4 or for a period of fifteen (15) business days (as observed in the location of our principal place of business) after such proceeding is concluded. You may transfer administration of your domain name registration to another registrar during a pending court action or arbitration, provided that the domain name you have registered with us shall continue to be subject to the proceedings commenced against you in accordance with the terms of this Policy. In the event that you transfer a domain name registration to us during the pendency of a court action or arbitration, such dispute shall remain subject to the domain name dispute policy of the registrar from which the domain name registration was transferred.

9. Policy Modifications. We reserve the right to modify this Policy at any time with the permission of ICANN. We will post our revised Policy . . . at least thirty (30) calendar days before it becomes effective. Unless this Policy has already been invoked by the submission of a complaint to a Provider, in which event the version of the Policy in effect at the time it was invoked will apply to you until the dispute is over, all such changes will be binding upon you with respect to any domain name registration dispute, whether the dispute arose before, on or after the effective date of our change. In the event that you object to a change in this Policy, your sole remedy is to cancel your domain name registration with us, provided that you will not be entitled to a refund of any fees you paid to us. The revised Policy will apply to you until you cancel your domain name registration.

PARIS CONVENTION FOR THE PROTECTION OF INDUSTRIAL PROPERTY (EXCERPTS)

of March 20, 1883,

as revised

At BRUSSELS on December 14, 1900, at WASHINGTON on June 2, 1911, at THE HAGUE on November 6, 1925, at LONDON on June 2, 1934, at LISBON on October 31, 1958, and at STOCKHOLM on July 14, 1967

NOTE: Headings enclosed in brackets are supplied by the World Intellectual Property Organization.

Article 1

[Establishment of the Union; Scope of Industrial Property]

(1) The countries to which this Convention applies constitute a Union for the protection of industrial property.

(2) The protection of industrial property has as its object patents, utility models, industrial designs, trademarks, service marks, trade names, indications of source or appellations of origin, and the repression of unfair competition.

(3) Industrial property shall be understood in the broadest sense and shall apply not only to industry and commerce proper, but likewise to agricultural and extractive industries and to all manufactured or natural products, for example, wines, grain, tobacco leaf, fruit, cattle, minerals, mineral waters, beer, flowers, and flour.

(4) Patents shall include the various kinds of industrial patents recognized by the laws of the countries of the Union, such as patents of importation, patents of improvement, patents and certificates of addition, etc.

Article 2

[National Treatment for Nationals of Countries of the Union]

(1) Nationals of any country of the Union shall, as regards the protection of industrial property, enjoy in all the other countries of the Union the advantages that their respective laws now grant, or may hereafter grant, to nationals; all without prejudice to the rights specially provided for by this Convention. Consequently, they shall have the same protection as the latter, and the same legal remedy against any infringement of their rights, provided that the conditions and formalities imposed upon nationals are complied with.

(2) However, no requirement as to domicile or establishment in the country where protection is claimed may be imposed upon nationals of countries of the Union for the enjoyment of any industrial property rights.

(3) The provisions of the laws of each of the countries of the Union relating to judicial and administrative procedure and to jurisdiction, and to the designation of an address for service or the appointment of an agent, which may be required by the laws on industrial property are expressly reserved.

Article 3

[Same Treatment for Certain Categories of Persons
as for Nationals of Countries of the Union]

Nationals of countries outside the Union who are domiciled or who have real and effective industrial or commercial establishments in the territory of one of the countries of the Union shall be treated in the same manner as nationals of the countries of the Union.

Article 4

[A to D, F. Patents, Utility Models, Industrial
Designs, Marks: Right of Priority]

A.—(1) Any person who has duly filed an application for a patent, or for the registration of a utility model, or of an industrial design, or of a trademark, in one of the countries of the Union, or his successor in title, shall enjoy, for the purpose of filing in the other countries, a right of priority during the periods hereinafter fixed.

(2) Any filing that is equivalent to a regular national filing under the domestic legislation of any country of the Union or under bilateral or multilateral treaties concluded between countries of the Union shall be recognized as giving rise to the right of priority.

(3) By a regular national filing is meant any filing that is adequate to establish the date on which the application was filed in the country concerned, whatever may be the subsequent fate of the application.

B.—Consequently, any subsequent filing in any of the other countries of the Union before the expiration of the periods referred to above shall not be invalidated by reason of any acts accomplished in the interval, in particular, another filing, the publication or exploitation of the invention, the putting on sale of copies of the design, or the use of the mark, and such acts cannot give rise to any third-party right or any right of personal possession. Rights acquired by third parties before the date of the first application that serves as the basis for the right of priority are reserved in accordance with the domestic legislation of each country of the Union.

C.—(1) The periods of priority referred to above shall be twelve months for patents and utility models, and six months for industrial designs and trademarks.

(2) These periods shall start from the date of filing of the first application; the day of filing shall not be included in the period.

(3) If the last day of the period is an official holiday, or a day when the Office is not open for the filing of applications in the country where protection is claimed, the period shall be extended until the first following working day.

(4) A subsequent application concerning the same subject as a previous first application within the meaning of paragraph (2), above, filed in the same country of the Union, shall be considered as the first application, of which the filing date shall be the starting point of the period of priority, if, at the time of filing the subsequent application, the said previous application has been withdrawn, abandoned, or refused, without having been laid open to public inspection and without leaving any rights outstanding, and if it has not yet served as a basis for claiming a right of priority. The previous application may not thereafter serve as a basis for claiming a right of priority.

D.—(1) Any person desiring to take advantage of the priority of a previous filing shall be required to make a declaration indicating the date of such filing and the country in which it was made. Each country shall determine the latest date on which such declaration must be made.

(2) These particulars shall be mentioned in the publications issued by the competent authority, and in particular in the patents and the specifications relating thereto.

(3) The countries of the Union may require any person making a declaration of priority to produce a copy of the application (description, drawings, etc.) previously filed. The copy, certified as correct by the authority which received such application, shall not require any authentication, and may in any case be filed, without fee, at any time within three months of the filing of the subsequent application. They may require it to be accompanied by a certificate from the same authority showing the date of filing, and by a translation.

(4) No other formalities may be required for the declaration of priority at the time of filing the application. Each country of the Union shall deter-

mine the consequences of failure to comply with the formalities prescribed by this Article, but such consequences shall in no case go beyond the loss of the right of priority.

(5) Subsequently, further proof may be required.

Any person who avails himself of the priority of a previous application shall be required to specify the number of that application; this number shall be published as provided for by paragraph (2), above.

. . .

Article 5

[C. *Marks:* Failure to Use; Different Forms; Use by Co-proprietors.—
D. *Patents, Utility Models, Marks, Industrial Designs.* Marking]

C.—(1) If, in any country, use of the registered mark is compulsory, the registration may be cancelled only after a reasonable period, and then only if the person concerned does not justify his inaction.

(2) Use of a trademark by the proprietor in a form differing in elements which do not alter the distinctive character of the mark in the form in which it was registered in one of the countries of the Union shall not entail invalidation of the registration and shall not diminish the protection granted to the mark.

(3) Concurrent use of the same mark on identical or similar goods by industrial or commercial establishments considered as co-proprietors of the mark according to the provisions of the domestic law of the country where protection is claimed shall not prevent registration or diminish in any way the protection granted to the said mark in any country of the Union, provided that such use does not result in misleading the public and is not contrary to the public interest.

D.—No indication or mention of the patent, of the utility model, of the registration of the trademark, or of the deposit of the industrial design, shall be required upon the goods as a condition of recognition of the right to protection.

Article 5bis

[*All Industrial Property Rights:* Period of Grace for the
Payment of Fees for the Maintenance of Rights]

(1) A period of grace of not less than six months shall be allowed for the payment of the fees prescribed for the maintenance of industrial property rights, subject, if the domestic legislation so provides, to the payment of a surcharge.

Article 6

[*Marks*: Conditions of Registration; Independence of Protection
of Same Mark in Different Countries]

(1) The conditions for the filing and registration of trademarks shall be determined in each country of the Union by its domestic legislation.

(2) However, an application for the registration of a mark filed by a national of a country of the Union in any country of the Union may not be refused, nor may a registration be invalidated, on the ground that filing, registration, or renewal, has not been effected in the country of origin.

(3) A mark duly registered in a country of the Union shall be regarded as independent of marks registered in the other countries of the Union, including the country of origin.

Article 6bis

[*Marks:* Well–Known Marks]

(1) The countries of the Union undertake, ex officio if their legislation so permits, or at the request of an interested party, to refuse or to cancel the registration, and to prohibit the use, of a trademark which constitutes a reproduction, an imitation, or a translation, liable to create confusion, of a mark considered by the competent authority of the country of registration or use to be well known in that country as being already the mark of a person entitled to the benefits of this Convention and used for identical or similar goods. These provisions shall also apply when the essential part of the mark constitutes a reproduction of any such well-known mark or an imitation liable to create confusion therewith.

(2) A period of at least five years from the date of registration shall be allowed for requesting the cancellation of such a mark. The countries of the Union may provide for a period within which the prohibition of use must be requested.

(3) No time limit shall be fixed for requesting the cancellation or the prohibition of the use of marks registered or used in bad faith.

Article 6ter

[*Marks:* Prohibitions Concerning State Emblems, Official Hallmarks, and Emblems of Intergovernmental Organizations]

(1)(a) The countries of the Union agree to refuse or to invalidate the registration, and to prohibit by appropriate measures the use, without authorization by the competent authorities, either as trademarks or as elements of trademarks, of armorial bearings, flags, and other State emblems, of the countries of the Union, official signs and hallmarks indicating control and warranty adopted by them, and any imitation from a heraldic point of view.

   (b) The provisions of subparagraph (a), above, shall apply equally to armorial bearings, flags, other emblems, abbreviations, and names, of international intergovernmental organizations of which one or more countries of the Union are members, with the exception of armorial bearings, flags, other emblems, abbreviations, and names, that are already the subject of international agreements in force, intended to ensure their protection.

(c) No country of the Union shall be required to apply the provisions of subparagraph (b), above, to the prejudice of the owners of rights acquired in good faith before the entry into force, in that country, of this Convention. The countries of the Union shall not be required to apply the said provisions when the use or registration referred to in subparagraph (a), above, is not of such a nature as to suggest to the public that a connection exists between the organization concerned and the armorial bearings, flags, emblems, abbreviations, and names, or if such use or registration is probably not of such a nature as to mislead the public as to the existence of a connection between the user and the organization.

(2) Prohibition of the use of official signs and hallmarks indicating control and warranty shall apply solely in cases where the marks in which they are incorporated are intended to be used on goods of the same or a similar kind.

(3)(a) For the application of these provisions, the countries of the Union agree to communicate reciprocally, through the intermediary of the International Bureau, the list of State emblems, and official signs and hallmarks indicating control and warranty, which they desire, or may hereafter desire, to place wholly or within certain limits under the protection of this Article, and all subsequent modifications of such list. Each country of the Union shall in due course make available to the public the lists so communicated.

Nevertheless such communication is not obligatory in respect of flags of States.

(b) The provisions of subparagraph (b) of paragraph (1) of this Article shall apply only to such armorial bearings, flags, other emblems, abbreviations, and names, of international intergovernmental organizations as the latter have communicated to the countries of the Union through the intermediary of the International Bureau.

(4) Any country of the Union may, within a period of twelve months from the receipt of the notification, transmit its objections, if any, through the intermediary of the International Bureau, to the country or international intergovernmental organization concerned.

(5) In the case of State flags, the measures prescribed by paragraph (1), above, shall apply solely to marks registered after November 6, 1925.

(6) In the case of State emblems other than flags, and of official signs and hallmarks of the countries of the Union, and in the case of armorial bearings, flags, other emblems, abbreviations, and names, of international intergovernmental organizations, these provisions shall apply only to marks registered more than two months after receipt of the communication provided for in paragraph (3), above.

(7) In cases of bad faith, the countries shall have the right to cancel even those marks incorporating State emblems, signs, and hallmarks, which were registered before November 6, 1925.

(8) Nationals of any country who are authorized to make use of the State emblems, signs, and hallmarks, of their country may use them even if they are similar to those of another country.

(9) The countries of the Union undertake to prohibit the unauthorized use in trade of the State armorial bearings of the other countries of the Union, when the use is of such a nature as to be misleading as to the origin of the goods.

(10) The above provisions shall not prevent the countries from exercising the right given in paragraph (3) of Article 6^{quinquies}, Section B, to refuse or to invalidate the registration of marks incorporating, without authorization, armorial bearings, flags, other State emblems, or official signs and hallmarks adopted by a country of the Union, as well as the distinctive signs of international intergovernmental organizations referred to in paragraph (1), above.

Article 6^{quater}

[*Marks:* Assignment of Marks]

(1) When, in accordance with the law of a country of the Union, the assignment of a mark is valid only if it takes place at the same time as the transfer of the business or goodwill to which the mark belongs, it shall suffice for the recognition of such validity that the portion of the business or goodwill located in that country be transferred to the assignee, together with the exclusive right to manufacture in the said country, or to sell therein, the goods bearing the mark assigned.

(2) The foregoing provision does not impose upon the countries of the Union any obligation to regard as valid the assignment of any mark the use of which by the assignee would, in fact, be of such a nature as to mislead the public, particularly as regards the origin, nature, or essential qualities, of the goods to which the mark is applied.

Article 6^{quinquies}

[*Marks:* Protection of Marks Registered in One Country of the Union in the Other Countries of the Union]

A.—(1) Every trademark duly registered in the country of origin shall be accepted for filing and protected as is in the other countries of the Union, subject to the reservations indicated in this Article. Such countries may, before proceeding to final registration, require the production of a certificate of registration in the country of origin, issued by the competent authority. No authentication shall be required for this certificate.

(2) Shall be considered the country of origin the country of the Union where the applicant has a real and effective industrial or commercial establishment, or, if he has no such establishment within the Union, the country of the Union where he has his domicile, or, if he has no domicile

within the Union but is a national of a country of the Union, the country of which he is a national.

B.—Trademarks covered by this Article may be neither denied registration nor invalidated except in the following cases:

1. when they are of such a nature as to infringe rights acquired by third parties in the country where protection is claimed;

2. when they are devoid of any distinctive character, or consist exclusively of signs or indications which may serve, in trade, to designate the kind, quality, quantity, intended purpose, value, place of origin, of the goods, or the time of production, or have become customary in the current language or in the bona fide and established practices of the trade of the country where protection is claimed;

3. when they are contrary to morality or public order and, in particular, of such a nature as to deceive the public. It is understood that a mark may not be considered contrary to public order for the sole reason that it does not conform to a provision of the legislation on marks, except if such provision itself relates to public order.

This provision is subject, however, to the application of Article 10bis.

C.—(1) In determining whether a mark is eligible for protection, all the factual circumstances must be taken into consideration, particularly the length of time the mark has been in use.

(2) No trademark shall be refused in the other countries of the Union for the sole reason that it differs from the mark protected in the country of origin only in respect of elements that do not alter its distinctive character and do not affect its identity in the form in which it has been registered in the said country of origin.

D.—No person may benefit from the provisions of this Article if the mark for which he claims protection is not registered in the country of origin.

E.—However, in no case shall the renewal of the registration of the mark in the country of origin involve an obligation to renew the registration in the other countries of the Union in which the mark has been registered.

F.—The benefit of priority shall remain unaffected for applications for the registration of marks filed within the period fixed by Article 4, even if registration in the country of origin is effected after the expiration of such period.

Article 6^{sexies}

[*Marks:* Service Marks]

The countries of the Union undertake to protect service marks. They shall not be required to provide for the registration of such marks.

Article 6^septies

[*Marks:* Registration in the Name of the Agent or Representative
of the Proprietor Without the Latter's Authorization]

(1) If the agent or representative of the person who is the proprietor of a mark in one of the countries of the Union applies, without such proprietor's authorization, for the registration of the mark in his own name, in one or more countries of the Union, the proprietor shall be entitled to oppose the registration applied for or demand its cancellation or, if the law of the country so allows, the assignment in his favor of the said registration, unless such agent or representative justifies his action.

(2) The proprietor of the mark shall, subject to the provisions of paragraph (1), above, be entitled to oppose the use of his mark by his agent or representative if he has not authorized such use.

(3) Domestic legislation may provide an equitable time limit within which the proprietor of a mark must exercise the rights provided for in this Article.

Article 7

[*Marks:* Nature of the Goods to Which the Mark Is Applied]

The nature of the goods to which a trademark is to be applied shall in no case form an obstacle to the registration of the mark.

Article 7bis

[*Marks:* Collective Marks]

(1) The countries of the Union undertake to accept for filing and to protect collective marks belonging to associations the existence of which is not contrary to the law of the country of origin, even if such associations do not possess an industrial or commercial establishment.

(2) Each country shall be the judge of the particular conditions under which a collective mark shall be protected and may refuse protection if the mark is contrary to the public interest.

(3) Nevertheless, the protection of these marks shall not be refused to any association the existence of which is not contrary to the law of the country of origin, on the ground that such association is not established in the country where protection is sought or is not constituted according to the law of the latter country.

Article 8

[*Trade Names*]

A trade name shall be protected in all the countries of the Union without the obligation of filing or registration, whether or not it forms part of a trademark.

Article 9

[*Marks, Trade Names:* Seizure, on Importation, etc., of Goods
Unlawfully Bearing a Mark or Trade Name]

(1) All goods unlawfully bearing a trademark or trade name shall be seized on importation into those countries of the Union where such mark or trade name is entitled to legal protection.

(2) Seizure shall likewise be effected in the country where the unlawful affixation occurred or in the country into which the goods were imported.

(3) Seizure shall take place at the request of the public prosecutor, or any other competent authority, or any interested party, whether a natural person or a legal entity, in conformity with the domestic legislation of each country.

(4) The authorities shall not be bound to effect seizure of goods in transit.

(5) If the legislation of a country does not permit seizure on importation, seizure shall be replaced by prohibition of importation or by seizure inside the country.

(6) If the legislation of a country permits neither seizure on importation nor prohibition of importation nor seizure inside the country, then, until such time as the legislation is modified accordingly, these measures shall be replaced by the actions and remedies available in such cases to nationals under the law of such country.

Article 10

[*False Indications:* Seizure, on Importation, etc., of Goods Bearing False
Indications as to Their Source or the Identity of the Producer]

(1) The provisions of the preceding Article shall apply in cases of direct or indirect use of a false indication of the source of the goods or the identity of the producer, manufacturer, or merchant.

(2) Any producer, manufacturer, or merchant, whether a natural person or a legal entity, engaged in the production or manufacture of or trade in such goods and established either in the locality falsely indicated as the source, or in the region where such locality is situated, or in the country falsely indicated, or in the country where the false indication of source is used, shall in any case be deemed an interested party.

Article 10[bis]

[*Unfair Competition*]

(1) The countries of the Union are bound to assure to nationals of such countries effective protection against unfair competition.

(2) Any act of competition contrary to honest practices in industrial or commercial matters constitutes an act of unfair competition.

(3) The following in particular shall be prohibited:

    1. all acts of such a nature as to create confusion by any means whatever with the establishment, the goods, or the industrial or commercial activities, of a competitor;

    2. false allegations in the course of trade of such a nature as to discredit the establishment, the goods, or the industrial or commercial activities, of a competitor;

    3. indications or allegations the use of which in the course of trade is liable to mislead the public as to the nature, the manufacturing process, the characteristics, the suitability for their purpose, or the quantity, of the goods.

Article 10ter

[Marks, Trade Names, False Indications, Unfair Competition: Remedies, Right to Sue]

(1) The countries of the Union undertake to assure to nationals of the other countries of the Union appropriate legal remedies effectively to repress all the acts referred to in Articles 9, 10, and 10bis.

(2) They undertake, further, to provide measures to permit federations and associations representing interested industrialists, producers, or merchants, provided that existence of such federations and associations is not contrary to the laws of their countries, to take action in the courts or before the administrative authorities, with a view to the repression of the acts referred to in Articles 9, 10, and 10bis, in so far as the law of the country in which protection is claimed allows such action by federations and associations of that country.

Article 11

[*Inventions, Utility Models, Industrial Designs, Marks:* Temporary Protection at Certain International Exhibitions]

(1) The countries of the Union shall, in conformity with their domestic legislation, grant temporary protection to patentable inventions, utility models, industrial designs, and trademarks, in respect of goods exhibited at official or officially recognized international exhibitions held in the territory of any of them.

(2) Such temporary protection shall not extend the periods provided by Article 4. If, later, the right of priority is invoked, the authorities of any country may provide that the period shall start from the date of introduction of the goods into the exhibition.

(3) Each country may require, as proof of the identity of the article exhibited and of the date of its introduction, such documentary evidence as it considers necessary.

Article 12

[Special National Industrial Property Services]

(1) Each country of the Union undertakes to establish a special industrial property service and a central office for the communication to the public of patents, utility models, industrial designs, and trademarks.

(2) This service shall publish an official periodical journal. It shall publish regularly:

.   .   .

(b) the reproductions of registered trademarks.

AGREEMENT ON TRADE-RELATED ASPECTS OF INTELLECTUAL PROPERTY RIGHTS (TRIPS) (EXCERPTS)

PART I
GENERAL PROVISIONS AND BASIC PRINCIPLES
Article 1
Nature and Scope of Obligations

1.   Members shall give effect to the provisions of this Agreement. Members may, but shall not be obliged to, implement in their law more extensive protection than is required by this Agreement, provided that such protection does not contravene the provisions of this Agreement. Members shall be free to determine the appropriate method of implementing the provisions of this Agreement within their own legal system and practice.

2.   For the purposes of this Agreement, the term "intellectual property" refers to all categories of intellectual property that are the subject of Sections 1 through 7 of Part II.

3.   Members shall accord the treatment provided for in this Agreement to the nationals of other Members.[1] In respect of the relevant intellectual property right, the nationals of other Members shall be understood as those natural or legal persons that would meet the criteria for eligibility for protection provided for in the Paris Convention (1967), the Berne Convention (1971), the Rome Convention and the Treaty on Intellectual Property in Respect of Integrated Circuits, were all Members of the WTO members of those conventions.[2] Any Member availing itself of the possibilities

---

1.   When "nationals" are referred to in this Agreement, they shall be deemed, in the case of a separate customs territory Member of the WTO, to mean persons, natural or legal, who are domiciled or who have a real and effective industrial or commercial establishment in that customs territory.

2.   In this Agreement, "Paris Convention" refers to the Paris Convention for the

Protection of Industrial Property; "Paris Convention (1967)" refers to the Stockholm Act of this Convention of 14 July 1967. "Berne Convention" refers to the Berne Convention for the Protection of Literary and Artistic Works; "Berne Convention (1971)" refers to the Paris Act of this Convention of 24 July 1971. "Rome Convention" refers to the International Convention for the Protec-

provided in paragraph 3 of Article 5 or paragraph 2 of Article 6 of the Rome Convention shall make a notification as foreseen in those provisions to the Council for Trade–Related Aspects of Intellectual Property Rights (the "Council for TRIPS").

Article 2

Intellectual Property Conventions

1. In respect of Parts II, III and IV of this Agreement, Members shall comply with Articles 1 through 12, and Article 19, of the Paris Convention (1967).

2. Nothing in Parts I to IV of this Agreement shall derogate from existing obligations that Members may have to each other under the Paris Convention, the Berne Convention, the Rome Convention and the Treaty on Intellectual Property in Respect of Integrated Circuits.

Article 3

National Treatment

1. Each Member shall accord to the nationals of other Members treatment no less favourable than that it accords to its own nationals with regard to the protection[3] of intellectual property, subject to the exceptions already provided in, respectively, the Paris Convention (1967), the Berne Convention (1971), the Rome Convention or the Treaty on Intellectual Property in Respect of Integrated Circuits. In respect of performers, producers of phonograms and broadcasting organizations, this obligation only applies in respect of the rights provided under this Agreement. Any Member availing itself of the possibilities provided in Article 6 of the Berne Convention (1971) or paragraph 1 (b) of Article 16 of the Rome Convention shall make a notification as foreseen in those provisions to the Council for TRIPS.

2. Members may avail themselves of the exceptions permitted under paragraph 1 in relation to judicial and administrative procedures, including the designation of an address for service or the appointment of an agent within the jurisdiction of a Member, only where such exceptions are necessary to secure compliance with laws and regulations which are not inconsistent with the provisions of this Agreement and where such practices are not applied in a manner which would constitute a disguised restriction on trade.

tion of Performers, Producers of Phonograms and Broadcasting Organizations, adopted at Rome on 26 October 1961. "Treaty on Intellectual Property in Respect of Integrated Circuits" (IPIC Treaty) refers to the Treaty on Intellectual Property in Respect of Integrated Circuits, adopted at Washington on 26 May 1989. "WTO Agreement" refers to the Agreement Establishing the WTO.

3. For the purposes of Articles 3 and 4, "protection" shall include matters affecting the availability, acquisition, scope, maintenance and enforcement of intellectual property rights as well as those matters affecting the use of intellectual property rights specifically addressed in this Agreement.

Article 4

Most–Favoured–Nation Treatment

With regard to the protection of intellectual property, any advantage, favour, privilege or immunity granted by a Member to the nationals of any other country shall be accorded immediately and unconditionally to the nationals of all other Members. Exempted from this obligation are any advantage, favour, privilege or immunity accorded by a Member:

(a) deriving from international agreements on judicial assistance or law enforcement of a general nature and not particularly confined to the protection of intellectual property;

(b) granted in accordance with the provisions of the Berne Convention (1971) or the Rome Convention authorizing that the treatment accorded be a function not of national treatment but of the treatment accorded in another country;

(c) in respect of the rights of performers, producers of phonograms and broadcasting organizations not provided under this Agreement;

(d) deriving from international agreements related to the protection of intellectual property which entered into force prior to the entry into force of the WTO Agreement, provided that such agreements are notified to the Council for TRIPS and do not constitute an arbitrary or unjustifiable discrimination against nationals of other Members.

Article 5

Multilateral Agreements on Acquisition or Maintenance of Protection

The obligations under Articles 3 and 4 do not apply to procedures provided in multilateral agreements concluded under the auspices of WIPO relating to the acquisition or maintenance of intellectual property rights.

Article 6

Exhaustion

For the purposes of dispute settlement under this Agreement, subject to the provisions of Articles 3 and 4 nothing in this Agreement shall be used to address the issue of the exhaustion of intellectual property rights.

Article 7

Objectives

The protection and enforcement of intellectual property rights should contribute to the promotion of technological innovation and to the transfer and dissemination of technology, to the mutual advantage of producers and users of technological knowledge and in a manner conducive to social and economic welfare, and to a balance of rights and obligations.

Article 8

Principles

1. Members may, in formulating or amending their laws and regulations, adopt measures necessary to protect public health and nutrition, and to promote the public interest in sectors of vital importance to their socio-economic and technological development, provided that such measures are consistent with the provisions of this Agreement.

2. Appropriate measures, provided that they are consistent with the provisions of this Agreement, may be needed to prevent the abuse of intellectual property rights by right holders or the resort to practices which unreasonably restrain trade or adversely affect the international transfer of technology.

PART II

STANDARDS CONCERNING THE AVAILABILITY, SCOPE AND USE OF INTELLECTUAL PROPERTY RIGHTS

. . .

SECTION 2: TRADEMARKS

Article 15

Protectable Subject Matter

1. Any sign, or any combination of signs, capable of distinguishing the goods or services of one undertaking from those of other undertakings, shall be capable of constituting a trademark. Such signs, in particular words including personal names, letters, numerals, figurative elements and combinations of colors as well as any combination of such signs, shall be eligible for registration as trademarks. Where signs are not inherently capable of distinguishing the relevant goods or services, Members may make registrability depend on distinctiveness acquired through use. Members may require, as a condition of registration that signs be visually perceptible.

2. Paragraph 1 above shall not be understood to prevent a Member from denying registration of a trademark on other grounds, provided that they do not derogate from the provisions of the Paris Convention (1967).

3. Members may make registrability depend on use. However, actual use of a trademark shall not be a condition for filing an application for registration. An application shall not be refused solely on the ground that intended use has not taken place before the expiry of a period of three years from the date of application.

4. The nature of the goods or services to which a trademark is to be applied shall in no case form an obstacle to registration of the trademark.

5. Members shall publish each trademark either before it is registered or promptly after it is registered and shall afford a reasonable opportunity for petitions to cancel the registration. In addition, Members may afford an opportunity for the registration of a trademark to be opposed.

Article 16

Rights Conferred

1. The owner of a registered trademark shall have the exclusive right to prevent all third parties not having his consent from using in the course of trade identical or similar signs for goods or services which are identical or similar to those in respect of which the trademark is registered where such use would result in a likelihood of confusion. In case of the use of an identical sign for identical goods or services, a likelihood of confusion shall be presumed. The rights described above shall not prejudice any existing prior rights, nor shall they affect the possibility of Members making rights available on the basis of use.

2. Article 6bis of the Paris Convention (1967) shall apply, mutatis mutandis, to services. In determining whether a trademark is well-known, account shall be taken of the knowledge of the trademark in the relevant sector of the public, including knowledge in that Member obtained as a result of the promotion of the trademark.

3. Article 6bis of the Paris Convention (1967) shall apply, mutatis mutandis, to goods or services which are not similar to those in respect of which a trademark is registered, provided that use of that trademark in relation to those goods or services would indicate a connection between those goods or services and the owner of the registered trademark and provided that the interests of the owner of the registered trademark are likely to be damaged by such use.

Article 17

Exceptions

Members may provide limited exceptions to the rights conferred by a trademark, such as fair use of descriptive terms, provided that such exceptions take account of the legitimate interests of the owner of the trademark and of third parties.

Article 18

Term of Protection

Initial registration, and each renewal of registration, of a trademark shall be for a term of no less than seven years. The registration of a trademark shall be renewable indefinitely.

Article 19

Requirement of Use

1. If use is required to maintain a registration, the registration may be cancelled only after an uninterrupted period of at least three years of non-

use, unless valid reasons based on the existence of obstacles to such use are shown by the trademark owner. Circumstances arising independently of the will of the owner of the trademark which constitute an obstacle to the use of the trademark, such as import restrictions on or other government requirements for goods or services protected by the trademark, shall be recognized as valid reasons for non-use.

2.   When subject to the control of its owner, use of a trademark by another person shall be recognized as use of the trademark for the purpose of maintaining the registration.

Article 20

Other Requirements

The use of a trademark in the course of trade shall not be unjustifiably encumbered by special requirements, such as use with another trademark, use in a special form or use in a manner detrimental to its capability to distinguish the goods or services of one undertaking from those of other undertakings. This will not preclude a requirement prescribing the use of the trademark identifying the undertaking producing the goods or services along with, but without linking it to, the trademark distinguishing the specific goods or services in question of that undertaking.

Article 21

Licensing and Assignment

Members may determine conditions on the licensing and assignment of trademarks, it being understood that the compulsory licensing of trademarks shall not be permitted and that the owner of a registered trademark shall have the right to assign his trademark with or without the transfer of the business to which the trademark belongs.

SECTION 3:   GEOGRAPHICAL INDICATIONS

Article 22

Protection of Geographical Indications

1.   Geographical indications are, for the purposes of this Agreement, indications which identify a good as originating in the territory of a Member, or a region or locality in that territory, where a given quality, reputation or other characteristic of the good is essentially attributable to its geographical origin.

2.   In respect of geographical indications, Members shall provide the legal means for interested parties to prevent:

   (a) the use of any means in the designation or presentation of a good that indicates or suggests that the good in question originates in a geographical area other than the true place of origin in a manner which misleads the public as to the geographical origin of the good;

(b) any use which constitutes an act of unfair competition within the meaning of Article 10bis of the Paris Convention (1967).

3. A Member shall, ex officio if its legislation so permits or at the request of an interested party, refuse or invalidate the registration of a trademark which contains or consists of a geographical indication with respect to goods not originating in the territory indicated, if use of the indication in the trademark for such goods in that Member is of such a nature as to mislead the public as to the true place of origin.

4. The provisions of the preceding paragraphs of this Article shall apply to a geographical indication which, although literally true as to the territory, region or locality in which the goods originate, falsely represents to the public that the goods originate in another territory.

Article 23

Additional Protection for Geographical Indications for Wines and Spirits

1. Each Member shall provide the legal means for interested parties to prevent use of a geographical indication identifying wines for wines not originating in the place indicated by the geographical indication in question or identifying spirits for spirits not originating in the place indicated by the geographical indication in question, even where the true origin of the goods is indicated or the geographical indication is used in translation or accompanied by expressions such as "kind," "type," "style," "imitation" or the like.[4]

2. The registration of a trademark for wines which contains or consists of a geographical indication identifying wines or for spirits which contains or consists of a geographical indication identifying spirits shall be refused or invalidated, ex officio if domestic legislation so permits or at the request of an interested party, with respect to such wines or spirits not having this origin.

3. In the case of homonymous geographical indications for wines, protection shall be accorded to each indication, subject to the provisions of paragraph 4 of Article 22 above. Each Member shall determine the practical conditions under which the homonymous indications in question will be differentiated from each other, taking into account the need to ensure equitable treatment of the producers concerned and that consumers are not misled.

4. In order to facilitate the protection of geographical indications for wines, negotiations shall be undertaken in the Council for Trade–Related Aspects of Intellectual Property Rights concerning the establishment of a multilateral system of notification and registration of geographical indica-

---

4. Notwithstanding the first sentence of Article 42, Members may, with respect to these obligations, instead provide for enforcement by administrative action.

tions for wines eligible for protection in those Members participating in the system.

Article 24

International Negotiations; Exceptions

1. Members agree to enter into negotiations aimed at increasing the protection of individual geographical indications under Article 23. The provisions of paragraphs 4–8 below shall not be used by a Member to refuse to conduct negotiations or to conclude bilateral or multilateral agreements. In the context of such negotiations, Members shall be willing to consider the continued applicability of these provisions to individual geographical indications whose use was the subject of such negotiations.

2. The Council for Trade–Related Aspects of Intellectual Property Rights shall keep under review the application of the provisions of this Section; the first such review shall take place within two years of the entry into force of the Agreement Establishing the MTO. Any matter affecting the compliance with the obligations under these provisions may be drawn to the attention of the Council, which, at the request of a Member, shall consult with any Member or Members in respect of such matter in respect of which it has not been possible to find a satisfactory solution through bilateral or pluralateral consultations between the Members concerned. The Council shall take such action as may be agreed to facilitate the operation and further the objectives of this Section.

3. In implementing this Section, a Member shall not diminish the protection of geographical indications that existed in that Member immediately prior to the date of entry into force of the Agreement Establishing the MTO.

4. Nothing in this Section shall require a Member to prevent continued and similar use of a particular geographical indication of another Member identifying wines or spirits in connection with goods or services by any of its nationals or domiciliaries who have used that geographical indication in a continuous manner with regard to the same or related goods or services in the territory of that Member either (a) for at least ten years preceding the date of the Ministerial Meeting concluding the Uruguay Round of Multilateral Trade Negotiations or (b) in good faith preceding that date.

5. Where a trademark has been applied for or registered in good faith, or where rights to a trademark have been acquired through use in good faith either:

(a) before the date of application of these provisions in that Member as defined in Part VI below; or

(b) before the geographical indication is protected in its county of origin; measures adopted to implement this Section shall not prejudice eligibility for or the validity of the registration of a trademark, or the right to use a trademark, on the basis that such a trademark is identical with, or similar to, a geographical indication.

6. Nothing in this Section shall require a Member to apply its provisions in respect of a geographical indication of any other Member with respect to goods or services for which the relevant indication is identical with the term customary in common language as the common name for such goods or services in the territory of that Member. Nothing in this Section shall require a Member to apply its provisions in respect of a geographical indication of any other Member with respect to products of the vine for which the relevant indication is identical with the customary name of a grape variety existing in the territory of that Member as of the date of entry into force of the Agreement Establishing the MTO.

7. A Member may provide that any request made under this Section in connection with the use or registration of a trademark must be presented within five years after the adverse use of the protected indication has become generally known in that Member or after the date of registration of the trademark in that Member provided that the trademark has been published by that date, if such date is earlier than the date on which the adverse use became generally known in that Member, provided that the geographical indication is not used or registered in bad faith.

8. The provisions of this Section shall in no way prejudice the right of any person to use, in the course of trade, his name or the name of his predecessor in business, except where such name is used in such a manner as to mislead the public.

9. There shall be no obligation under this Agreement to protect geographical indications which are not or cease to be protected in their country of origin, or which have fallen into disuse in that country.

NORTH AMERICAN FREE TRADE AGREEMENT (EXCERPTS)

Article 1708: Trademarks

1. For purposes of this Agreement, a trademark consists of any sign, or any combination of signs, capable of distinguishing the goods or services of one person from those of another, including personal names, designs, letters, numerals, colors, figurative elements, or the shape of goods or of their packaging. Trademarks shall include service marks and collective marks, and may include certification marks. A Party may require, as a condition for registration that a sign be visually perceptible.

2. Each Party shall provide to the owner of a registered trademark the right to prevent all persons not having the owner's consent from using in commerce identical or similar signs for goods or services that are identical or similar to those goods or services in respect of which the owner's trademark is registered, where such use would result in a likelihood of confusion. In the case of the use of an identical sign for identical goods or services, a likelihood of confusion shall be presumed. The rights described above shall not prejudice any prior rights, nor shall they affect the possibility of a Party making rights available on the basis of use.

3. A Party may make registrability depend on use. However, actual use of a trademark shall not be a condition for filing an application for registration. No Party may refuse an application solely on the ground that intended use has not taken place before the expiry of a period of three years from the date of application for registration.

4. Each Party shall provide a system for the registration of trademarks, which shall include:

   (a) examination of applications;

   (b) notice to be given to an applicant of the reasons for the refusal to register a trademark;

   (c) a reasonable opportunity for the applicant to respond to the notice;

   (d) publication of each trademark either before or promptly after it is registered; and

   (e) a reasonable opportunity for interested persons to petition to cancel the registration of a trademark.

A Party may provide for a reasonable opportunity for interested persons to oppose the registration of a trademark.

5.   The nature of the goods or services to which a trademark is to be applied shall in no case form an obstacle to the registration of the trademark.

6.   Article 6bis of the Paris Convention shall apply, with such modifications as may be necessary, to services. In determining whether a trademark is well-known, account shall be taken of the knowledge of the trademark in the relevant sector of the public, including knowledge in the Party's territory obtained as a result of the promotion of the trademark. No Party may require that the reputation of the trademark extend beyond the sector of the public that normally deals with the relevant goods or services.

7.   Each Party shall provide that the initial registration of a trademark be for a term of at least 10 years and that the registration be indefinitely renewable for terms of not less than 10 years when conditions for renewal have been met.

8.   Each Party shall require the use of a trademark to maintain a registration. The registration may be cancelled for the reason of non-use only after an uninterrupted period of at least two years of non-use, unless valid reasons based on the existence of obstacles to such use are shown by the trademark owner. Each Party shall recognize, as valid reasons for non-use, circumstances arising independently of the will of the trademark owner that constitute an obstacle to the use of the trademark, such as import restrictions on, or other government requirements for, goods or services identified by the trademark.

9.   Each Party shall recognize use of a trademark by a person other than the trademark owner, where such use is subject to the owner's control, as use of the trademark for purposes of maintaining the registration.

10.   No Party may encumber the use of a trademark in commerce by special requirements, such as a use that reduces the trademark's function as an indication of source or a use with another trademark.

11.   A Party may determine conditions on the licensing and assignment of trademarks, it being understood that the compulsory licensing of trademarks shall not be permitted and that the owner of a registered trademark shall have the right to assign its trademark with or without the transfer of the business to which the trademark belongs.

12.   A Party may provide limited exceptions to the rights conferred by a trademark, such as fair use of descriptive terms, provided that such exceptions take into account the legitimate interests of the trademark owner and of other persons.

13.   Each Party shall prohibit the registration as a trademark of words, at least in English, French or Spanish, that generically designate goods or services or types of goods or services to which the trademark applies.

14. Each Party shall refuse to register trademarks that consist of or comprise immoral, deceptive or scandalous matter, or matter that may disparage or falsely suggest a connection with persons, living or dead, institutions, beliefs or any Party's national symbols, or bring them into contempt or disrepute.

†